ISBN 978-1-4278-1624-5

51099

9 781427 816245

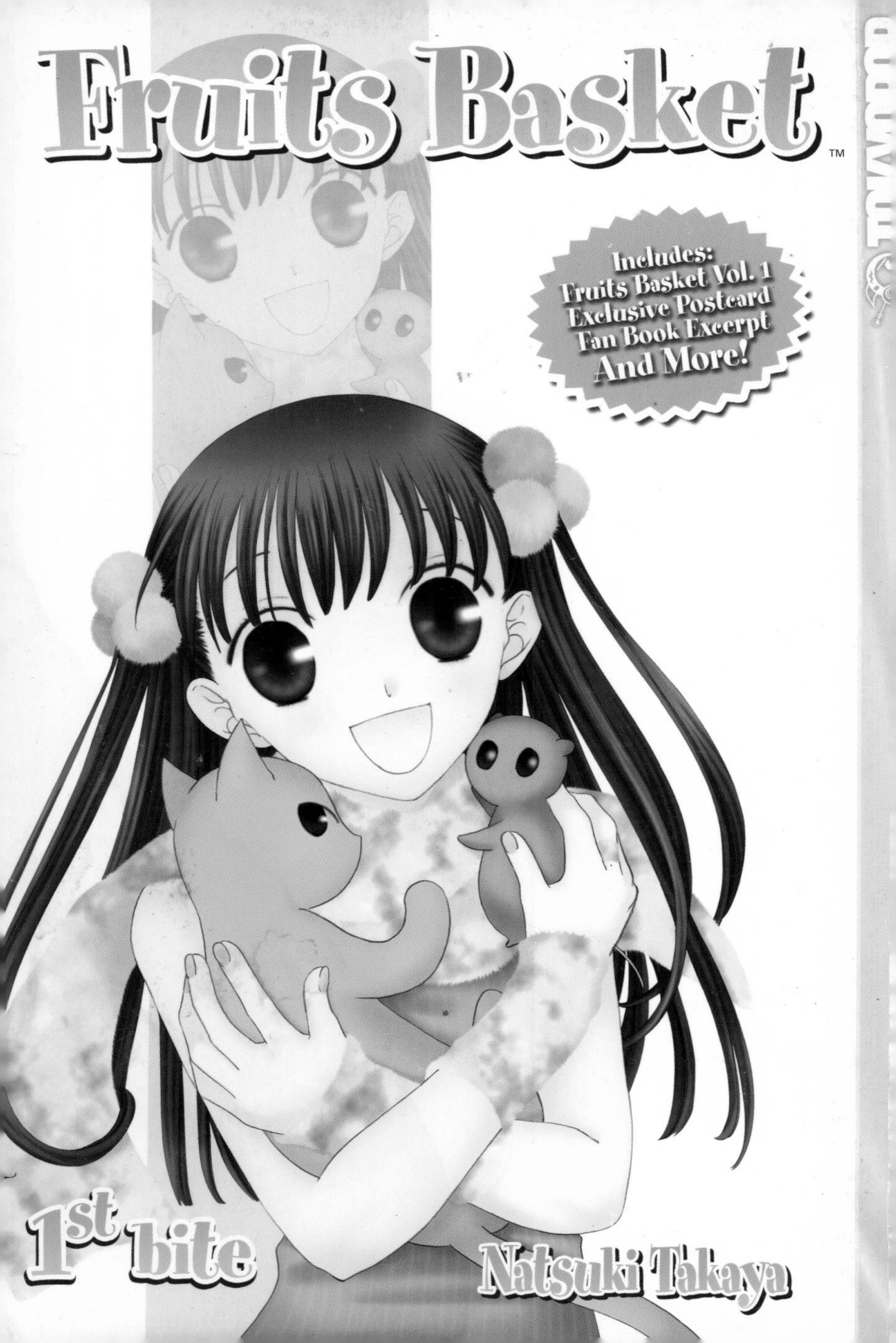
Fruits Basket™
Includes:
Fruits Basket Vol. 1
Exclusive Postcard
Fan Book Excerpt
And More!
1st bite
Natsuki Takaya
TOKYOPOP

Fruits Basket 1st Bite
Created by Natsuki Takaya

Production Artist - Lucas Rivera
Cover Design - James Lee

Editor - Alexis Kirsch
Pre-Production Supervisor - Vicente Rivera, Jr.
Pre-Production Specialist - Lucas Rivera
Managing Editor - Vy Nguyen
Senior Designer - Louis Csontos
Senior Designer - James Lee
Senior Editor - Bryce P. Coleman
Senior Editor - Jenna Winterberg
Associate Publisher - Marco F. Pavia
President and C.O.O. - John Parker
C.E.O. and Chief Creative Officer - Stu Levy

A  Manga

TOKYOPOP and 🐭 are trademarks or registered trademarks of TOKYOPOP Inc.

TOKYOPOP Inc.
5900 Wilshire Blvd. Suite 2000
Los Angeles, CA 90036

E-mail: info@TOKYOPOP.com
Come visit us online at www.TOKYOPOP.com

ISBN: 978-1-4278-1624-5

First TOKYOPOP printing: December 2008
10 9 8 7 6 5 4 3 2 1
Printed in the USA

Fruits Basket™

1st Bite

Natsuki Takaya

Fruits Basket™

1st Bite

Table of Contents

Fruits Basket™

What exactly is *Fruits Basket?* It doesn't fit into the ordinary manga categories, but then, it's not an ordinary manga. Take two parts drama, one part comedy, add a spoonful of romance and a pinch of magic and you're partway there, but…something about *Fruits Basket* is special. What that special ingredient is, you'll have to discover for yourself. But to help you get started, here's a brief history of the series.

Natsuki Takaya's *Fruits Basket* (or *"Furuba"* as it's known to fans) began its life in the pages of *Hana to Yume* magazine, the shojo manga anthology from Japanese publisher Hakusensha that is also home to *Kare Kano* and *Angel Sanctuary*. This wasn't the first time Takaya-sensei worked with the publisher. Since the early '90s she has created a steady flow of series and short stories for Hakusensha's various anthologies. Her two biggest pre-Fruits series were Geneimusou, a dark fantasy romance, and *Tsubasa O Motsu Mono (Those with Wings)*, a story about an orphaned thief in a totalitarian future. When *Fruits Basket* premiered in 1999, it took Takaya-sensei to new levels of success.

2001 was a big year for *Furuba*. The series became a huge fan-favorite in Japan, jumping to the top of manga sales. Takaya-sensei won one of the manga world's highest recognitions, the prestigious Kodansha Manga Award (she won for Shojo manga the same year Ken Akamatsu won the shonen award for *Love Hina!*). And beginning that summer, Hakusensha and TV Tokyo teamed up to turn *Fruits Basket* into a 26 episode anime series.

An established hit in Japan, *"Furuba"* fever" quickly spread throughout the American fan community. In 2002 the anime was released in English by FUNimation (see the interview with voice actress Laura Bailey at the back of the book!), but for several years the manga remained in limbo. We conducted a poll on TOKYOPOP.com in which fans could send in their wish list of manga series they'd like to see translated. *Fruits Basket* didn't just top the poll—it DOMINATED. Now, at long last, the English manga is here!

TOKYOPOP's presentation of *Fruits Basket* is published in the original right-to-left format with original sound effects retained to preserve the art. Also retained are "honorifics," the suffixes used with characters names. At the back of each book you'll find bonus features and exclusive interviews—look for some big surprises in the books to come! Future volumes will also include a special Reader Feedback section with letters, fan art and more. Please send us your pictures, questions, poetry, or whatever Furuba inspires you to send and we'll try to include it!

Fruits Basket Fan Mail
c/o TOKYOPOP
5900 Wilshire Blvd.
Suite 2000
Los Angeles, CA 90036

We look forward to hearing from you, and we hope you'll enjoy the #1 most wanted manga in America!

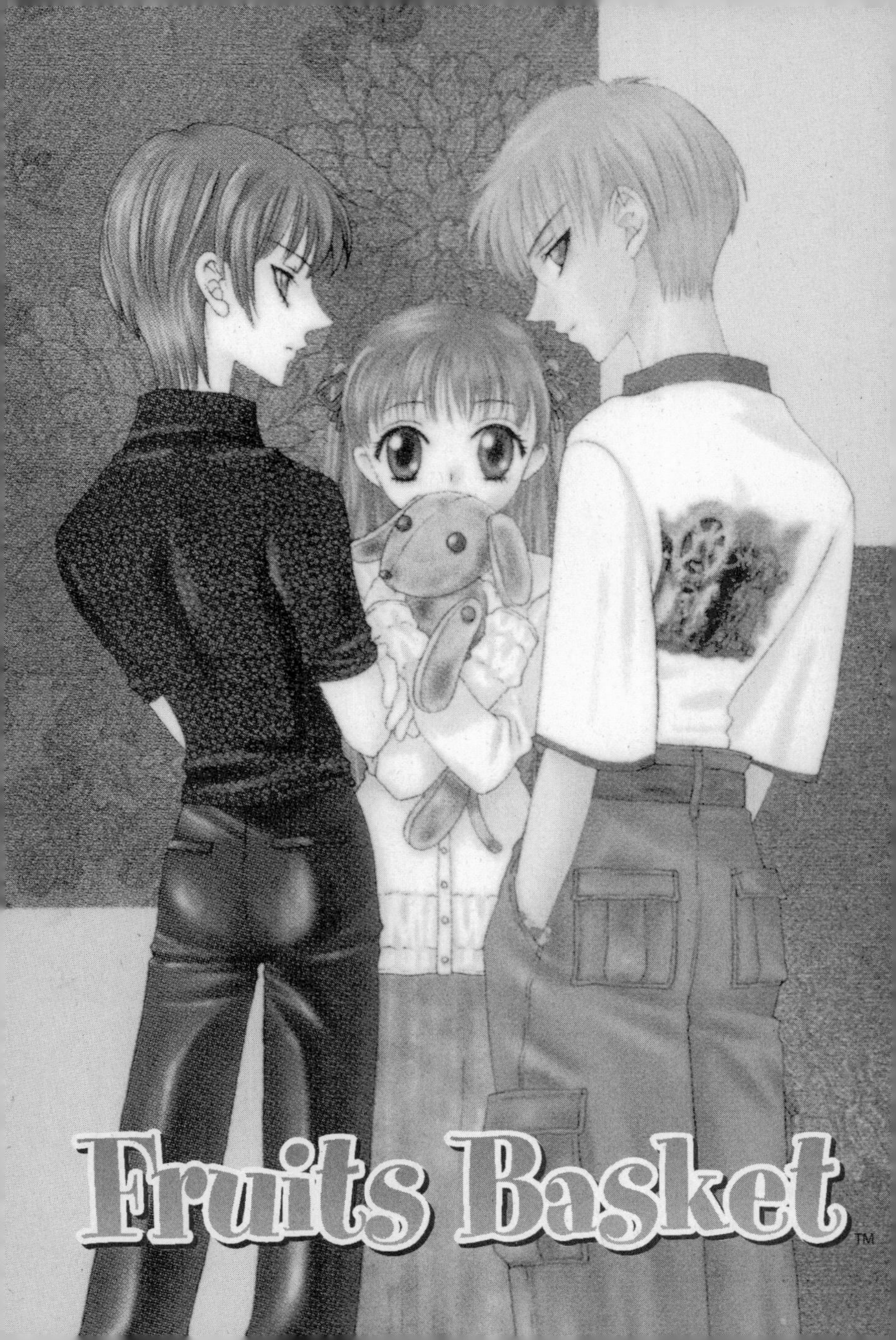
Fruits Basket™

Omake Theater 1: Life in the Sohma Household, pre- Tohru

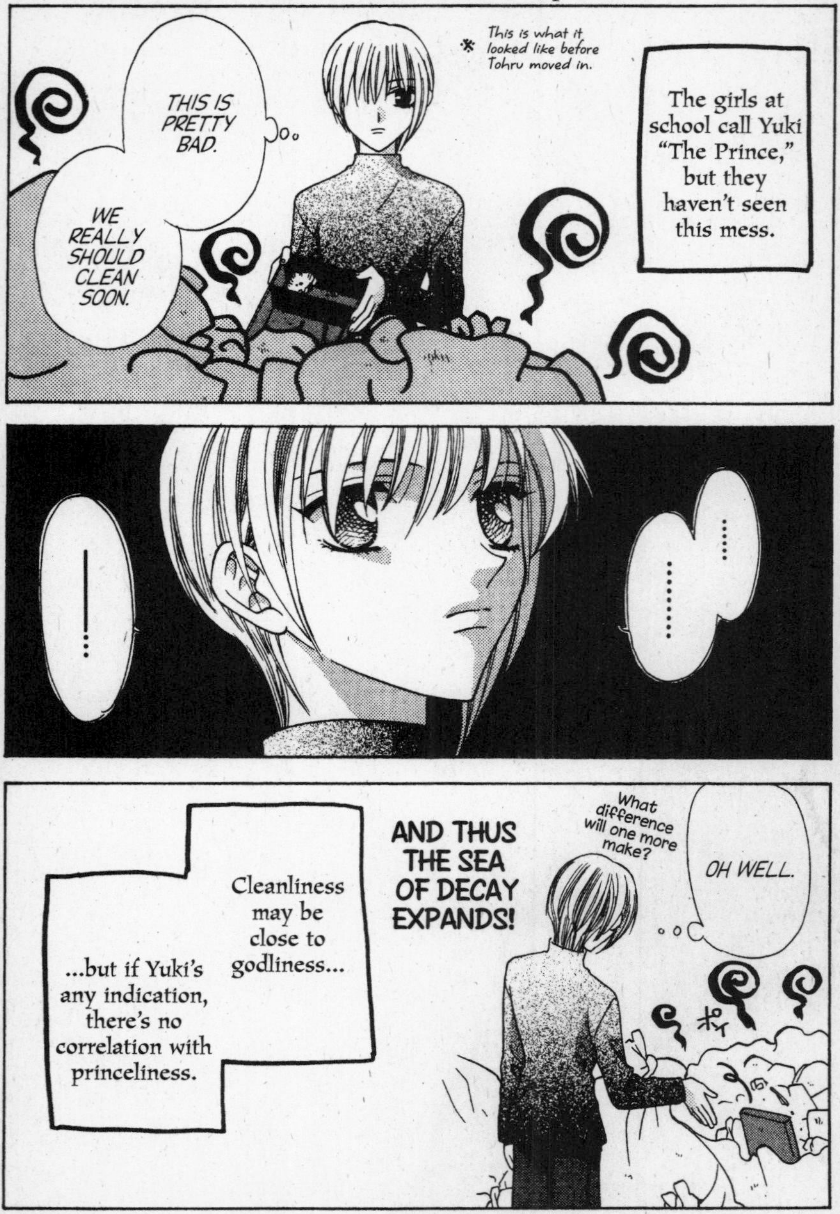
The girls at school call Yuki "The Prince," but they haven't seen this mess.
※ This is what it looked like before Tohru moved in.
THIS IS PRETTY BAD.
WE REALLY SHOULD CLEAN SOON.
......
—!...
OH WELL.
What difference will one more make?
ポイ
AND THUS THE SEA OF DECAY EXPANDS!
Cleanliness may be close to godliness...
...but if Yuki's any indication, there's no correlation with princeliness.

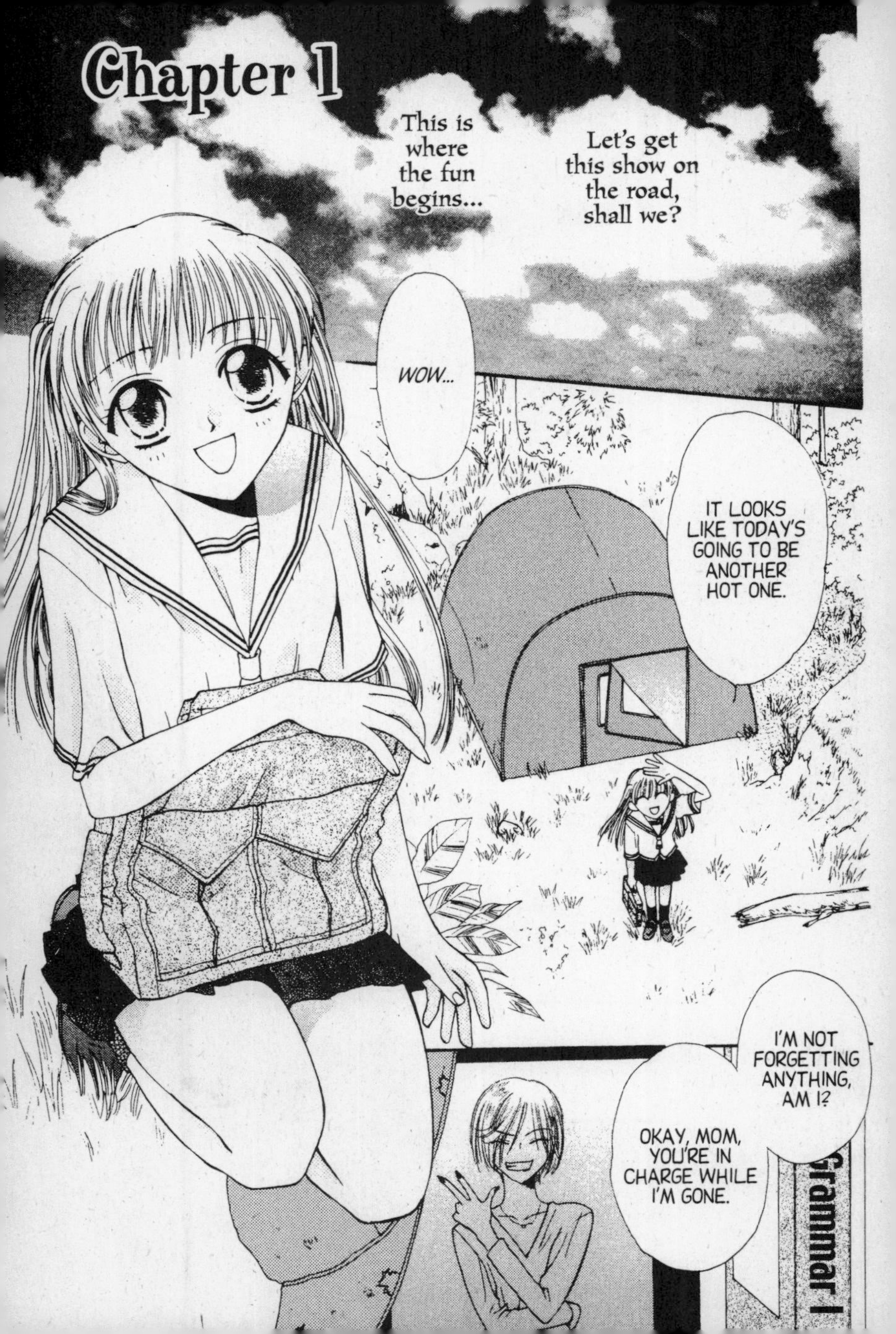
Chapter 1
Let's get this show on the road, shall we?
This is where the fun begins...
WOW...
IT LOOKS LIKE TODAY'S GOING TO BE ANOTHER HOT ONE.
I'M NOT FORGETTING ANYTHING, AM I?
OKAY, MOM, YOU'RE IN CHARGE WHILE I'M GONE.
Grammar 1

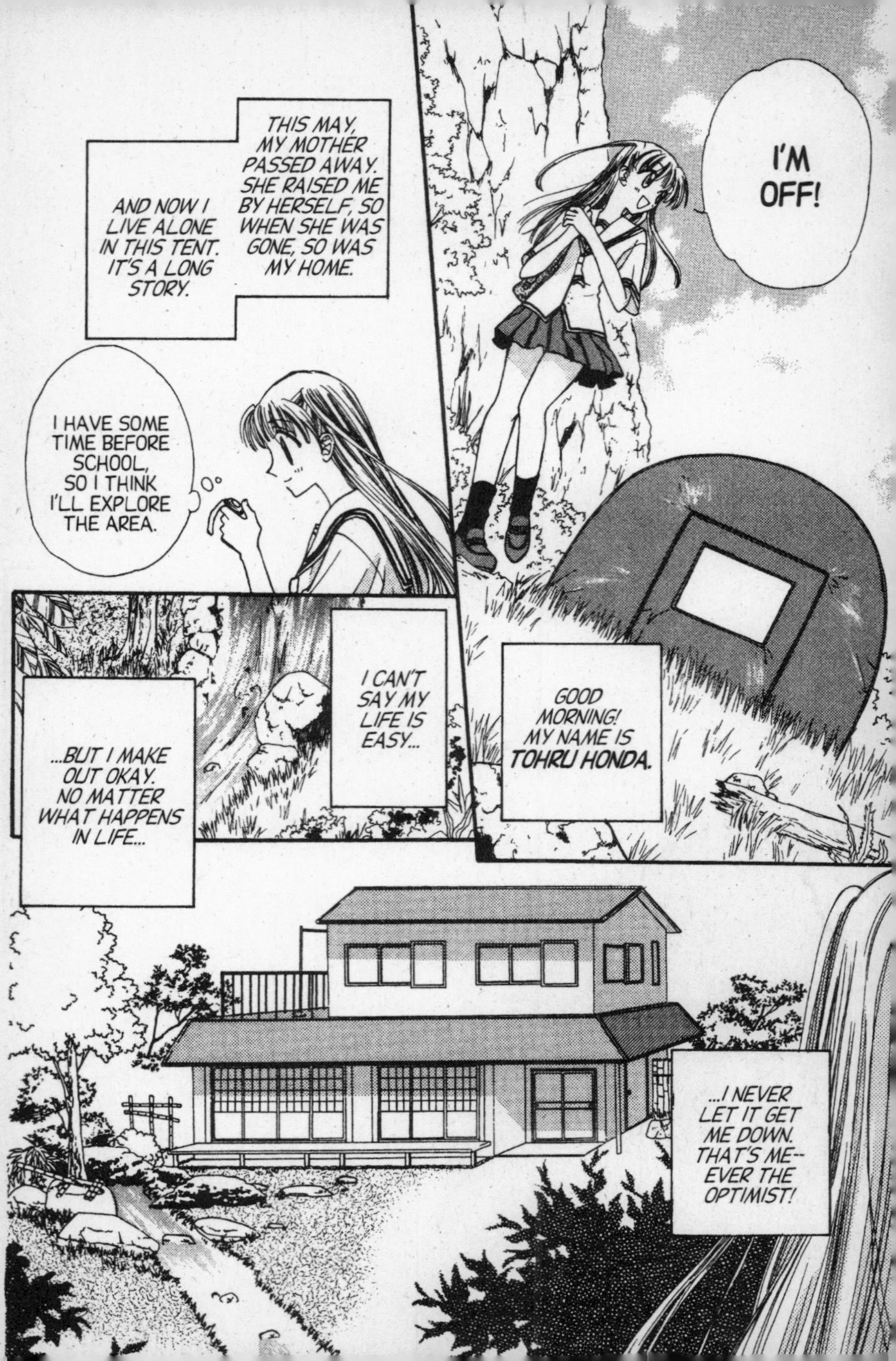
I'M OFF!
GOOD MORNING! MY NAME IS TOHRU HONDA.
THIS MAY, MY MOTHER PASSED AWAY. SHE RAISED ME BY HERSELF, SO WHEN SHE WAS GONE, SO WAS MY HOME.
AND NOW I LIVE ALONE IN THIS TENT. IT'S A LONG STORY.
I HAVE SOME TIME BEFORE SCHOOL, SO I THINK I'LL EXPLORE THE AREA.
I CAN'T SAY MY LIFE IS EASY...
...BUT I MAKE OUT OKAY. NO MATTER WHAT HAPPENS IN LIFE...
...I NEVER LET IT GET ME DOWN. THAT'S ME--EVER THE OPTIMIST!

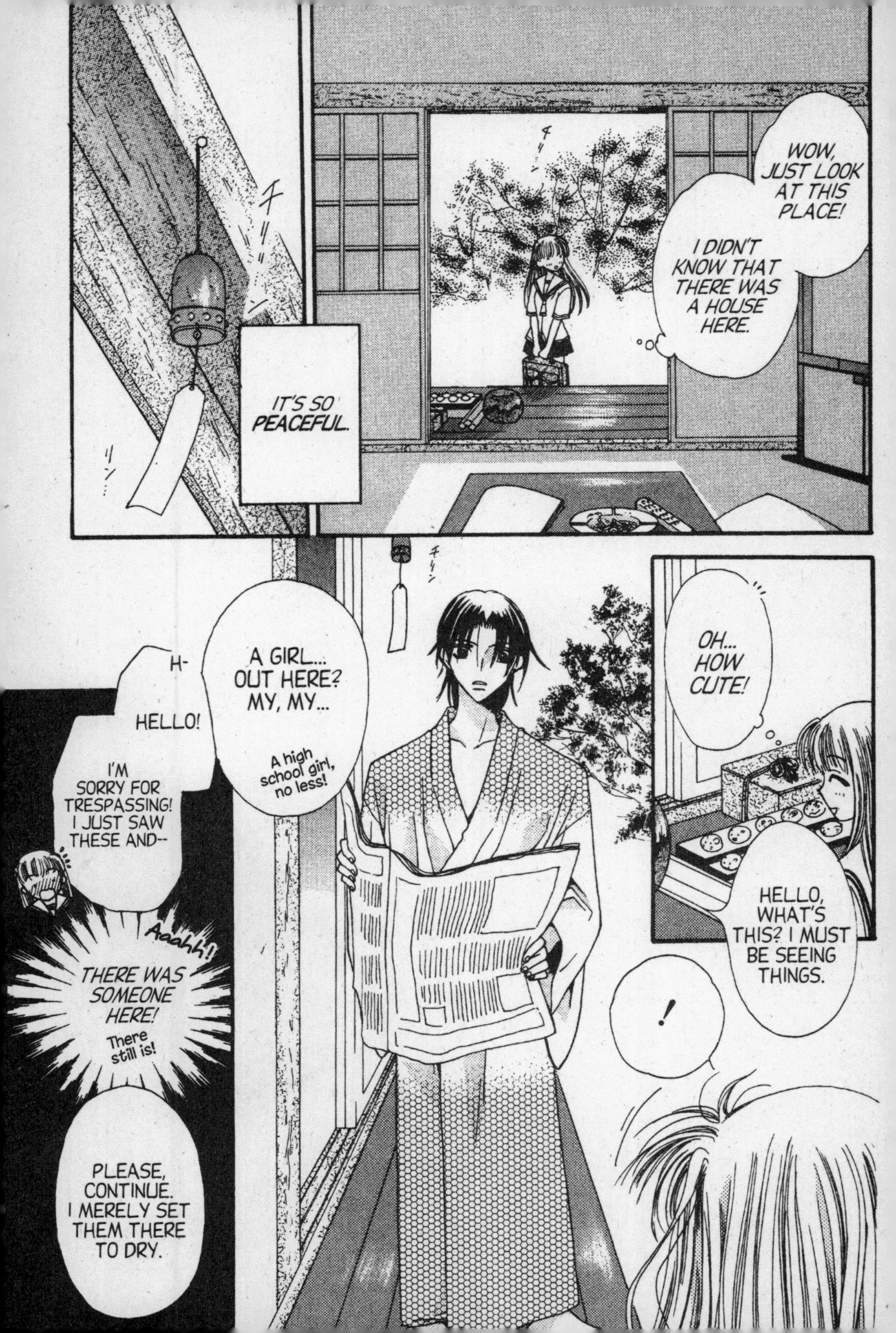
WOW, JUST LOOK AT THIS PLACE!
I DIDN'T KNOW THAT THERE WAS A HOUSE HERE.
IT'S SO PEACEFUL.
OH... HOW CUTE!
HELLO, WHAT'S THIS? I MUST BE SEEING THINGS.
!
A GIRL... OUT HERE? MY, MY...
A high school girl, no less!
H-
HELLO!
I'M SORRY FOR TRESPASSING! I JUST SAW THESE AND--
Aaahh!
THERE WAS SOMEONE HERE!
There still is!
PLEASE, CONTINUE. I MERELY SET THEM THERE TO DRY.

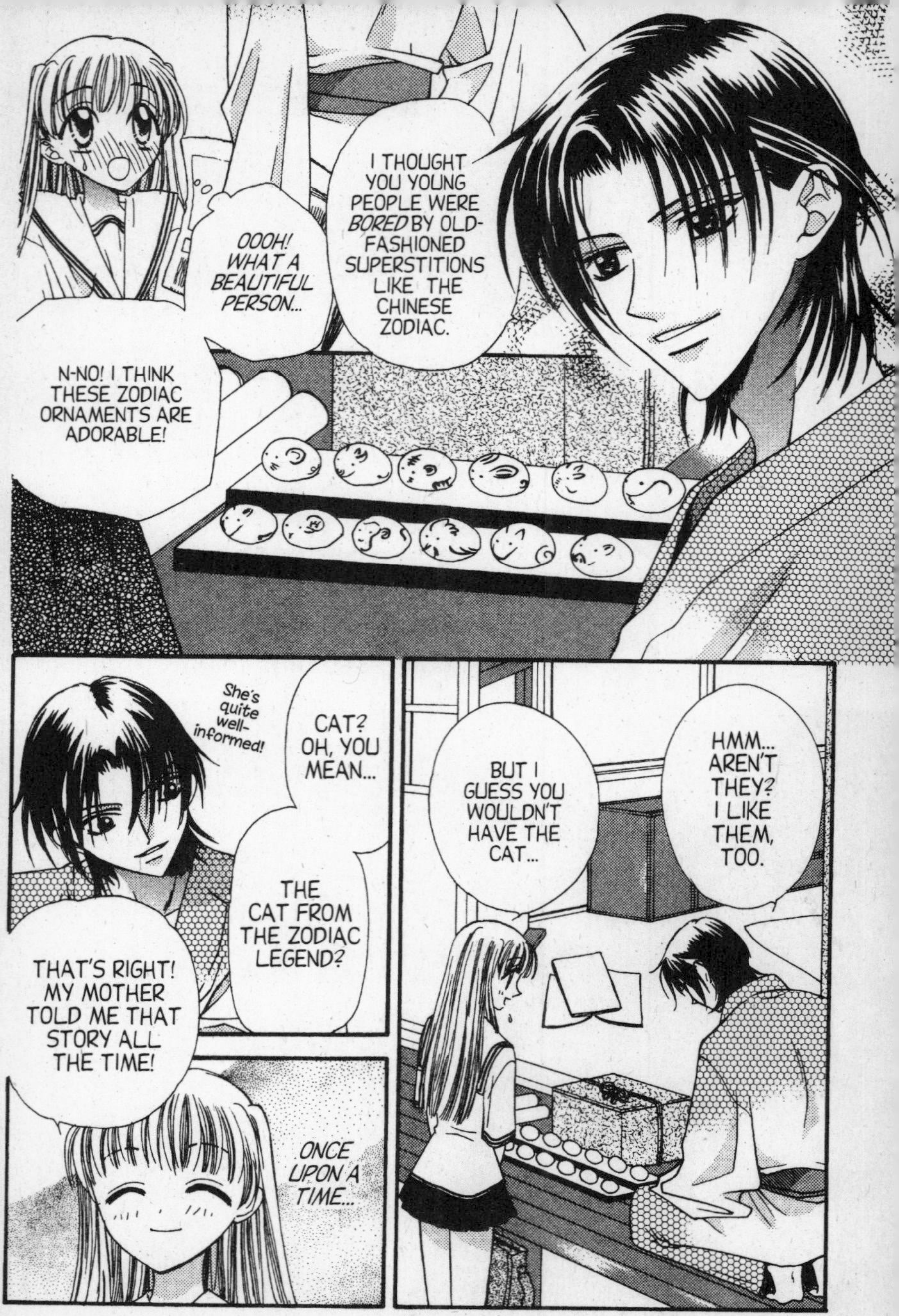
I THOUGHT YOU YOUNG PEOPLE WERE *BORED* BY OLD-FASHIONED SUPERSTITIONS LIKE THE CHINESE ZODIAC.
OOOH! WHAT A BEAUTIFUL PERSON...
N-NO! I THINK THESE ZODIAC ORNAMENTS ARE ADORABLE!
HMM... AREN'T THEY? I LIKE THEM, TOO.
BUT I GUESS YOU WOULDN'T HAVE THE CAT...
CAT? OH, YOU MEAN...
She's quite well-informed!
THE CAT FROM THE ZODIAC LEGEND?
THAT'S RIGHT! MY MOTHER TOLD ME THAT STORY ALL THE TIME!
ONCE UPON A TIME...

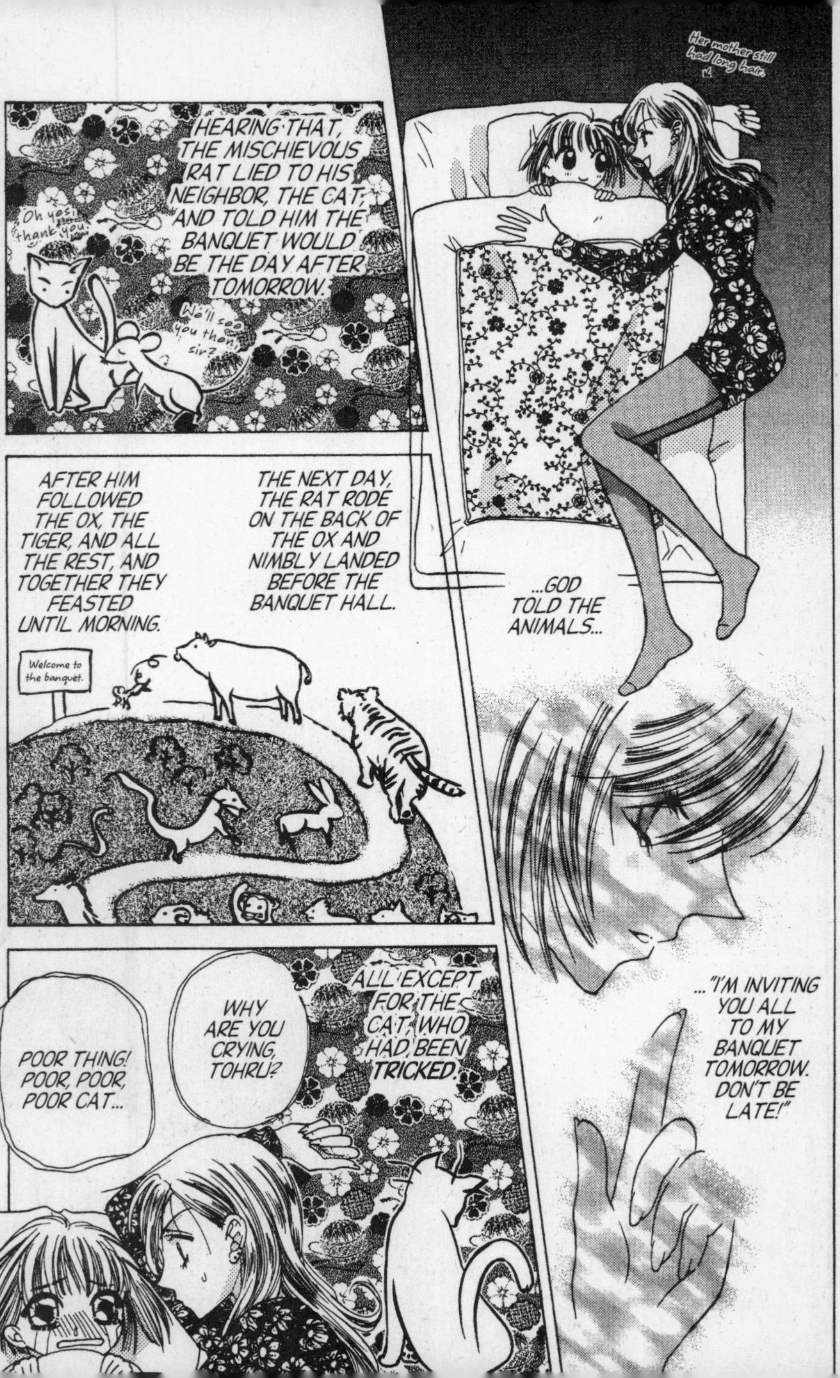
Her mother still had long hair.
...GOD TOLD THE ANIMALS...
..."I'M INVITING YOU ALL TO MY BANQUET TOMORROW. DON'T BE LATE!"
HEARING THAT, THE MISCHIEVOUS RAT LIED TO HIS NEIGHBOR, THE CAT, AND TOLD HIM THE BANQUET WOULD BE THE DAY AFTER TOMORROW.
Oh yes, thank you.
We'll see you then, sir.
THE NEXT DAY, THE RAT RODE ON THE BACK OF THE OX AND NIMBLY LANDED BEFORE THE BANQUET HALL.
AFTER HIM FOLLOWED THE OX, THE TIGER, AND ALL THE REST, AND TOGETHER THEY FEASTED UNTIL MORNING.
Welcome to the banquet.
ALL EXCEPT FOR THE CAT, WHO HAD BEEN **TRICKED**.
WHY ARE YOU CRYING, TOHRU?
POOR THING! POOR, POOR, POOR CAT...

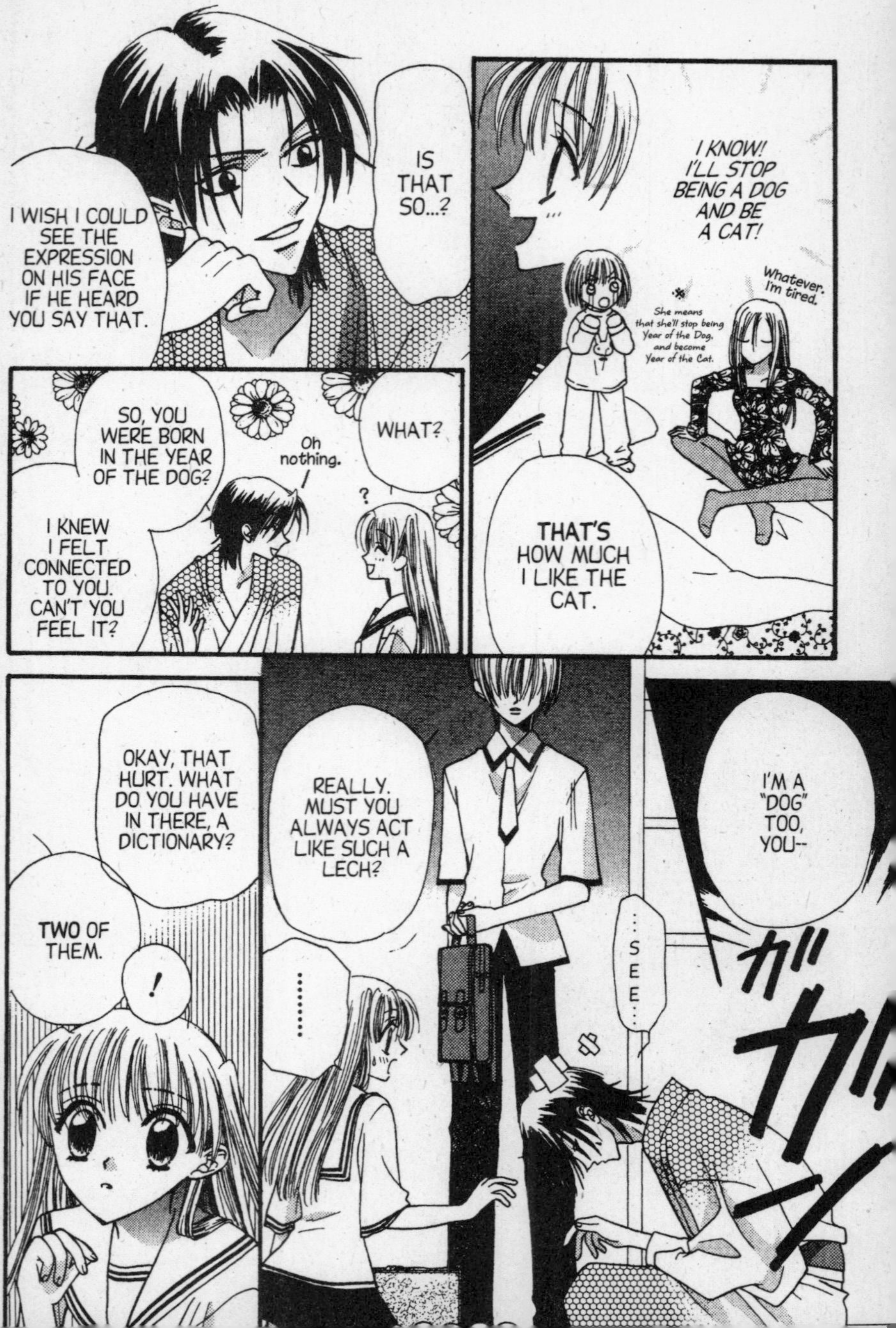
I KNOW! I'LL STOP BEING A DOG AND BE A CAT!
Whatever. I'm tired.
※ She means that she'll stop being Year of the Dog, and become Year of the Cat.
THAT'S HOW MUCH I LIKE THE CAT.
IS THAT SO...?
I WISH I COULD SEE THE EXPRESSION ON HIS FACE IF HE HEARD YOU SAY THAT.
WHAT?
Oh nothing.
SO, YOU WERE BORN IN THE YEAR OF THE DOG?
I KNEW I FELT CONNECTED TO YOU. CAN'T YOU FEEL IT?
I'M A "DOG" TOO, YOU--
ガッ
...SEE...
REALLY. MUST YOU ALWAYS ACT LIKE SUCH A LECH?
....
OKAY, THAT HURT. WHAT DO YOU HAVE IN THERE, A DICTIONARY?
TWO OF THEM.
!

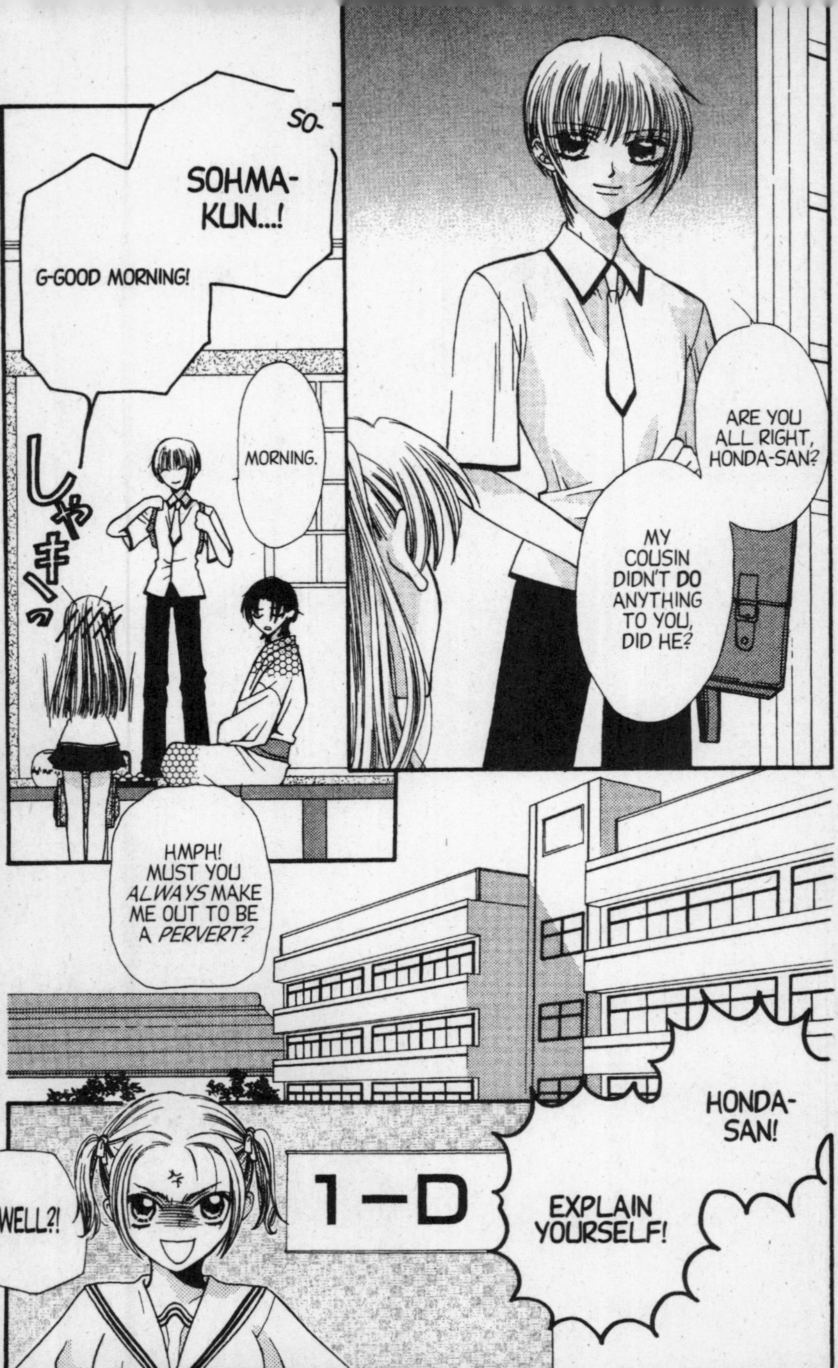
ARE YOU ALL RIGHT, HONDA-SAN?
MY COUSIN DIDN'T DO ANYTHING TO YOU, DID HE?
SO-
SOHMA-KUN...!
G-GOOD MORNING!
MORNING.
しゃキーっ
HMPH! MUST YOU ALWAYS MAKE ME OUT TO BE A PERVERT?
HONDA-SAN!
EXPLAIN YOURSELF!
1-D
WELL?!

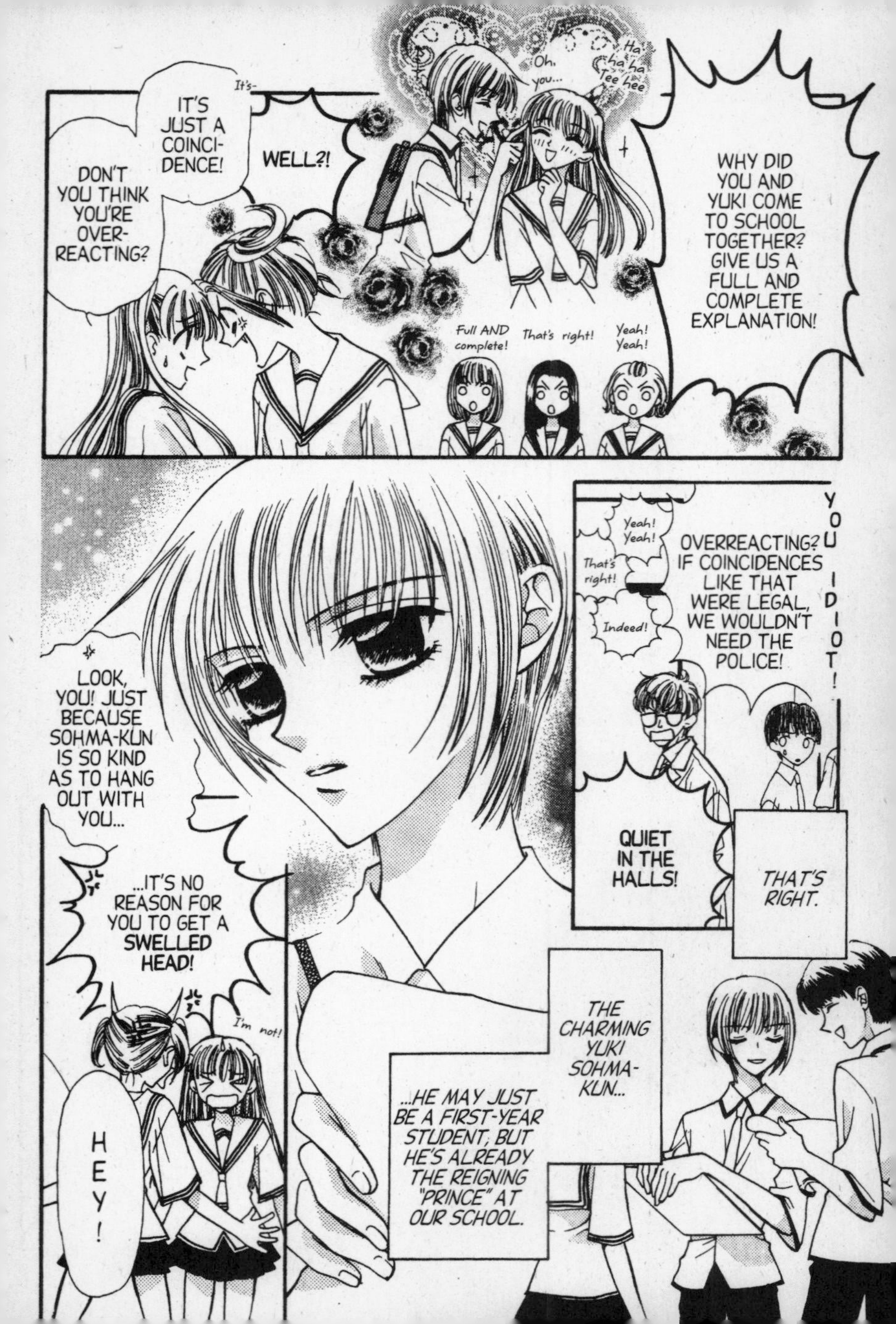
WHY DID YOU AND YUKI COME TO SCHOOL TOGETHER? GIVE US A FULL AND COMPLETE EXPLANATION!
Ha ha ha Tee hee
Oh, you...
Yeah! Yeah!
That's right!
Full AND complete!
WELL?!
It's-
IT'S JUST A COINCI-DENCE!
DON'T YOU THINK YOU'RE OVER-REACTING?
YOU IDIOT!
OVERREACTING? IF COINCIDENCES LIKE THAT WERE LEGAL, WE WOULDN'T NEED THE POLICE!
Yeah! Yeah!
That's right!
Indeed!
QUIET IN THE HALLS!
THAT'S RIGHT.
LOOK, YOU! JUST BECAUSE SOHMA-KUN IS SO KIND AS TO HANG OUT WITH YOU...
...IT'S NO REASON FOR YOU TO GET A SWELLED HEAD!
I'm not!
HEY!
THE CHARMING YUKI SOHMA-KUN...
...HE MAY JUST BE A FIRST-YEAR STUDENT, BUT HE'S ALREADY THE REIGNING "PRINCE" AT OUR SCHOOL.

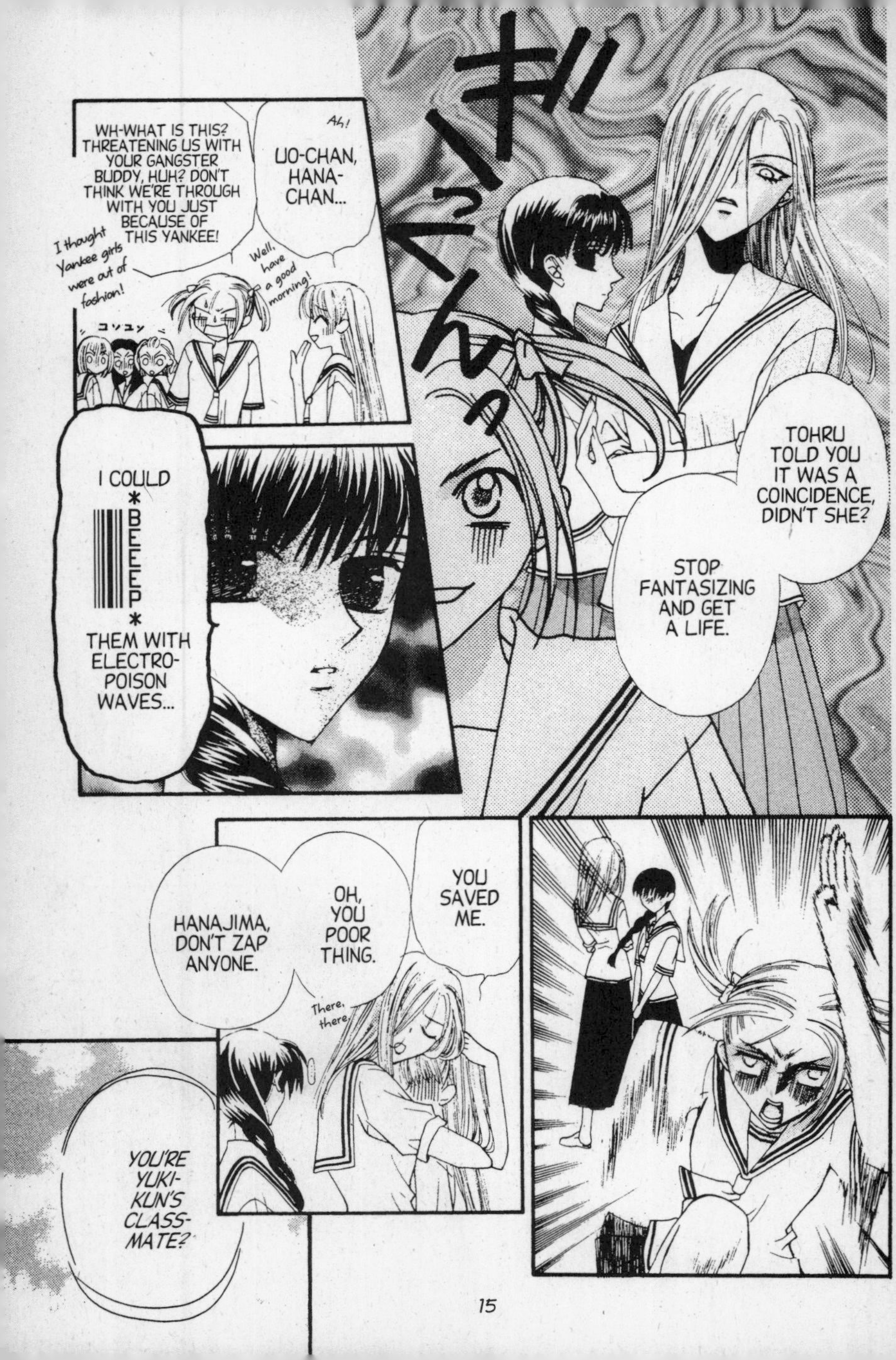
ギッくんっ
TOHRU TOLD YOU IT WAS A COINCIDENCE, DIDN'T SHE?
STOP FANTASIZING AND GET A LIFE.
Ah!
UO-CHAN, HANA-CHAN...
WH-WHAT IS THIS? THREATENING US WITH YOUR GANGSTER BUDDY, HUH? DON'T THINK WE'RE THROUGH WITH YOU JUST BECAUSE OF THIS YANKEE!
Well, have a good morning!
I thought Yankee girls were out of fashion!
コソコソ
I COULD *BEEEP* THEM WITH ELECTRO-POISON WAVES...
YOU SAVED ME.
OH, YOU POOR THING.
HANAJIMA, DON'T ZAP ANYONE.
There, there.
YOU'RE YUKI-KUN'S CLASSMATE?

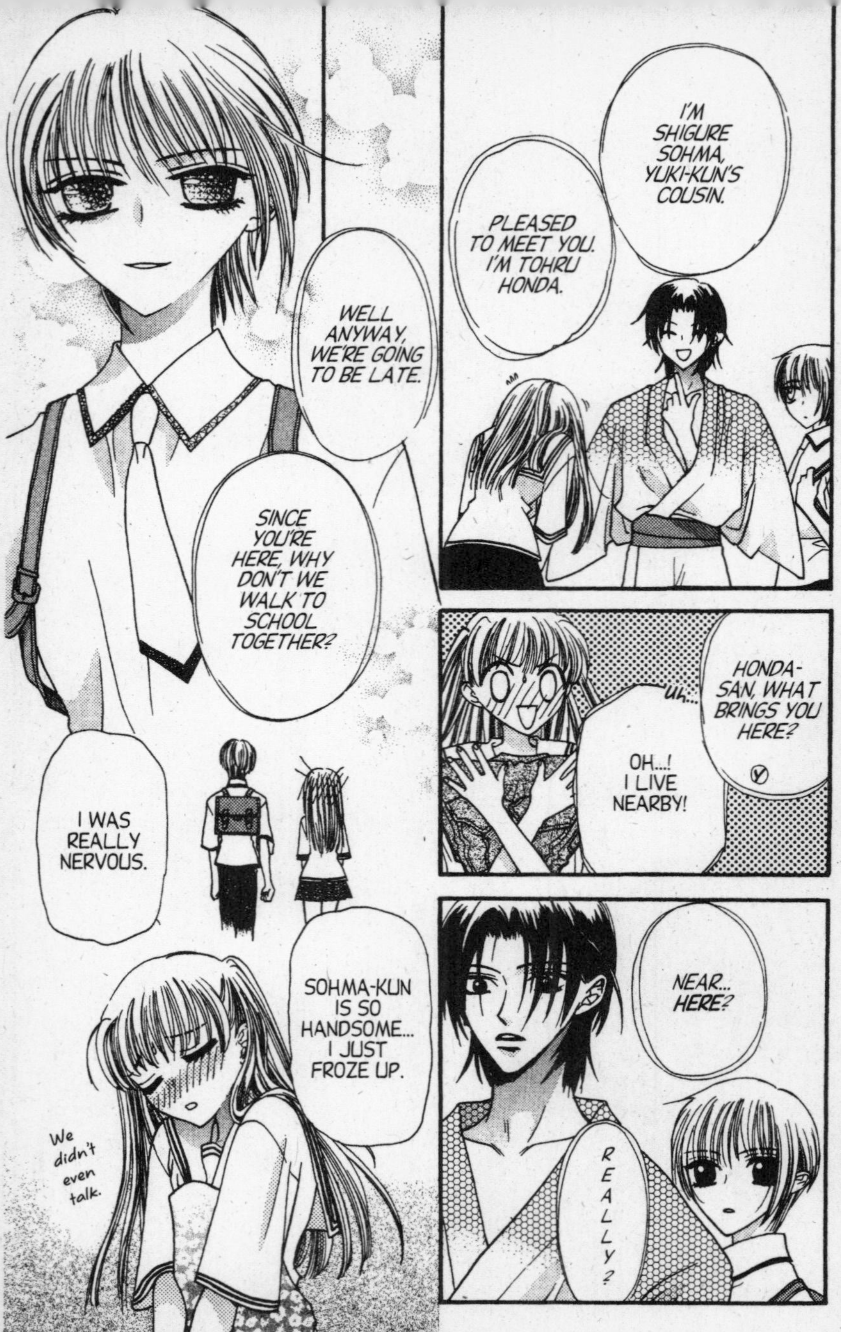
I'M SHIGURE SOHMA, YUKI-KUN'S COUSIN.
PLEASED TO MEET YOU. I'M TOHRU HONDA.
HONDA-SAN, WHAT BRINGS YOU HERE?
UH...
OH...! I LIVE NEARBY!
NEAR... HERE?
REALLY?
WELL ANYWAY, WE'RE GOING TO BE LATE.
SINCE YOU'RE HERE, WHY DON'T WE WALK TO SCHOOL TOGETHER?
I WAS REALLY NERVOUS.
SOHMA-KUN IS SO HANDSOME... I JUST FROZE UP.
We didn't even talk.

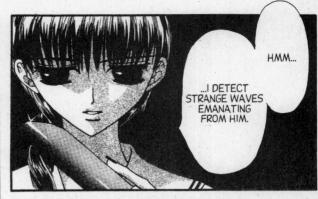

HMM...
...I DETECT STRANGE WAVES EMANATING FROM HIM.
TIME FOR HANAJIMA'S WAVE REPORT.
Kyaaaaa!
You put in too much!
The heat's too high!
It's burnt!
"STRANGE?"
I DON'T REALLY KNOW HOW ELSE TO EXPLAIN.
SHING
WHAT'S TO EXPLAIN? THE GUY'S A WALKING ENIGMA. NEVER TALKS ABOUT HIMSELF.
Not like I care.
I HEAR A SECOND YEAR GIRL CONFESSED HER LOVE FOR HIM ONCE...
...AND WHEN SHE TRIED TO HUG HIM, HE FLUNG HER AWAY. TOTALLY FREAKED HER OUT.
THE PRINCE'S CRAB-WALK
I-I DIDN'T KNOW THAT. I WONDER WHY.
Uh, um...

Fruits Basket Number 1:

Hello! Nice to meet you, I'm Takaya. To those of you who have been waiting--and to those of you who haven't been waiting, too--I am proud to present Fruits Basket Volume 1. It's a new world, different from my last manga, "Tsubasa," but I think you'll find similarities, too. (Because I'm drawing all the people, basically. Even if the details are different, I am still me!) But if there were any parts in "Tsubasa" that were weird or confusing to you, I blame my lack of sleep. Ah, sleep. I remember sleep. Maybe I should try that again one day...? In the meantime, please enjoy Fruits Basket Vol. 1!

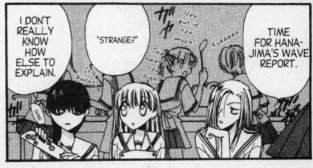

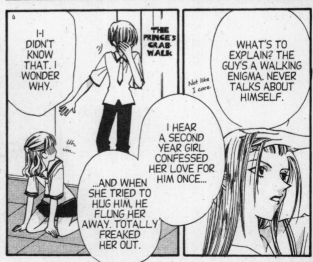

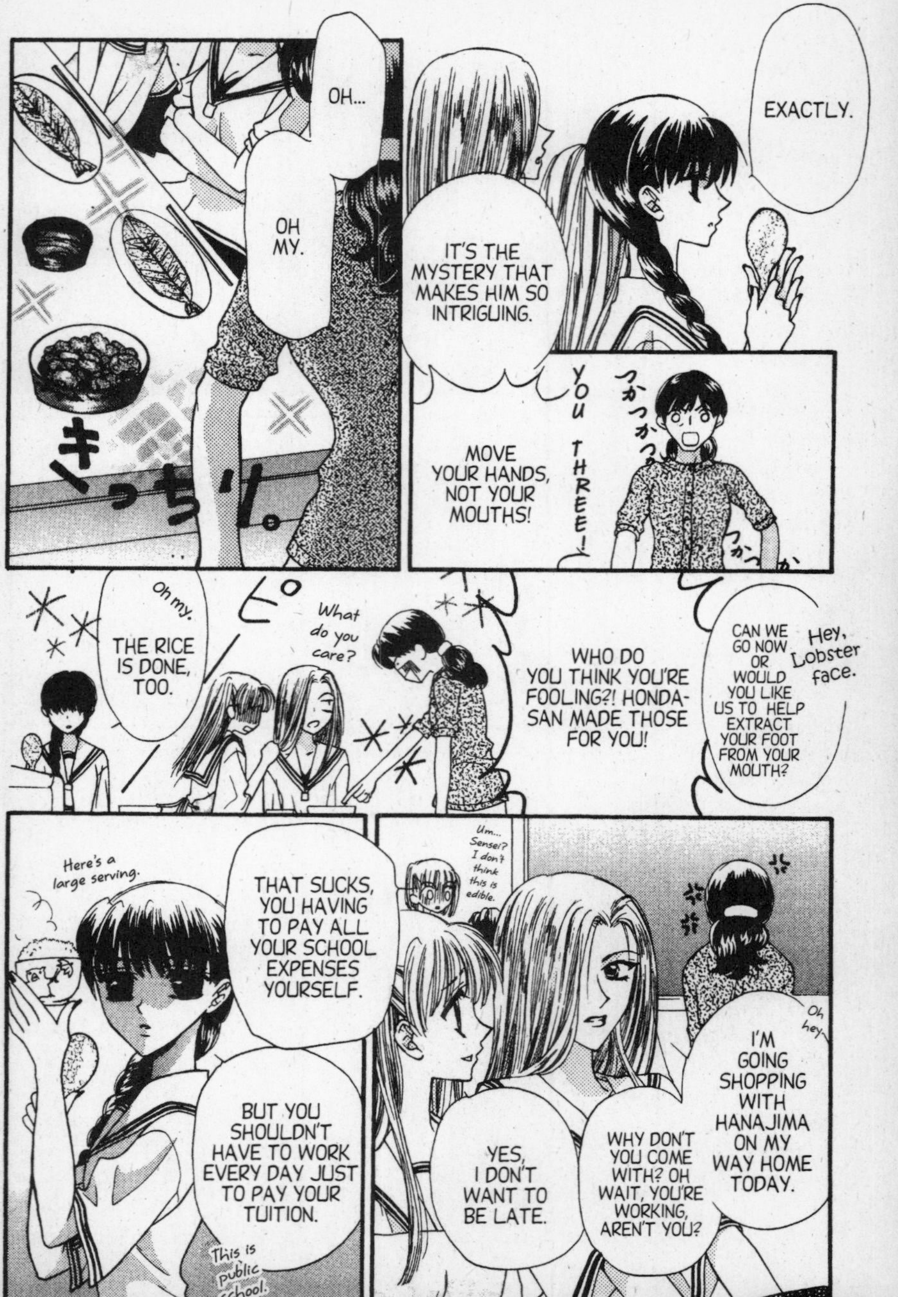
EXACTLY.
IT'S THE MYSTERY THAT MAKES HIM SO INTRIGUING.
つかつかつか
YOU THREE!
MOVE YOUR HANDS, NOT YOUR MOUTHS!
つかつか
OH...
OH MY.
キッチリ。
Hey, Lobster face.
CAN WE GO NOW OR WOULD YOU LIKE US TO HELP EXTRACT YOUR FOOT FROM YOUR MOUTH?
WHO DO YOU THINK YOU'RE FOOLING?! HONDA-SAN MADE THOSE FOR YOU!
What do you care?
ピ
Oh my.
THE RICE IS DONE, TOO.
Oh hey.
I'M GOING SHOPPING WITH HANAJIMA ON MY WAY HOME TODAY.
WHY DON'T YOU COME WITH? OH WAIT, YOU'RE WORKING, AREN'T YOU?
YES, I DON'T WANT TO BE LATE.
Um... Sensei? I don't think this is edible.
THAT SUCKS, YOU HAVING TO PAY ALL YOUR SCHOOL EXPENSES YOURSELF.
Here's a large serving.
BUT YOU SHOULDN'T HAVE TO WORK EVERY DAY JUST TO PAY YOUR TUITION.
This is public school.

The Yankee has a soft spot for her friends.

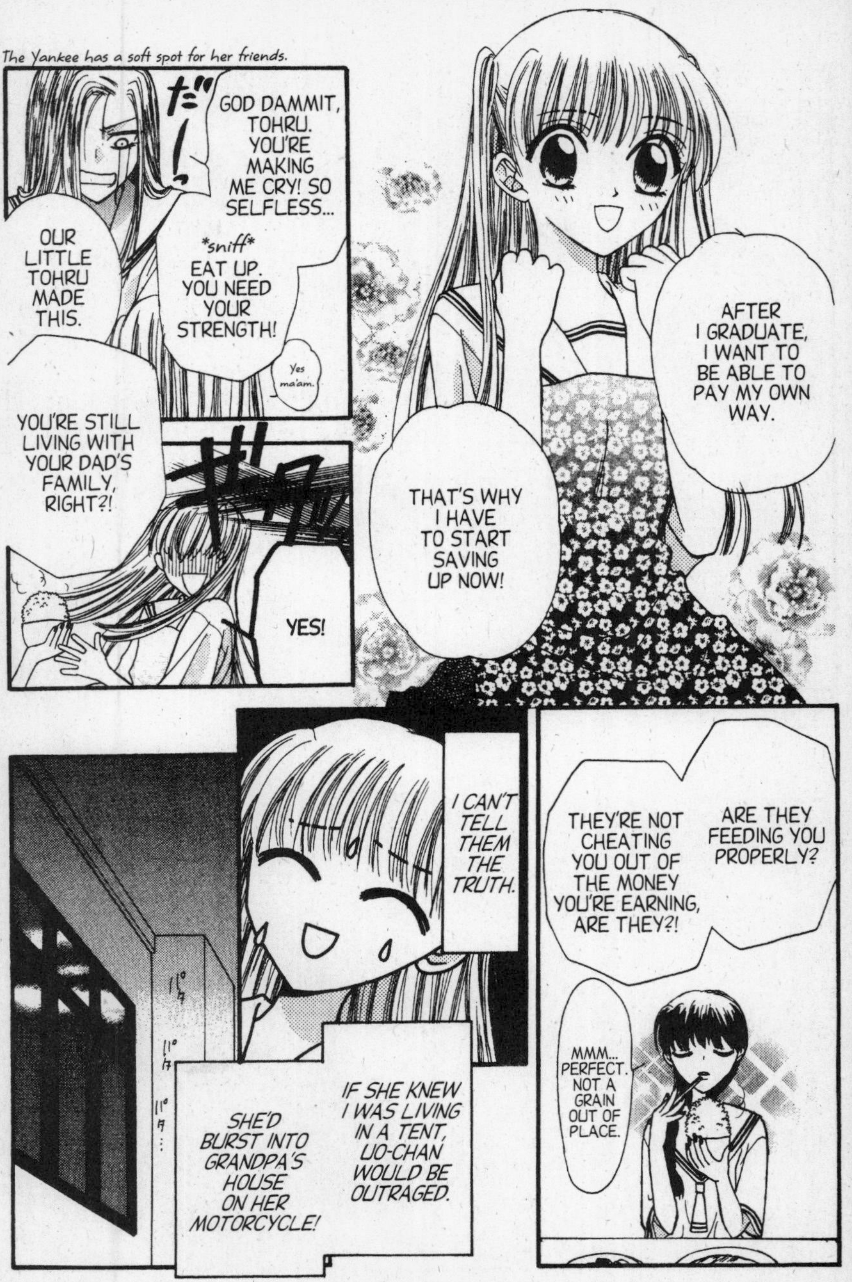

AFTER I GRADUATE, I WANT TO BE ABLE TO PAY MY OWN WAY.
THAT'S WHY I HAVE TO START SAVING UP NOW!
GOD DAMMIT, TOHRU. YOU'RE MAKING ME CRY! SO SELFLESS...
sniff EAT UP. YOU NEED YOUR STRENGTH!
OUR LITTLE TOHRU MADE THIS.
Yes ma'am.
YOU'RE STILL LIVING WITH YOUR DAD'S FAMILY, RIGHT?!
YES!
ARE THEY FEEDING YOU PROPERLY?
THEY'RE NOT CHEATING YOU OUT OF THE MONEY YOU'RE EARNING, ARE THEY?!
MMM... PERFECT. NOT A GRAIN OUT OF PLACE.
I CAN'T TELL THEM THE TRUTH.
IF SHE KNEW I WAS LIVING IN A TENT, UO-CHAN WOULD BE OUTRAGED.
SHE'D BURST INTO GRANDPA'S HOUSE ON HER MOTORCYCLE!

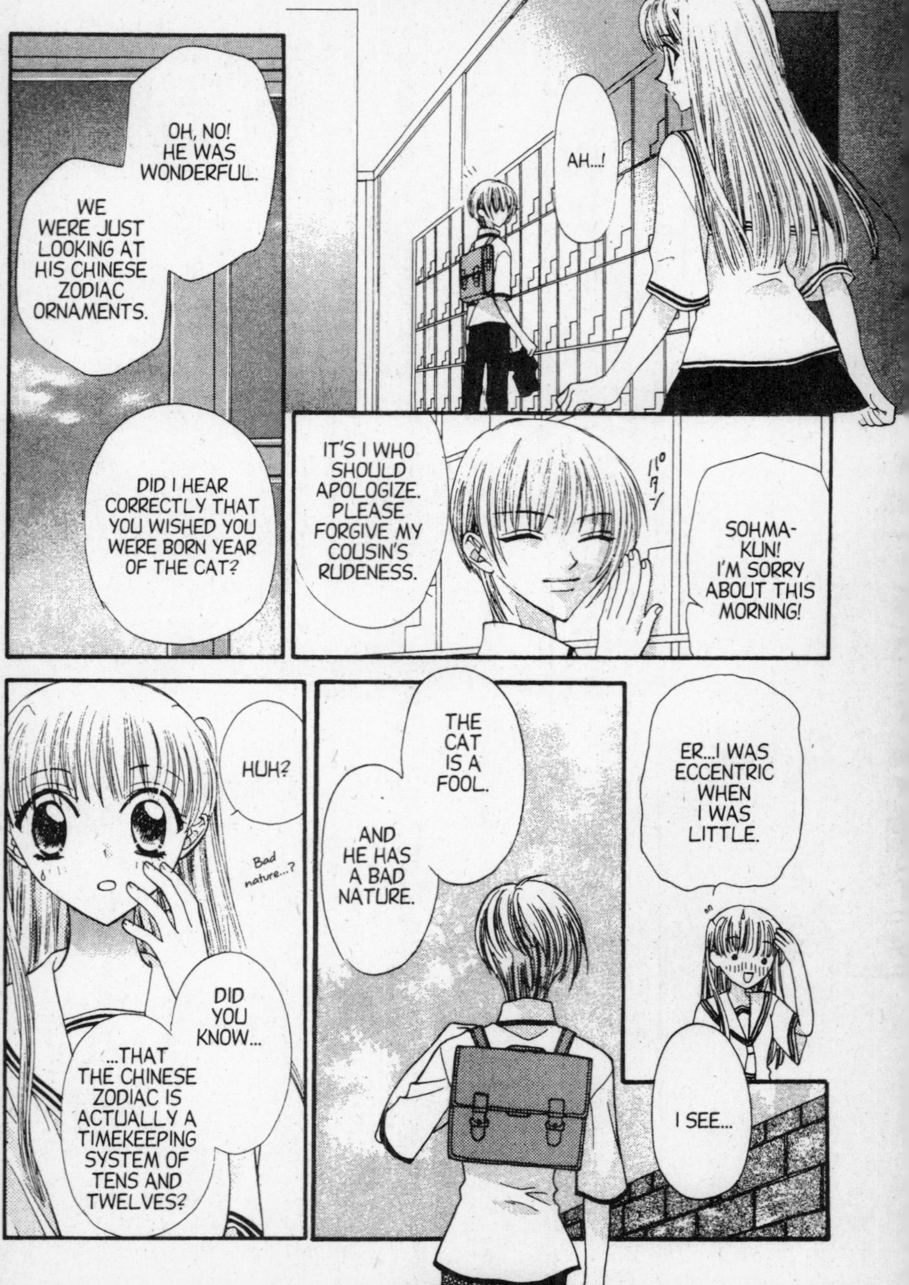
AH...!
SOHMA-KUN! I'M SORRY ABOUT THIS MORNING!
IT'S I WHO SHOULD APOLOGIZE. PLEASE FORGIVE MY COUSIN'S RUDENESS.
OH, NO! HE WAS WONDERFUL.
WE WERE JUST LOOKING AT HIS CHINESE ZODIAC ORNAMENTS.
DID I HEAR CORRECTLY THAT YOU WISHED YOU WERE BORN YEAR OF THE CAT?
ER...I WAS ECCENTRIC WHEN I WAS LITTLE.
THE CAT IS A FOOL.
AND HE HAS A BAD NATURE.
I SEE...
HUH?
Bad nature...?
DID YOU KNOW...
...THAT THE CHINESE ZODIAC IS ACTUALLY A TIMEKEEPING SYSTEM OF TENS AND TWELVES?

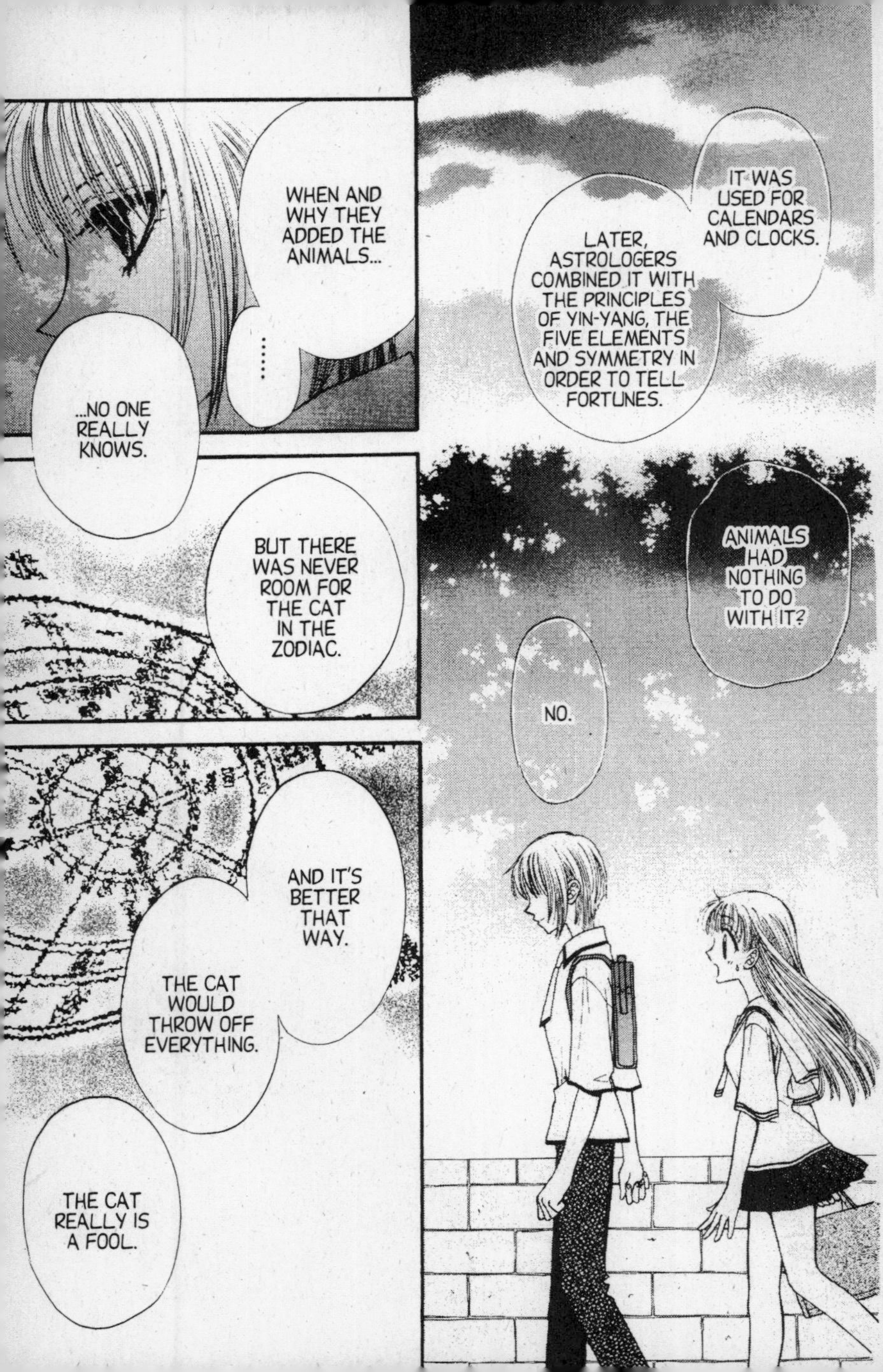
IT WAS USED FOR CALENDARS AND CLOCKS.
LATER, ASTROLOGERS COMBINED IT WITH THE PRINCIPLES OF YIN-YANG, THE FIVE ELEMENTS AND SYMMETRY IN ORDER TO TELL FORTUNES.
ANIMALS HAD NOTHING TO DO WITH IT?
NO.
WHEN AND WHY THEY ADDED THE ANIMALS...
......
...NO ONE REALLY KNOWS.
BUT THERE WAS NEVER ROOM FOR THE CAT IN THE ZODIAC.
AND IT'S BETTER THAT WAY.
THE CAT WOULD THROW OFF EVERYTHING.
THE CAT REALLY IS A FOOL.

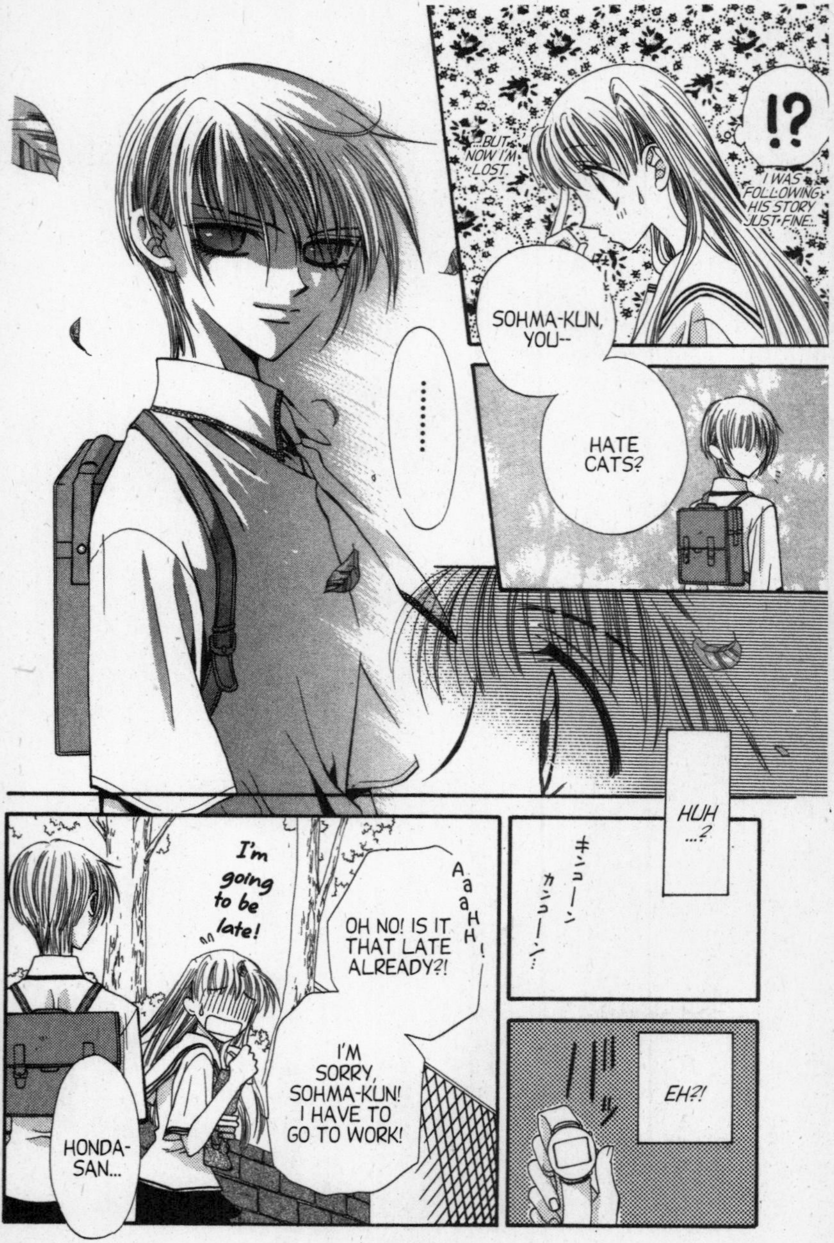
!?
I WAS FOLLOWING HIS STORY JUST FINE...
...BUT NOW I'M LOST.
SOHMA-KUN, YOU--
HATE CATS?
......
HUH...?
キンコーン
カンコーン...
EH?!
AaaHH!
OH NO! IS IT THAT LATE ALREADY?!
I'M SORRY, SOHMA-KUN! I HAVE TO GO TO WORK!
I'm going to be late!
HONDA-SAN...

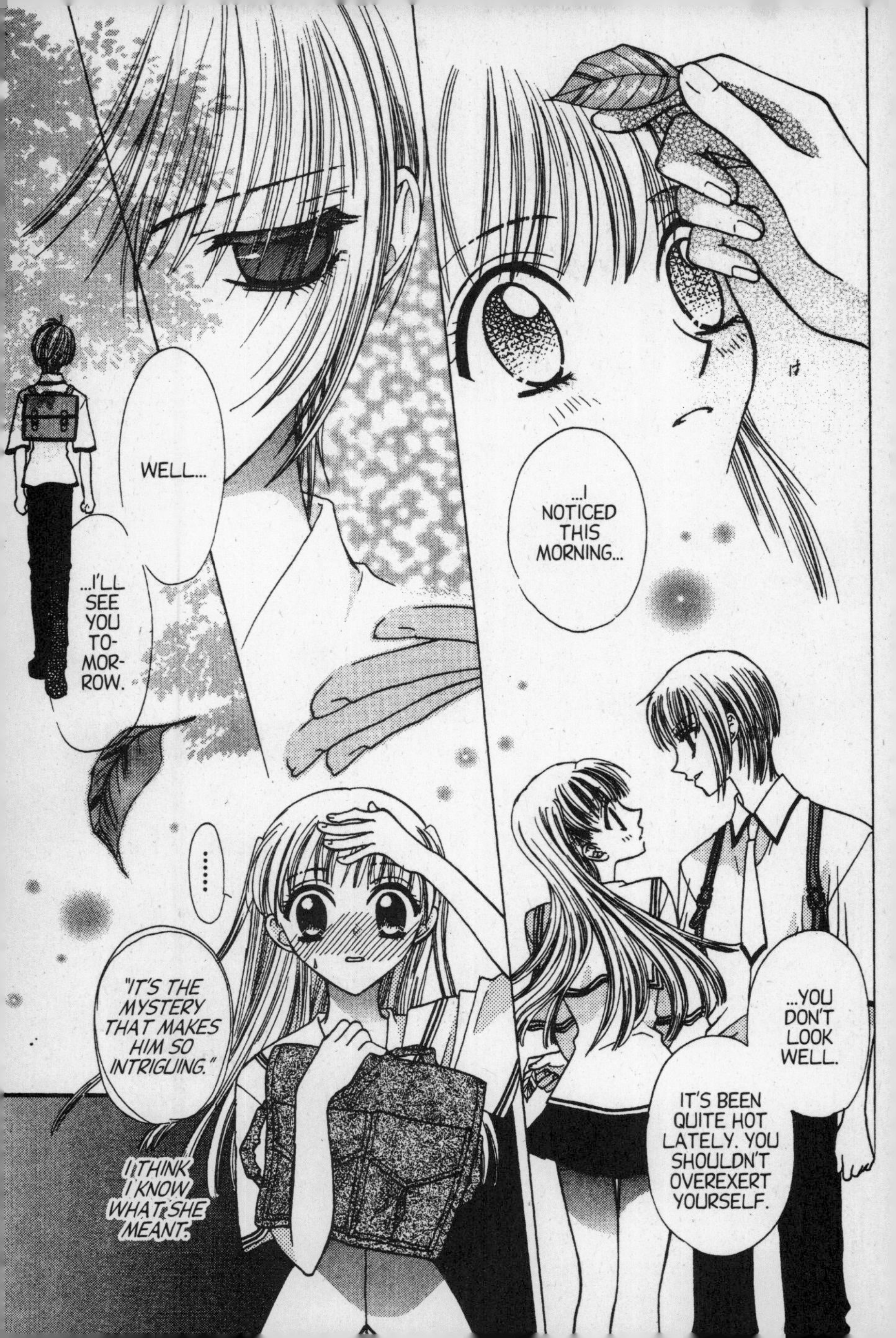
...I NOTICED THIS MORNING...
WELL...
...I'LL SEE YOU TO-MOR-ROW.
...YOU DON'T LOOK WELL.
IT'S BEEN QUITE HOT LATELY. YOU SHOULDN'T OVEREXERT YOURSELF.
......
"IT'S THE MYSTERY THAT MAKES HIM SO INTRIGUING."
I THINK I KNOW WHAT SHE MEANT.

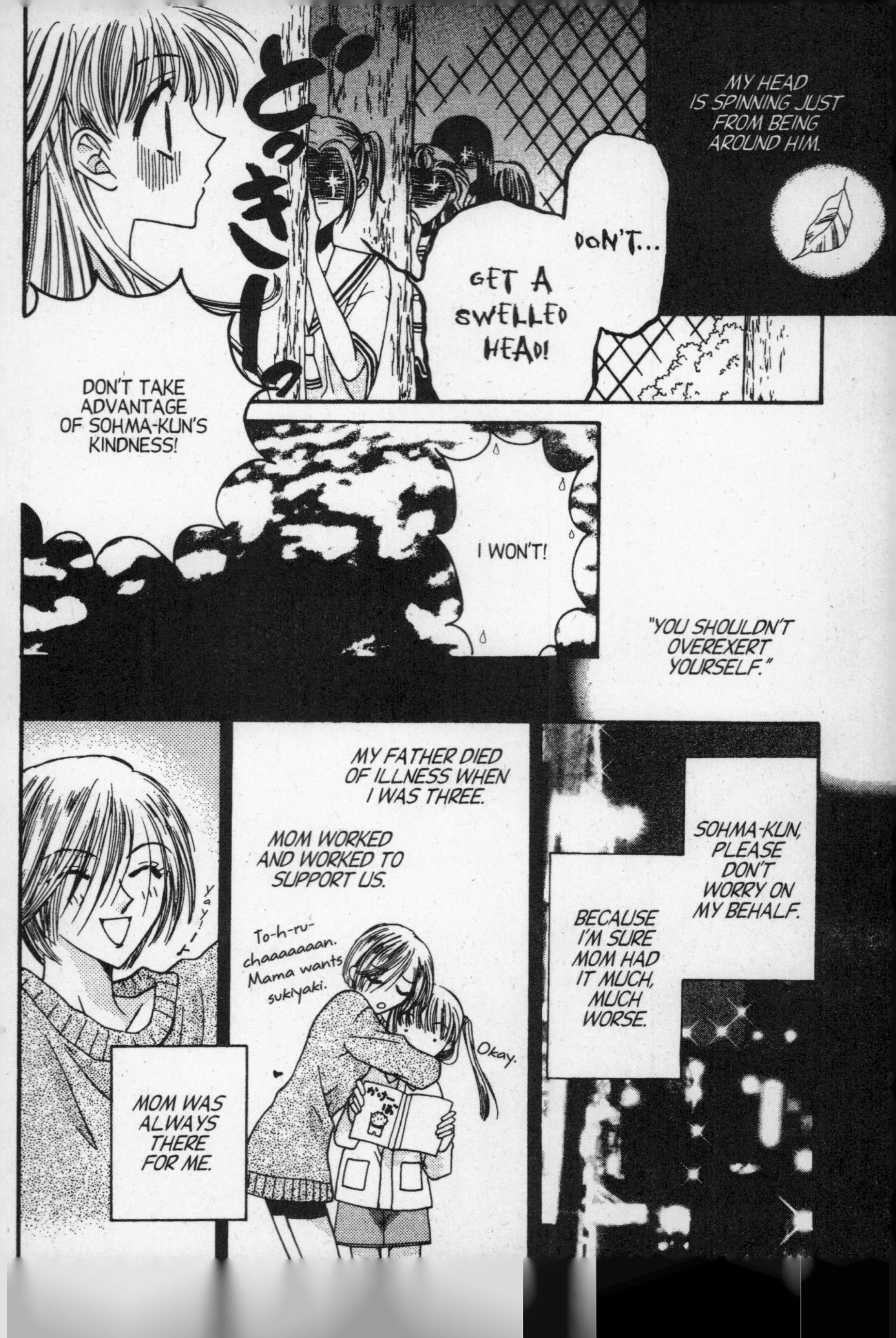

MY HEAD IS SPINNING JUST FROM BEING AROUND HIM.
どっきーっ
DON'T...
GET A SWELLED HEAD!
DON'T TAKE ADVANTAGE OF SOHMA-KUN'S KINDNESS!
I WON'T!
"YOU SHOULDN'T OVEREXERT YOURSELF."
SOHMA-KUN, PLEASE DON'T WORRY ON MY BEHALF.
BECAUSE I'M SURE MOM HAD IT MUCH, MUCH WORSE.
MY FATHER DIED OF ILLNESS WHEN I WAS THREE.
MOM WORKED AND WORKED TO SUPPORT US.
To-h-ru-chaaaaaaan. Mama wants sukiyaki.
Okay.
Yay!!
MOM WAS ALWAYS THERE FOR ME.

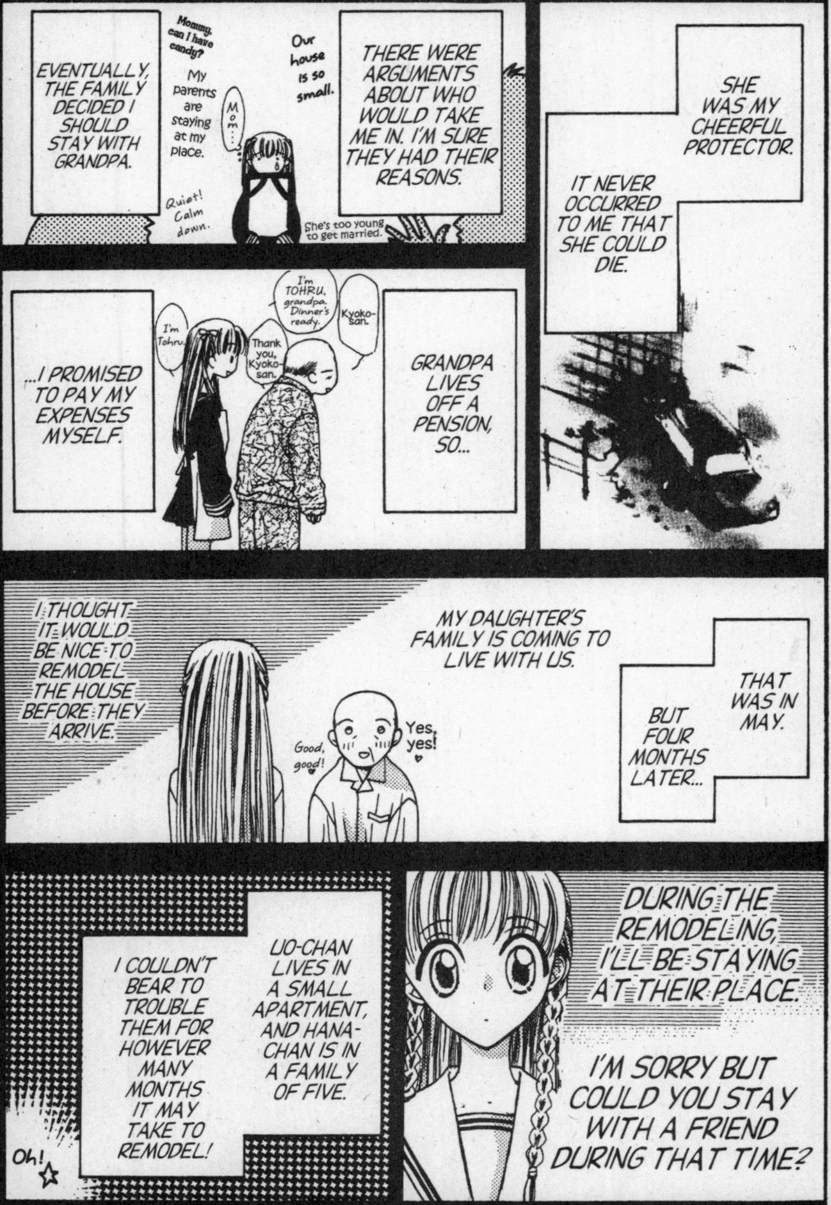
SHE WAS MY CHEERFUL PROTECTOR.
IT NEVER OCCURRED TO ME THAT SHE COULD DIE.
THERE WERE ARGUMENTS ABOUT WHO WOULD TAKE ME IN. I'M SURE THEY HAD THEIR REASONS.
Our house is so small.
Mommy, can I have candy?
My parents are staying at my place.
Mom...
She's too young to get married.
Quiet! Calm down.
EVENTUALLY, THE FAMILY DECIDED I SHOULD STAY WITH GRANDPA.
GRANDPA LIVES OFF A PENSION, SO...
Kyoko-san.
I'm TOHRU, grandpa. Dinner's ready.
Thank you, Kyoko-san.
I'm Tohru.
...I PROMISED TO PAY MY EXPENSES MYSELF.
THAT WAS IN MAY.
BUT FOUR MONTHS LATER...
MY DAUGHTER'S FAMILY IS COMING TO LIVE WITH US.
Yes, yes!
Good, good!
I THOUGHT IT WOULD BE NICE TO REMODEL THE HOUSE BEFORE THEY ARRIVE.
DURING THE REMODELING, I'LL BE STAYING AT THEIR PLACE.
I'M SORRY BUT COULD YOU STAY WITH A FRIEND DURING THAT TIME?
UO-CHAN LIVES IN A SMALL APARTMENT, AND HANA-CHAN IS IN A FAMILY OF FIVE.
I COULDN'T BEAR TO TROUBLE THEM FOR HOWEVER MANY MONTHS IT MAY TAKE TO REMODEL!
Oh!

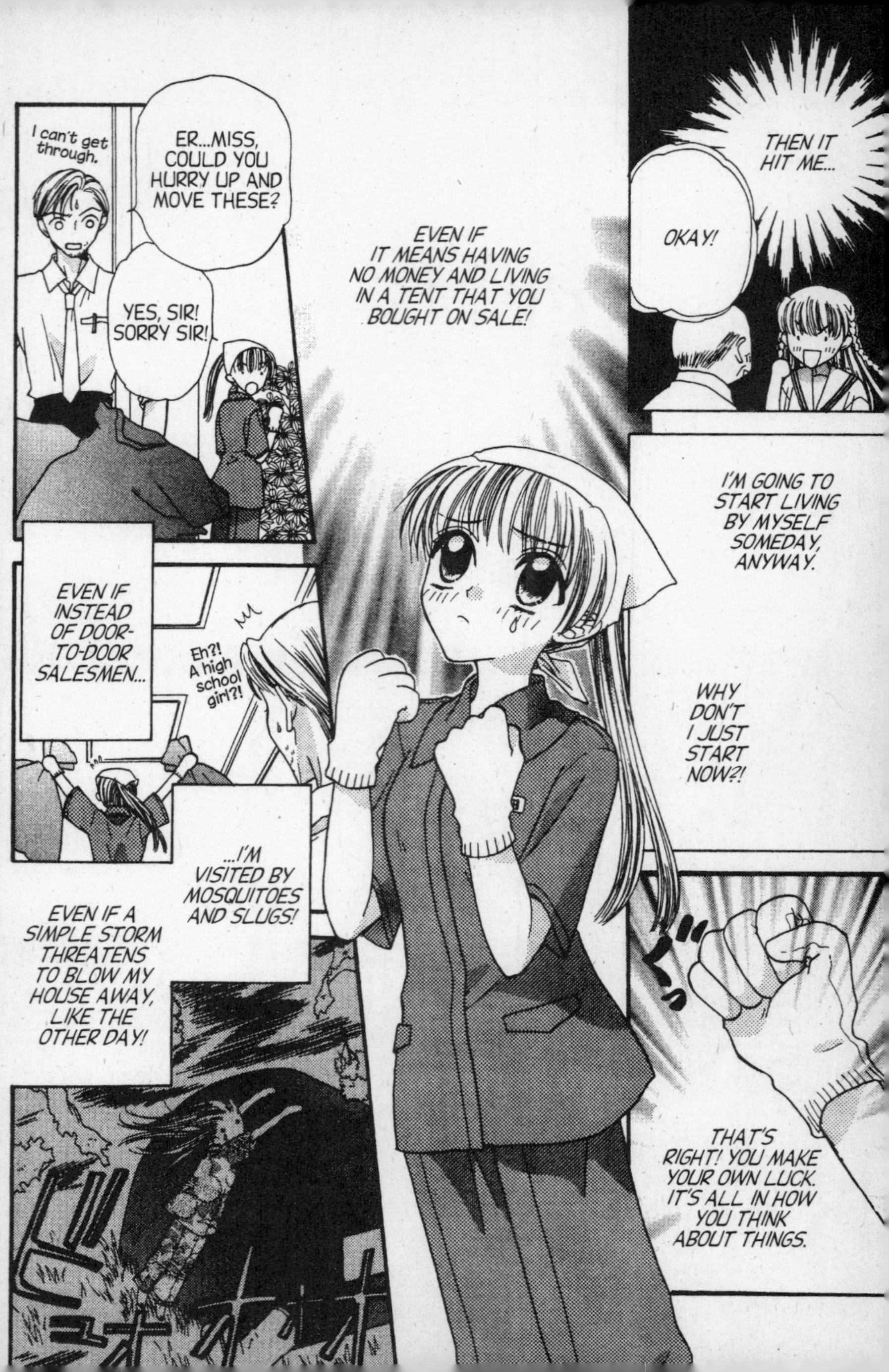
THEN IT HIT ME...
OKAY!
I'M GOING TO START LIVING BY MYSELF SOMEDAY, ANYWAY.
WHY DON'T I JUST START NOW?!
THAT'S RIGHT! YOU MAKE YOUR OWN LUCK. IT'S ALL IN HOW YOU THINK ABOUT THINGS.
EVEN IF IT MEANS HAVING NO MONEY AND LIVING IN A TENT THAT YOU BOUGHT ON SALE!
ER...MISS, COULD YOU HURRY UP AND MOVE THESE?
I can't get through.
YES, SIR! SORRY SIR!
EVEN IF INSTEAD OF DOOR-TO-DOOR SALESMEN...
Eh?! A high school girl?!
...I'M VISITED BY MOSQUITOES AND SLUGS!
EVEN IF A SIMPLE STORM THREATENS TO BLOW MY HOUSE AWAY, LIKE THE OTHER DAY!

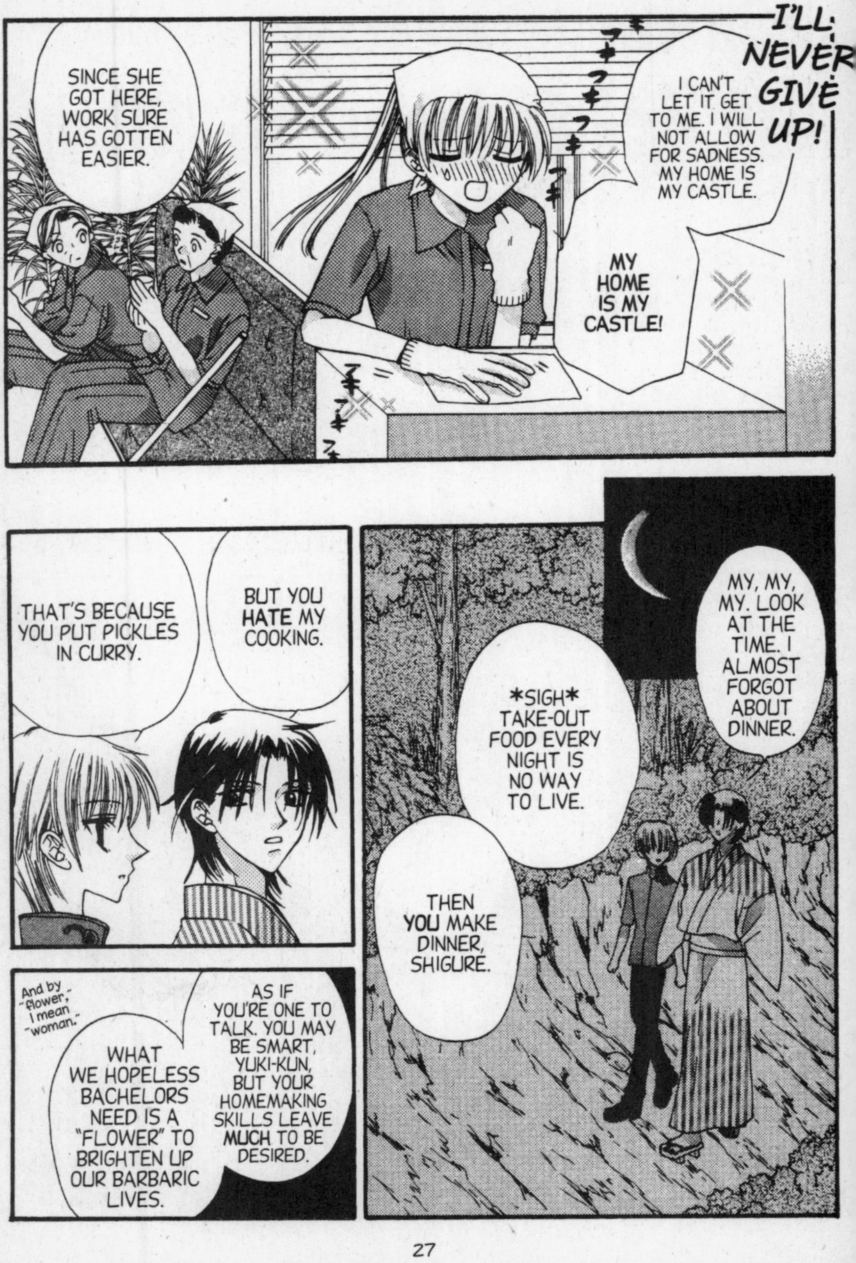
I'LL NEVER GIVE UP!
I CAN'T LET IT GET TO ME. I WILL NOT ALLOW FOR SADNESS. MY HOME IS MY CASTLE.
MY HOME IS MY CASTLE!
SINCE SHE GOT HERE, WORK SURE HAS GOTTEN EASIER.
MY, MY, MY. LOOK AT THE TIME. I ALMOST FORGOT ABOUT DINNER.
SIGH TAKE-OUT FOOD EVERY NIGHT IS NO WAY TO LIVE.
THEN YOU MAKE DINNER, SHIGURE.
BUT YOU HATE MY COOKING.
THAT'S BECAUSE YOU PUT PICKLES IN CURRY.
AS IF YOU'RE ONE TO TALK. YOU MAY BE SMART, YUKI-KUN, BUT YOUR HOMEMAKING SKILLS LEAVE MUCH TO BE DESIRED.
WHAT WE HOPELESS BACHELORS NEED IS A "FLOWER" TO BRIGHTEN UP OUR BARBARIC LIVES.
And by "flower," I mean "woman."

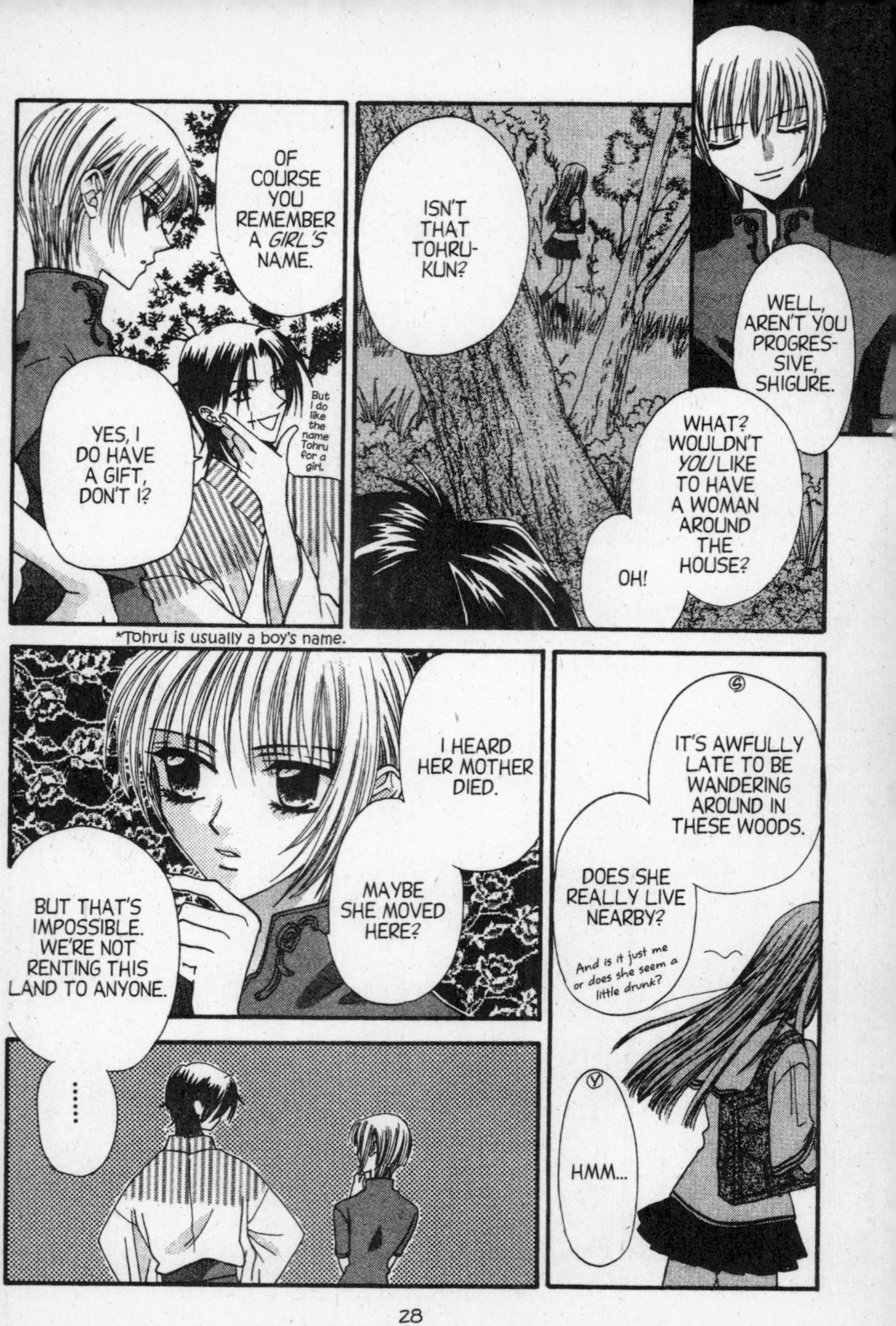
WELL, AREN'T YOU PROGRES-SIVE, SHIGURE.
WHAT? WOULDN'T *YOU* LIKE TO HAVE A WOMAN AROUND THE HOUSE?
OH!
ISN'T THAT TOHRU-KUN?
OF COURSE YOU REMEMBER A *GIRL'S* NAME.
But I do like the name Tohru for a girl.
YES, I DO HAVE A GIFT, DON'T I?
*Tohru is usually a boy's name.
IT'S AWFULLY LATE TO BE WANDERING AROUND IN THESE WOODS.
DOES SHE REALLY LIVE NEARBY?
And is it just me or does she seem a little drunk?
HMM...
I HEARD HER MOTHER DIED.
MAYBE SHE MOVED HERE?
BUT THAT'S IMPOSSIBLE. WE'RE NOT RENTING THIS LAND TO ANYONE.
......

Number 2:

I get mail from people who started with "Furuba" asking me to introduce myself, so here I go: Natsuki Takaya (pen name)/ July 7th/Cancer/ Blood type A/ Tokyo (I moved)/ left-handed. People say that left-handers are natural students—not me! I couldn't study. I didn't ever feel like it, and when I did study, my grades stayed the same anyway. I like games and music and I'm not that interested in talking about myself. It's way more fun to talk about my favorite things and favorite characters. Like, "Pikachu is adorable!" (Ha ha!)

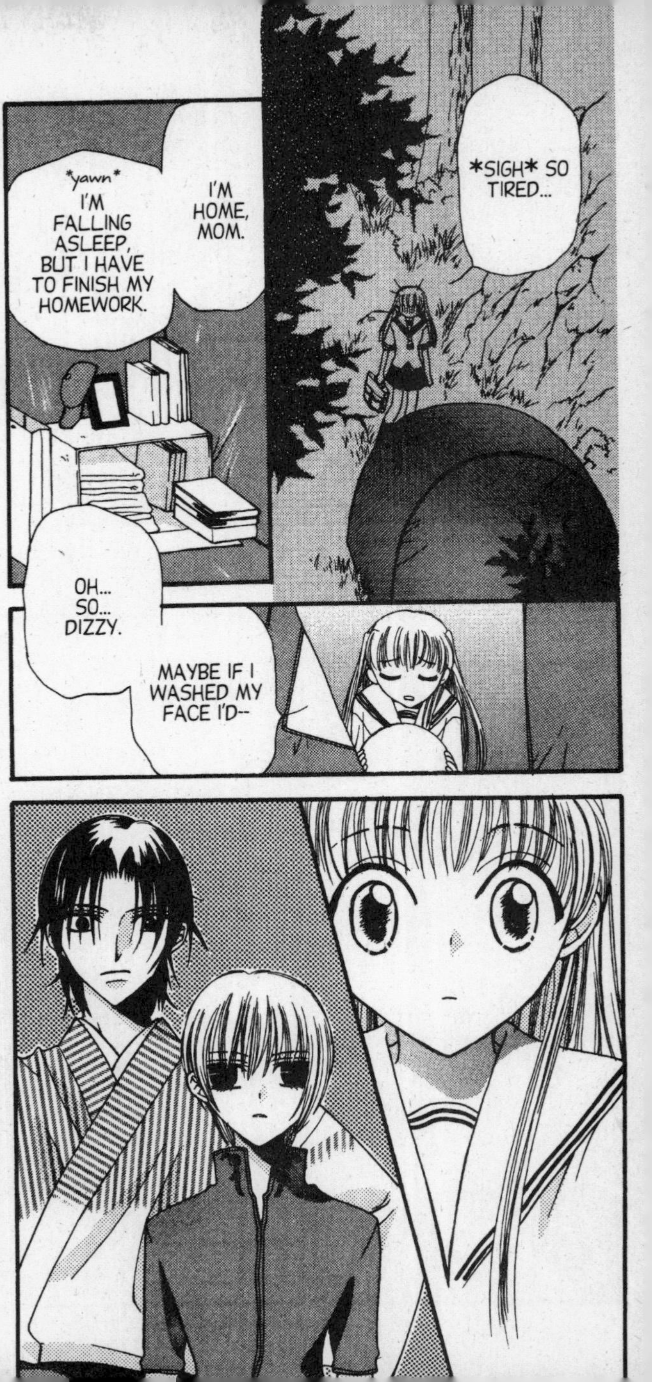

SIGH SO TIRED...
I'M HOME, MOM.
yawn I'M FALLING ASLEEP, BUT I HAVE TO FINISH MY HOMEWORK.
OH... SO... DIZZY.
MAYBE IF I WASHED MY FACE I'D--

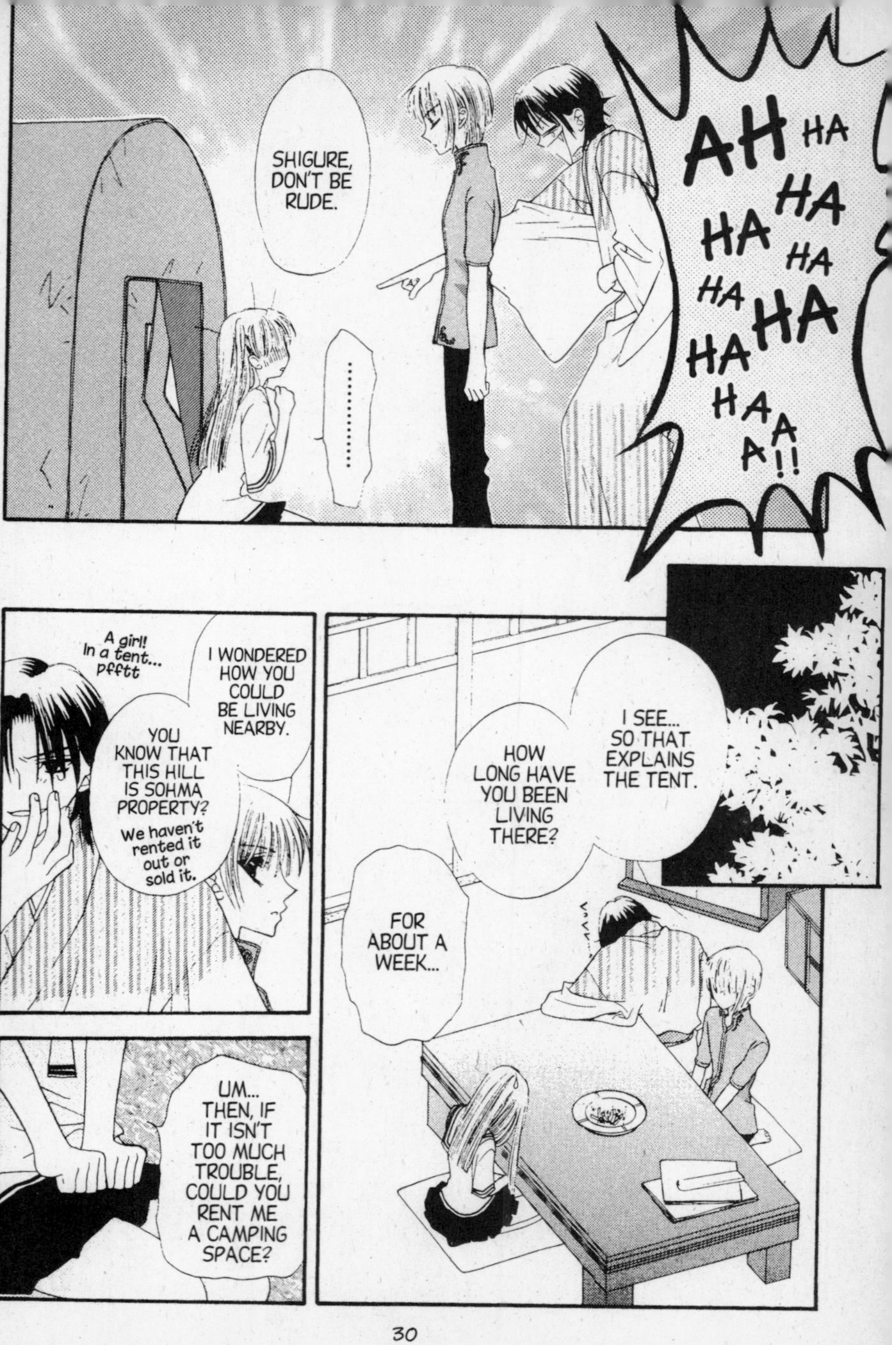
AH HA HA HA HA HA HA HA HA HAAA!!
SHIGURE, DON'T BE RUDE.
......
I SEE... SO THAT EXPLAINS THE TENT.
HOW LONG HAVE YOU BEEN LIVING THERE?
FOR ABOUT A WEEK...
I WONDERED HOW YOU COULD BE LIVING NEARBY.
A girl! In a tent... pfftt
YOU KNOW THAT THIS HILL IS SOHMA PROPERTY?
We haven't rented it out or sold it.
UM... THEN, IF IT ISN'T TOO MUCH TROUBLE, COULD YOU RENT ME A CAMPING SPACE?

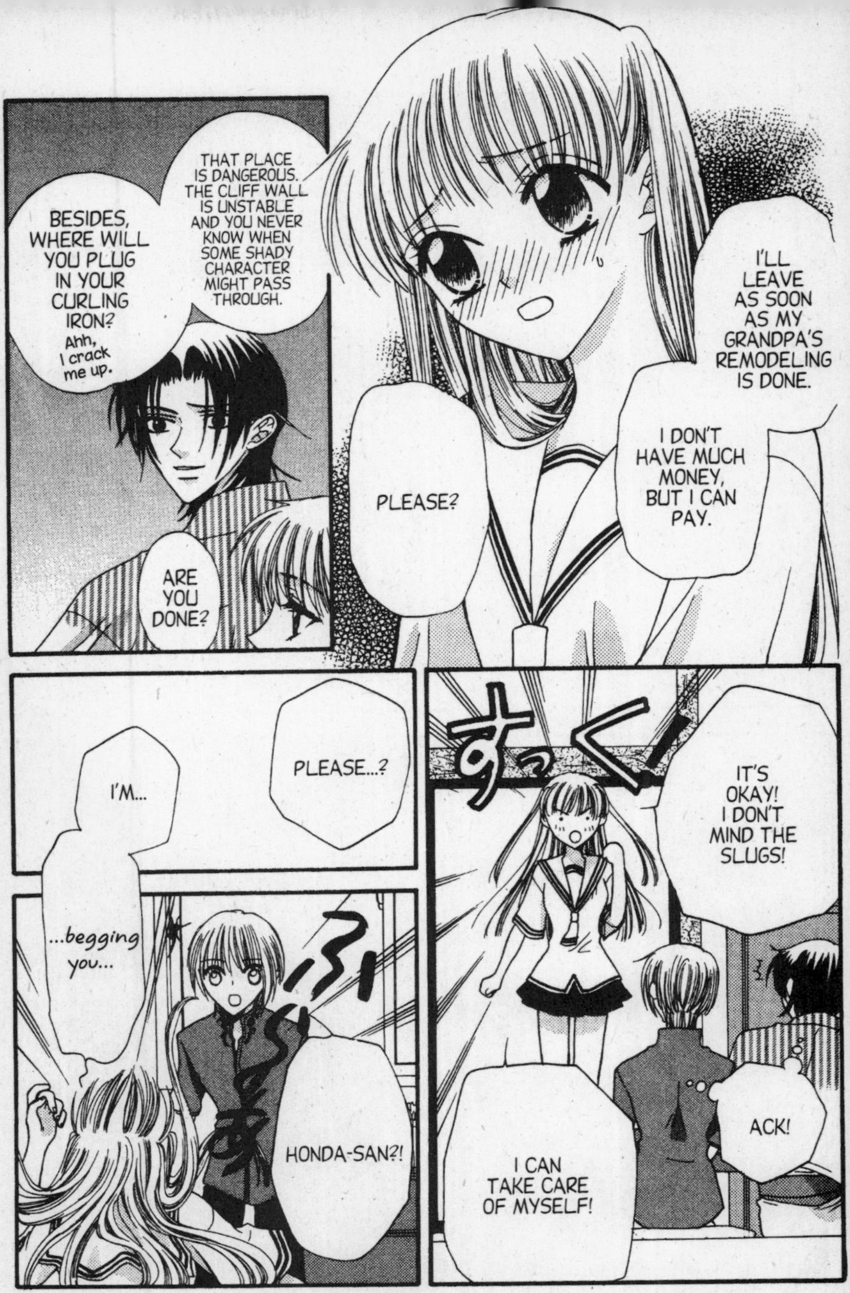
I'LL LEAVE AS SOON AS MY GRANDPA'S REMODELING IS DONE.
I DON'T HAVE MUCH MONEY, BUT I CAN PAY.
PLEASE?
THAT PLACE IS DANGEROUS. THE CLIFF WALL IS UNSTABLE AND YOU NEVER KNOW WHEN SOME SHADY CHARACTER MIGHT PASS THROUGH.
BESIDES, WHERE WILL YOU PLUG IN YOUR CURLING IRON?
Ahh, I crack me up.
ARE YOU DONE?
すっく
IT'S OKAY! I DON'T MIND THE SLUGS!
ACK!
I CAN TAKE CARE OF MYSELF!
PLEASE...?
I'M...
...begging you...
HONDA-SAN?!

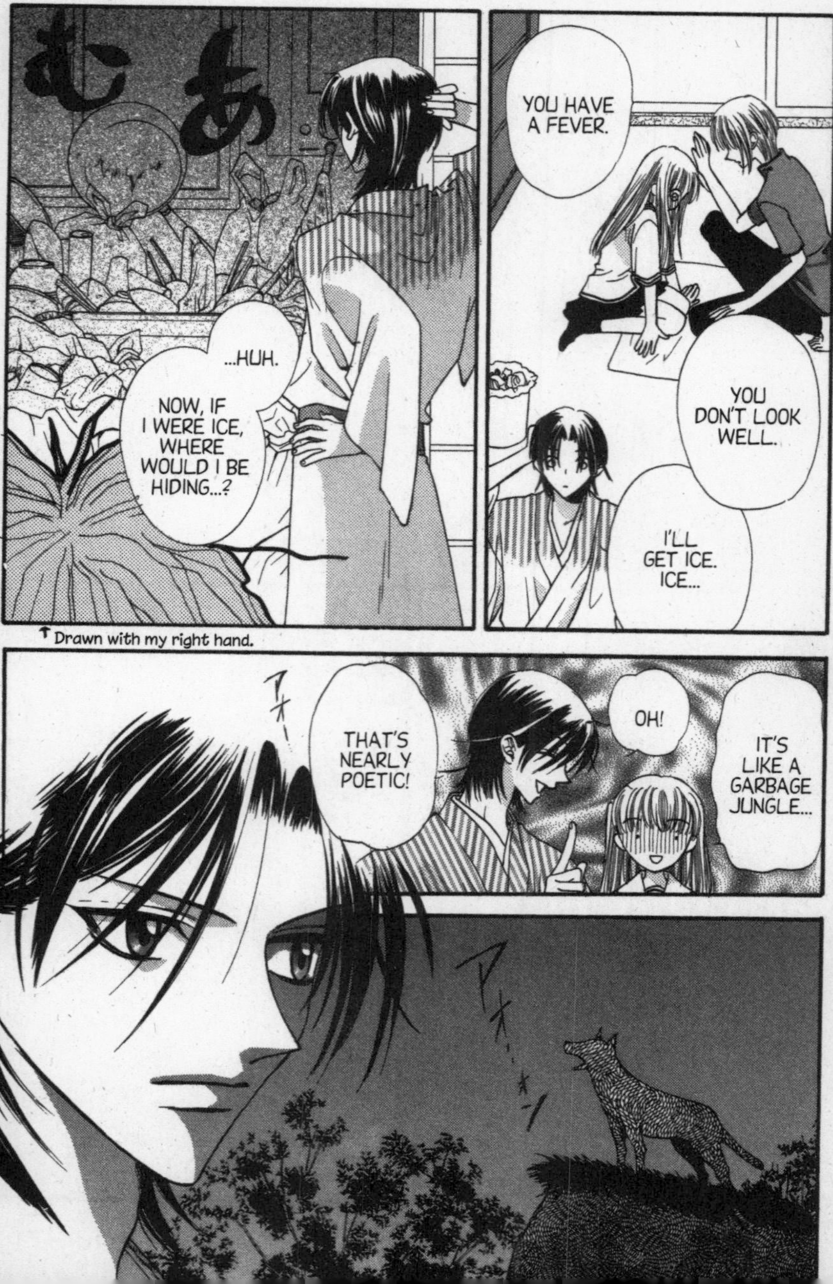
YOU HAVE A FEVER.
YOU DON'T LOOK WELL.
I'LL GET ICE. ICE...
むあ
...HUH.
NOW, IF I WERE ICE, WHERE WOULD I BE HIDING...?
IT'S LIKE A GARBAGE JUNGLE...
OH!
THAT'S NEARLY POETIC!
アオー
アオーー

↑ Drawn with my right hand.

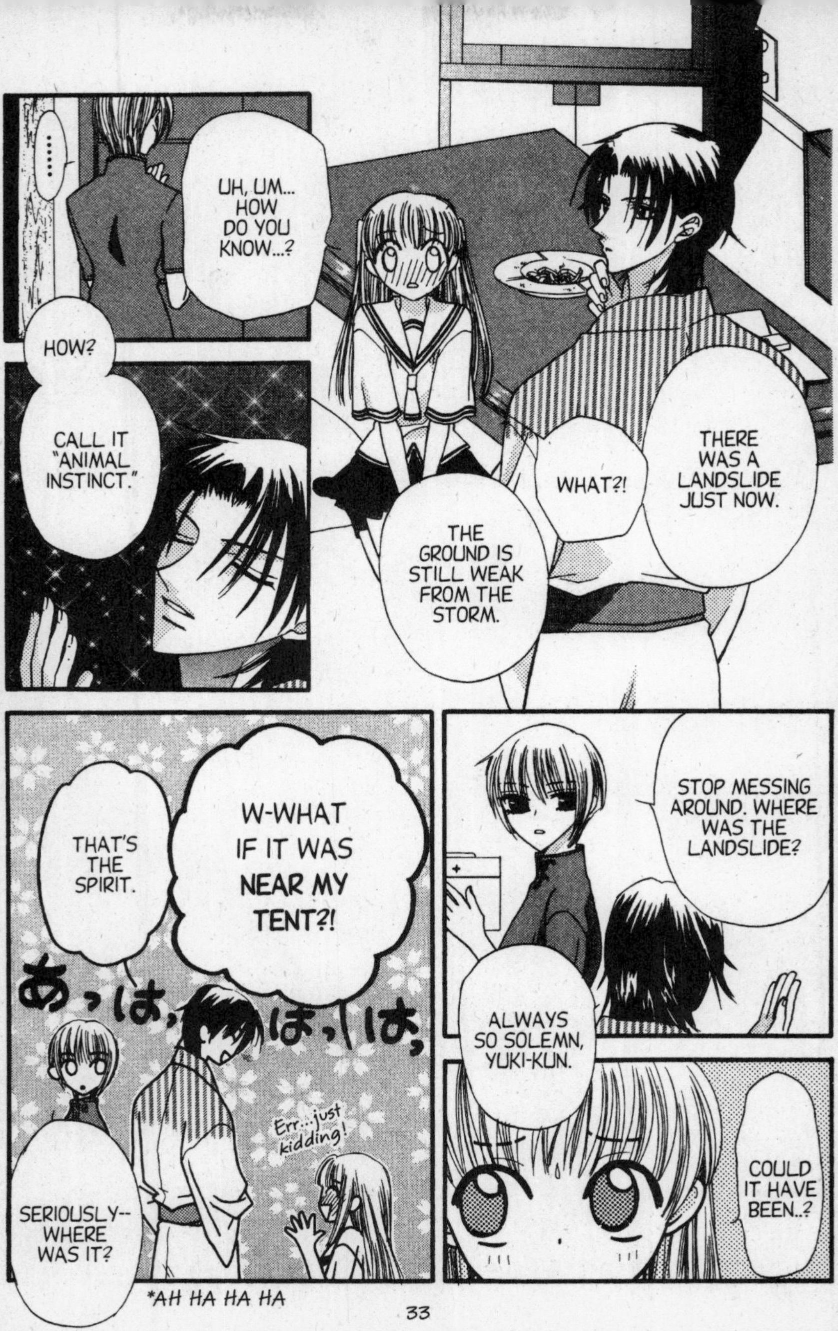

THERE WAS A LANDSLIDE JUST NOW.
WHAT?!
THE GROUND IS STILL WEAK FROM THE STORM.
......
UH, UM... HOW DO YOU KNOW...?
HOW?
CALL IT "ANIMAL INSTINCT."
STOP MESSING AROUND. WHERE WAS THE LANDSLIDE?
ALWAYS SO SOLEMN, YUKI-KUN.
COULD IT HAVE BEEN..?
W-WHAT IF IT WAS NEAR MY TENT?!
THAT'S THE SPIRIT.
あっは、はっは、
Err...just kidding!
SERIOUSLY-- WHERE WAS IT?

*AH HA HA HA

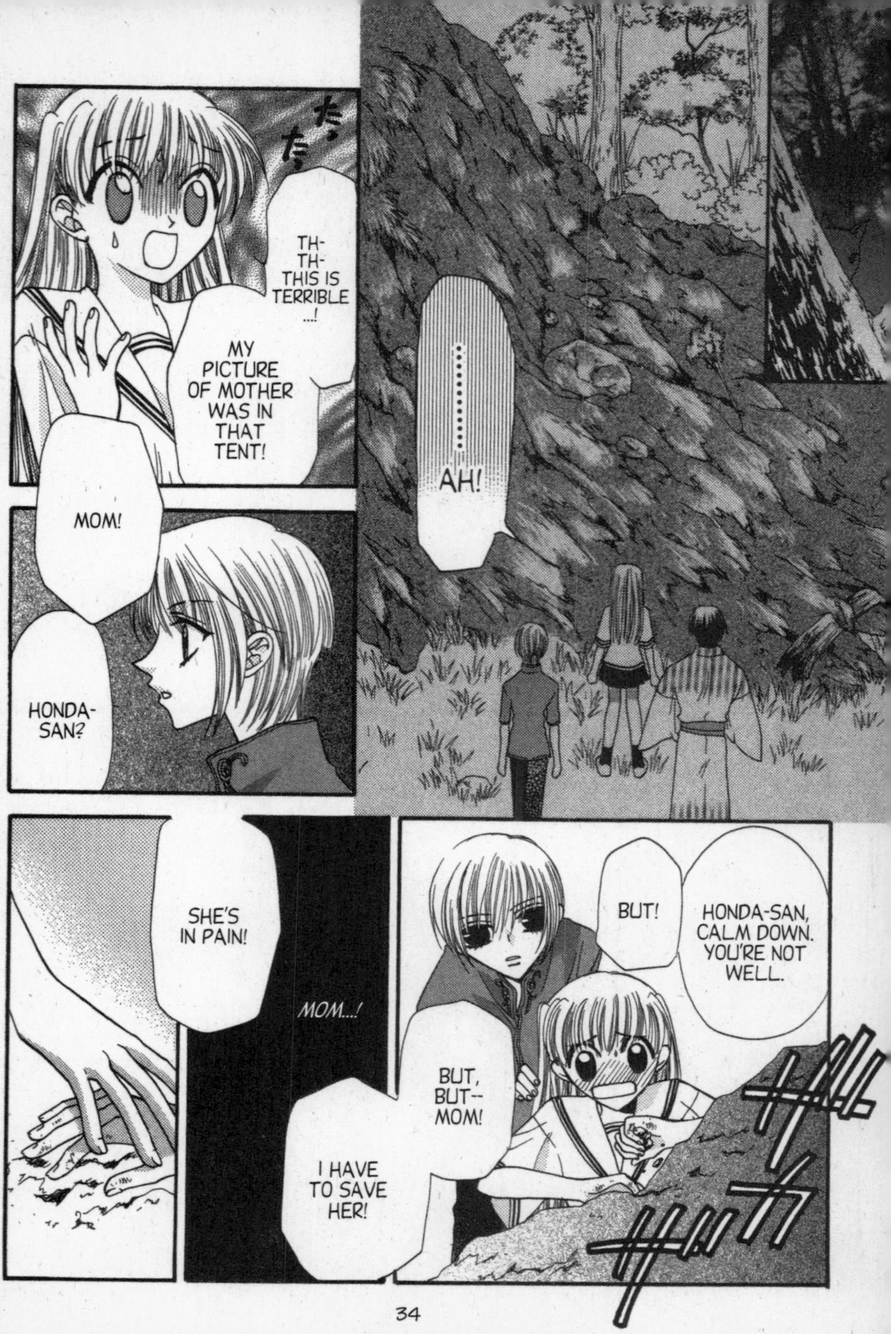
......
AH!
たた
TH-TH-THIS IS TERRIBLE...!
MY PICTURE OF MOTHER WAS IN THAT TENT!
MOM!
HONDA-SAN?
HONDA-SAN, CALM DOWN. YOU'RE NOT WELL.
BUT!
BUT, BUT-- MOM!
I HAVE TO SAVE HER!
MOM...!
SHE'S IN PAIN!

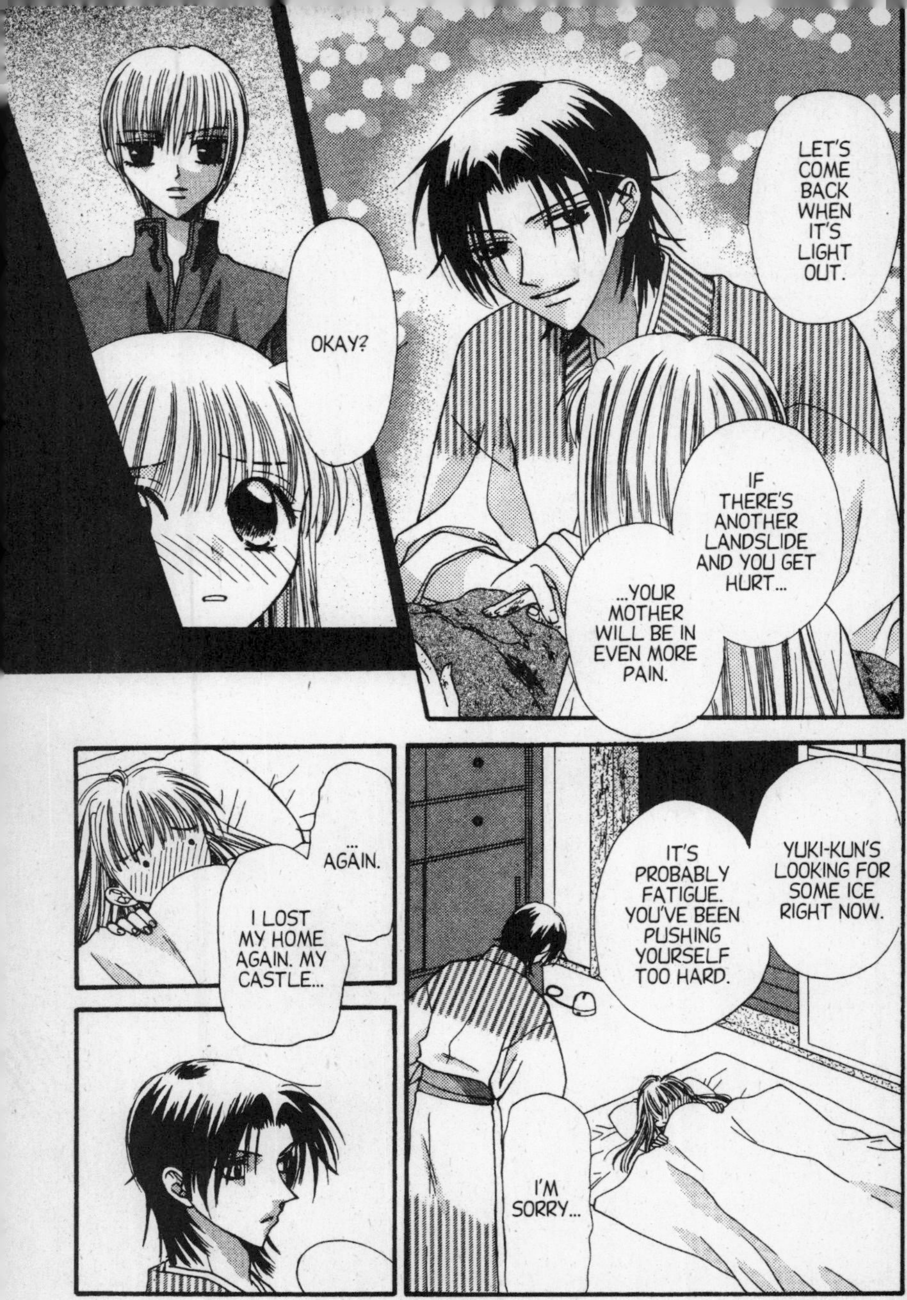
LET'S COME BACK WHEN IT'S LIGHT OUT.
IF THERE'S ANOTHER LANDSLIDE AND YOU GET HURT...
...YOUR MOTHER WILL BE IN EVEN MORE PAIN.
OKAY?
YUKI-KUN'S LOOKING FOR SOME ICE RIGHT NOW.
IT'S PROBABLY FATIGUE. YOU'VE BEEN PUSHING YOURSELF TOO HARD.
I'M SORRY...
...AGAIN.
I LOST MY HOME AGAIN. MY CASTLE...

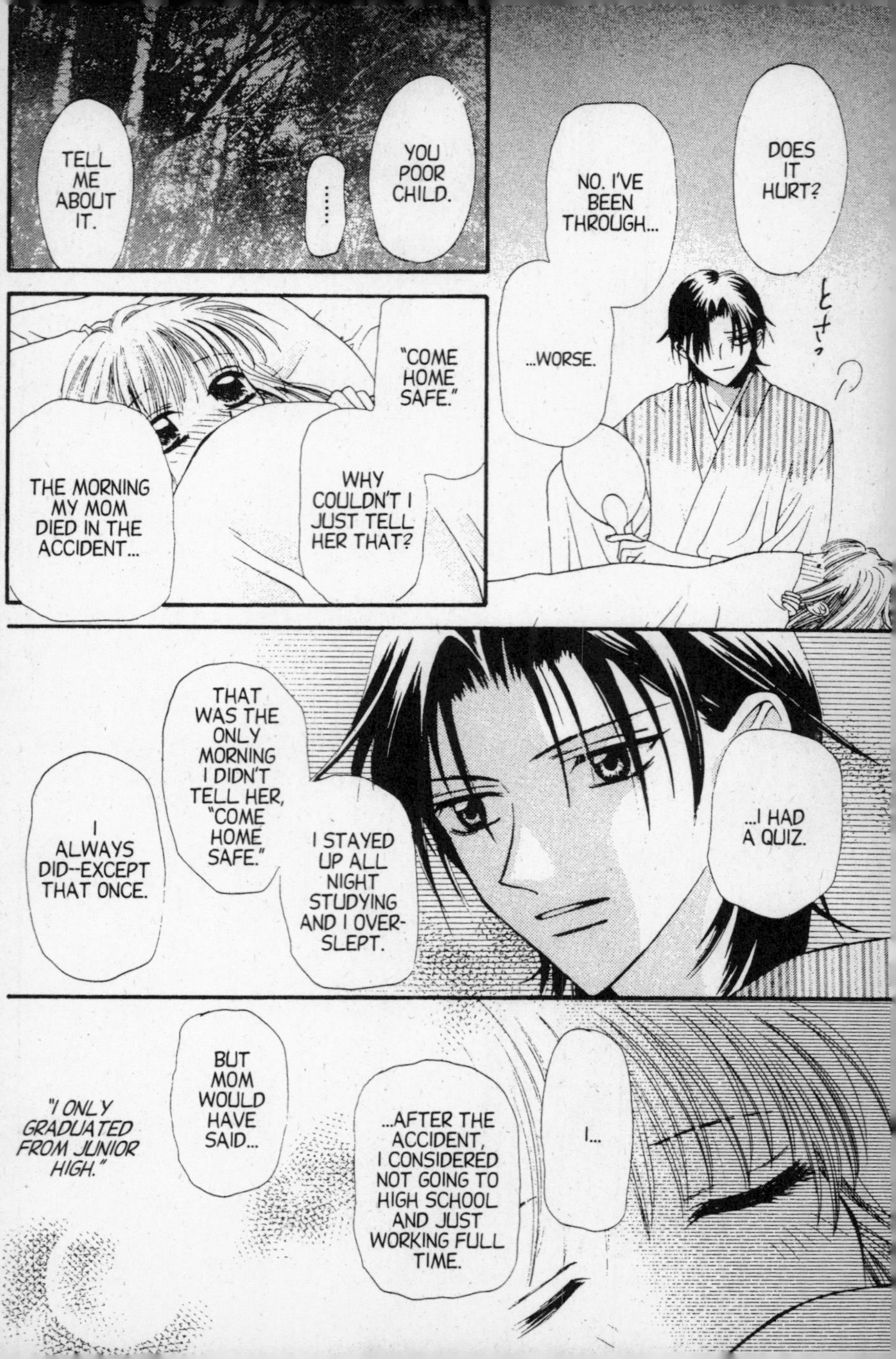
DOES IT HURT?
とさっ
NO. I'VE BEEN THROUGH...
...WORSE.
YOU POOR CHILD.
......
TELL ME ABOUT IT.
"COME HOME SAFE."
WHY COULDN'T I JUST TELL HER THAT?
THE MORNING MY MOM DIED IN THE ACCIDENT...
...I HAD A QUIZ.
I STAYED UP ALL NIGHT STUDYING AND I OVER-SLEPT.
THAT WAS THE ONLY MORNING I DIDN'T TELL HER, "COME HOME SAFE."
I ALWAYS DID--EXCEPT THAT ONCE.
I...
...AFTER THE ACCIDENT, I CONSIDERED NOT GOING TO HIGH SCHOOL AND JUST WORKING FULL TIME.
BUT MOM WOULD HAVE SAID...
"I ONLY GRADUATED FROM JUNIOR HIGH."

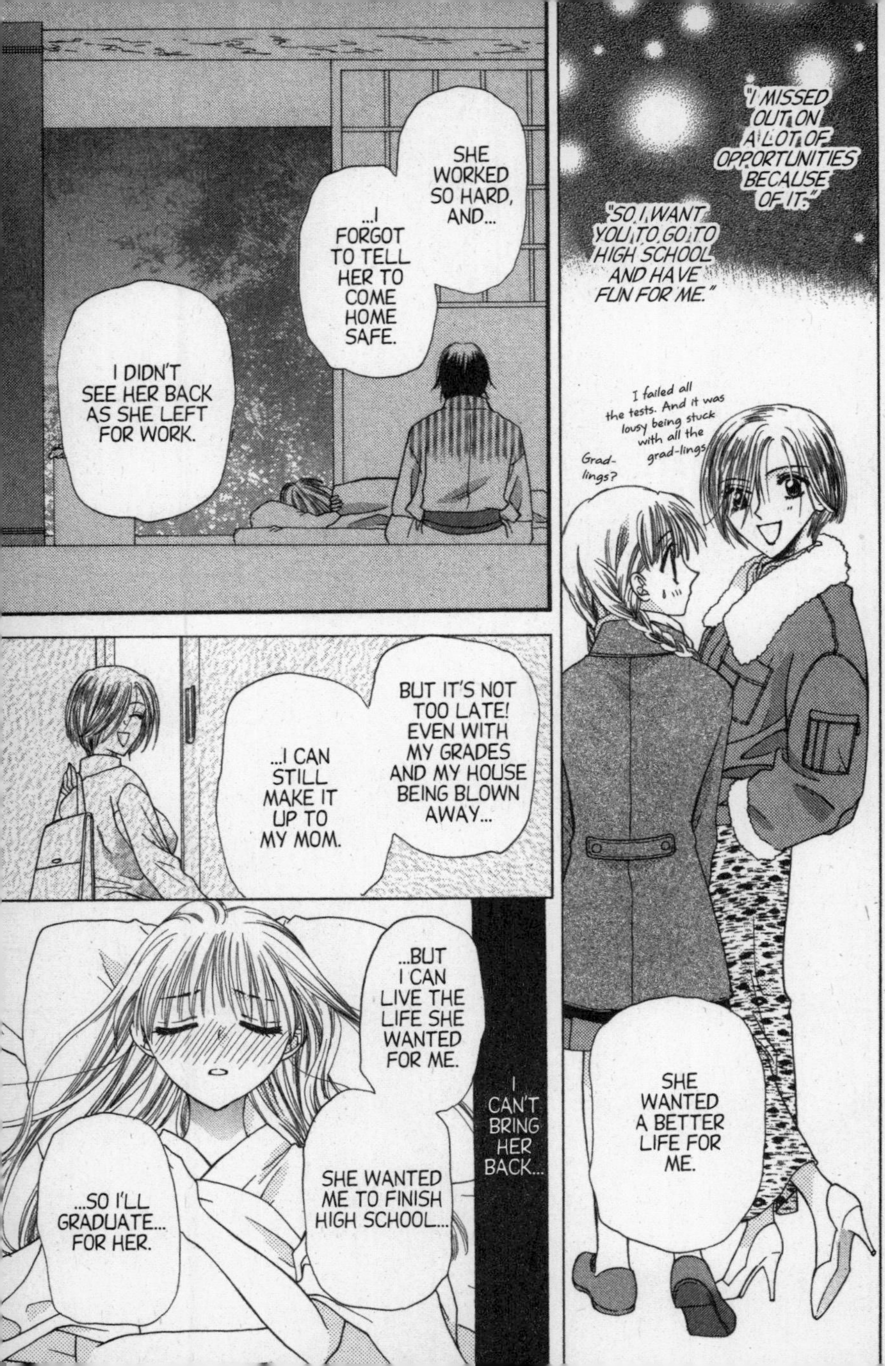
"I MISSED OUT ON A LOT OF OPPORTUNITIES BECAUSE OF IT."
"SO I WANT YOU TO GO TO HIGH SCHOOL AND HAVE FUN FOR ME."
I failed all the tests. And it was lousy being stuck with all the grad-lings.
Grad-lings?
SHE WANTED A BETTER LIFE FOR ME.
SHE WORKED SO HARD, AND...
...I FORGOT TO TELL HER TO COME HOME SAFE.
I DIDN'T SEE HER BACK AS SHE LEFT FOR WORK.
BUT IT'S NOT TOO LATE! EVEN WITH MY GRADES AND MY HOUSE BEING BLOWN AWAY...
...I CAN STILL MAKE IT UP TO MY MOM.
I CAN'T BRING HER BACK...
...BUT I CAN LIVE THE LIFE SHE WANTED FOR ME.
SHE WANTED ME TO FINISH HIGH SCHOOL...
...SO I'LL GRADUATE... FOR HER.

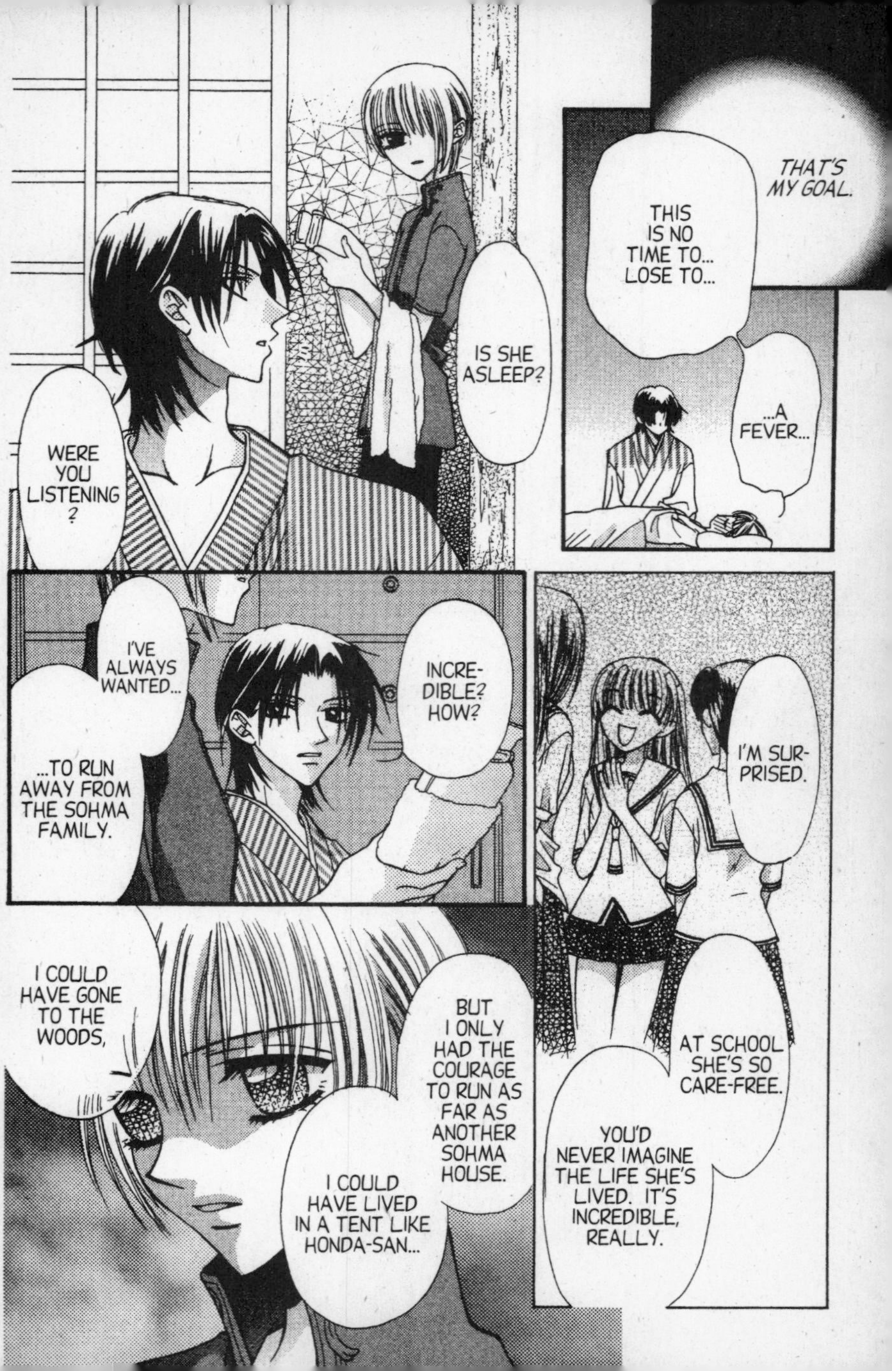
THAT'S MY GOAL.
THIS IS NO TIME TO... LOSE TO...
...A FEVER...
IS SHE ASLEEP?
WERE YOU LISTENING?
I'M SUR-PRISED.
AT SCHOOL SHE'S SO CARE-FREE.
YOU'D NEVER IMAGINE THE LIFE SHE'S LIVED. IT'S INCREDIBLE, REALLY.
INCRE-DIBLE? HOW?
I'VE ALWAYS WANTED...
...TO RUN AWAY FROM THE SOHMA FAMILY.
I COULD HAVE GONE TO THE WOODS,
I COULD HAVE LIVED IN A TENT LIKE HONDA-SAN...
BUT I ONLY HAD THE COURAGE TO RUN AS FAR AS ANOTHER SOHMA HOUSE.

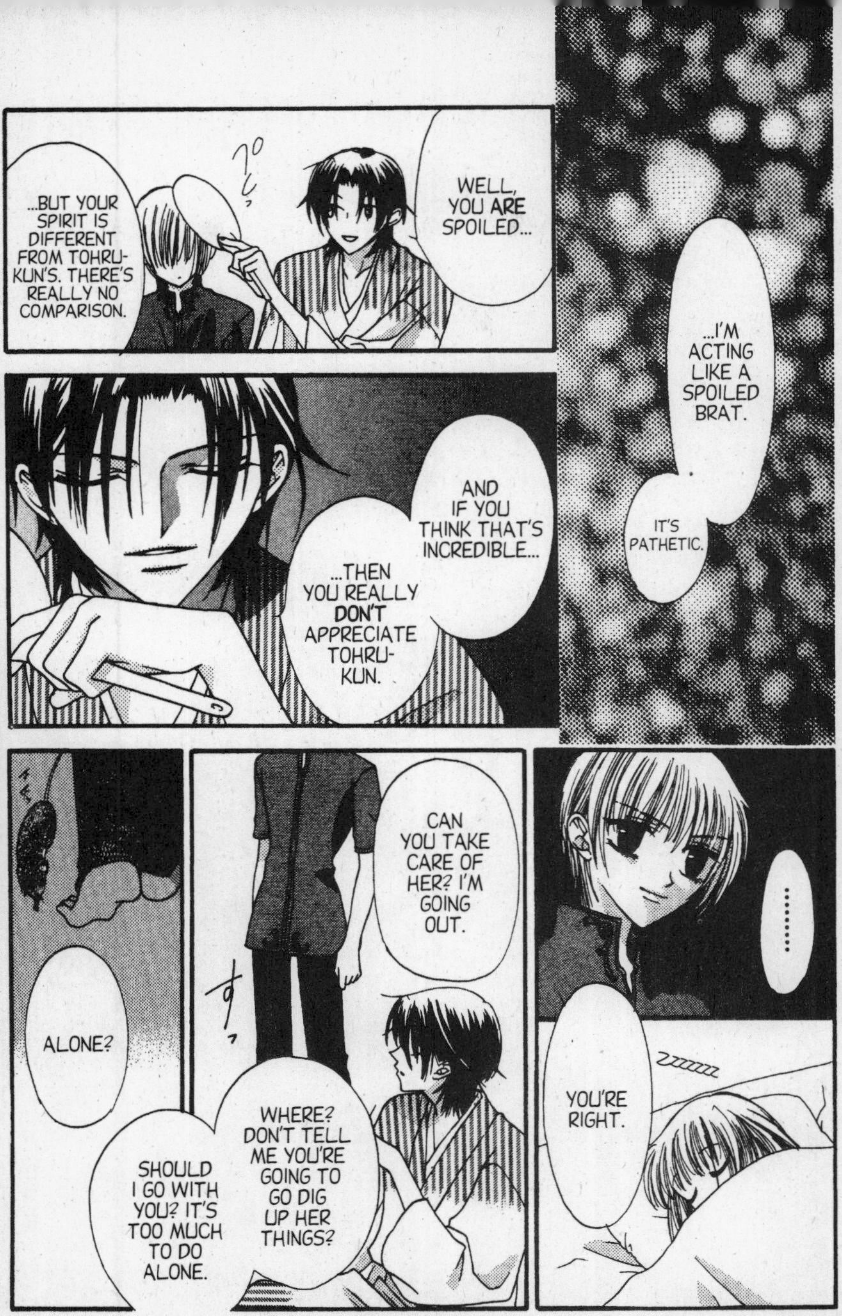
...I'M ACTING LIKE A SPOILED BRAT.
IT'S PATHETIC.
WELL, YOU ARE SPOILED...
...BUT YOUR SPIRIT IS DIFFERENT FROM TOHRU-KUN'S. THERE'S REALLY NO COMPARISON.
AND IF YOU THINK THAT'S INCREDIBLE...
...THEN YOU REALLY DON'T APPRECIATE TOHRU-KUN.
......
YOU'RE RIGHT.
CAN YOU TAKE CARE OF HER? I'M GOING OUT.
WHERE? DON'T TELL ME YOU'RE GOING TO GO DIG UP HER THINGS?
SHOULD I GO WITH YOU? IT'S TOO MUCH TO DO ALONE.
ALONE?

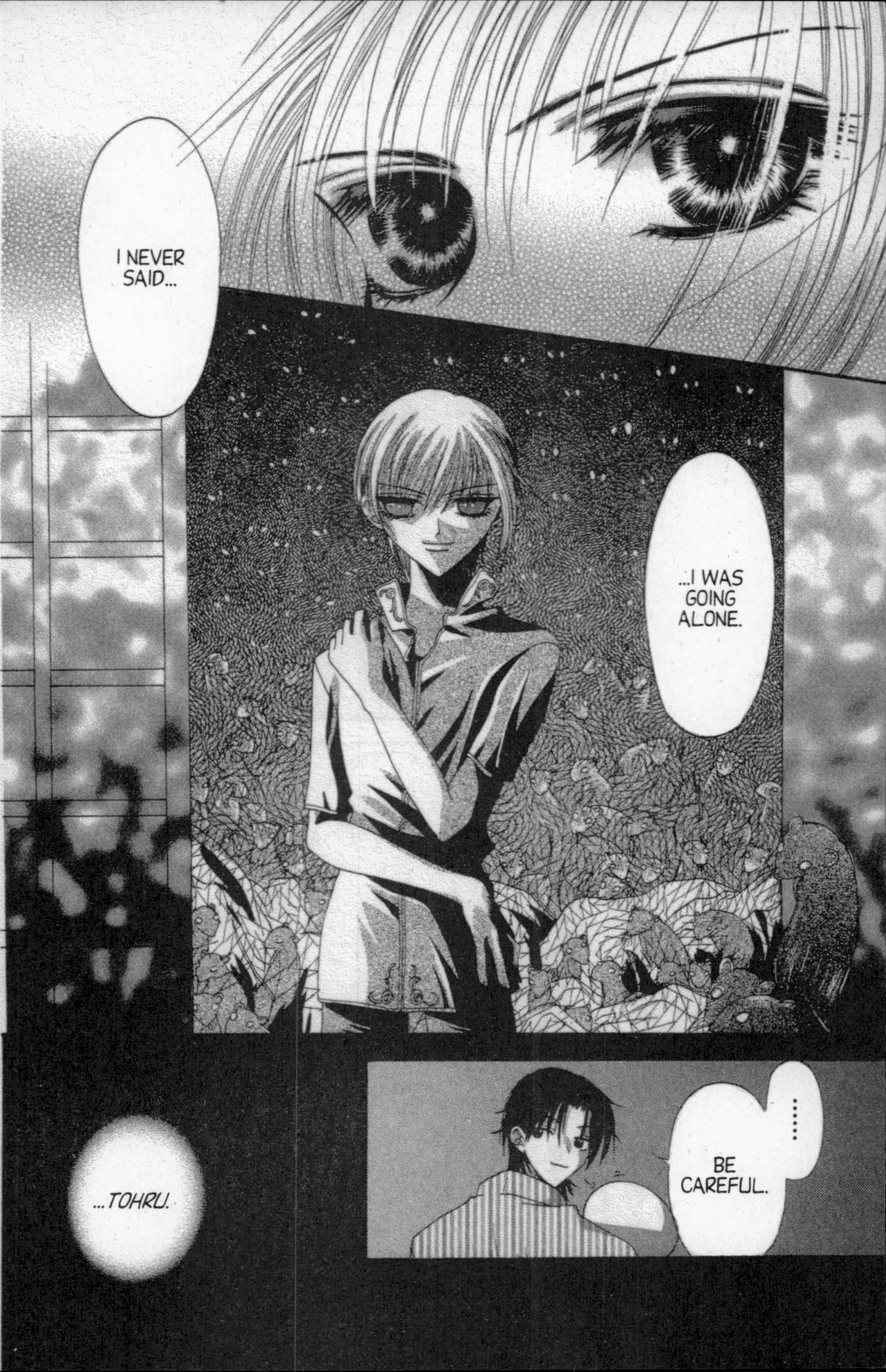
I NEVER SAID...
...I WAS GOING ALONE.
......
BE CAREFUL.
...TOHRU.

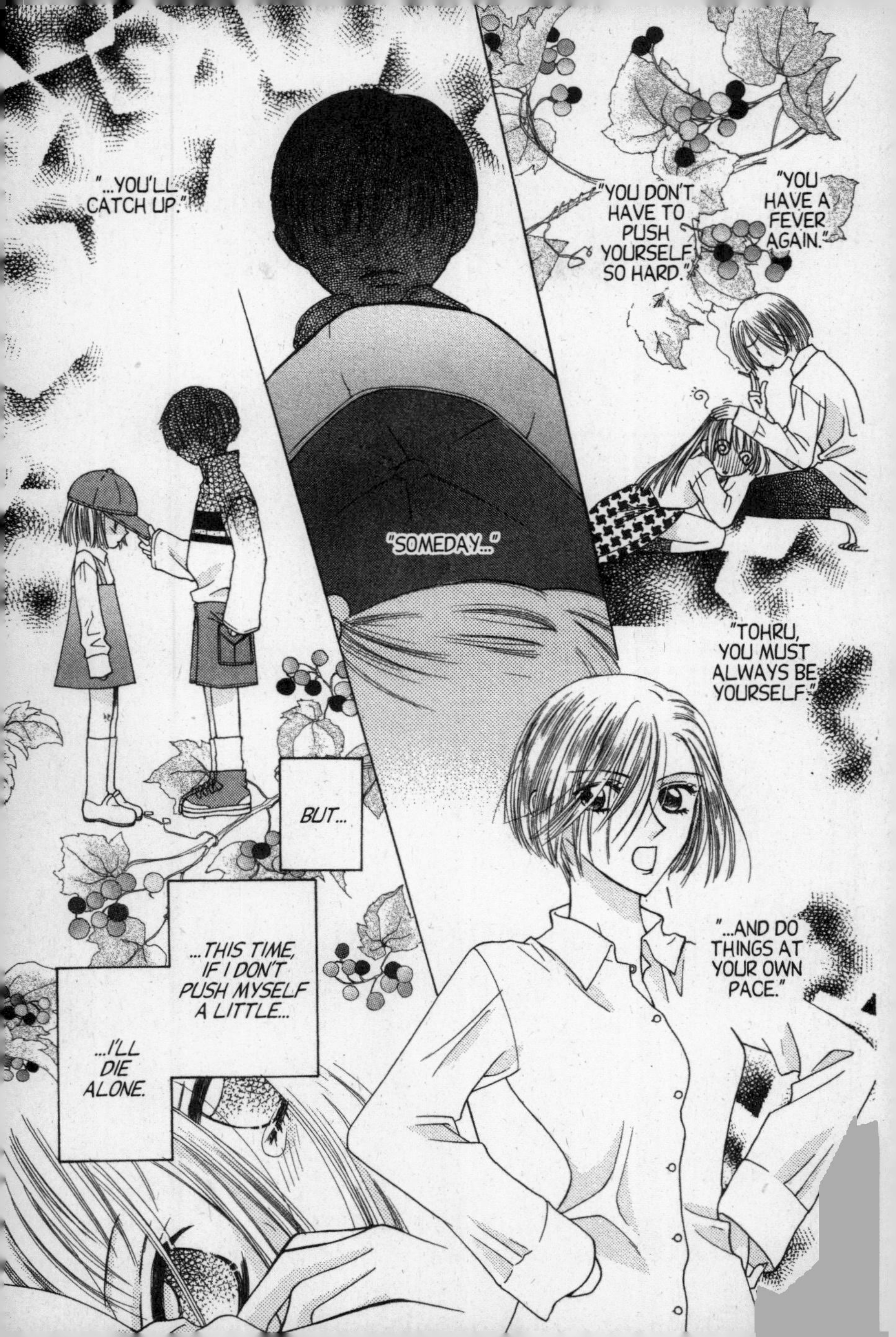
"YOU HAVE A FEVER AGAIN."
"YOU DON'T HAVE TO PUSH YOURSELF SO HARD."
"TOHRU, YOU MUST ALWAYS BE YOURSELF."
"...AND DO THINGS AT YOUR OWN PACE."
"SOMEDAY..."
"...YOU'LL CATCH UP."
BUT...
...THIS TIME, IF I DON'T PUSH MYSELF A LITTLE...
...I'LL DIE ALONE.

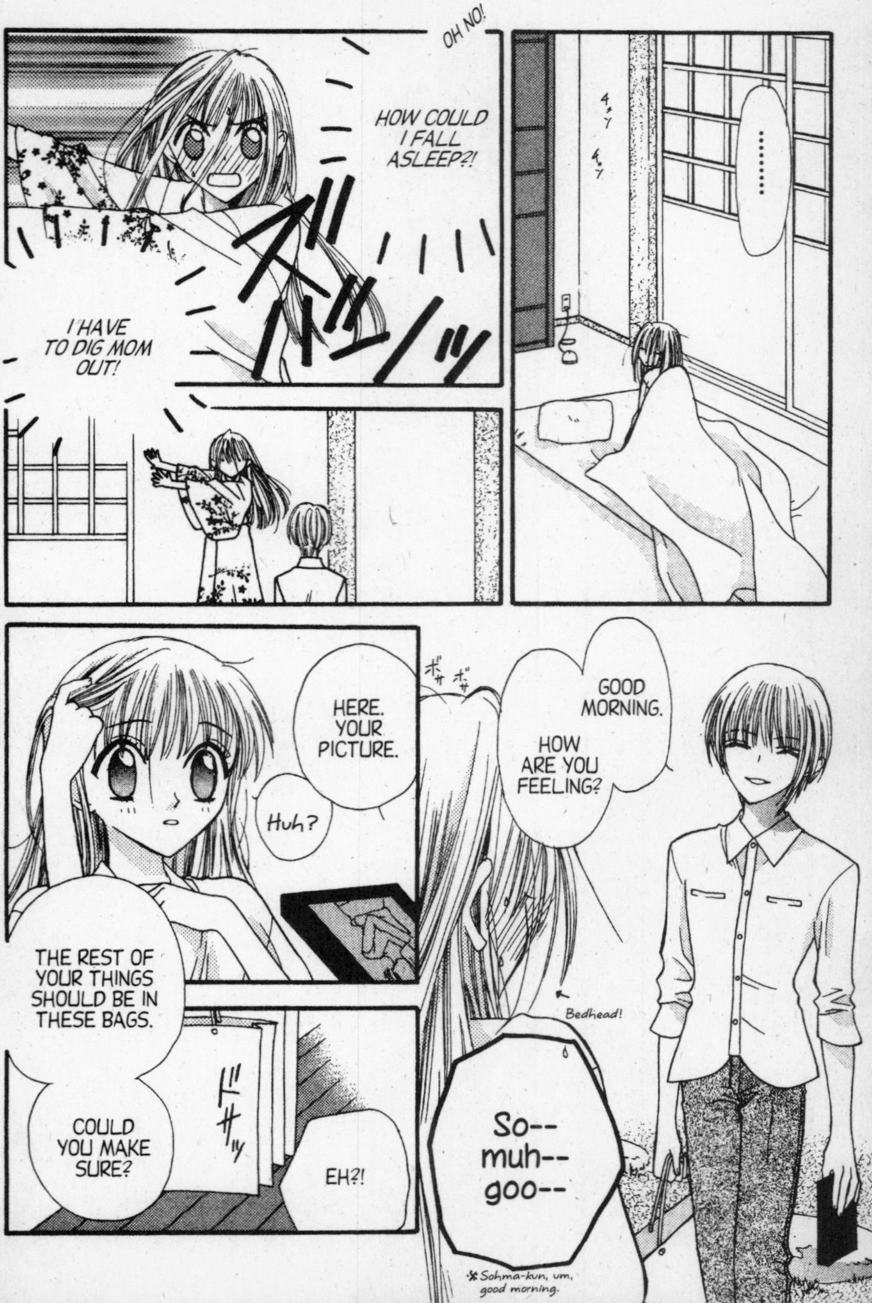
......
OH NO!
HOW COULD I FALL ASLEEP?!
I HAVE TO DIG MOM OUT!
GOOD MORNING.
HOW ARE YOU FEELING?
Bedhead!
So--muh--goo--
※Sohma-kun, um, good morning.
HERE. YOUR PICTURE.
Huh?
THE REST OF YOUR THINGS SHOULD BE IN THESE BAGS.
COULD YOU MAKE SURE?
EH?!

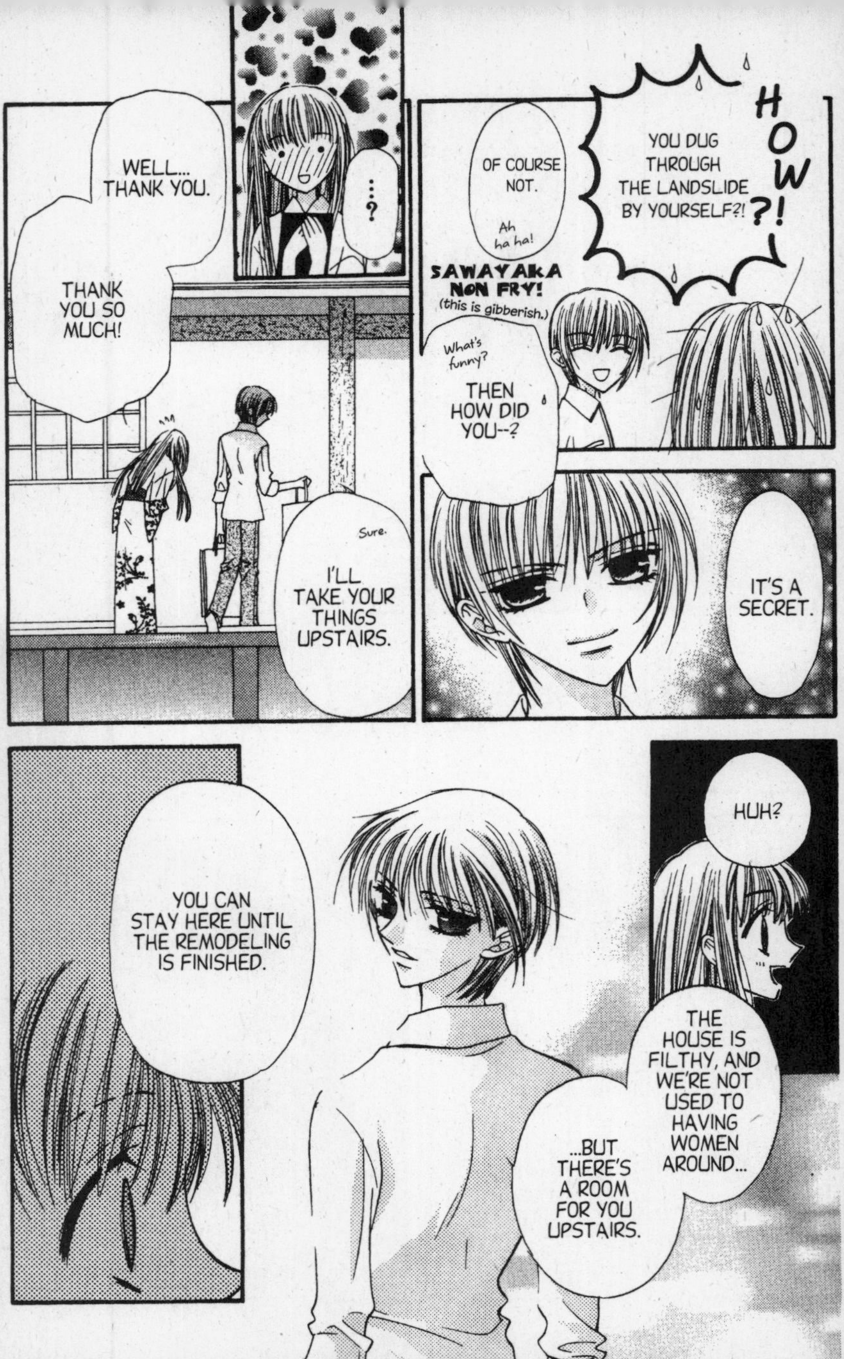
HOW?!
YOU DUG THROUGH THE LANDSLIDE BY YOURSELF?!
OF COURSE NOT.
Ah ha ha!
SAWAYAKA NON FRY!
(this is gibberish.)
What's funny?
THEN HOW DID YOU--?
IT'S A SECRET.
...?
WELL... THANK YOU.
THANK YOU SO MUCH!
Sure.
I'LL TAKE YOUR THINGS UPSTAIRS.
HUH?
THE HOUSE IS FILTHY, AND WE'RE NOT USED TO HAVING WOMEN AROUND...
...BUT THERE'S A ROOM FOR YOU UPSTAIRS.
YOU CAN STAY HERE UNTIL THE REMODELING IS FINISHED.

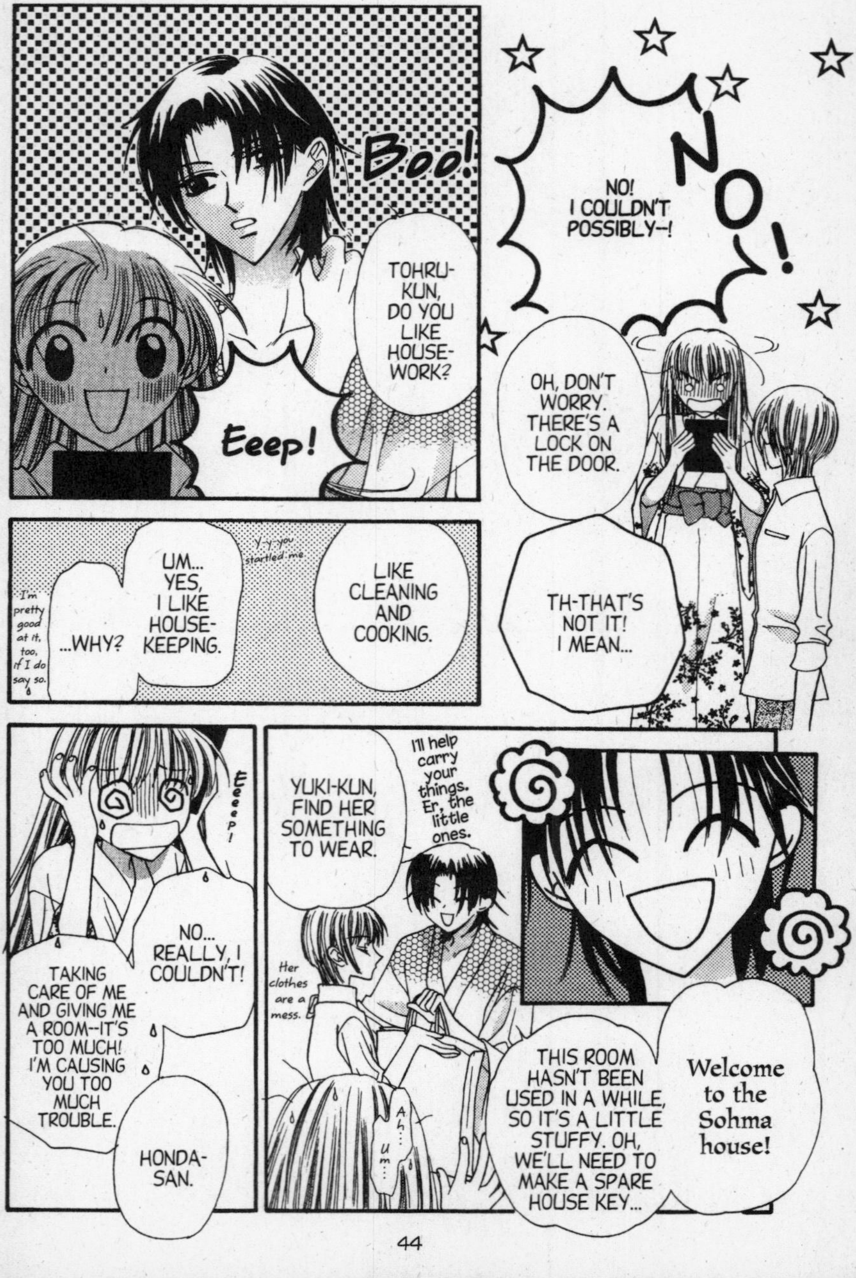
NO!
NO! I COULDN'T POSSIBLY--!
OH, DON'T WORRY. THERE'S A LOCK ON THE DOOR.
TH-THAT'S NOT IT! I MEAN...
Boo!
TOHRU-KUN, DO YOU LIKE HOUSE-WORK?
Eeep!
LIKE CLEANING AND COOKING.
Y-y-you startled me
UM... YES, I LIKE HOUSE-KEEPING.
...WHY?
I'm pretty good at it, too, if I do say so.
Welcome to the Sohma house!
THIS ROOM HASN'T BEEN USED IN A WHILE, SO IT'S A LITTLE STUFFY. OH, WE'LL NEED TO MAKE A SPARE HOUSE KEY...
YUKI-KUN, FIND HER SOMETHING TO WEAR.
I'll help carry your things. Er, the little ones.
Her clothes are a mess.
Ah... Um...
Eeeep!
NO... REALLY, I COULDN'T!
TAKING CARE OF ME AND GIVING ME A ROOM--IT'S TOO MUCH! I'M CAUSING YOU TOO MUCH TROUBLE.
HONDA-SAN.

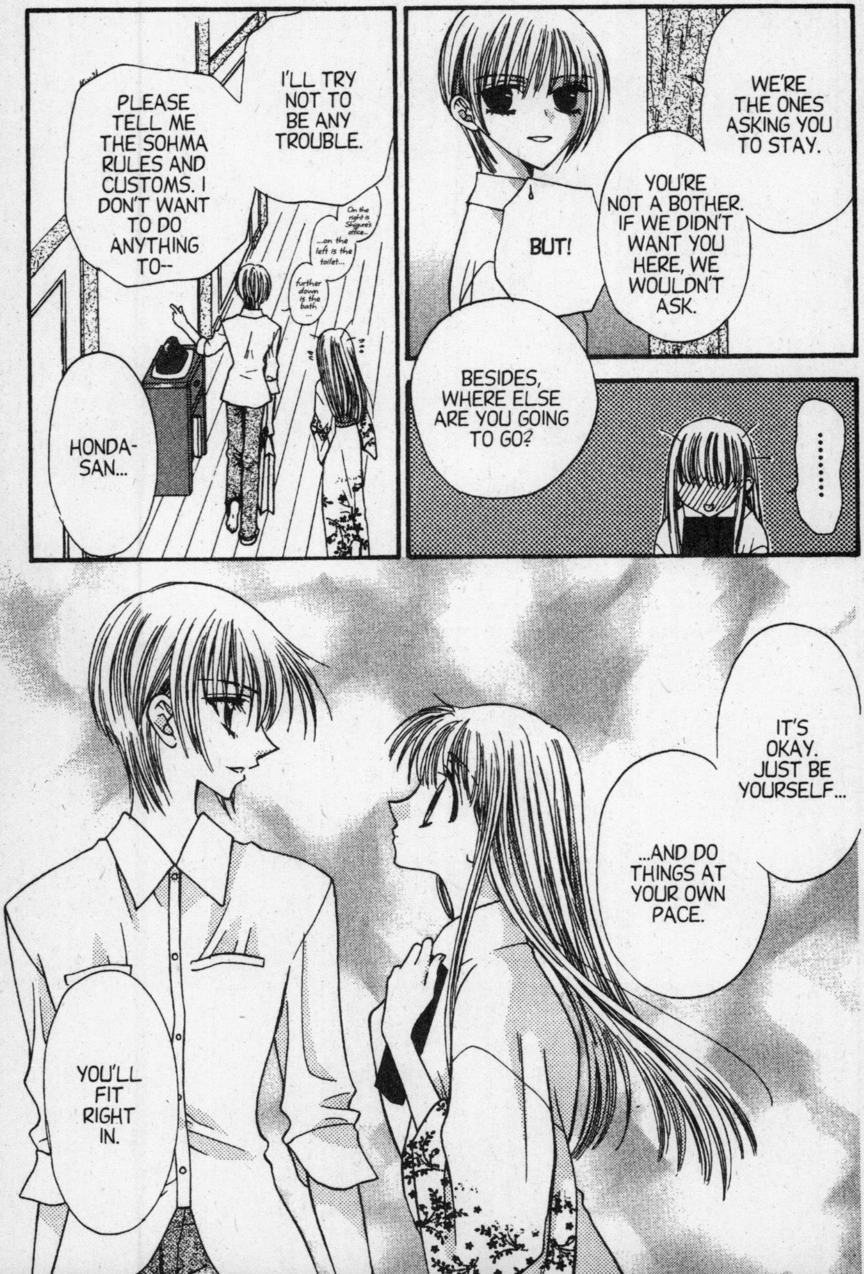
On the right is Shigure's office...
...on the left is the toilet...
further down is the bath...
I'LL TRY NOT TO BE ANY TROUBLE.
PLEASE TELL ME THE SOHMA RULES AND CUSTOMS. I DON'T WANT TO DO ANYTHING TO--
HONDA-SAN...
WE'RE THE ONES ASKING YOU TO STAY.
YOU'RE NOT A BOTHER. IF WE DIDN'T WANT YOU HERE, WE WOULDN'T ASK.
BUT!
BESIDES, WHERE ELSE ARE YOU GOING TO GO?
......
IT'S OKAY. JUST BE YOURSELF...
...AND DO THINGS AT YOUR OWN PACE.
YOU'LL FIT RIGHT IN.

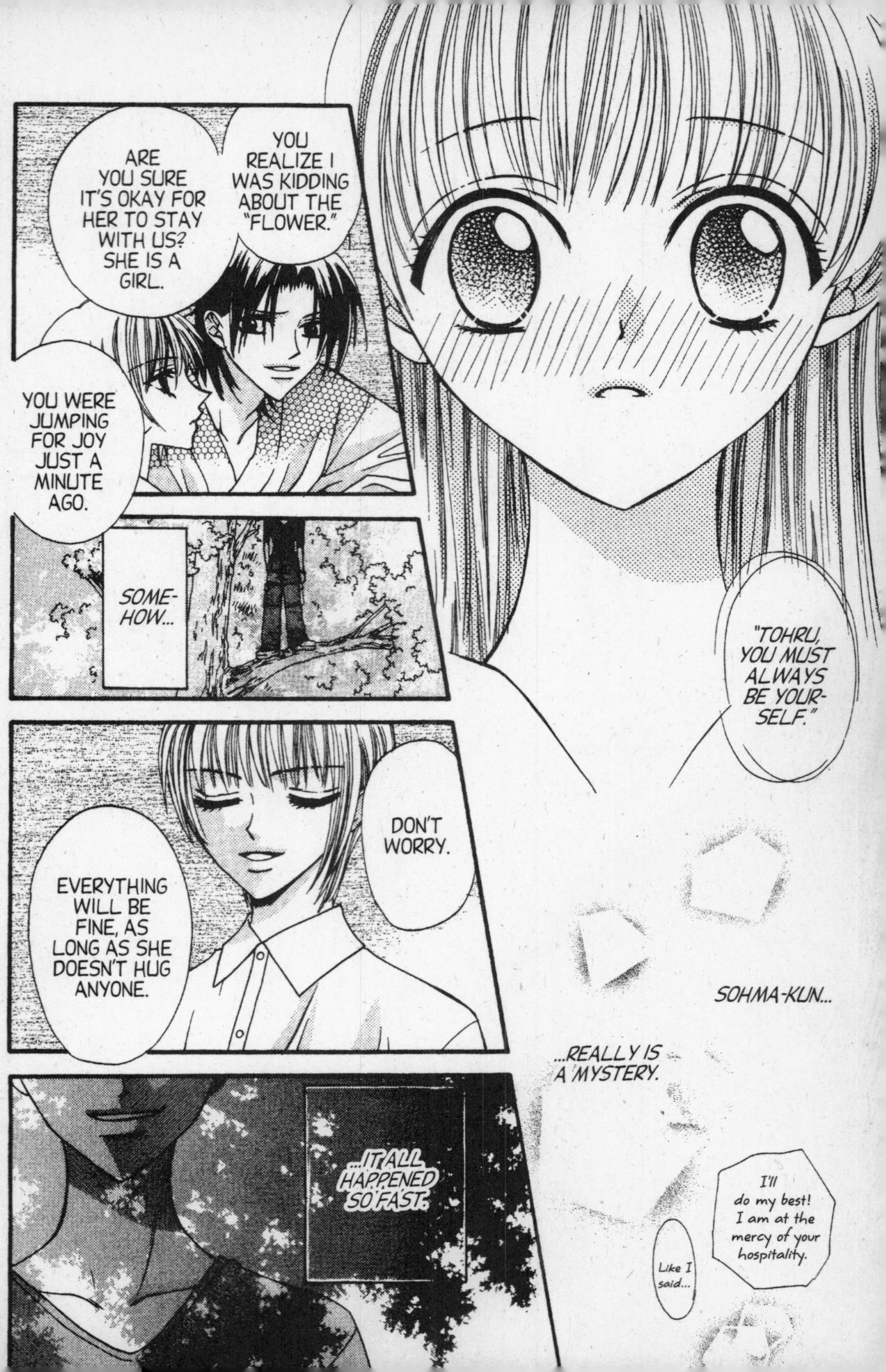
"TOHRU, YOU MUST ALWAYS BE YOURSELF."
SOHMA-KUN...
...REALLY IS A MYSTERY.
I'll do my best! I am at the mercy of your hospitality.
Like I said...
YOU REALIZE I WAS KIDDING ABOUT THE "FLOWER."
ARE YOU SURE IT'S OKAY FOR HER TO STAY WITH US? SHE IS A GIRL.
YOU WERE JUMPING FOR JOY JUST A MINUTE AGO.
SOME-HOW...
DON'T WORRY.
EVERYTHING WILL BE FINE, AS LONG AS SHE DOESN'T HUG ANYONE.
...IT ALL HAPPENED SO FAST.

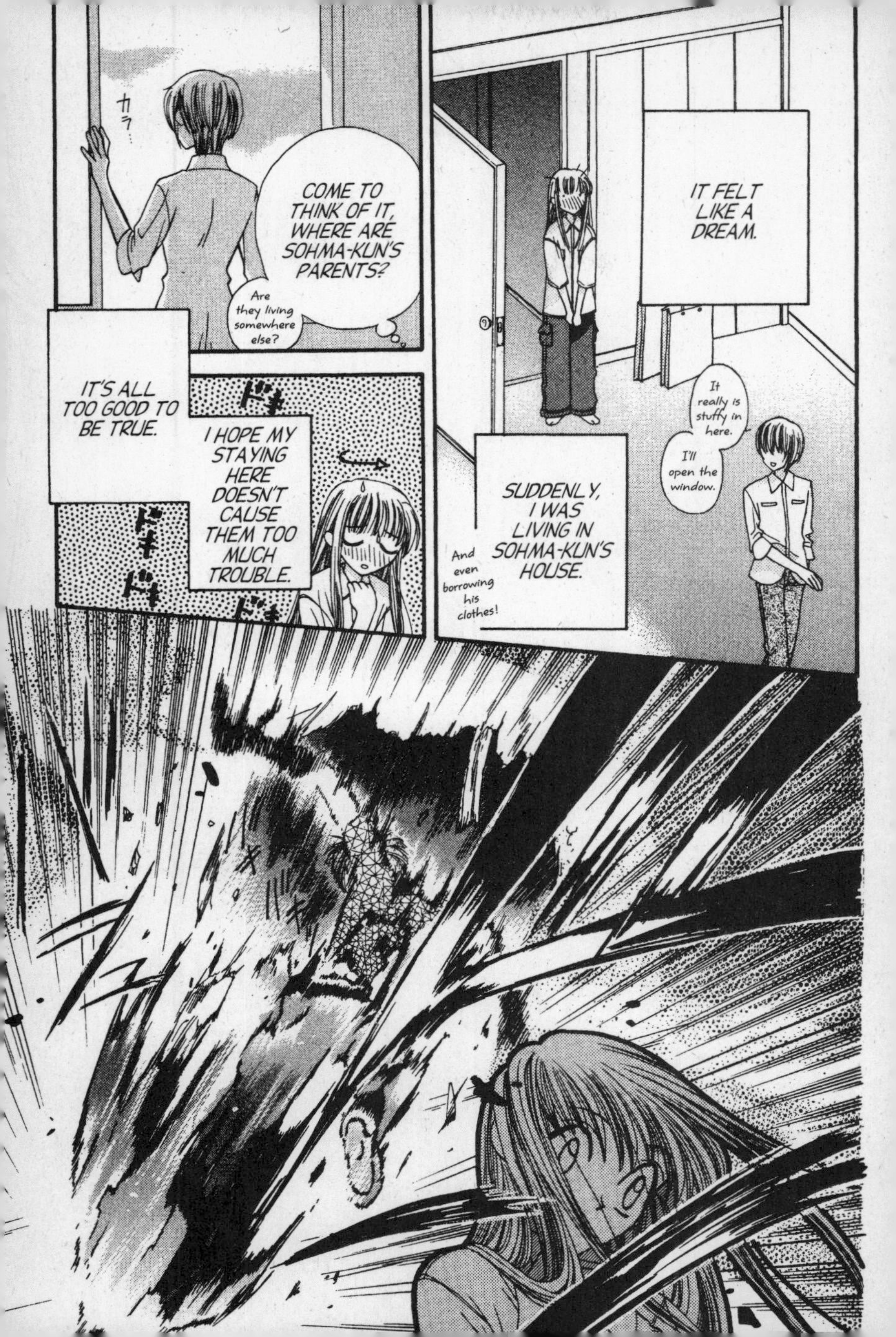
IT FELT LIKE A DREAM.
SUDDENLY, I WAS LIVING IN SOHMA-KUN'S HOUSE.
And even borrowing his clothes!
It really is stuffy in here.
I'll open the window.
カラ…
COME TO THINK OF IT, WHERE ARE SOHMA-KUN'S PARENTS?
Are they living somewhere else?
IT'S ALL TOO GOOD TO BE TRUE.
I HOPE MY STAYING HERE DOESN'T CAUSE THEM TOO MUCH TROUBLE.
ドキ
ドキ
ドキ
ドキ

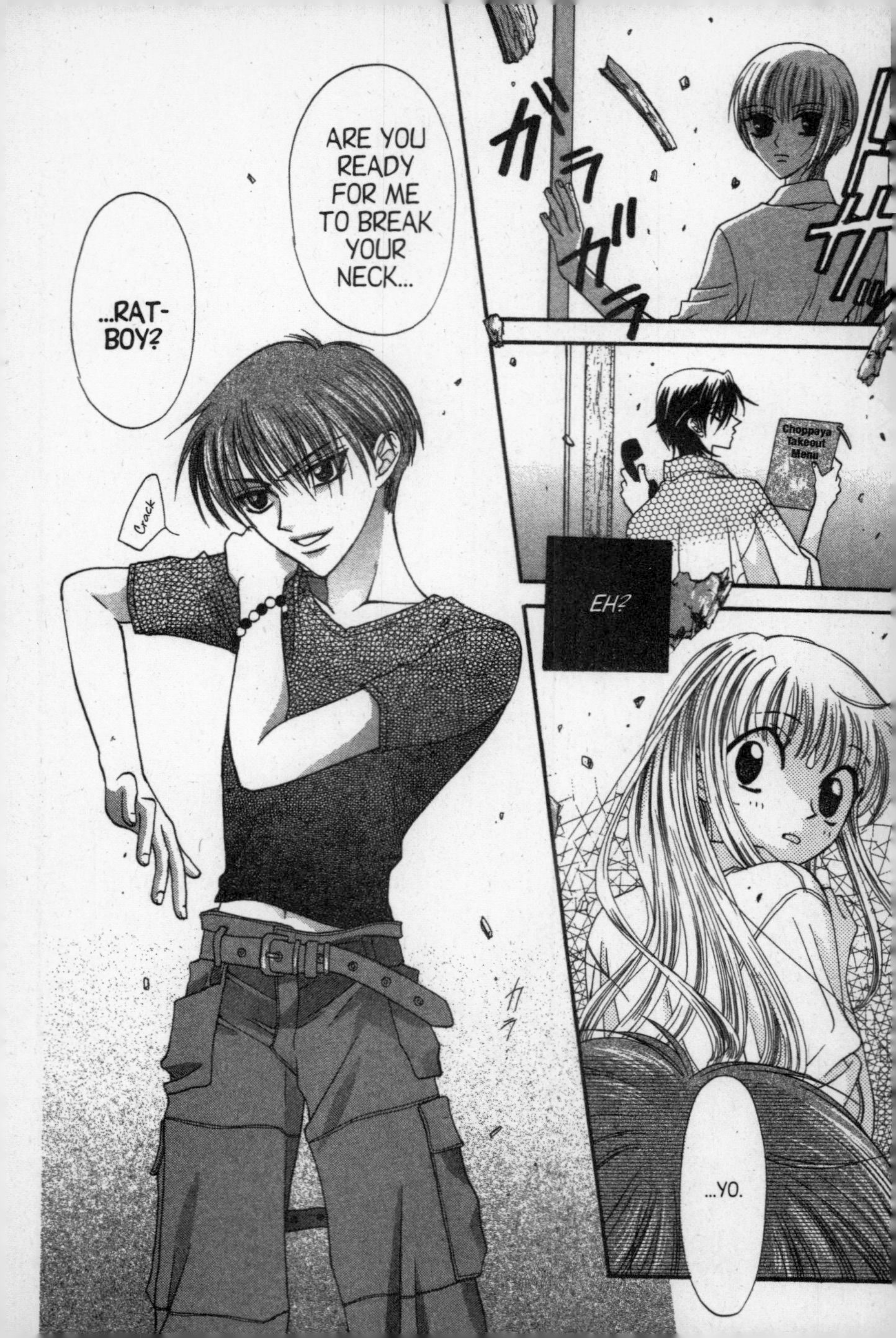
ガラ
ガラ
Choppaya Takeout Menu
EH?
...YO.
ARE YOU READY FOR ME TO BREAK YOUR NECK...
...RAT-BOY?
Crack
カラ

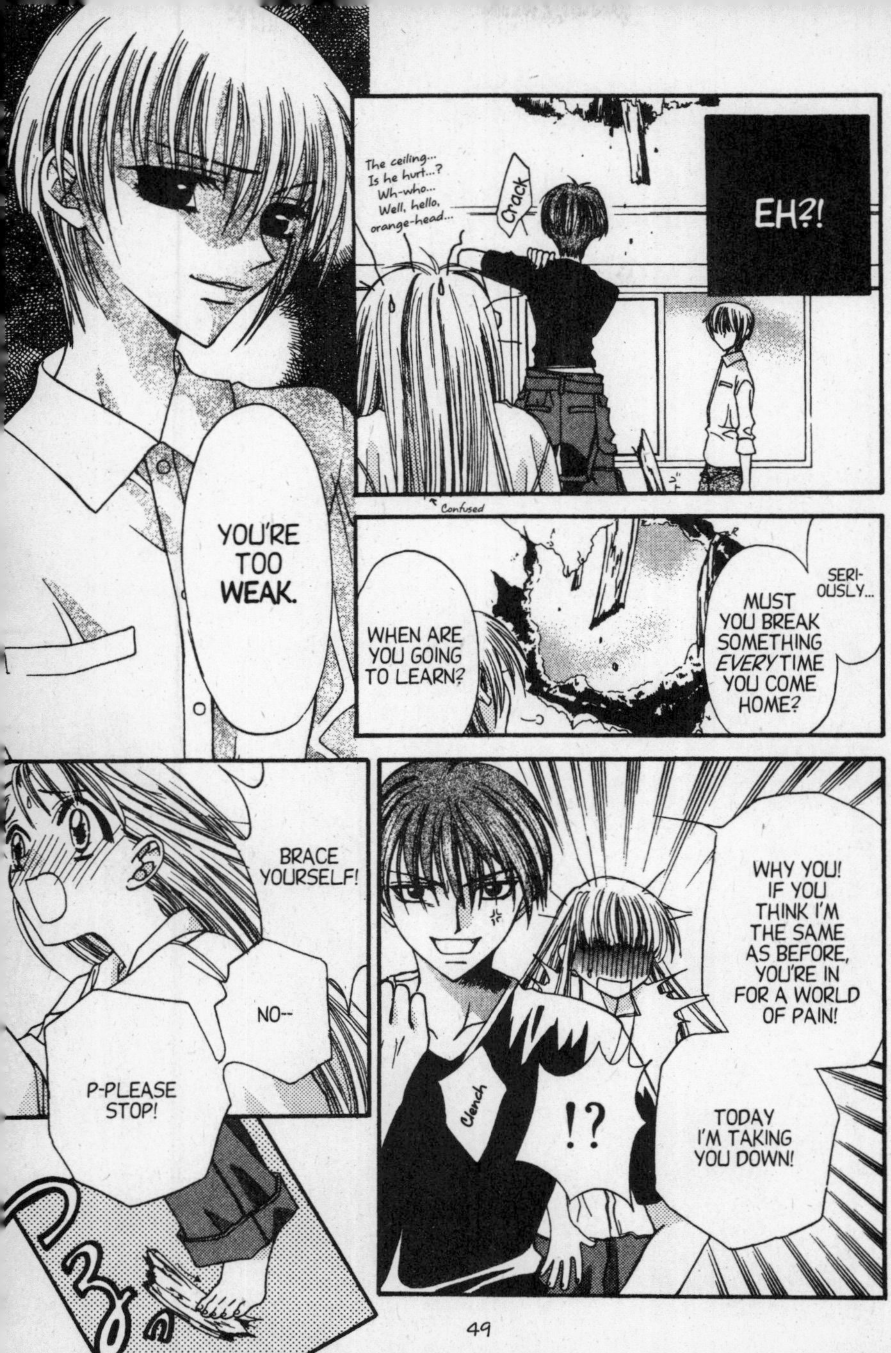
EH?!
The ceiling... Is he hurt...? Wh-who... Well, hello, orange-head...
Crack
Confused
SERIOUSLY...
MUST YOU BREAK SOMETHING EVERY TIME YOU COME HOME?
WHEN ARE YOU GOING TO LEARN?
YOU'RE TOO WEAK.
WHY YOU! IF YOU THINK I'M THE SAME AS BEFORE, YOU'RE IN FOR A WORLD OF PAIN!
TODAY I'M TAKING YOU DOWN!
!?
Clench
BRACE YOURSELF!
NO--
P-PLEASE STOP!

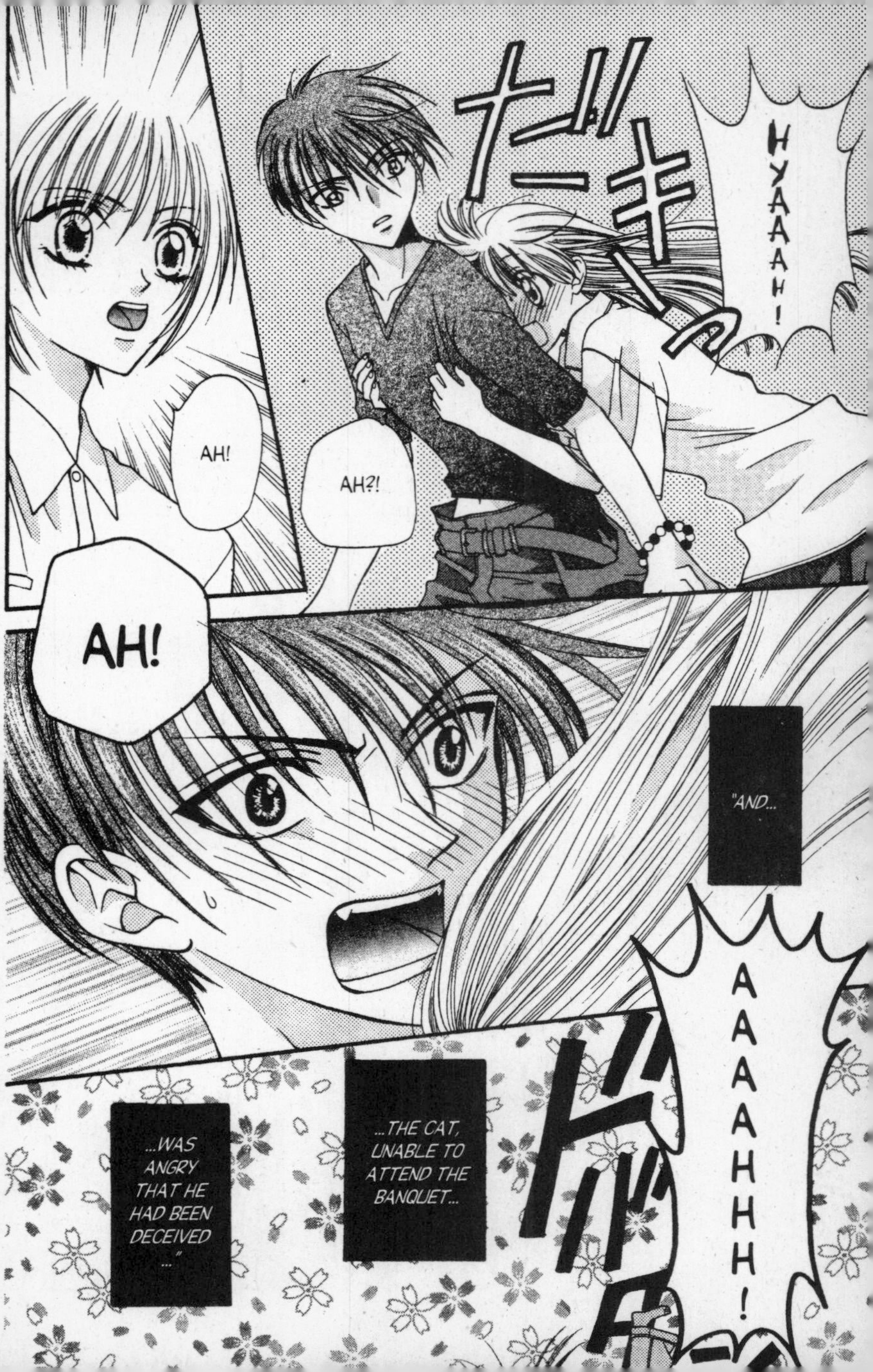
HYAAAAH!
AH?!
AH!
AH!
"AND...
AAAAAHHH!
...THE CAT, UNABLE TO ATTEND THE BANQUET...
...WAS ANGRY THAT HE HAD BEEN DECEIVED"...

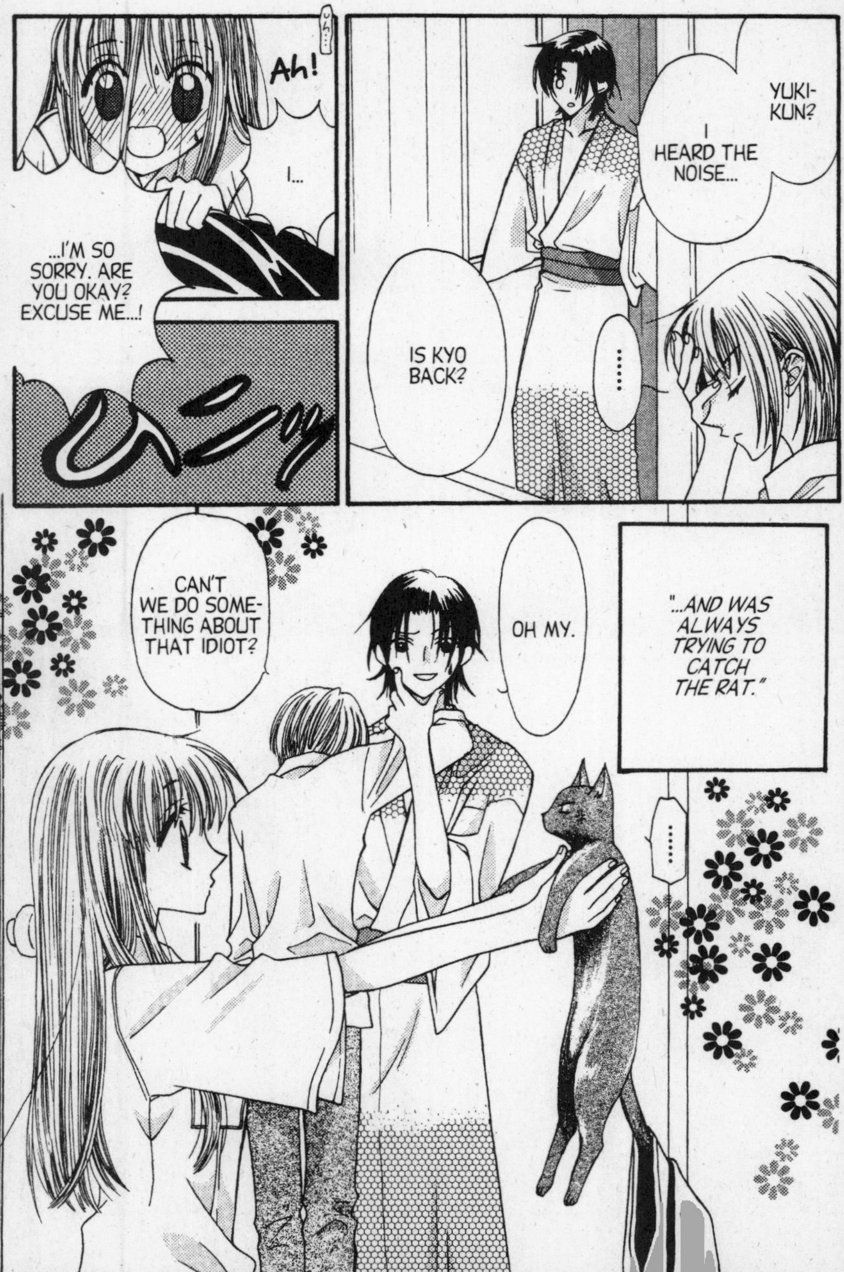
YUKI-KUN?
I HEARD THE NOISE...
......
IS KYO BACK?
Ah!
I...
...I'M SO SORRY. ARE YOU OKAY? EXCUSE ME...!
"...AND WAS ALWAYS TRYING TO CATCH THE RAT."
......
OH MY.
CAN'T WE DO SOMETHING ABOUT THAT IDIOT?

Omake Theater 2: It's part of his charm.

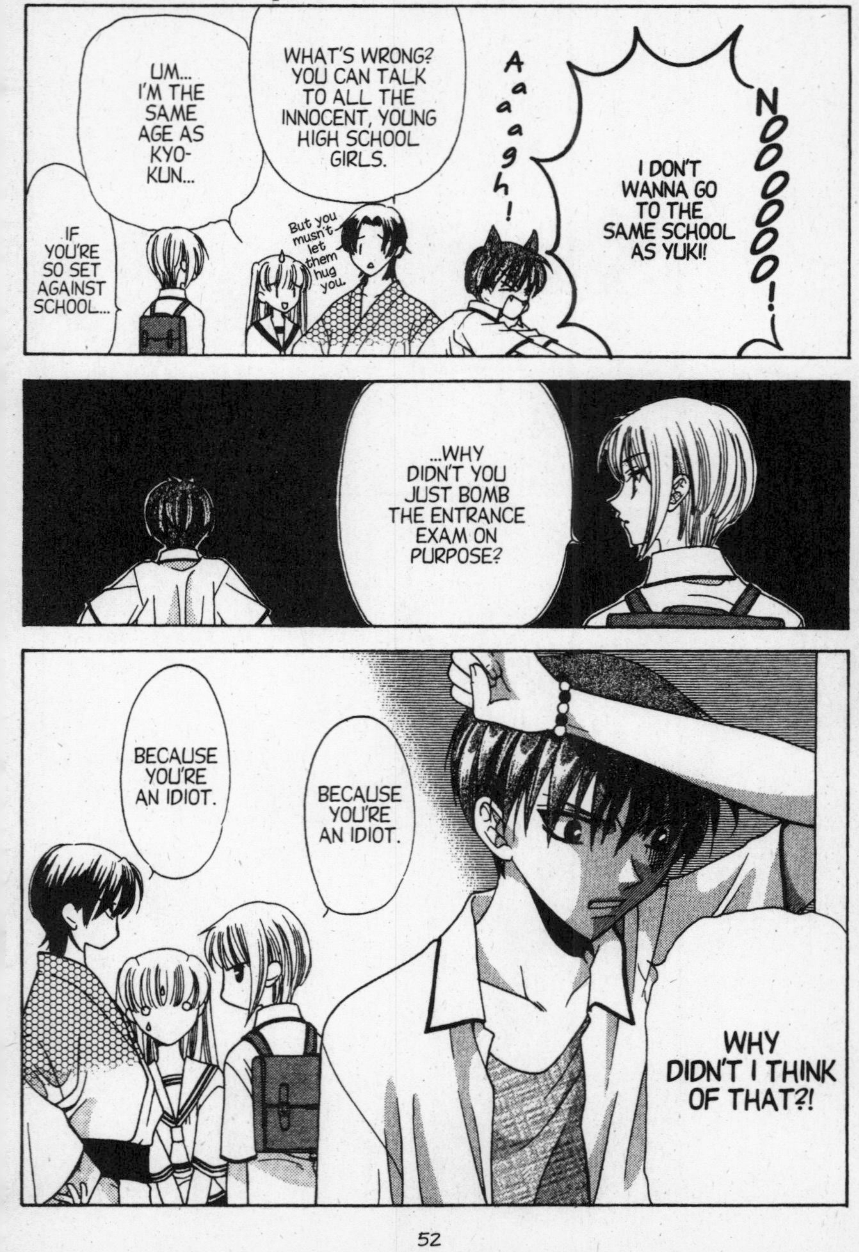
NOOOOOO!
I DON'T WANNA GO TO THE SAME SCHOOL AS YUKI!
Aaaagh!
WHAT'S WRONG? YOU CAN TALK TO ALL THE INNOCENT, YOUNG HIGH SCHOOL GIRLS.
But you musn't let them hug you.
UM... I'M THE SAME AGE AS KYO-KUN...
IF YOU'RE SO SET AGAINST SCHOOL...
...WHY DIDN'T YOU JUST BOMB THE ENTRANCE EXAM ON PURPOSE?
WHY DIDN'T I THINK OF THAT?!
BECAUSE YOU'RE AN IDIOT.
BECAUSE YOU'RE AN IDIOT.

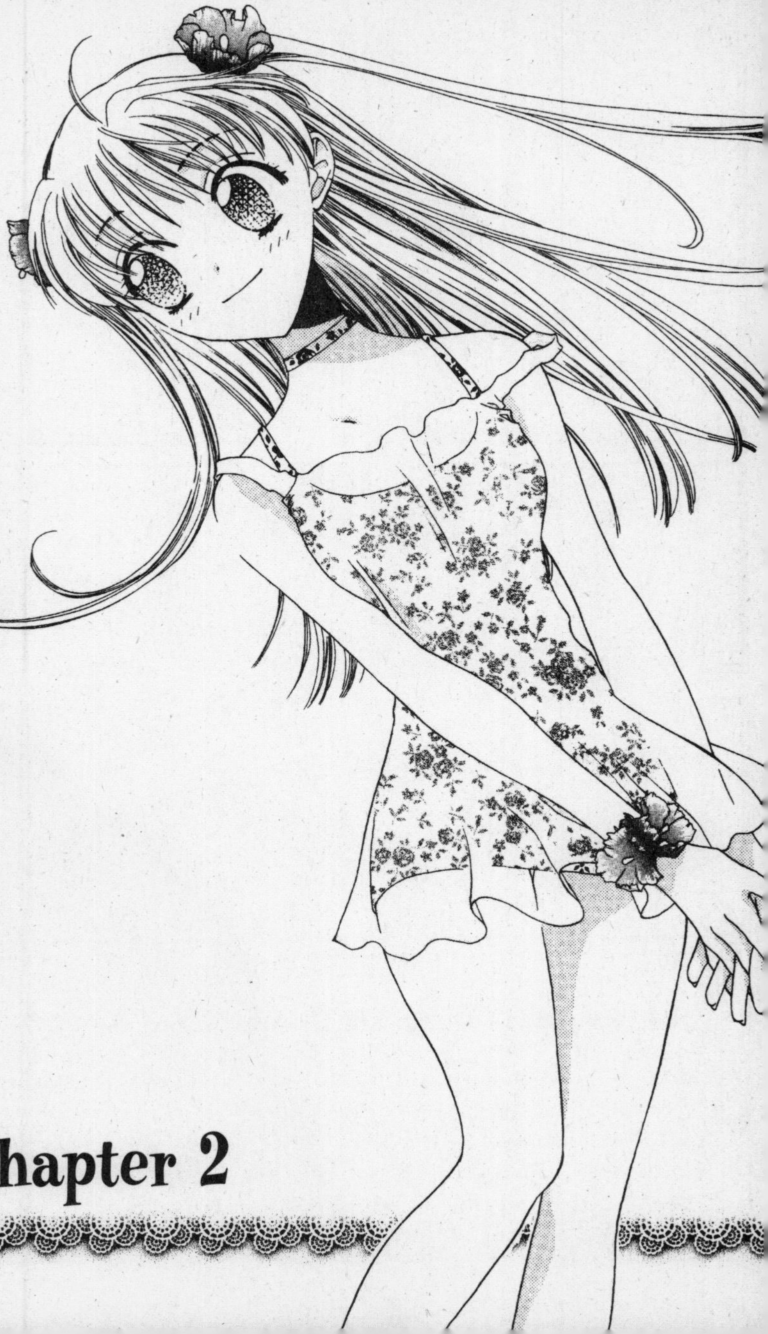

Chapter 2

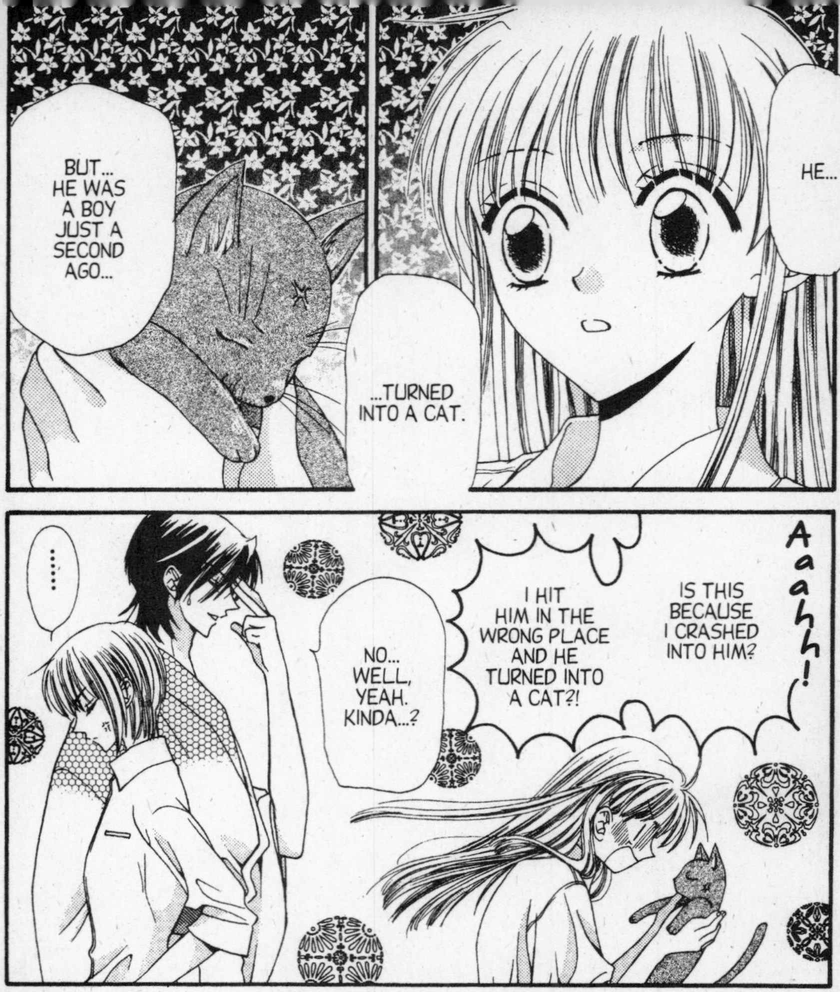
HE...
...TURNED INTO A CAT.
BUT... HE WAS A BOY JUST A SECOND AGO...
Aaahh!
IS THIS BECAUSE I CRASHED INTO HIM?
I HIT HIM IN THE WRONG PLACE AND HE TURNED INTO A CAT?!
NO... WELL, YEAH. KINDA...?
......

ULTRA SPECIAL BLAH BLAH BLAH, NUMBER 1:

I got a letter from some smart aleck reminding me, "Didn't you say you wouldn't use English titles?" Well... I guess I did say that... And, actually, this book did have a Japanese title at first. But things happened (nothing really big) and it became "Fruits Basket." Sometimes that's just how it works.

Number 3:

Now I'm going to talk about games. I once wrote that I wouldn't play Sakura Wars 2... well, I played it. And...
IT WAS AWESOME!
I'm hooked. Seriously, it's really good. And I ended up playing the first one, too (because I was so obsessed). It's weird that I'm more into SW2 than some of the games I worked on!

(Of course, **I** do all the best endings.)

It's also weird that K-chan (who has been a Sakura Wars fan from the beginning of time and is in love with Ren and Ohgami-san) and I are now having success with those two characters' storylines.

K-chan: thank you always for everything!

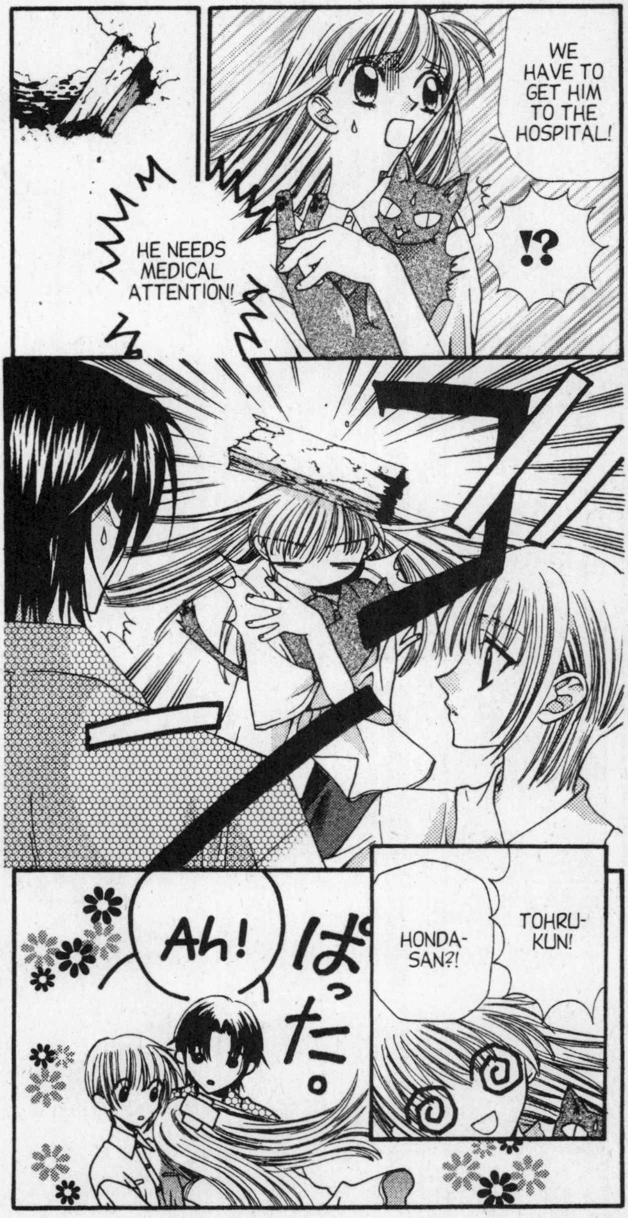
WE HAVE TO GET HIM TO THE HOSPITAL!
!?
HE NEEDS MEDICAL ATTENTION!
TOHRU-KUN!
HONDA-SAN?!
Ah!
ぱった。

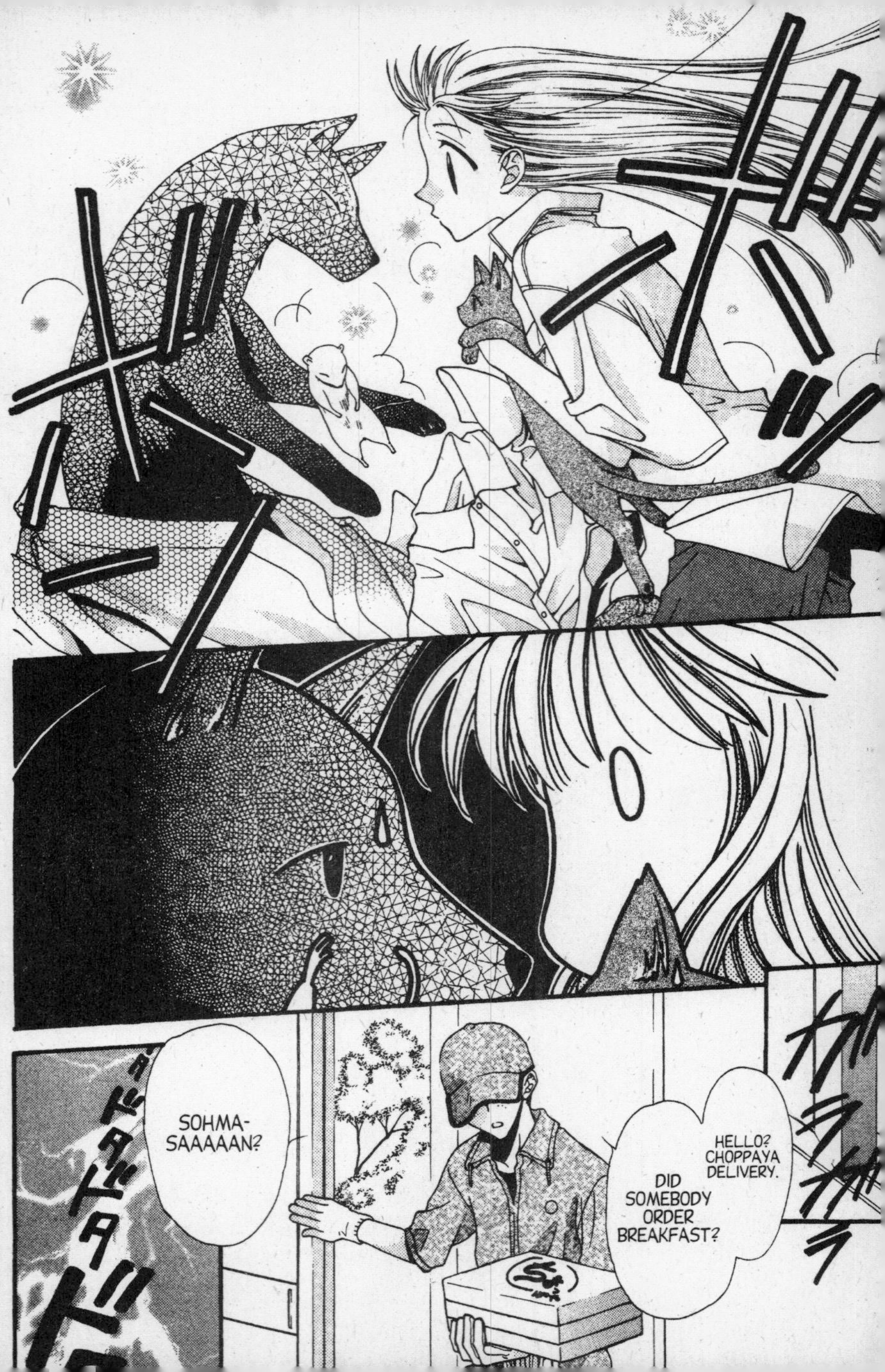
HELLO? CHOPPAYA DELIVERY.
DID SOMEBODY ORDER BREAKFAST?
SOHMA-SAAAAAN?

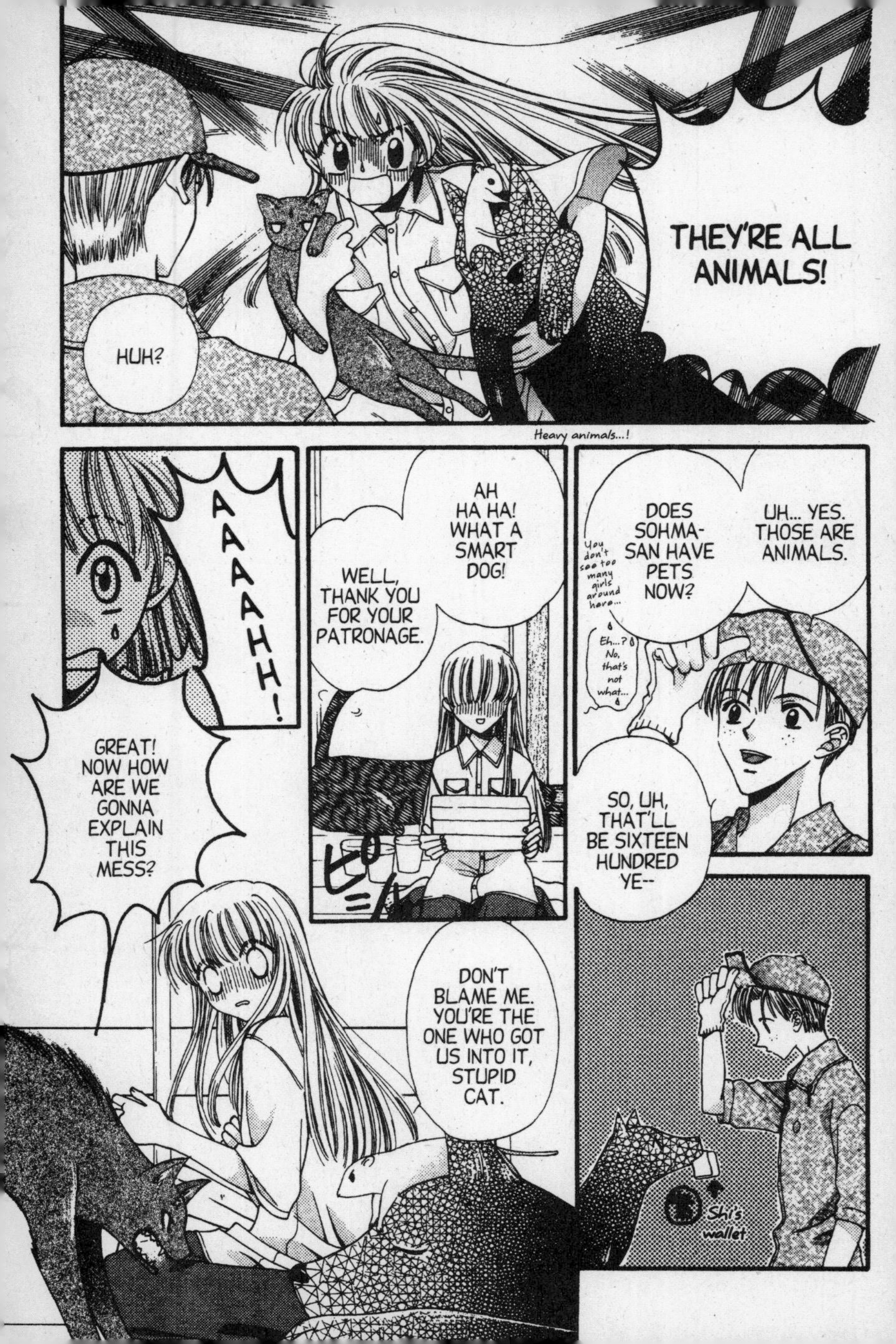
THEY'RE ALL ANIMALS!
HUH?
Heavy animals...!
UH... YES. THOSE ARE ANIMALS.
DOES SOHMA-SAN HAVE PETS NOW?
You don't see too many girls around here...
Eh...? No, that's not what...
SO, UH, THAT'LL BE SIXTEEN HUNDRED YE--
AH HA HA! WHAT A SMART DOG!
WELL, THANK YOU FOR YOUR PATRONAGE.
AAAAAHH!
Shi's wallet
GREAT! NOW HOW ARE WE GONNA EXPLAIN THIS MESS?
DON'T BLAME ME. YOU'RE THE ONE WHO GOT US INTO IT, STUPID CAT.

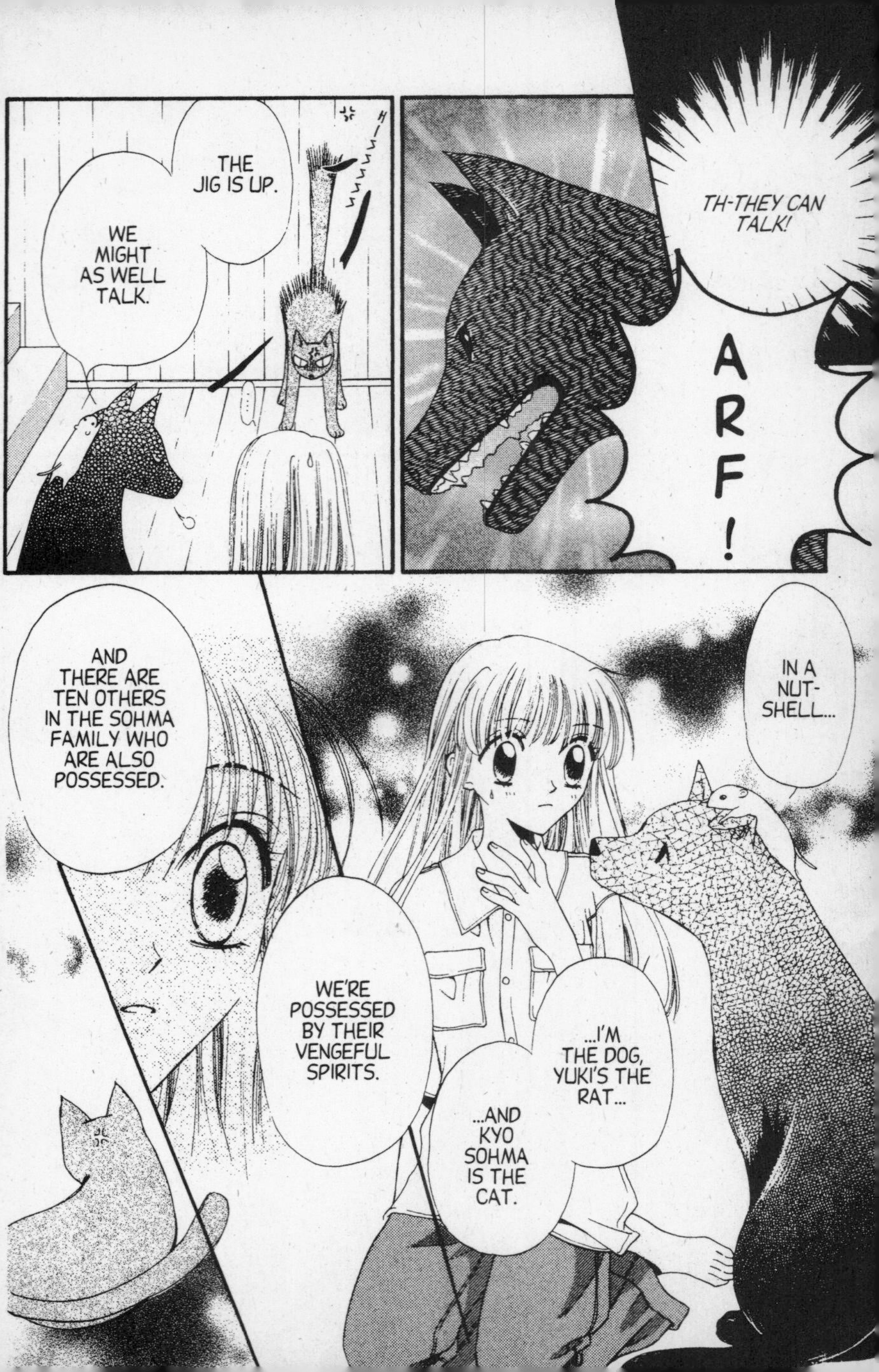
TH-THEY CAN TALK!
ARF!
THE JIG IS UP.
WE MIGHT AS WELL TALK.
...
IN A NUT-SHELL...
...I'M THE DOG, YUKI'S THE RAT...
...AND KYO SOHMA IS THE CAT.
WE'RE POSSESSED BY THEIR VENGEFUL SPIRITS.
AND THERE ARE TEN OTHERS IN THE SOHMA FAMILY WHO ARE ALSO POSSESSED.

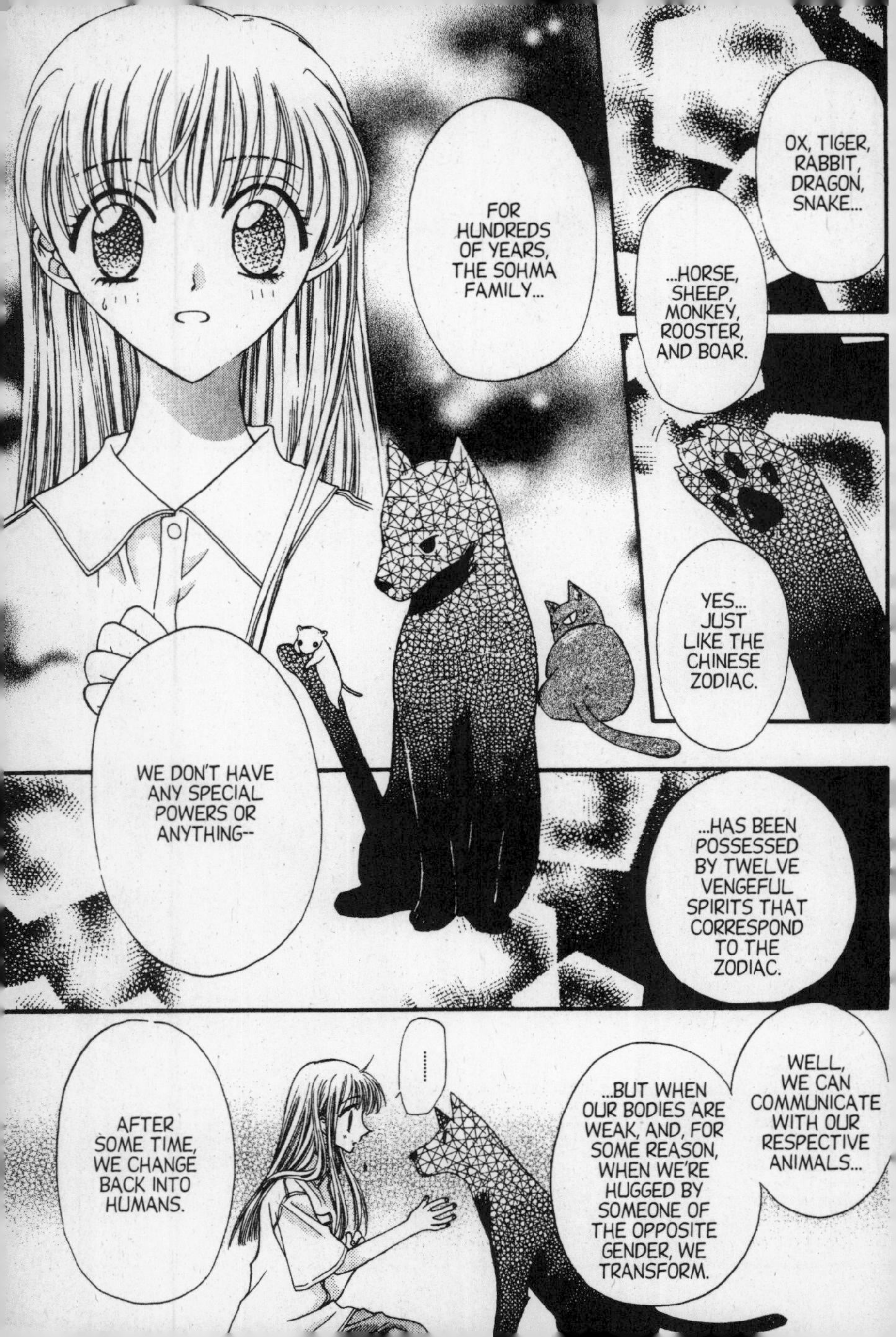
FOR HUNDREDS OF YEARS, THE SOHMA FAMILY...
...HAS BEEN POSSESSED BY TWELVE VENGEFUL SPIRITS THAT CORRESPOND TO THE ZODIAC.
OX, TIGER, RABBIT, DRAGON, SNAKE...
...HORSE, SHEEP, MONKEY, ROOSTER, AND BOAR.
YES... JUST LIKE THE CHINESE ZODIAC.
WE DON'T HAVE ANY SPECIAL POWERS OR ANYTHING--
WELL, WE CAN COMMUNICATE WITH OUR RESPECTIVE ANIMALS...
...BUT WHEN OUR BODIES ARE WEAK, AND, FOR SOME REASON, WHEN WE'RE HUGGED BY SOMEONE OF THE OPPOSITE GENDER, WE TRANSFORM.
......
AFTER SOME TIME, WE CHANGE BACK INTO HUMANS.

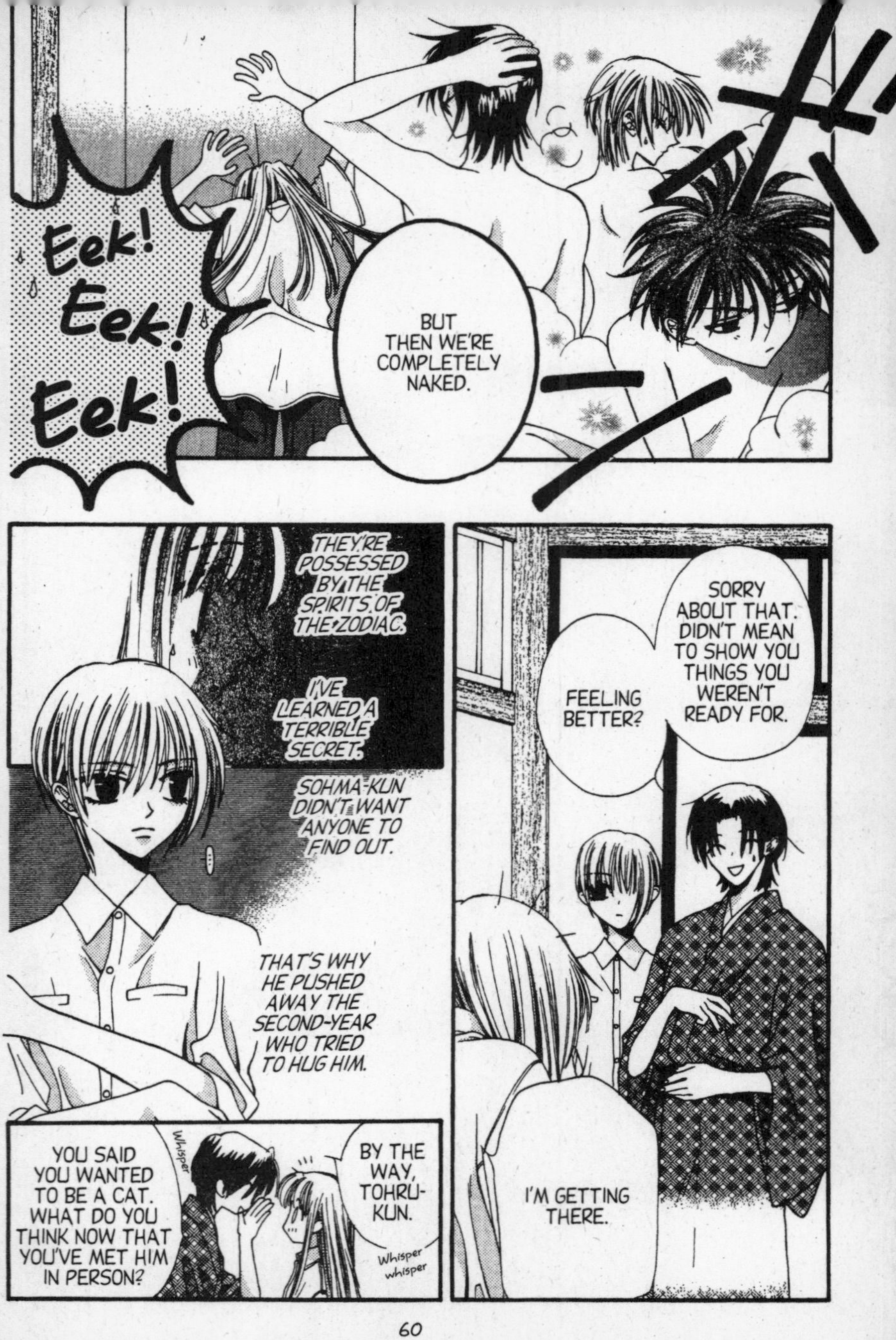
BUT THEN WE'RE COMPLETELY NAKED.
Eek! Eek! Eek!
SORRY ABOUT THAT. DIDN'T MEAN TO SHOW YOU THINGS YOU WEREN'T READY FOR.
FEELING BETTER?
I'M GETTING THERE.
THEY'RE POSSESSED BY THE SPIRITS OF THE ZODIAC.
I'VE LEARNED A TERRIBLE SECRET.
SOHMA-KUN DIDN'T WANT ANYONE TO FIND OUT.
...
THAT'S WHY HE PUSHED AWAY THE SECOND-YEAR WHO TRIED TO HUG HIM.
BY THE WAY, TOHRU-KUN.
Whisper whisper
Whisper
YOU SAID YOU WANTED TO BE A CAT. WHAT DO YOU THINK NOW THAT YOU'VE MET HIM IN PERSON?

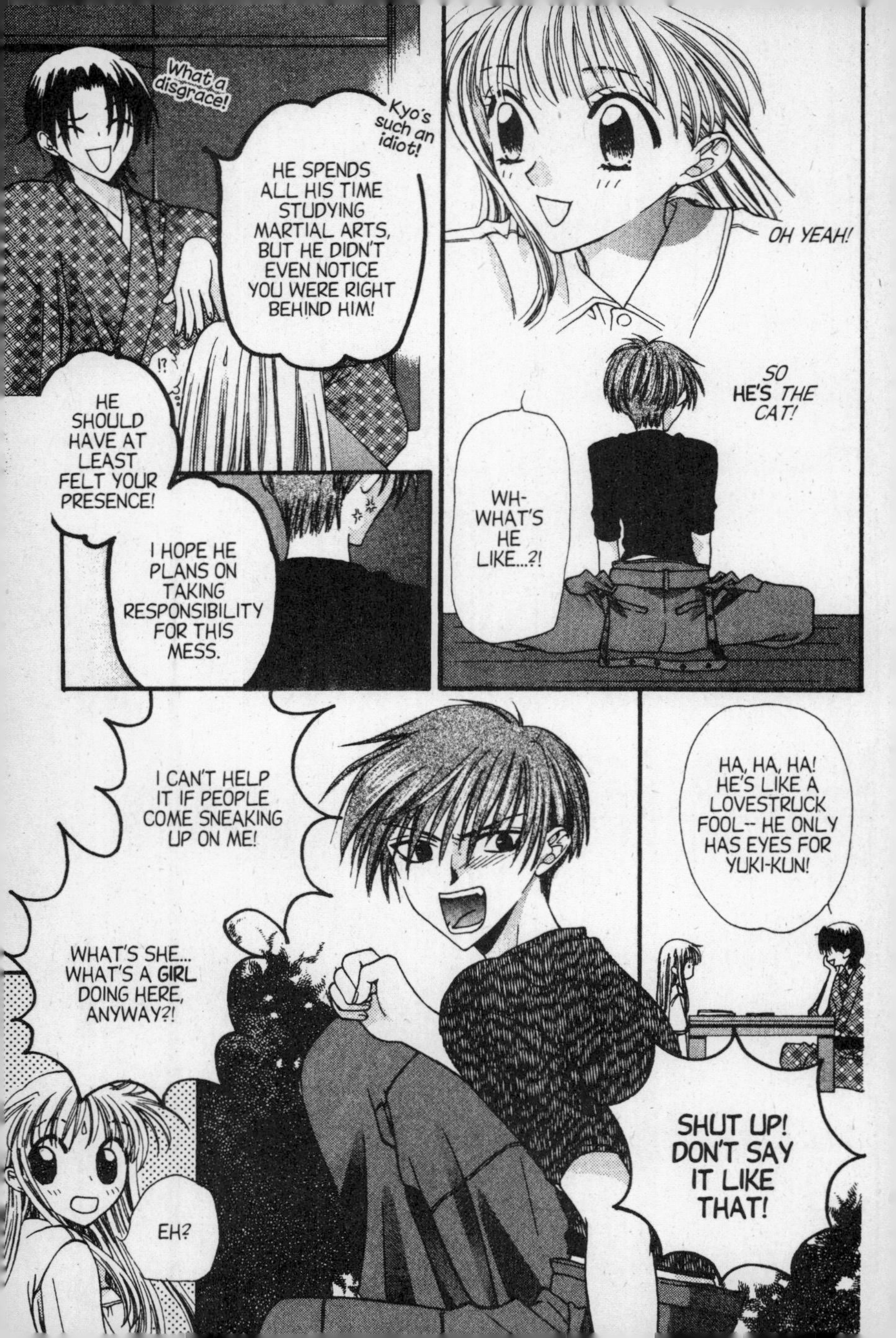
OH YEAH!
SO HE'S THE CAT!
WH-WHAT'S HE LIKE...?!
What a disgrace!
Kyo's such an idiot!
HE SPENDS ALL HIS TIME STUDYING MARTIAL ARTS, BUT HE DIDN'T EVEN NOTICE YOU WERE RIGHT BEHIND HIM!
!?
HE SHOULD HAVE AT LEAST FELT YOUR PRESENCE!
I HOPE HE PLANS ON TAKING RESPONSIBILITY FOR THIS MESS.
HA, HA, HA! HE'S LIKE A LOVESTRUCK FOOL-- HE ONLY HAS EYES FOR YUKI-KUN!
SHUT UP! DON'T SAY IT LIKE THAT!
I CAN'T HELP IT IF PEOPLE COME SNEAKING UP ON ME!
WHAT'S SHE... WHAT'S A GIRL DOING HERE, ANYWAY?!
EH?

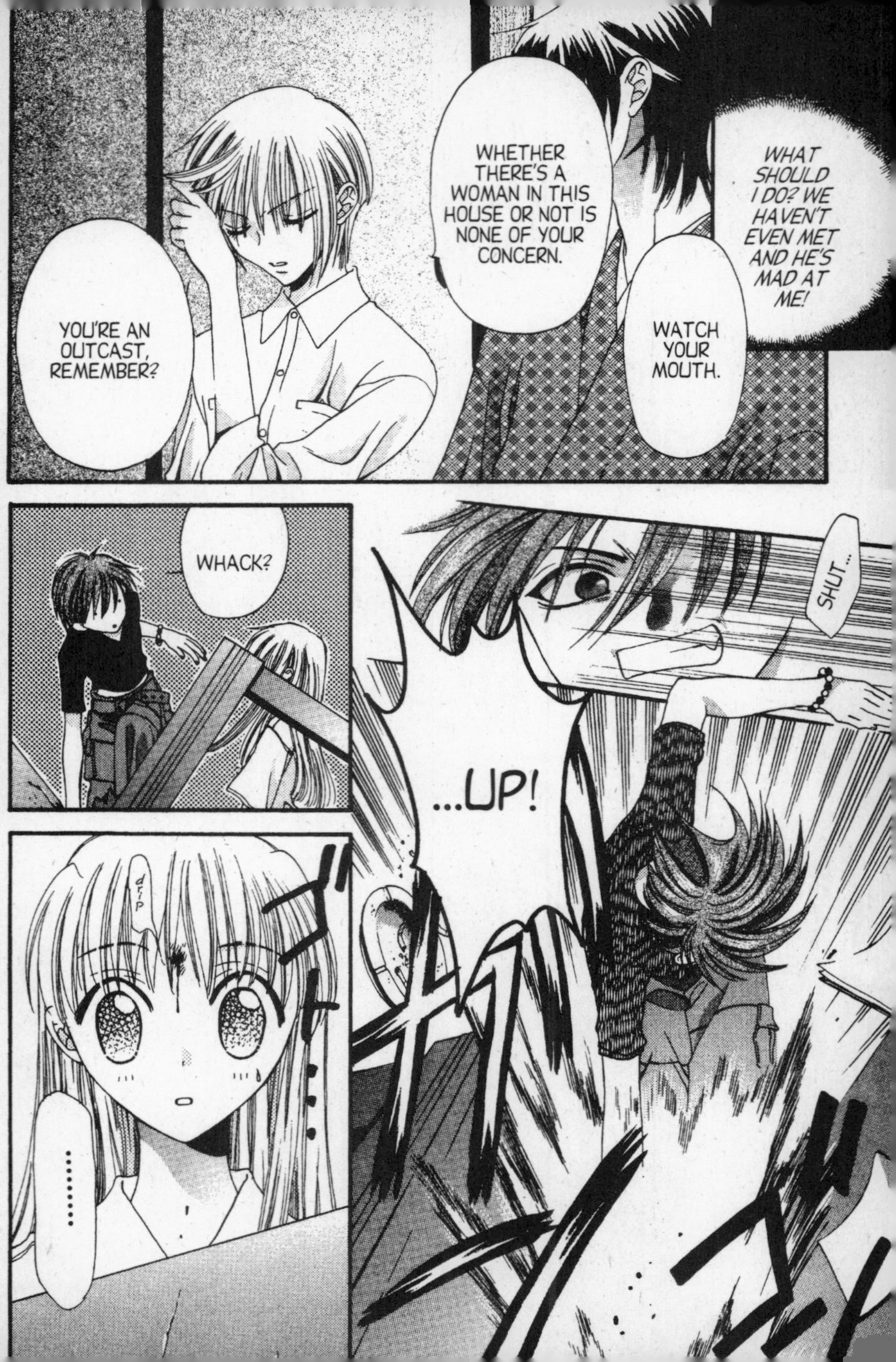
WHAT SHOULD I DO? WE HAVEN'T EVEN MET AND HE'S MAD AT ME!
WHETHER THERE'S A WOMAN IN THIS HOUSE OR NOT IS NONE OF YOUR CONCERN.
WATCH YOUR MOUTH.
YOU'RE AN OUTCAST, REMEMBER?
SHUT...
...UP!
WHACK?
drip
....

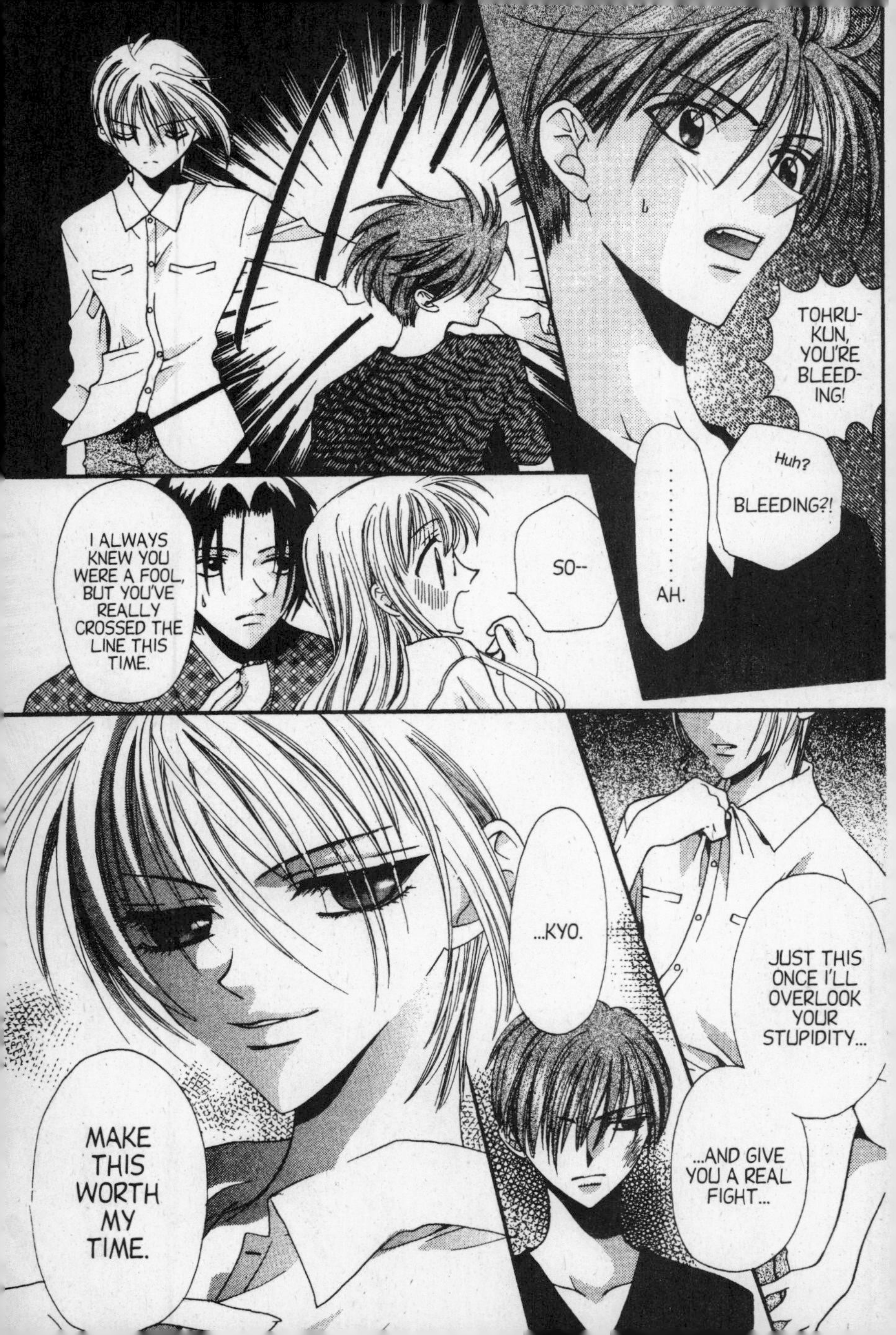
TOHRU-KUN, YOU'RE BLEEDING!
Huh? BLEEDING?!
...AH.
SO--
I ALWAYS KNEW YOU WERE A FOOL, BUT YOU'VE REALLY CROSSED THE LINE THIS TIME.
...KYO.
JUST THIS ONCE I'LL OVERLOOK YOUR STUPIDITY...
...AND GIVE YOU A REAL FIGHT...
MAKE THIS WORTH MY TIME.

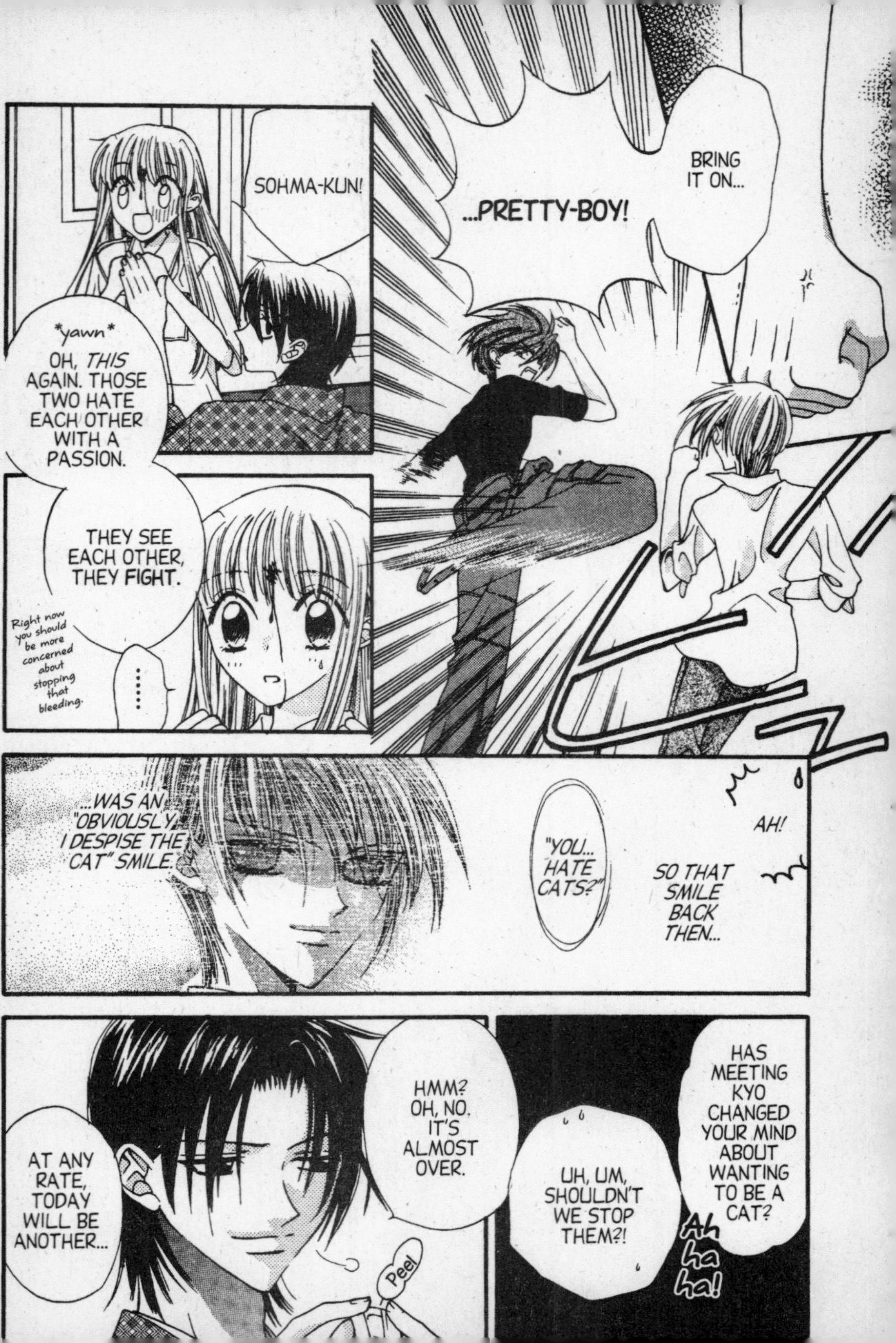
BRING IT ON...
...PRETTY-BOY!
SOHMA-KUN!
yawn OH, *THIS* AGAIN. THOSE TWO HATE EACH OTHER WITH A PASSION.
THEY SEE EACH OTHER, THEY **FIGHT**.
Right now you should be more concerned about stopping that bleeding.
......
AH!
SO THAT SMILE BACK THEN...
"YOU... HATE CATS?"
...WAS AN "OBVIOUSLY I DESPISE THE CAT" SMILE.
HAS MEETING KYO CHANGED YOUR MIND ABOUT WANTING TO BE A CAT?
Ah ha ha!
UH, UM, SHOULDN'T WE STOP THEM?!
HMM? OH, NO. IT'S ALMOST OVER.
AT ANY RATE, TODAY WILL BE ANOTHER...
Peel

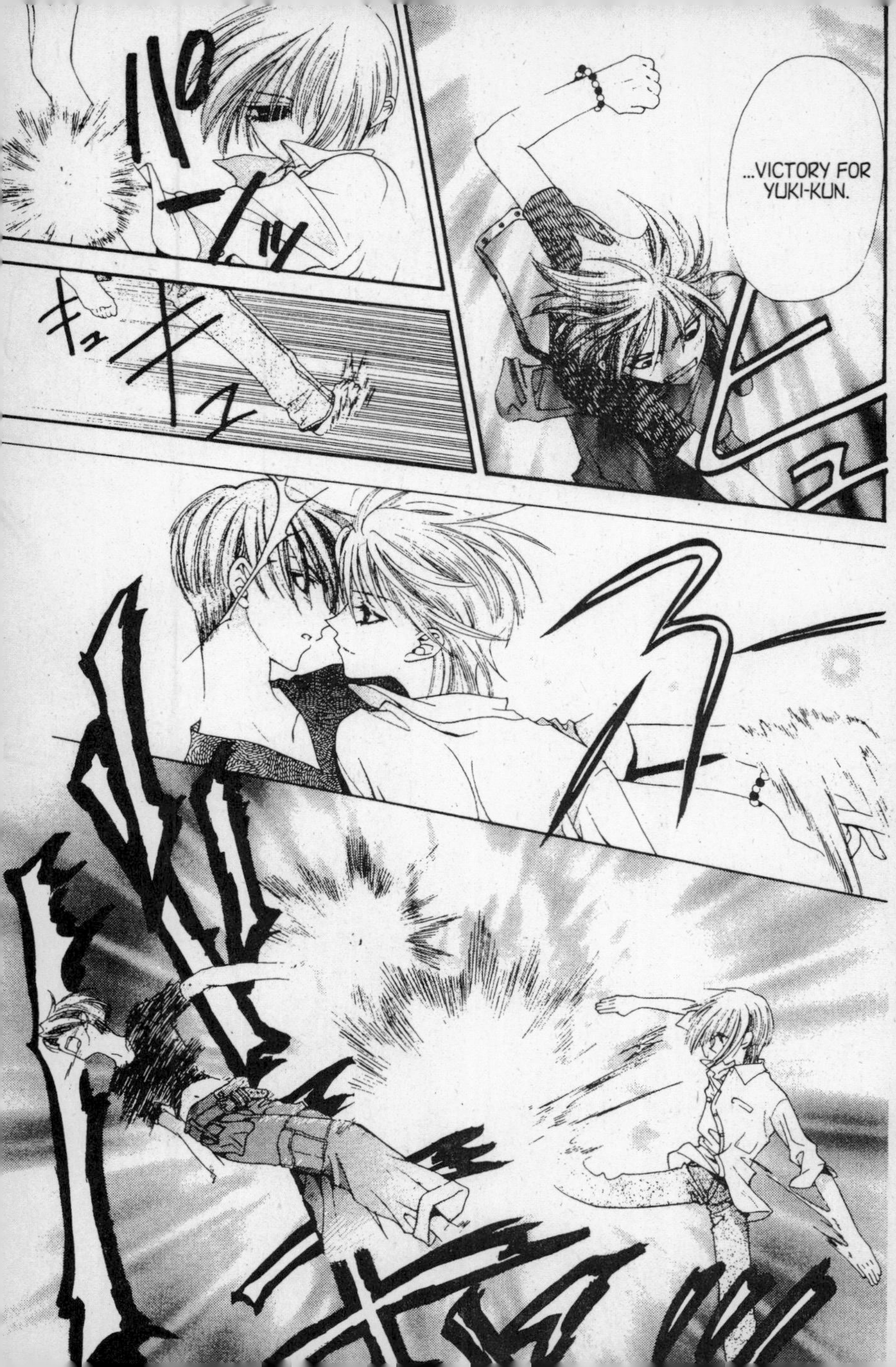
...VICTORY FOR YUKI-KUN.

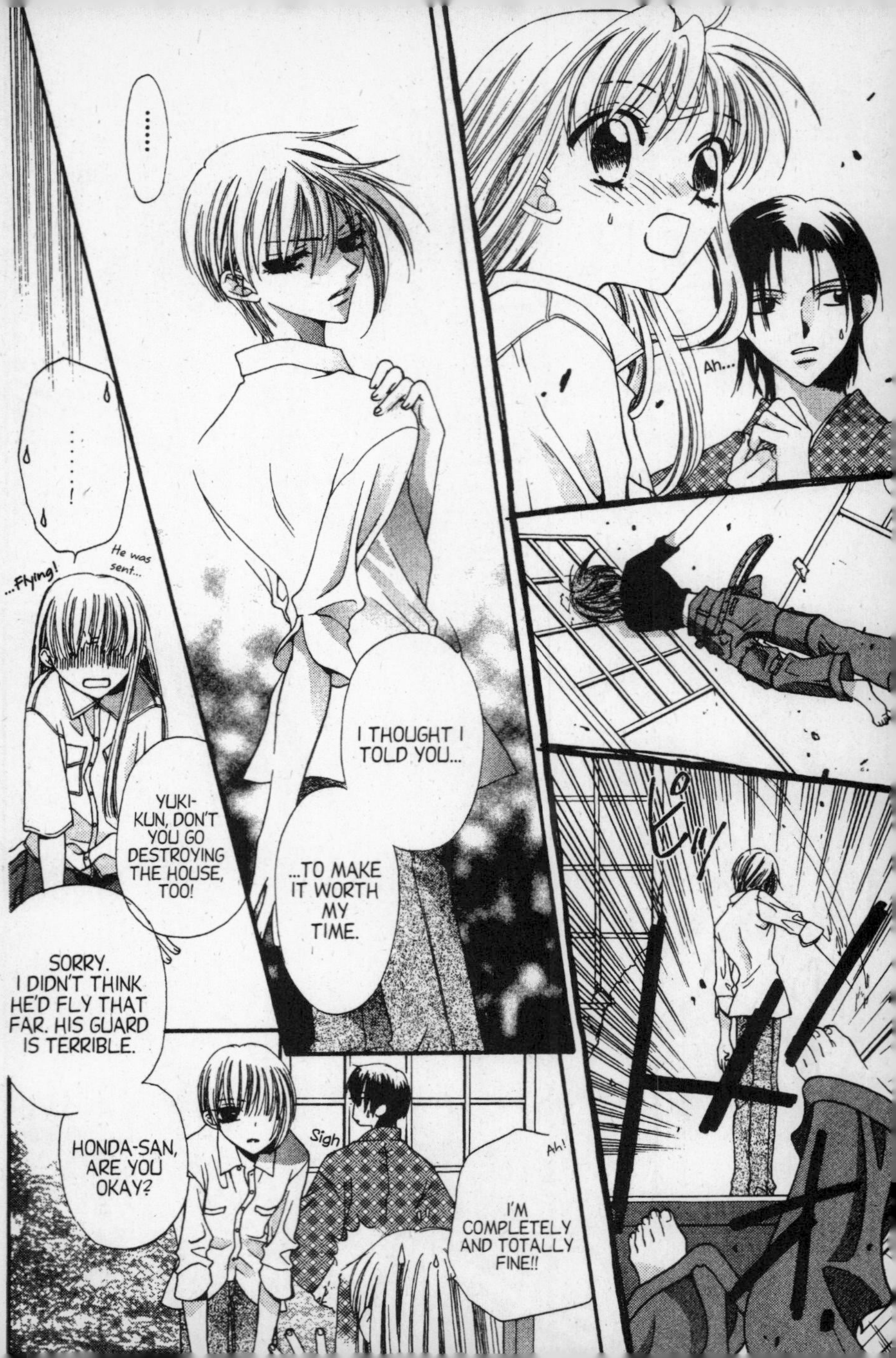
Ah...
I THOUGHT I TOLD YOU...
...TO MAKE IT WORTH MY TIME.
......
......!
He was sent...
...Flying!
YUKI-KUN, DON'T YOU GO DESTROYING THE HOUSE, TOO!
SORRY. I DIDN'T THINK HE'D FLY THAT FAR. HIS GUARD IS TERRIBLE.
Ah!
I'M COMPLETELY AND TOTALLY FINE!!
Sigh
HONDA-SAN, ARE YOU OKAY?

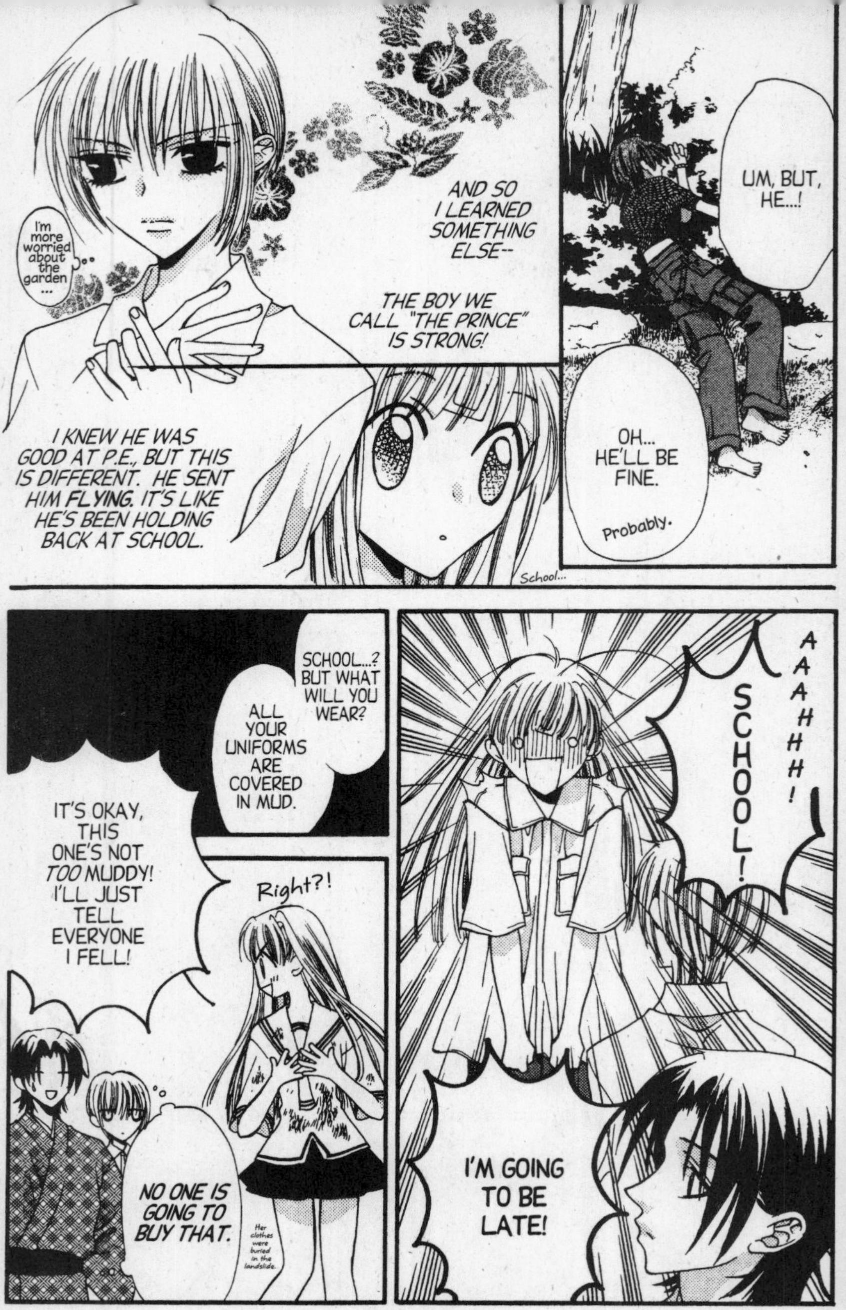
UM, BUT, HE...!
OH... HE'LL BE FINE.
Probably.
AND SO I LEARNED SOMETHING ELSE--
THE BOY WE CALL "THE PRINCE" IS STRONG!
I'm more worried about the garden...
I KNEW HE WAS GOOD AT P.E., BUT THIS IS DIFFERENT. HE SENT HIM FLYING. IT'S LIKE HE'S BEEN HOLDING BACK AT SCHOOL.
School...
AAAHHH!
SCHOOL!
I'M GOING TO BE LATE!
SCHOOL...? BUT WHAT WILL YOU WEAR?
ALL YOUR UNIFORMS ARE COVERED IN MUD.
IT'S OKAY, THIS ONE'S NOT TOO MUDDY! I'LL JUST TELL EVERYONE I FELL!
Right?!
NO ONE IS GOING TO BUY THAT.
Her clothes were buried in the landslide.

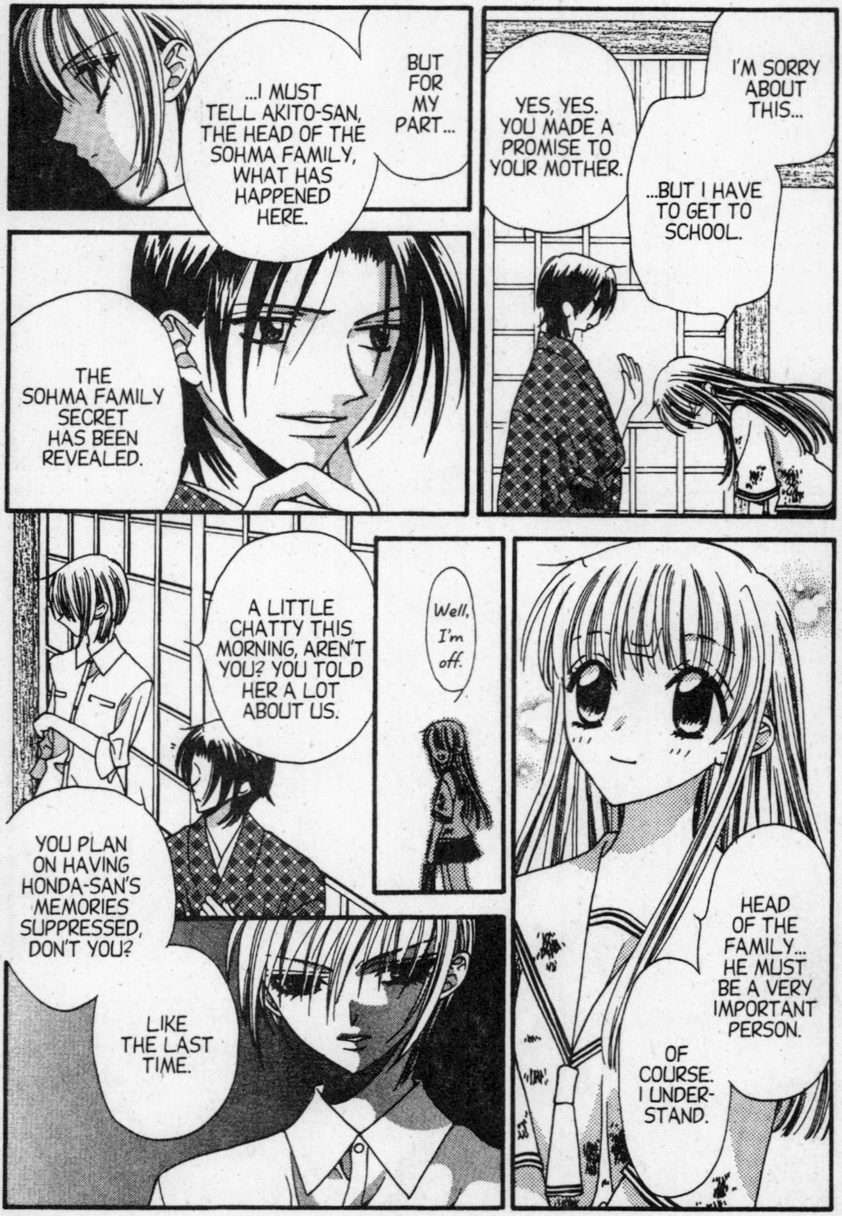
I'M SORRY ABOUT THIS...
...BUT I HAVE TO GET TO SCHOOL.
YES, YES. YOU MADE A PROMISE TO YOUR MOTHER.
BUT FOR MY PART...
...I MUST TELL AKITO-SAN, THE HEAD OF THE SOHMA FAMILY, WHAT HAS HAPPENED HERE.
THE SOHMA FAMILY SECRET HAS BEEN REVEALED.
HEAD OF THE FAMILY... HE MUST BE A VERY IMPORTANT PERSON.
OF COURSE. I UNDER-STAND.
Well, I'm off.
A LITTLE CHATTY THIS MORNING, AREN'T YOU? YOU TOLD HER A LOT ABOUT US.
YOU PLAN ON HAVING HONDA-SAN'S MEMORIES SUPPRESSED, DON'T YOU?
LIKE THE LAST TIME.

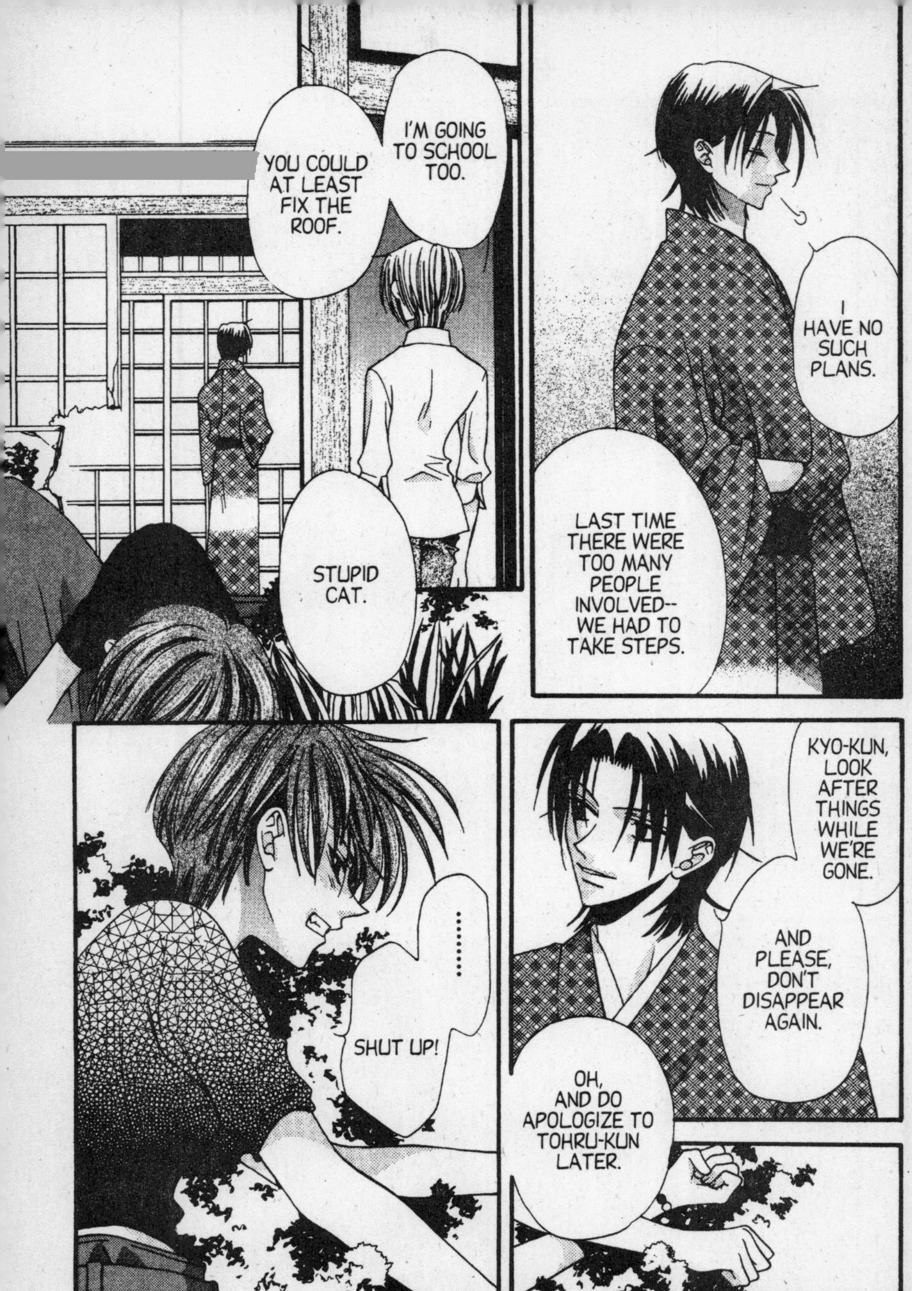
I HAVE NO SUCH PLANS.
LAST TIME THERE WERE TOO MANY PEOPLE INVOLVED-- WE HAD TO TAKE STEPS.
I'M GOING TO SCHOOL TOO.
YOU COULD AT LEAST FIX THE ROOF.
STUPID CAT.
KYO-KUN, LOOK AFTER THINGS WHILE WE'RE GONE.
AND PLEASE, DON'T DISAPPEAR AGAIN.
OH, AND DO APOLOGIZE TO TOHRU-KUN LATER.
......
SHUT UP!

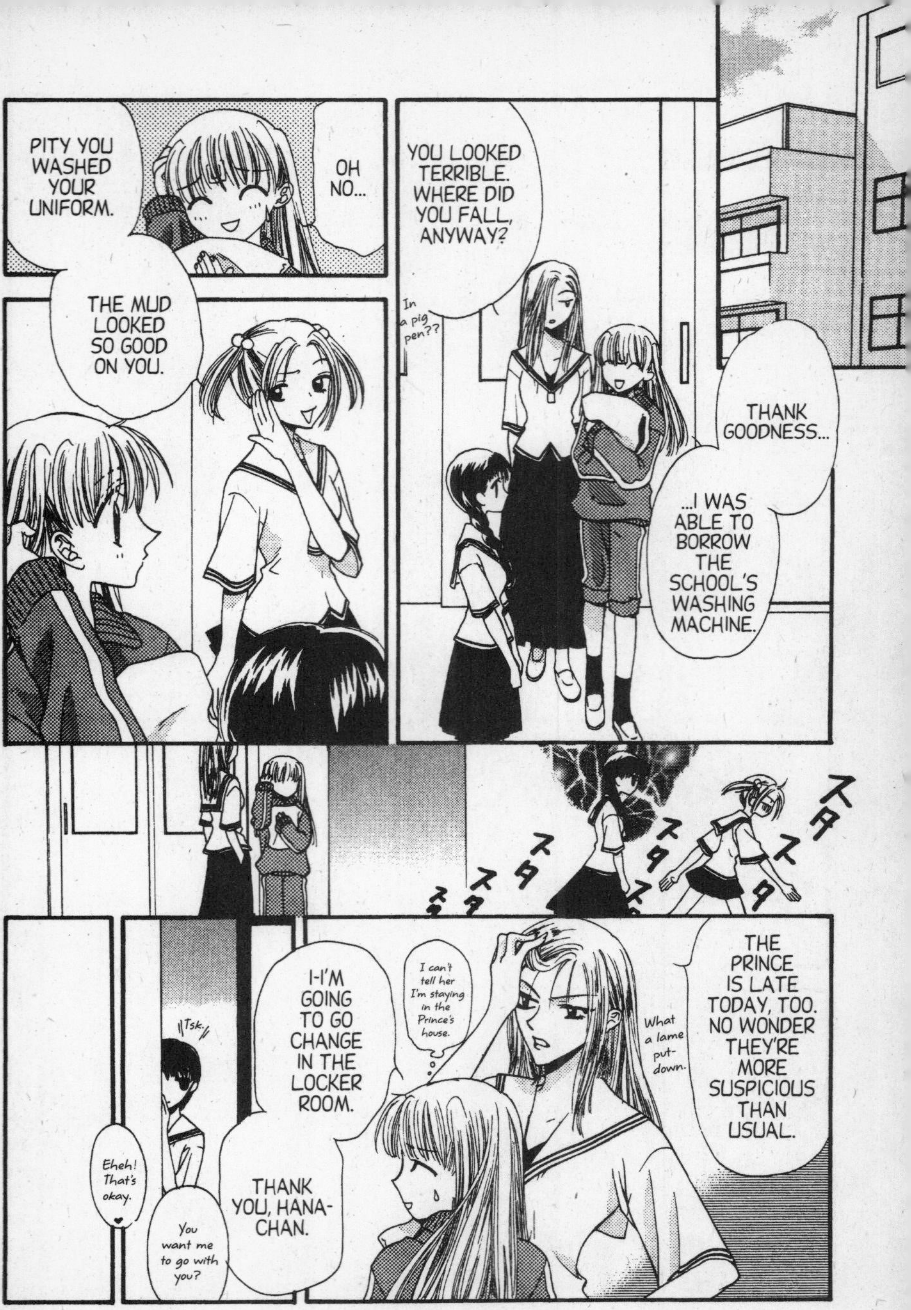
THANK GOODNESS...
...I WAS ABLE TO BORROW THE SCHOOL'S WASHING MACHINE.
YOU LOOKED TERRIBLE. WHERE DID YOU FALL, ANYWAY?
In a pig pen??
OH NO...
PITY YOU WASHED YOUR UNIFORM.
THE MUD LOOKED SO GOOD ON YOU.
スタスタ
スタスタ
スタスタ
THE PRINCE IS LATE TODAY, TOO. NO WONDER THEY'RE MORE SUSPICIOUS THAN USUAL.
What a lame put-down.
I can't tell her I'm staying in the Prince's house.
I-I'M GOING TO GO CHANGE IN THE LOCKER ROOM.
Tsk.
THANK YOU, HANA-CHAN.
You want me to go with you?
Eheh! That's okay.

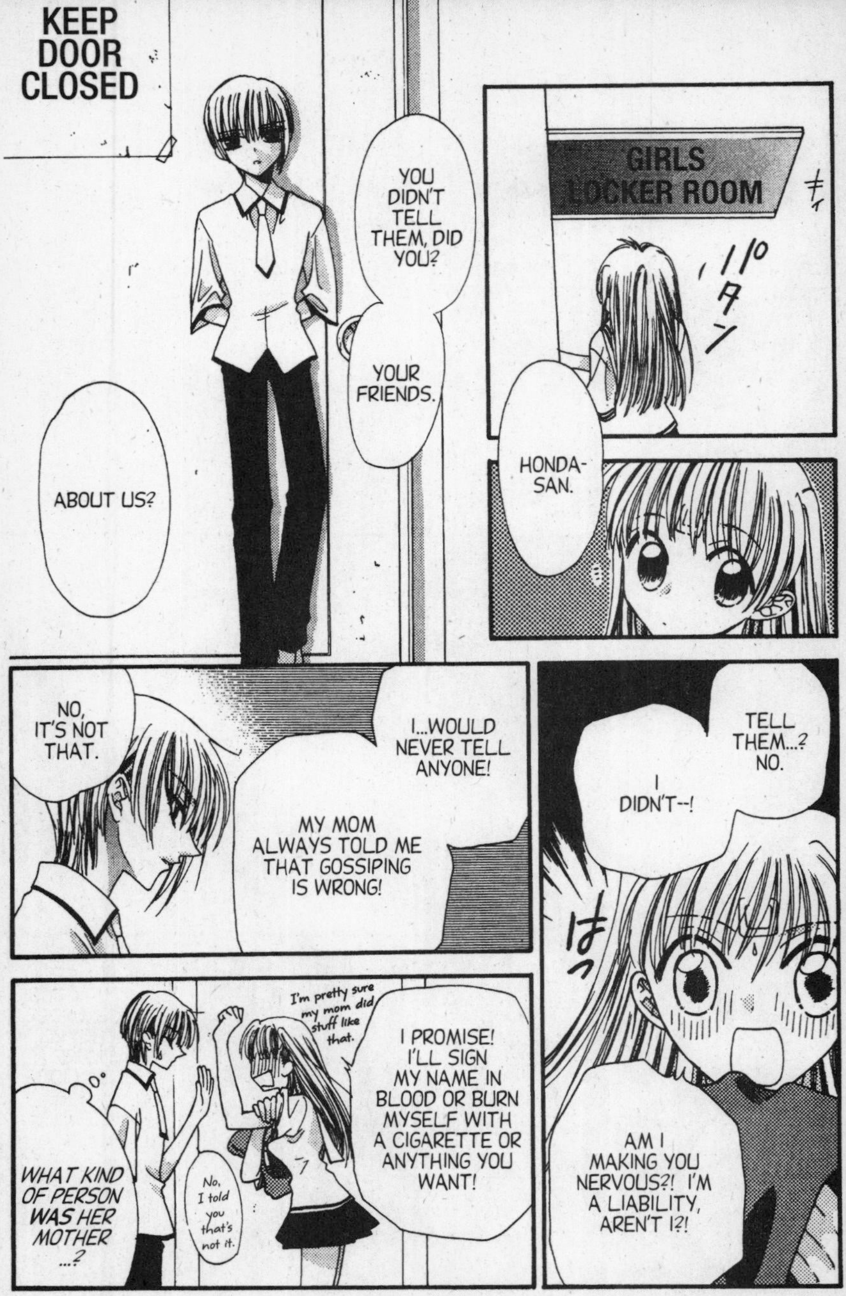
GIRLS LOCKER ROOM
キィ
パタン
HONDA-SAN.
KEEP DOOR CLOSED
YOU DIDN'T TELL THEM, DID YOU?
YOUR FRIENDS.
ABOUT US?
TELL THEM...? NO.
I DIDN'T--!
はっ
AM I MAKING YOU NERVOUS?! I'M A LIABILITY, AREN'T I?!
I...WOULD NEVER TELL ANYONE!
MY MOM ALWAYS TOLD ME THAT GOSSIPING IS WRONG!
NO, IT'S NOT THAT.
I PROMISE! I'LL SIGN MY NAME IN BLOOD OR BURN MYSELF WITH A CIGARETTE OR ANYTHING YOU WANT!
I'm pretty sure my mom did stuff like that.
No, I told you that's not it.
WHAT KIND OF PERSON WAS HER MOTHER ...?

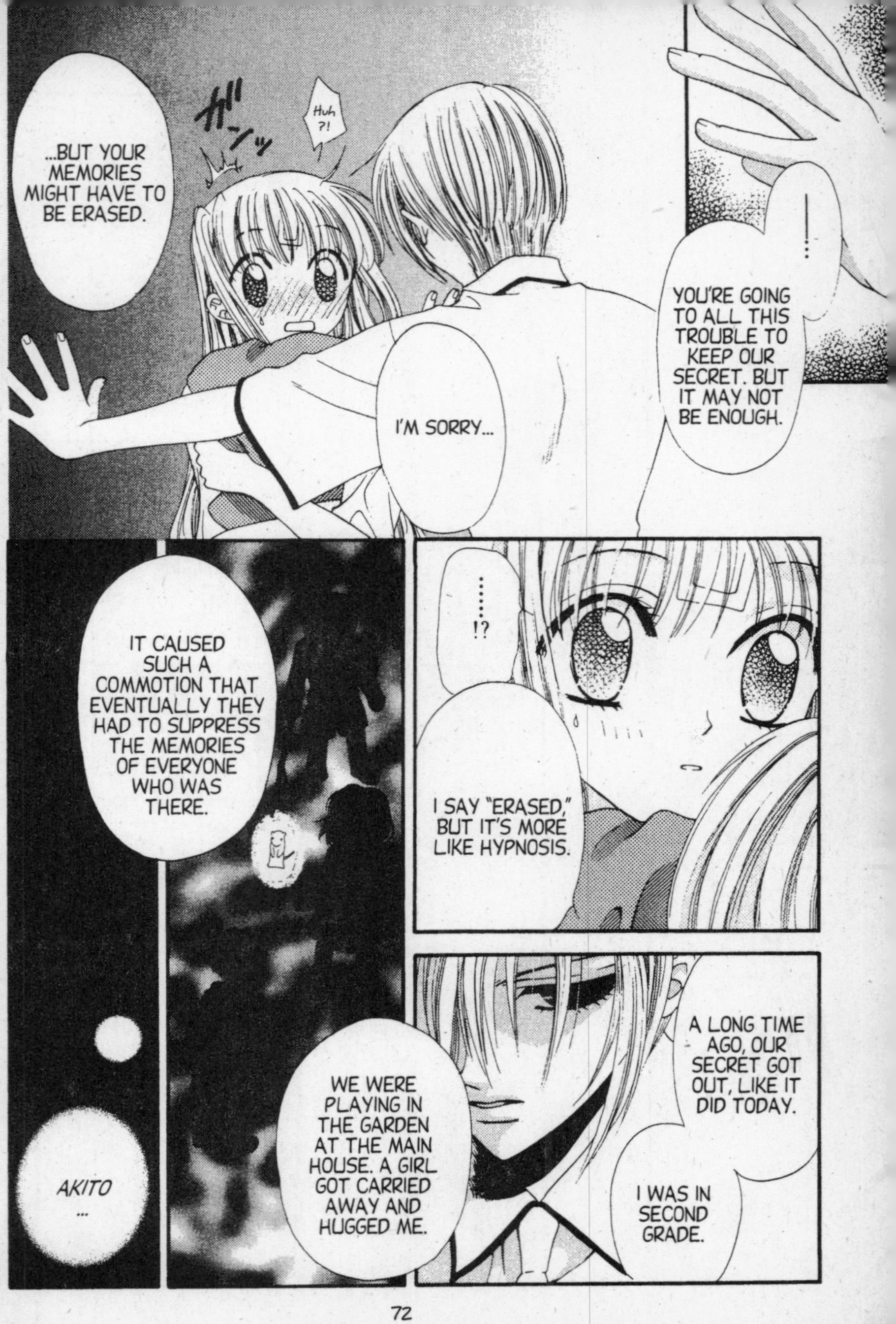
......
YOU'RE GOING TO ALL THIS TROUBLE TO KEEP OUR SECRET. BUT IT MAY NOT BE ENOUGH.
I'M SORRY...
...BUT YOUR MEMORIES MIGHT HAVE TO BE ERASED.
Huh ?!
......!?
I SAY "ERASED," BUT IT'S MORE LIKE HYPNOSIS.
A LONG TIME AGO, OUR SECRET GOT OUT, LIKE IT DID TODAY.
I WAS IN SECOND GRADE.
WE WERE PLAYING IN THE GARDEN AT THE MAIN HOUSE. A GIRL GOT CARRIED AWAY AND HUGGED ME.
IT CAUSED SUCH A COMMOTION THAT EVENTUALLY THEY HAD TO SUPPRESS THE MEMORIES OF EVERYONE WHO WAS THERE.
AKITO ...

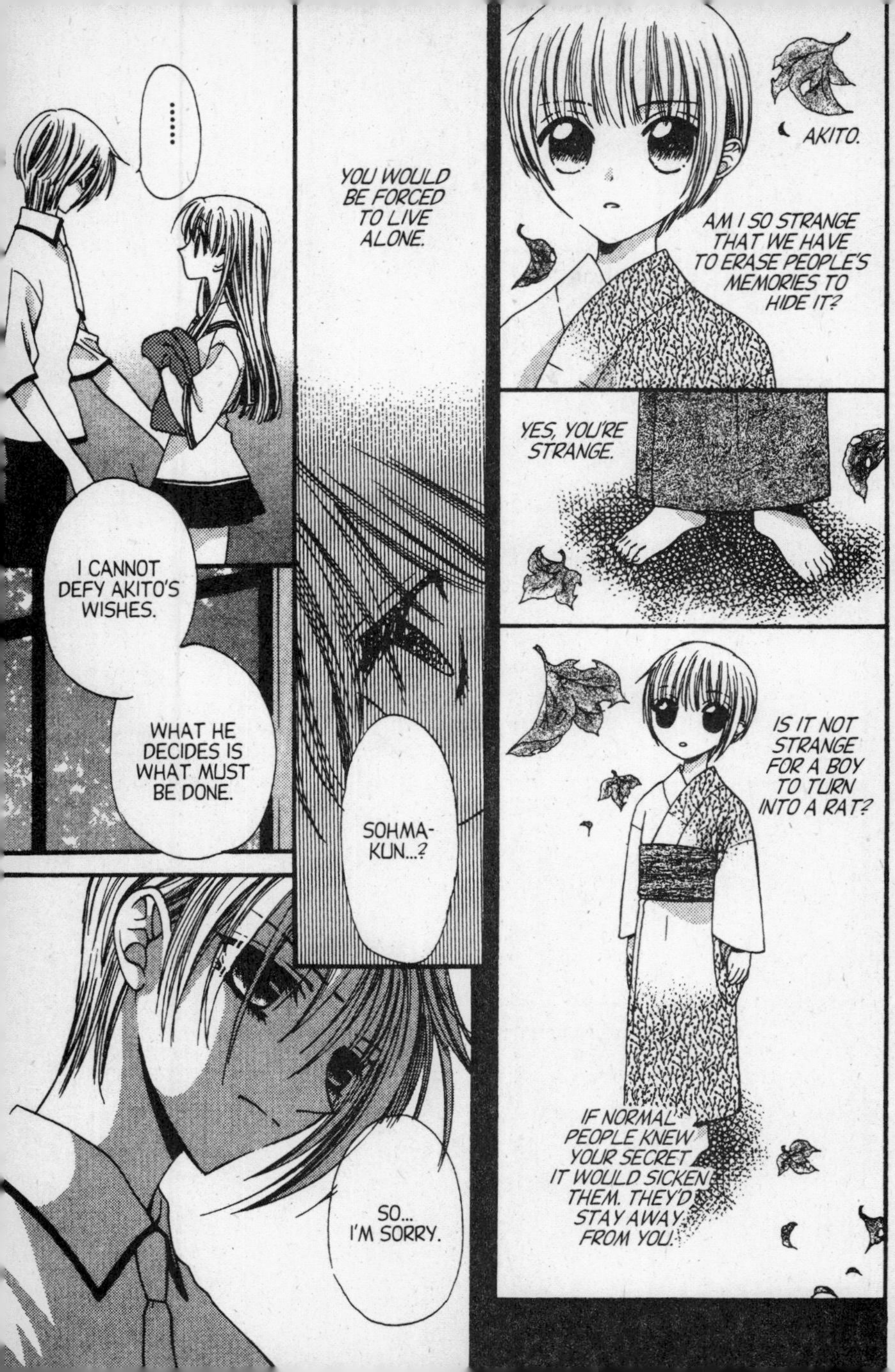
AKITO.
AM I SO STRANGE THAT WE HAVE TO ERASE PEOPLE'S MEMORIES TO HIDE IT?
YES, YOU'RE STRANGE.
IS IT NOT STRANGE FOR A BOY TO TURN INTO A RAT?
IF NORMAL PEOPLE KNEW YOUR SECRET IT WOULD SICKEN THEM. THEY'D STAY AWAY FROM YOU.
YOU WOULD BE FORCED TO LIVE ALONE.
......
I CANNOT DEFY AKITO'S WISHES.
WHAT HE DECIDES IS WHAT MUST BE DONE.
SOHMA-KUN...?
SO... I'M SORRY.

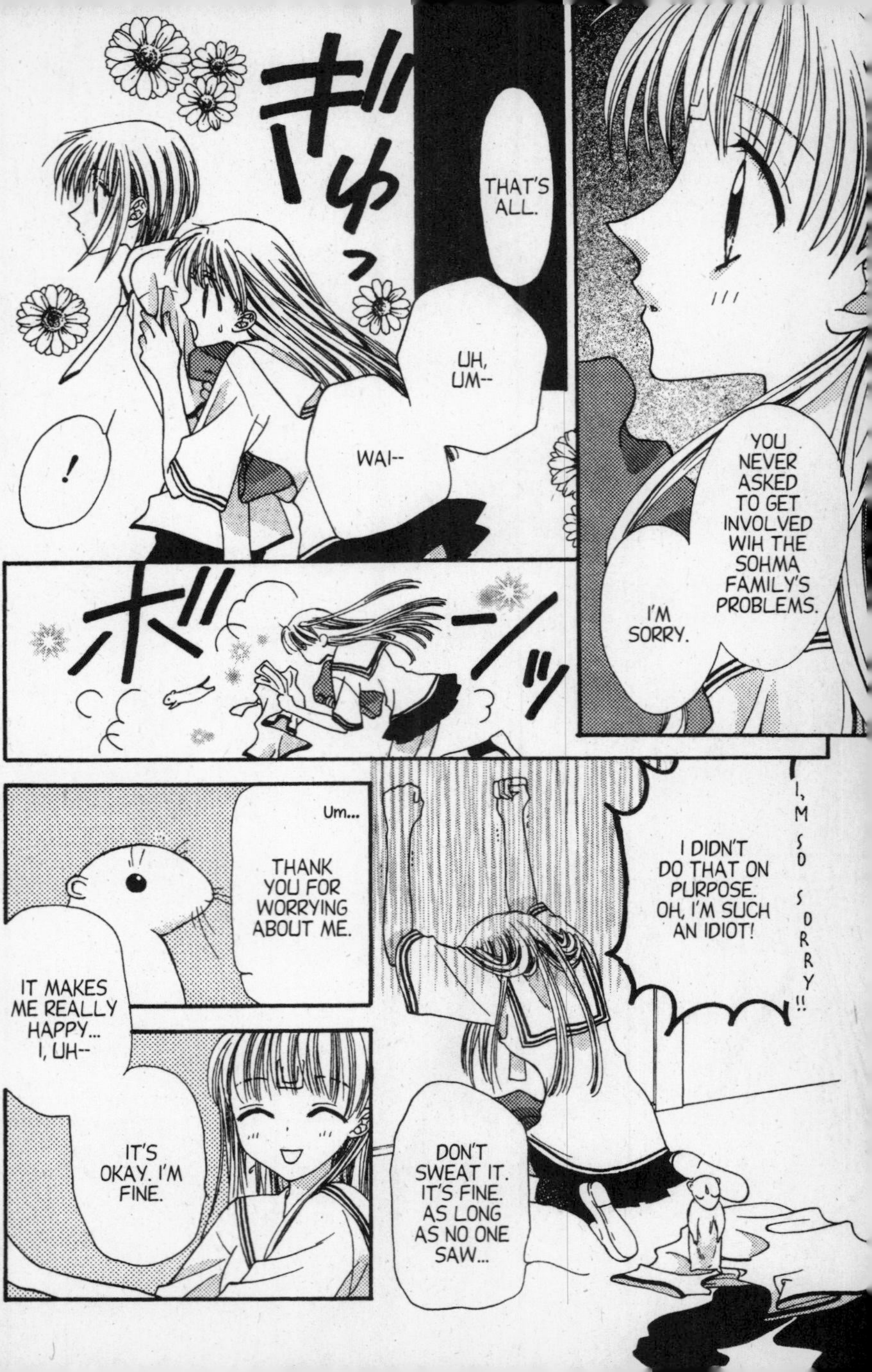
YOU NEVER ASKED TO GET INVOLVED WIH THE SOHMA FAMILY'S PROBLEMS.
I'M SORRY.
THAT'S ALL.
ぎゅっ
UH, UM--
WAI--
!
ボーンッ
I, M SO SORRY!!
I DIDN'T DO THAT ON PURPOSE. OH, I'M SUCH AN IDIOT!
DON'T SWEAT IT. IT'S FINE. AS LONG AS NO ONE SAW...
Um...
THANK YOU FOR WORRYING ABOUT ME.
IT MAKES ME REALLY HAPPY... I, UH--
IT'S OKAY. I'M FINE.

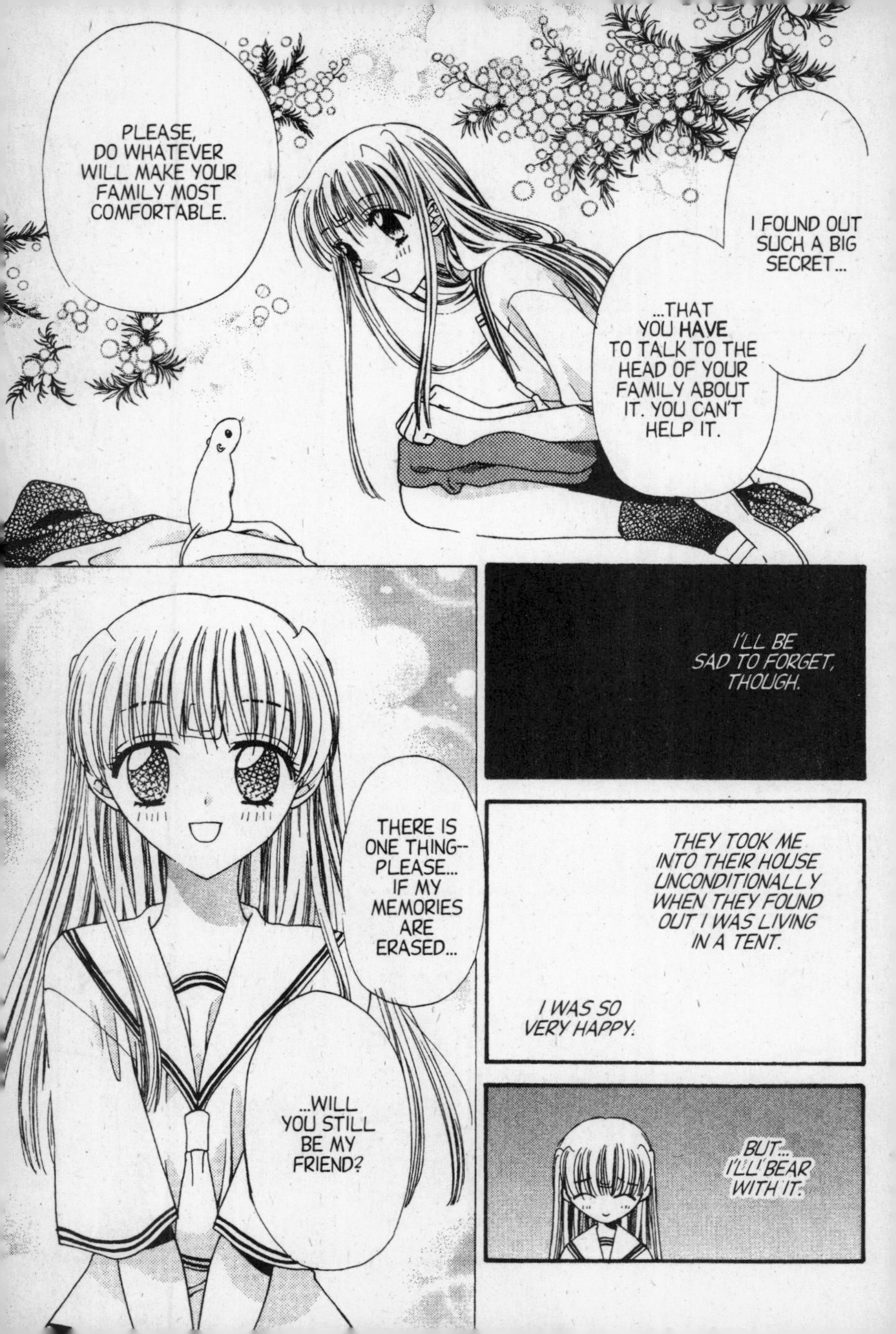
I FOUND OUT SUCH A BIG SECRET...
...THAT YOU **HAVE** TO TALK TO THE HEAD OF YOUR FAMILY ABOUT IT. YOU CAN'T HELP IT.
PLEASE, DO WHATEVER WILL MAKE YOUR FAMILY MOST COMFORTABLE.
I'LL BE SAD TO FORGET, THOUGH.
THEY TOOK ME INTO THEIR HOUSE UNCONDITIONALLY WHEN THEY FOUND OUT I WAS LIVING IN A TENT.
I WAS SO VERY HAPPY.
BUT... I'LL BEAR WITH IT.
THERE IS ONE THING-- PLEASE... IF MY MEMORIES ARE ERASED...
...WILL YOU STILL BE MY FRIEND?

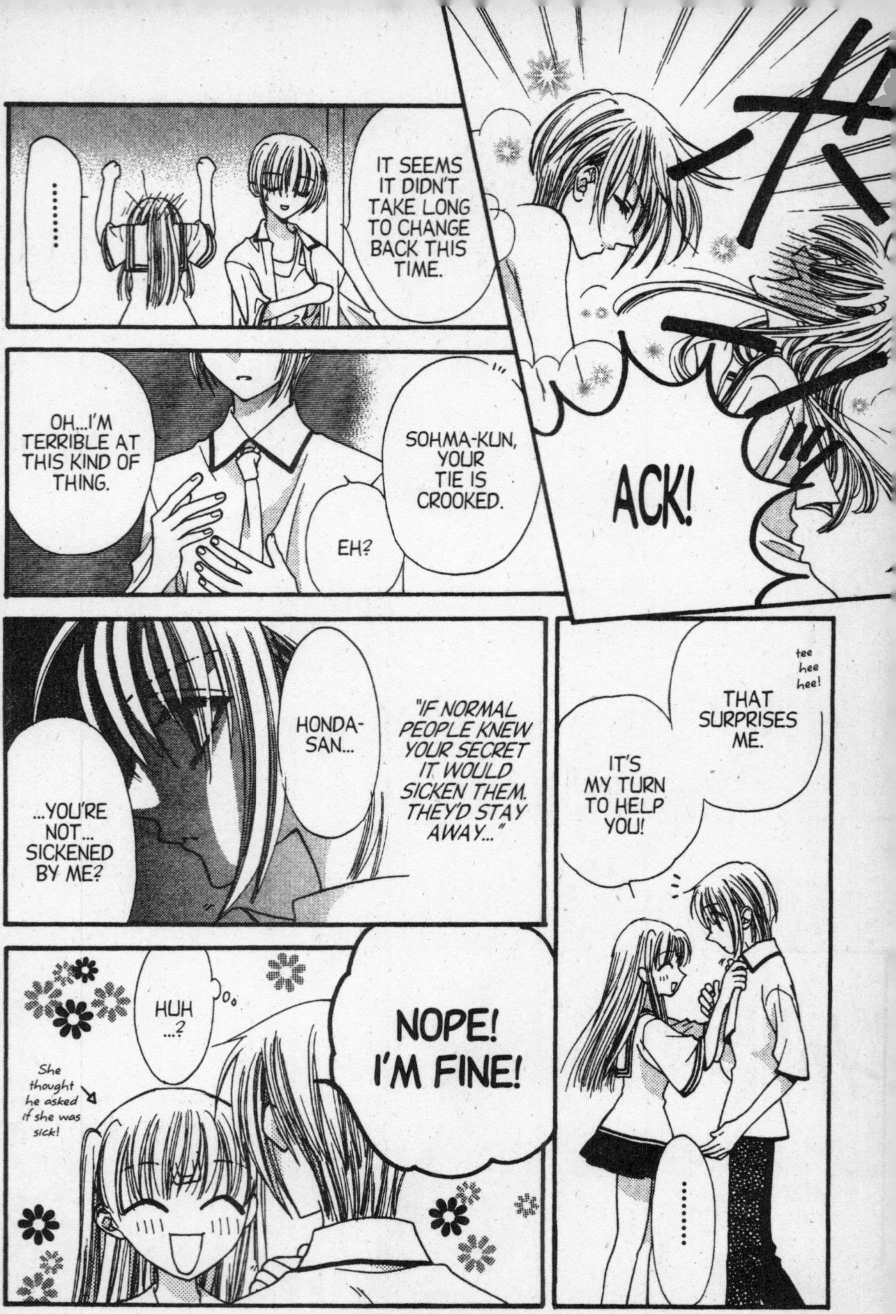
ACK!
IT SEEMS IT DIDN'T TAKE LONG TO CHANGE BACK THIS TIME.
......
SOHMA-KUN, YOUR TIE IS CROOKED.
EH?
OH...I'M TERRIBLE AT THIS KIND OF THING.
tee hee hee!
THAT SURPRISES ME.
IT'S MY TURN TO HELP YOU!
......
HONDA-SAN...
"IF NORMAL PEOPLE KNEW YOUR SECRET IT WOULD SICKEN THEM. THEY'D STAY AWAY..."
...YOU'RE NOT... SICKENED BY ME?
NOPE! I'M FINE!
HUH ...?
She thought he asked if she was sick!

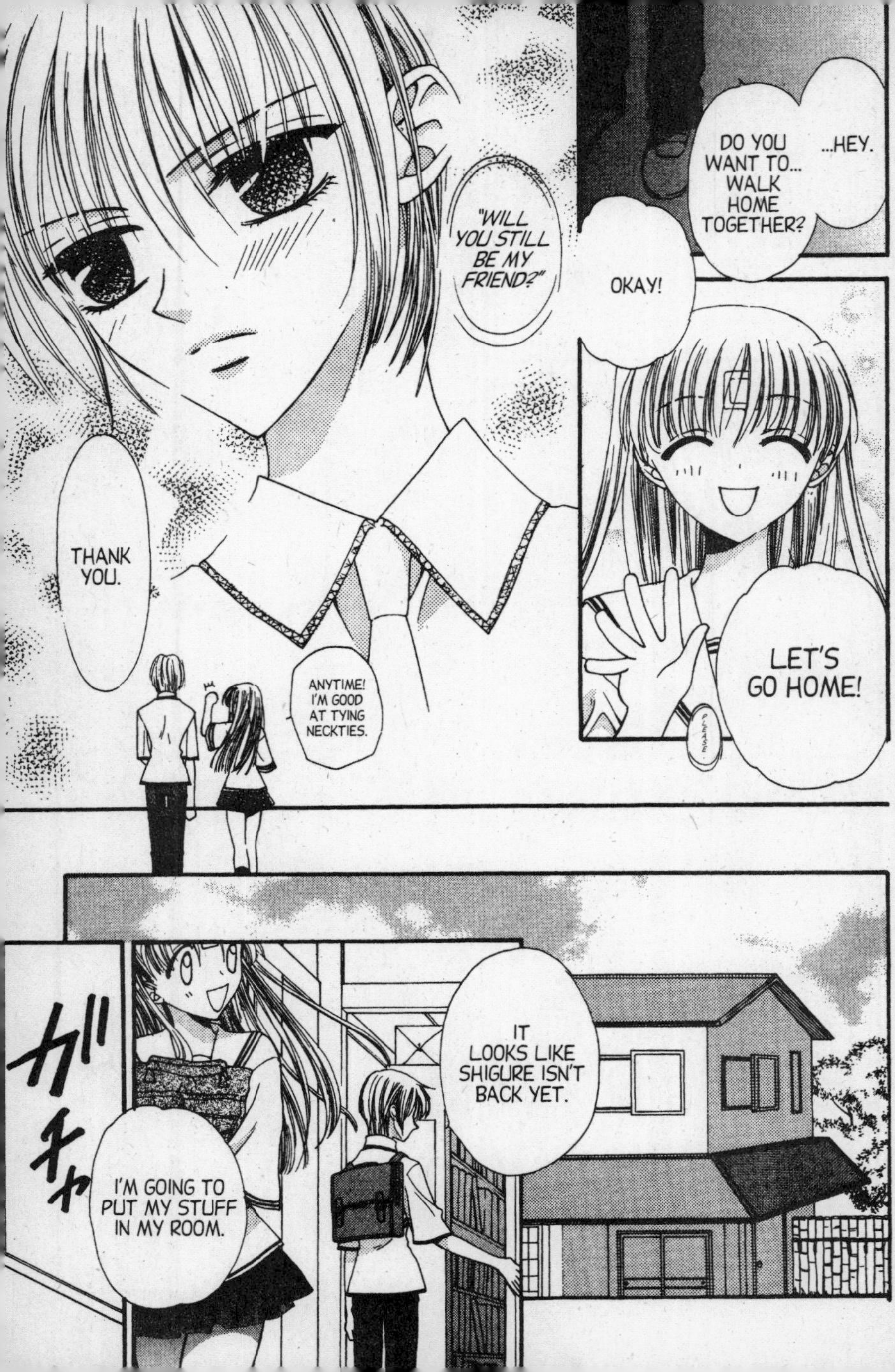
...HEY.
DO YOU WANT TO... WALK HOME TOGETHER?
OKAY!
LET'S GO HOME!
PLEASE
"WILL YOU STILL BE MY FRIEND?"
THANK YOU.
ANYTIME! I'M GOOD AT TYING NECKTIES.
ガチャ
IT LOOKS LIKE SHIGURE ISN'T BACK YET.
I'M GOING TO PUT MY STUFF IN MY ROOM.

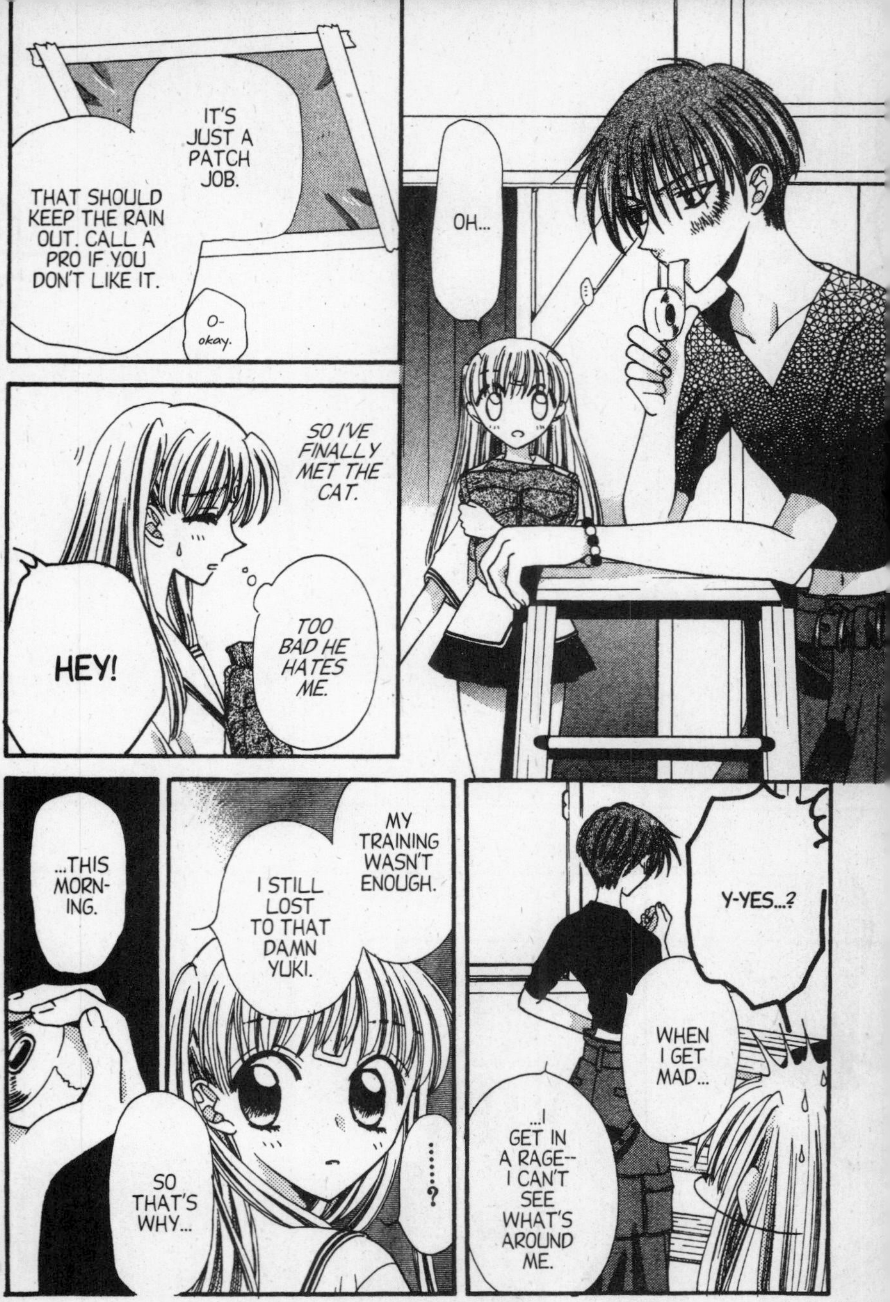
OH...
...
IT'S JUST A PATCH JOB.
THAT SHOULD KEEP THE RAIN OUT. CALL A PRO IF YOU DON'T LIKE IT.
O-okay.
SO I'VE FINALLY MET THE CAT.
TOO BAD HE HATES ME.
HEY!
Y-YES...?
WHEN I GET MAD...
...I GET IN A RAGE-- I CAN'T SEE WHAT'S AROUND ME.
MY TRAINING WASN'T ENOUGH.
I STILL LOST TO THAT DAMN YUKI.
......?
SO THAT'S WHY...
...THIS MORNING.

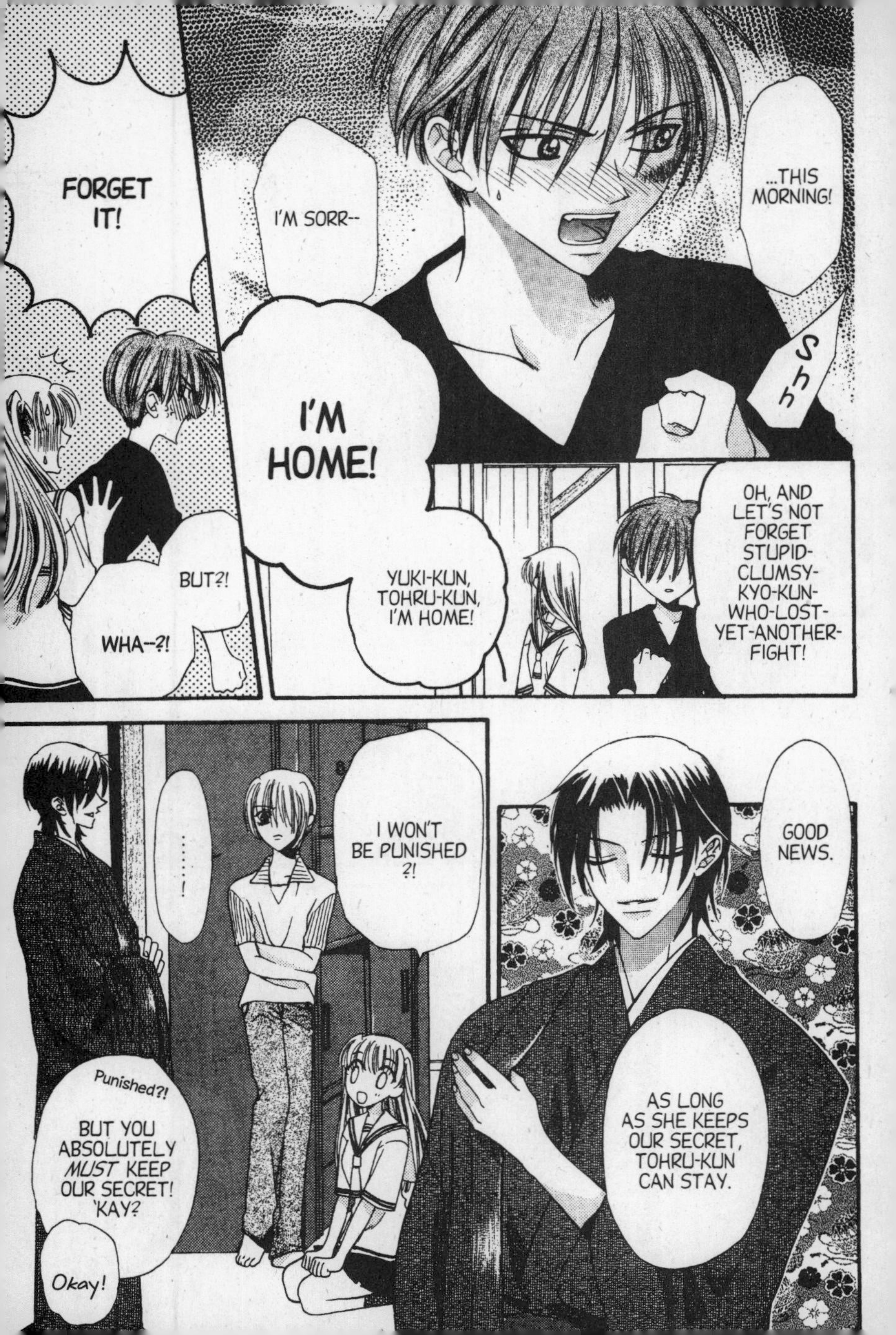
...THIS MORNING!
Shh
I'M SORR--
I'M HOME!
OH, AND LET'S NOT FORGET STUPID-CLUMSY-KYO-KUN-WHO-LOST-YET-ANOTHER-FIGHT!
YUKI-KUN, TOHRU-KUN, I'M HOME!
FORGET IT!
BUT?!
WHA--?!
GOOD NEWS.
AS LONG AS SHE KEEPS OUR SECRET, TOHRU-KUN CAN STAY.
I WON'T BE PUNISHED ?!
......!
Punished?!
BUT YOU ABSOLUTELY *MUST* KEEP OUR SECRET! 'KAY?
Okay!

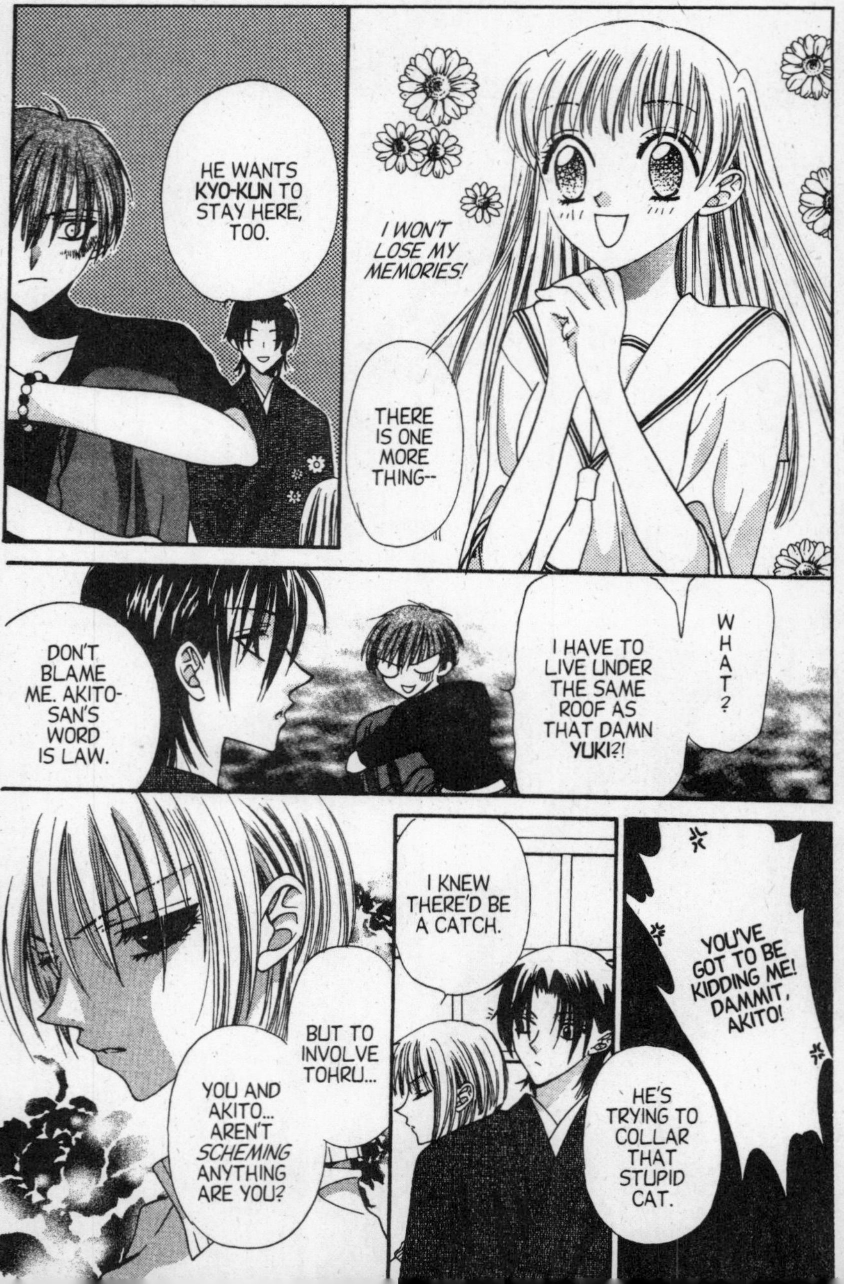
I WON'T LOSE MY MEMORIES!
THERE IS ONE MORE THING--
HE WANTS KYO-KUN TO STAY HERE, TOO.
WHAT?
I HAVE TO LIVE UNDER THE SAME ROOF AS THAT DAMN YUKI?!
DON'T BLAME ME. AKITO-SAN'S WORD IS LAW.
YOU'VE GOT TO BE KIDDING ME! DAMMIT, AKITO!
HE'S TRYING TO COLLAR THAT STUPID CAT.
I KNEW THERE'D BE A CATCH.
BUT TO INVOLVE TOHRU...
YOU AND AKITO... AREN'T SCHEMING ANYTHING ARE YOU?

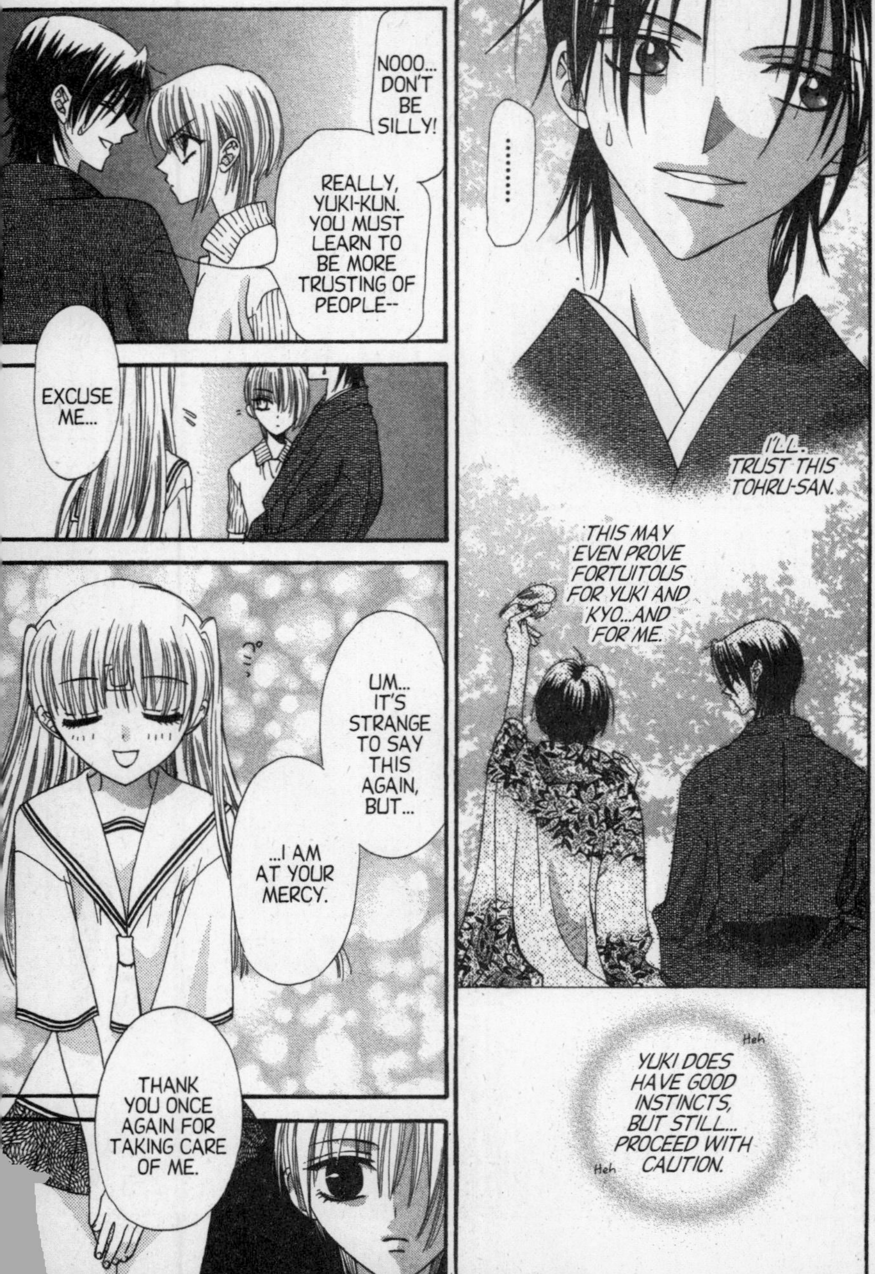
......
I'LL. TRUST THIS TOHRU-SAN.
THIS MAY EVEN PROVE FORTUITOUS FOR YUKI AND KYO...AND FOR ME.
Heh
YUKI DOES HAVE GOOD INSTINCTS, BUT STILL... PROCEED WITH CAUTION.
Heh
NOOO... DON'T BE SILLY!
REALLY, YUKI-KUN. YOU MUST LEARN TO BE MORE TRUSTING OF PEOPLE--
EXCUSE ME...
UM... IT'S STRANGE TO SAY THIS AGAIN, BUT...
...I AM AT YOUR MERCY.
THANK YOU ONCE AGAIN FOR TAKING CARE OF ME.

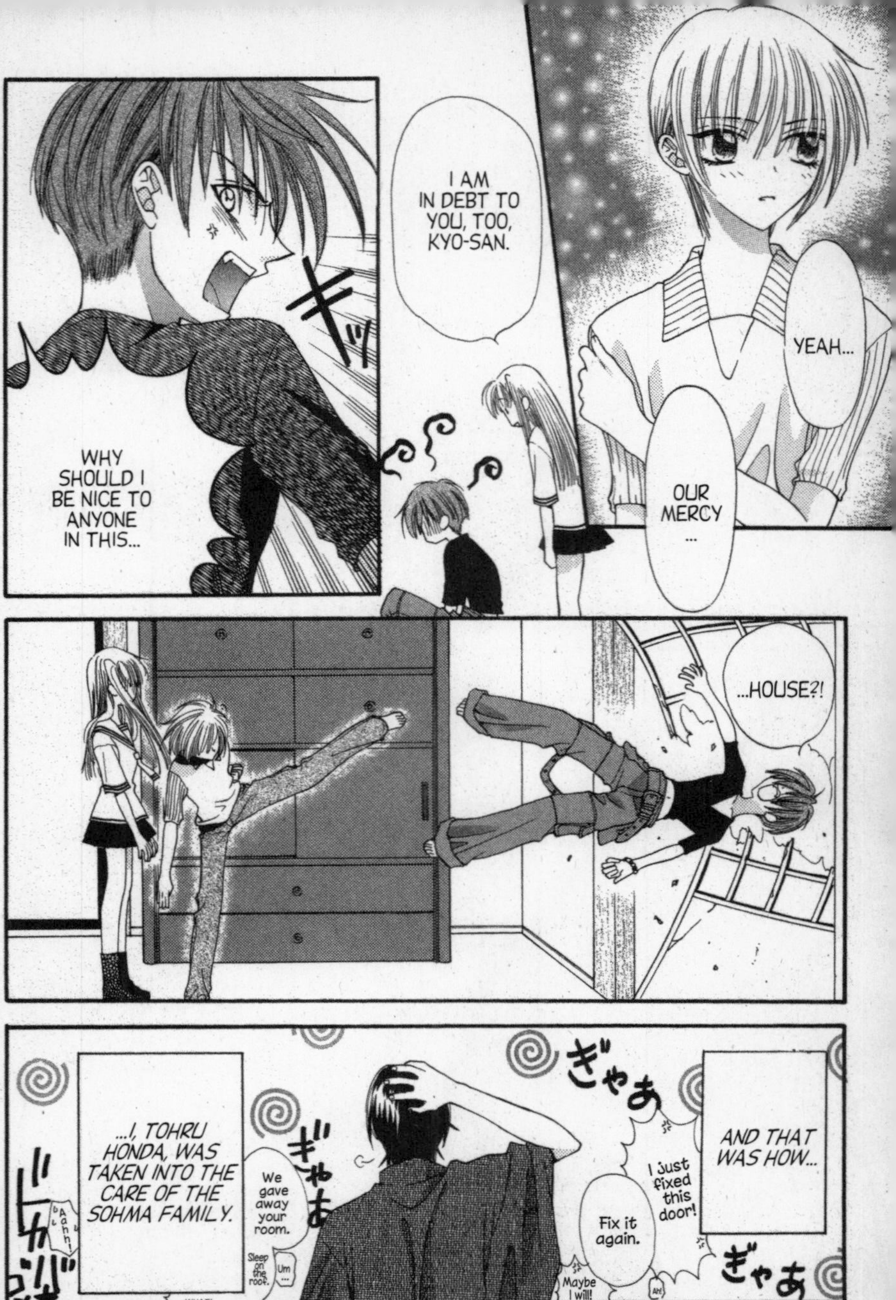
YEAH...
OUR MERCY ...
I AM IN DEBT TO YOU, TOO, KYO-SAN.
キッ
WHY SHOULD I BE NICE TO ANYONE IN THIS...
...HOUSE?!
AND THAT WAS HOW...
ぎゃあ
I just fixed this door!
Fix it again.
Maybe I will!
Ah!
ぎゃあ
ぎゃあ
We gave away your room.
Sleep on the roof.
Um ...
Aahh!
WHAT!
...I, TOHRU HONDA, WAS TAKEN INTO THE CARE OF THE SOHMA FAMILY.

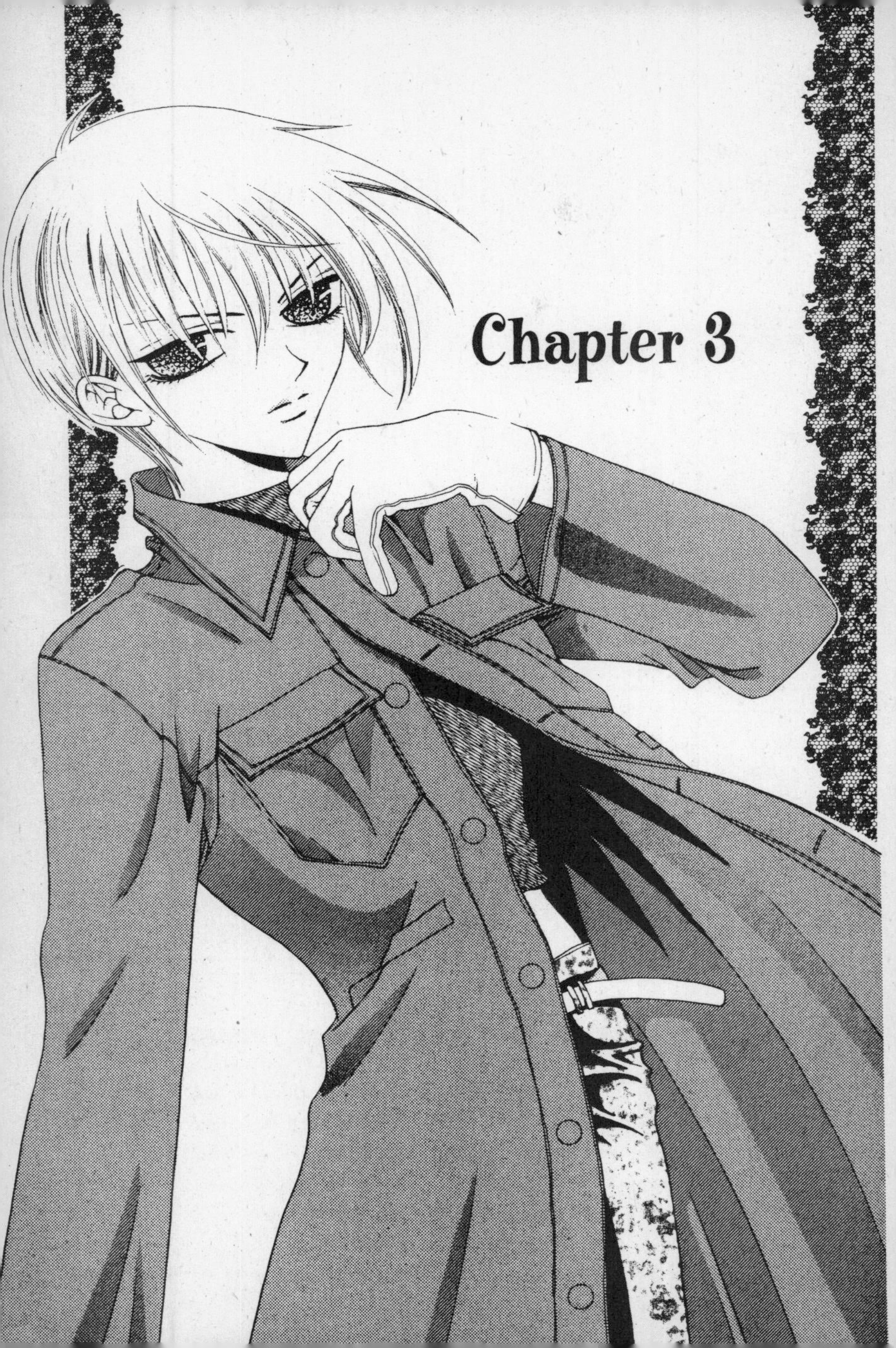

Chapter 3

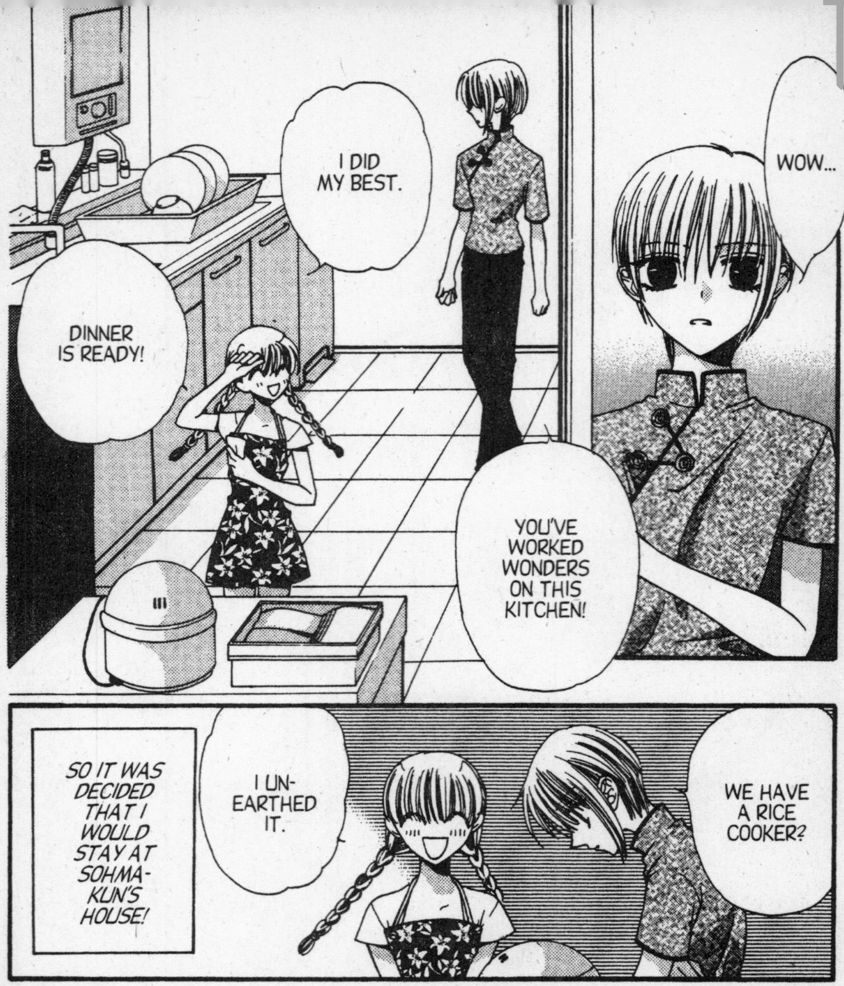
WOW...
YOU'VE WORKED WONDERS ON THIS KITCHEN!
I DID MY BEST.
DINNER IS READY!
WE HAVE A RICE COOKER?
I UN-EARTHED IT.
SO IT WAS DECIDED THAT I WOULD STAY AT SOHMA-KUN'S HOUSE!

ULTRA SPECIAL BLAH BLAH BLAH, NUMBER 2.

A martial artist has to have a firm body. They have to have muscles. But Yuki and Kyo are scrawny (ha ha). That's just because I don't like drawing muscles very much. I prefer a slender aesthetic for my men. Don't worry too much about it. Not that people had been pointing it out to me; I was just worried about it myself.

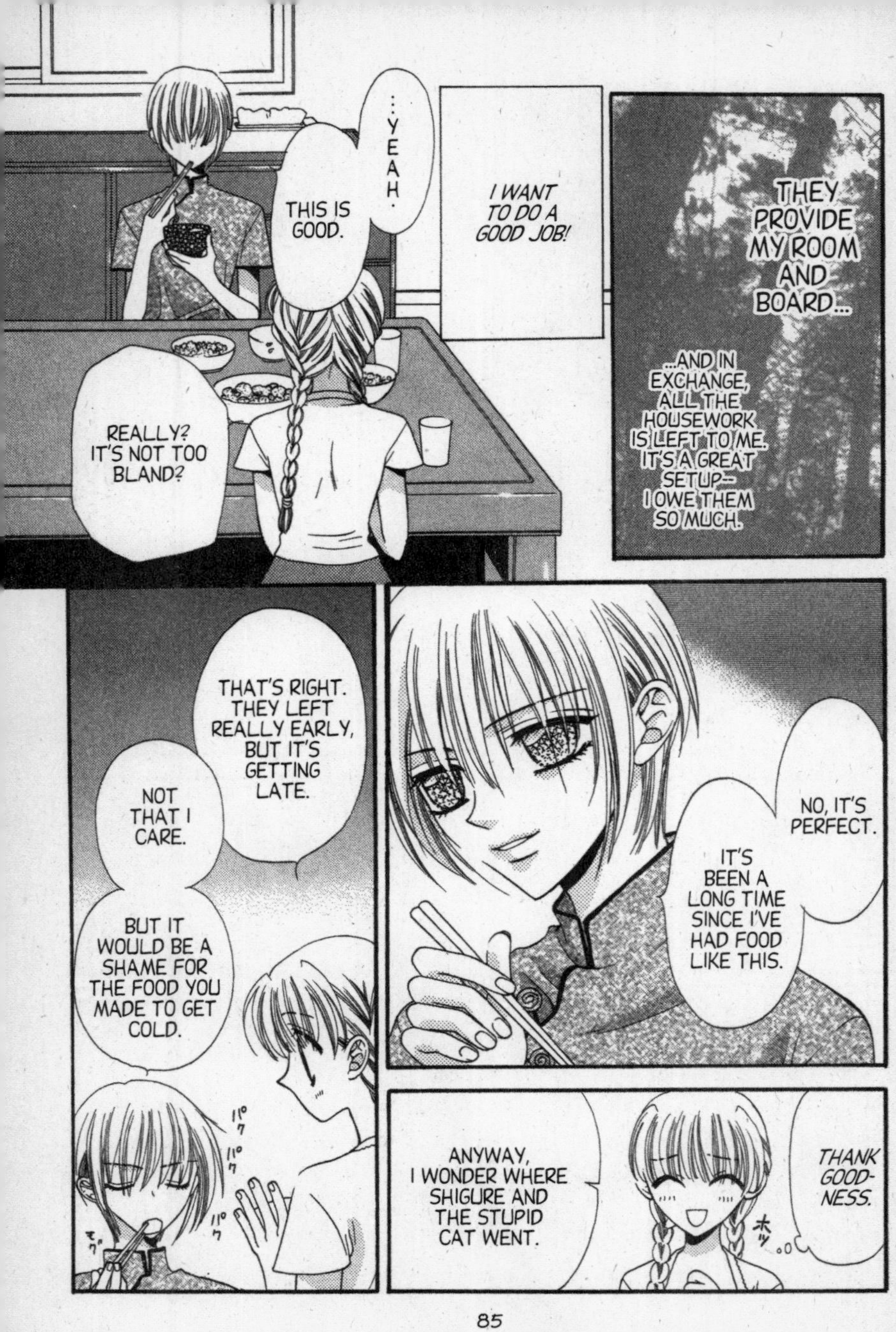
THEY PROVIDE MY ROOM AND BOARD...
...AND IN EXCHANGE, ALL THE HOUSEWORK IS LEFT TO ME. IT'S A GREAT SETUP-- I OWE THEM SO MUCH.
I WANT TO DO A GOOD JOB!
...YEAH.
THIS IS GOOD.
REALLY? IT'S NOT TOO BLAND?
NO, IT'S PERFECT.
IT'S BEEN A LONG TIME SINCE I'VE HAD FOOD LIKE THIS.
THANK GOODNESS.
ANYWAY, I WONDER WHERE SHIGURE AND THE STUPID CAT WENT.
THAT'S RIGHT. THEY LEFT REALLY EARLY, BUT IT'S GETTING LATE.
NOT THAT I CARE.
BUT IT WOULD BE A SHAME FOR THE FOOD YOU MADE TO GET COLD.

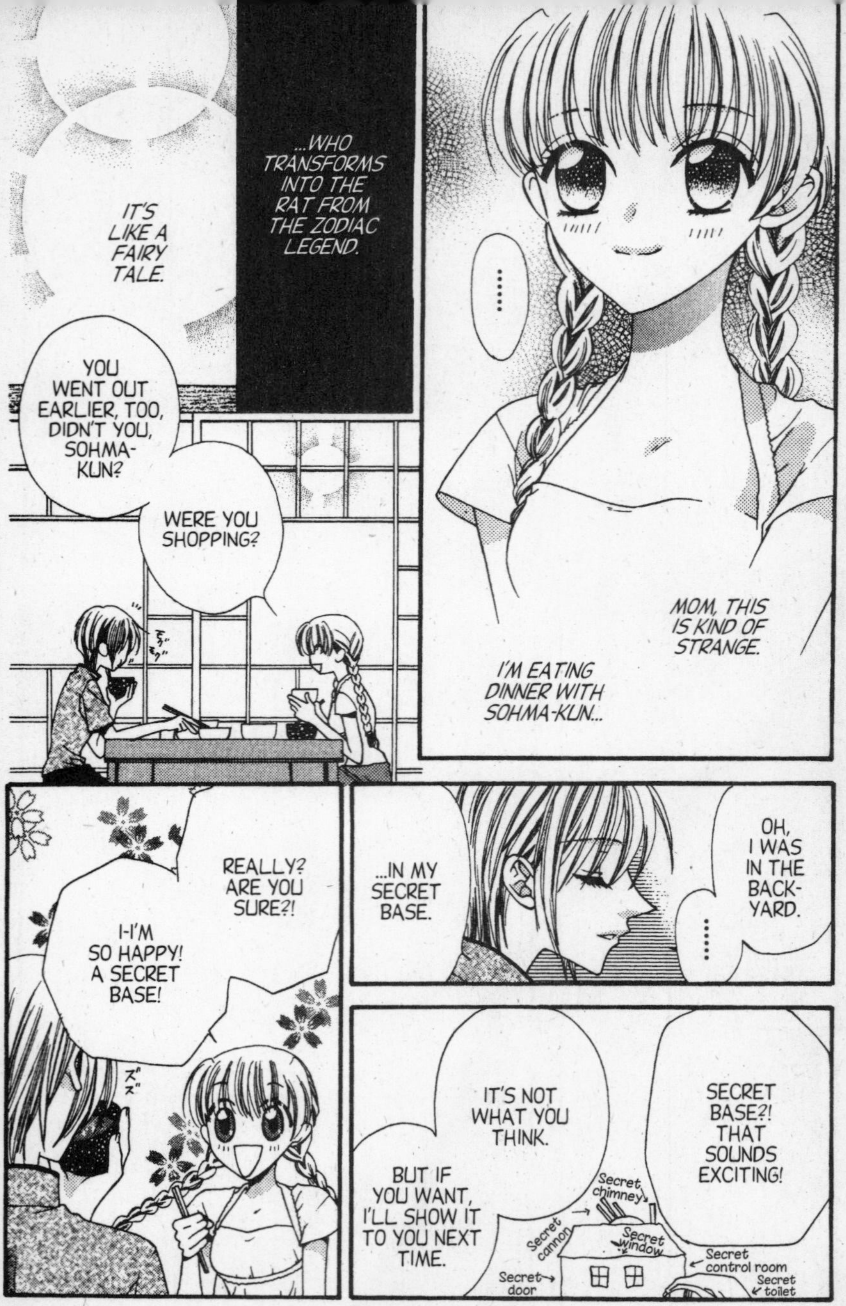
……
MOM, THIS IS KIND OF STRANGE.
I'M EATING DINNER WITH SOHMA-KUN...
...WHO TRANSFORMS INTO THE RAT FROM THE ZODIAC LEGEND.
IT'S LIKE A FAIRY TALE.
YOU WENT OUT EARLIER, TOO, DIDN'T YOU, SOHMA-KUN?
WERE YOU SHOPPING?
OH, I WAS IN THE BACK-YARD.
……
...IN MY SECRET BASE.
SECRET BASE?! THAT SOUNDS EXCITING!
Secret chimney
Secret cannon
Secret window
Secret control room
Secret door
Secret toilet
IT'S NOT WHAT YOU THINK.
BUT IF YOU WANT, I'LL SHOW IT TO YOU NEXT TIME.
REALLY? ARE YOU SURE?!
I-I'M SO HAPPY! A SECRET BASE!

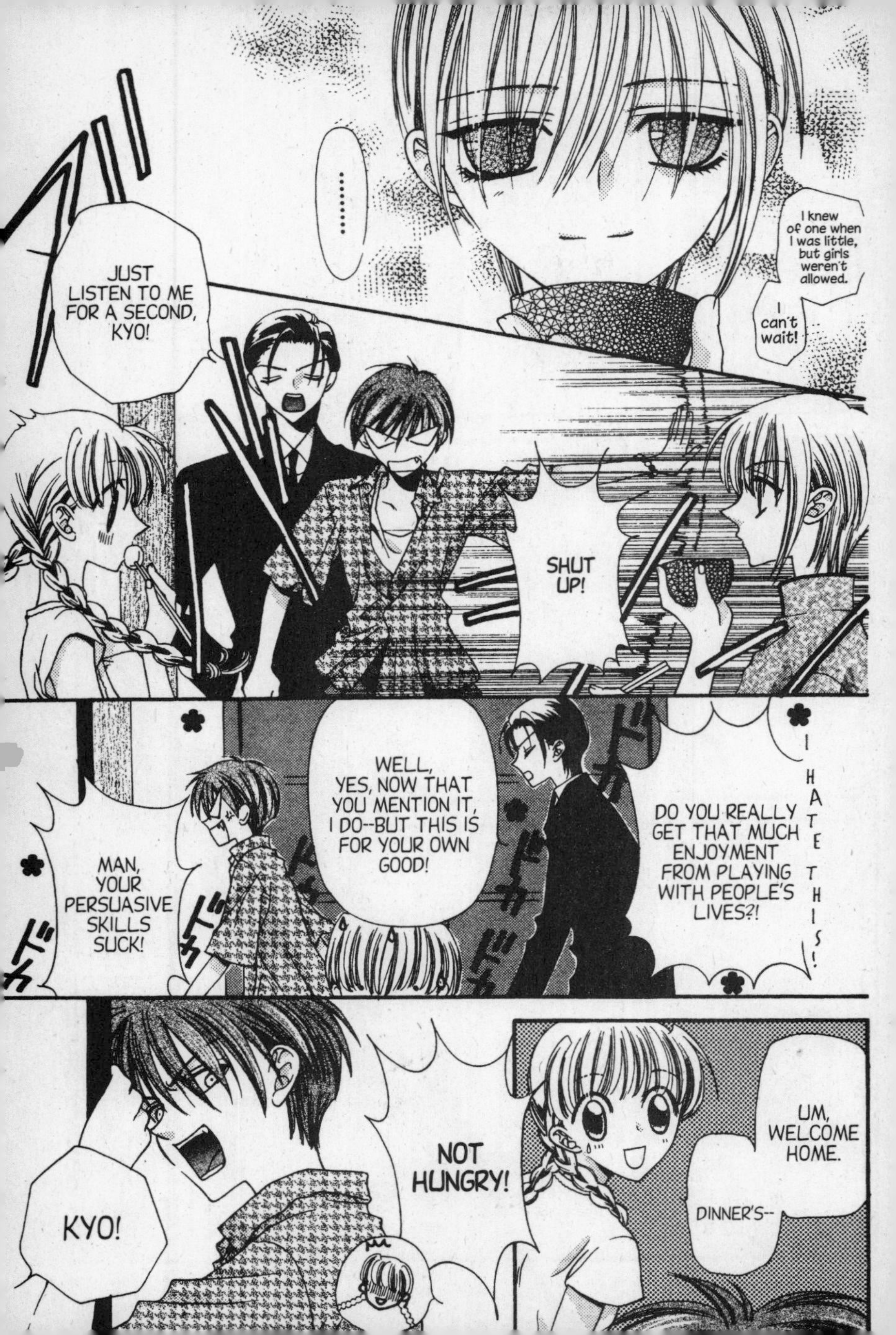
I knew of one when I was little, but girls weren't allowed.
I can't wait!
......
SHUT UP!
JUST LISTEN TO ME FOR A SECOND, KYO!
I HATE THIS!
DO YOU REALLY GET THAT MUCH ENJOYMENT FROM PLAYING WITH PEOPLE'S LIVES?!
WELL, YES, NOW THAT YOU MENTION IT, I DO--BUT THIS IS FOR YOUR OWN GOOD!
MAN, YOUR PERSUASIVE SKILLS SUCK!
UM, WELCOME HOME.
DINNER'S--
NOT HUNGRY!
KYO!

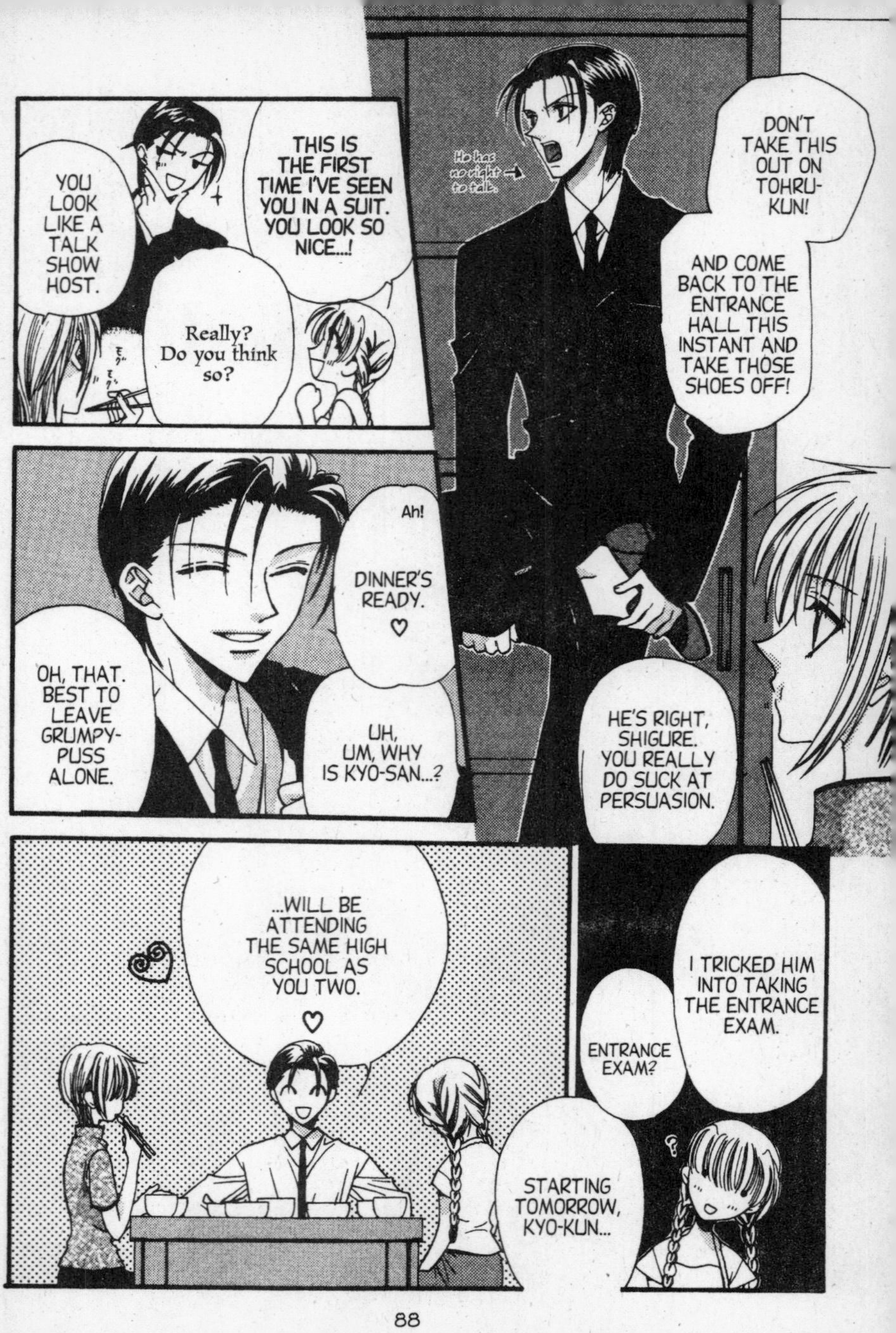

DON'T TAKE THIS OUT ON TOHRU-KUN!
He has no right to talk.
AND COME BACK TO THE ENTRANCE HALL THIS INSTANT AND TAKE THOSE SHOES OFF!
HE'S RIGHT, SHIGURE. YOU REALLY DO SUCK AT PERSUASION.
THIS IS THE FIRST TIME I'VE SEEN YOU IN A SUIT. YOU LOOK SO NICE...!
YOU LOOK LIKE A TALK SHOW HOST.
Really? Do you think so?
Ah!
DINNER'S READY. ♡
UH, UM, WHY IS KYO-SAN...?
OH, THAT. BEST TO LEAVE GRUMPY-PUSS ALONE.
I TRICKED HIM INTO TAKING THE ENTRANCE EXAM.
ENTRANCE EXAM?
STARTING TOMORROW, KYO-KUN...
...WILL BE ATTENDING THE SAME HIGH SCHOOL AS YOU TWO. ♡

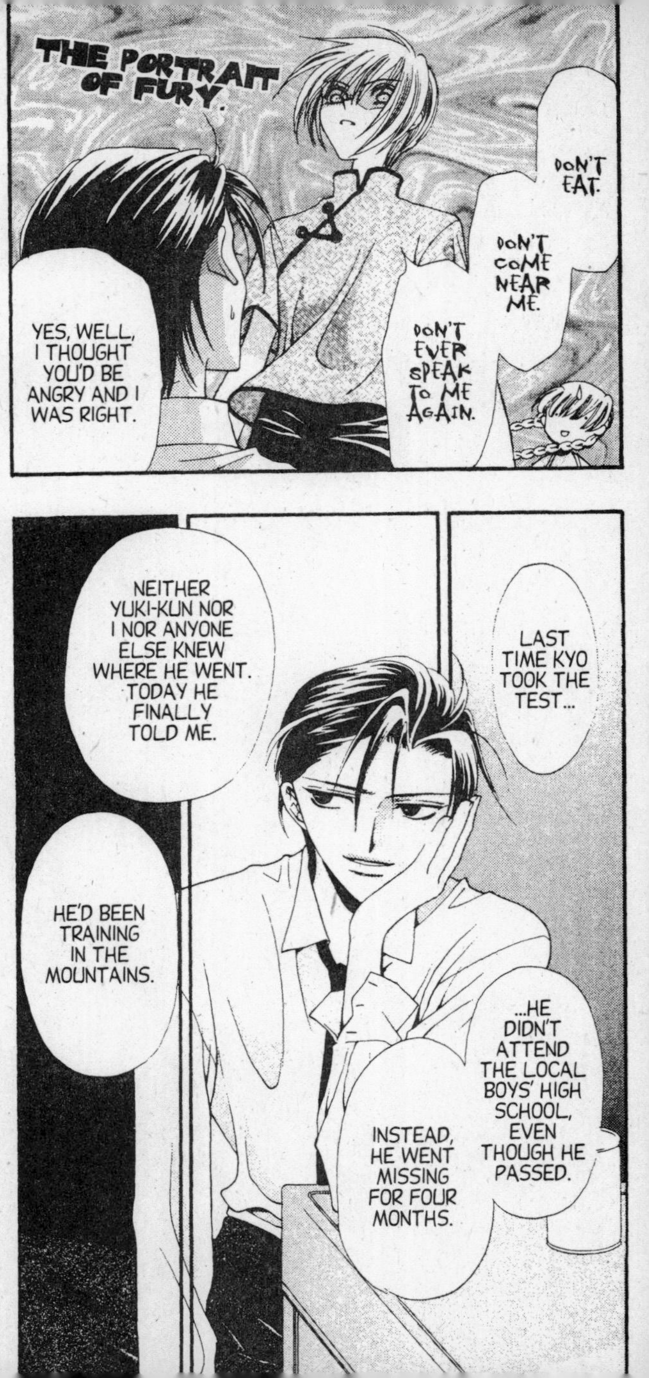
THE PORTRAIT OF FURY.
DON'T EAT.
DON'T COME NEAR ME.
DON'T EVER SPEAK TO ME AGAIN.
YES, WELL, I THOUGHT YOU'D BE ANGRY AND I WAS RIGHT.
LAST TIME KYO TOOK THE TEST...
...HE DIDN'T ATTEND THE LOCAL BOYS' HIGH SCHOOL, EVEN THOUGH HE PASSED.
INSTEAD, HE WENT MISSING FOR FOUR MONTHS.
NEITHER YUKI-KUN NOR I NOR ANYONE ELSE KNEW WHERE HE WENT. TODAY HE FINALLY TOLD ME.
HE'D BEEN TRAINING IN THE MOUNTAINS.

Number 4:

I finished "Romance of the Three Kingdoms," "Black Matrix" and "Pretty League." My characters were so strong that I won all the battles. I'm happy, but a little dramatic tension would've been nice, too (ha ha). I'll finish "Tokyo Friend" soon, too. It's a shame that all the main characters are guys, it would've been nice to play a girl! The one I'm waiting for now is "Teigaku Graph." (K-chan is looking forward to it more than I am.) I'm looking forward to "Knight R." And "Hey You, Pikachu!" Where will I ever find the time? I'll just sleep less! Then faint.

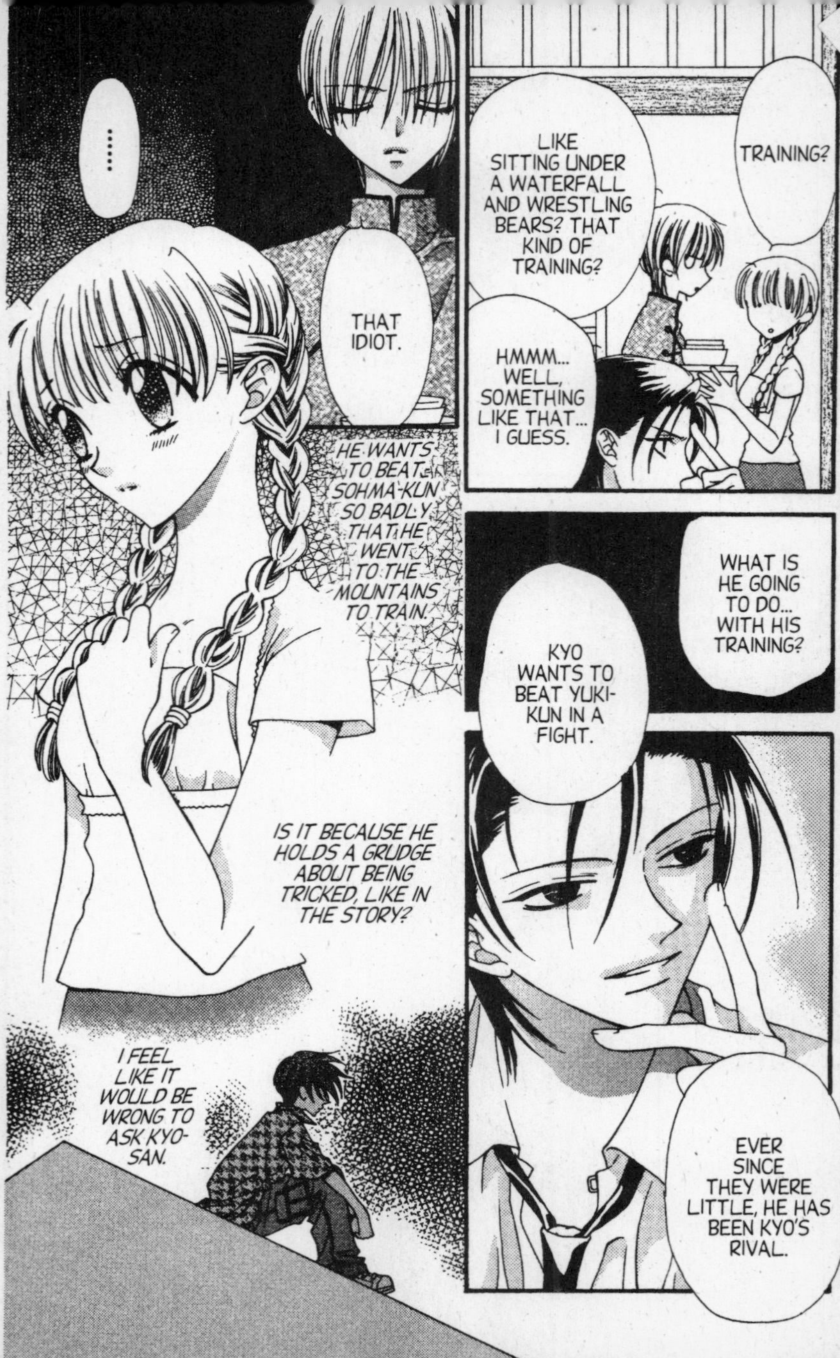
TRAINING?
LIKE SITTING UNDER A WATERFALL AND WRESTLING BEARS? THAT KIND OF TRAINING?
HMMM... WELL, SOMETHING LIKE THAT... I GUESS.
......
THAT IDIOT.
HE WANTS TO BEAT SOHMA-KUN SO BADLY THAT HE WENT TO THE MOUNTAINS TO TRAIN.
WHAT IS HE GOING TO DO... WITH HIS TRAINING?
KYO WANTS TO BEAT YUKI-KUN IN A FIGHT.
EVER SINCE THEY WERE LITTLE, HE HAS BEEN KYO'S RIVAL.
IS IT BECAUSE HE HOLDS A GRUDGE ABOUT BEING TRICKED, LIKE IN THE STORY?
I FEEL LIKE IT WOULD BE WRONG TO ASK KYO-SAN.

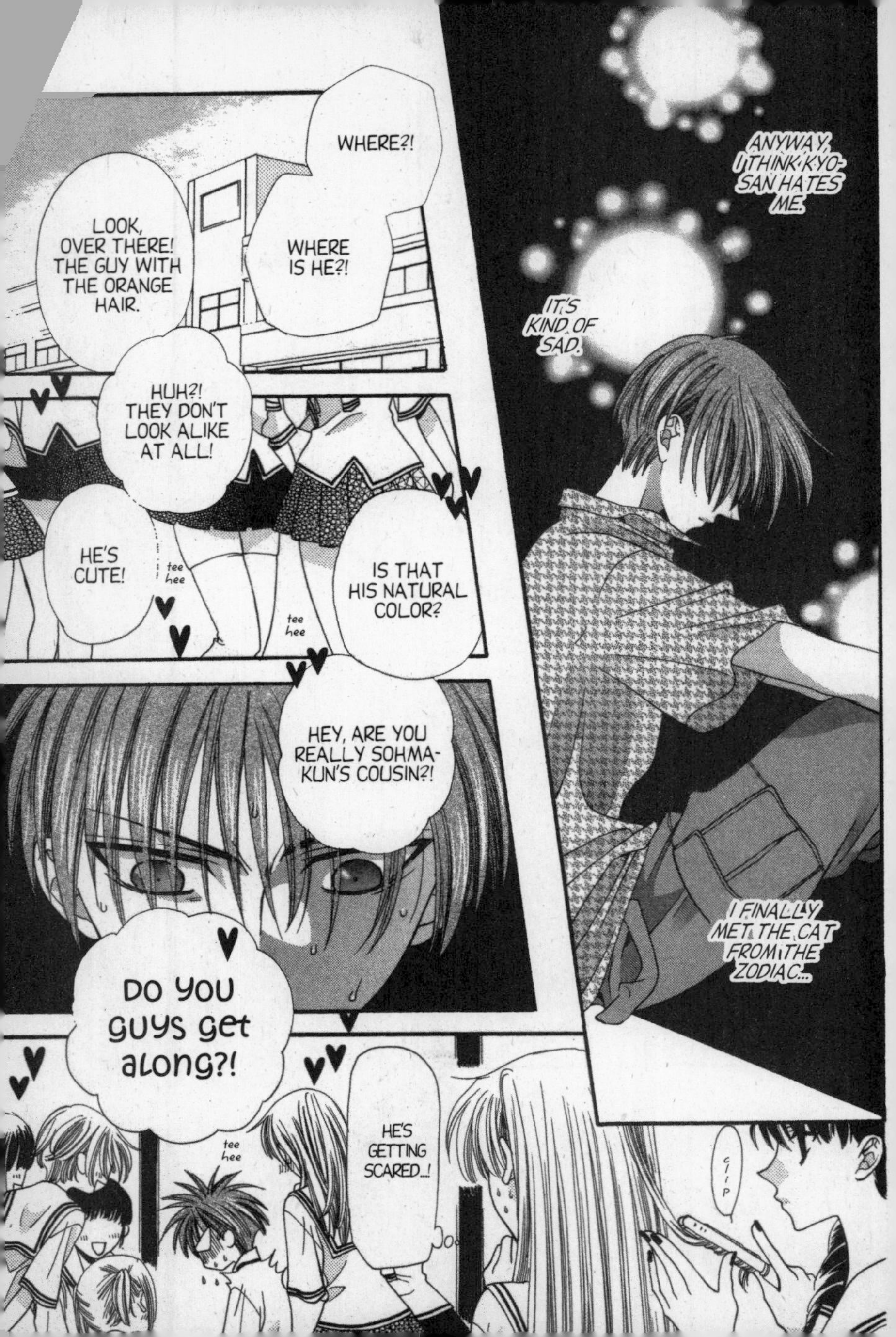
ANYWAY, I THINK KYO-SAN HATES ME.
IT'S KIND OF SAD.
I FINALLY MET THE CAT FROM THE ZODIAC...
WHERE?!
LOOK, OVER THERE! THE GUY WITH THE ORANGE HAIR.
WHERE IS HE?!
HUH?! THEY DON'T LOOK ALIKE AT ALL!
IS THAT HIS NATURAL COLOR?
tee hee
HE'S CUTE!
tee hee
HEY, ARE YOU REALLY SOHMA-KUN'S COUSIN?!
DO YOU GUYS GET ALONG?!
clip
HE'S GETTING SCARED...!
tee hee

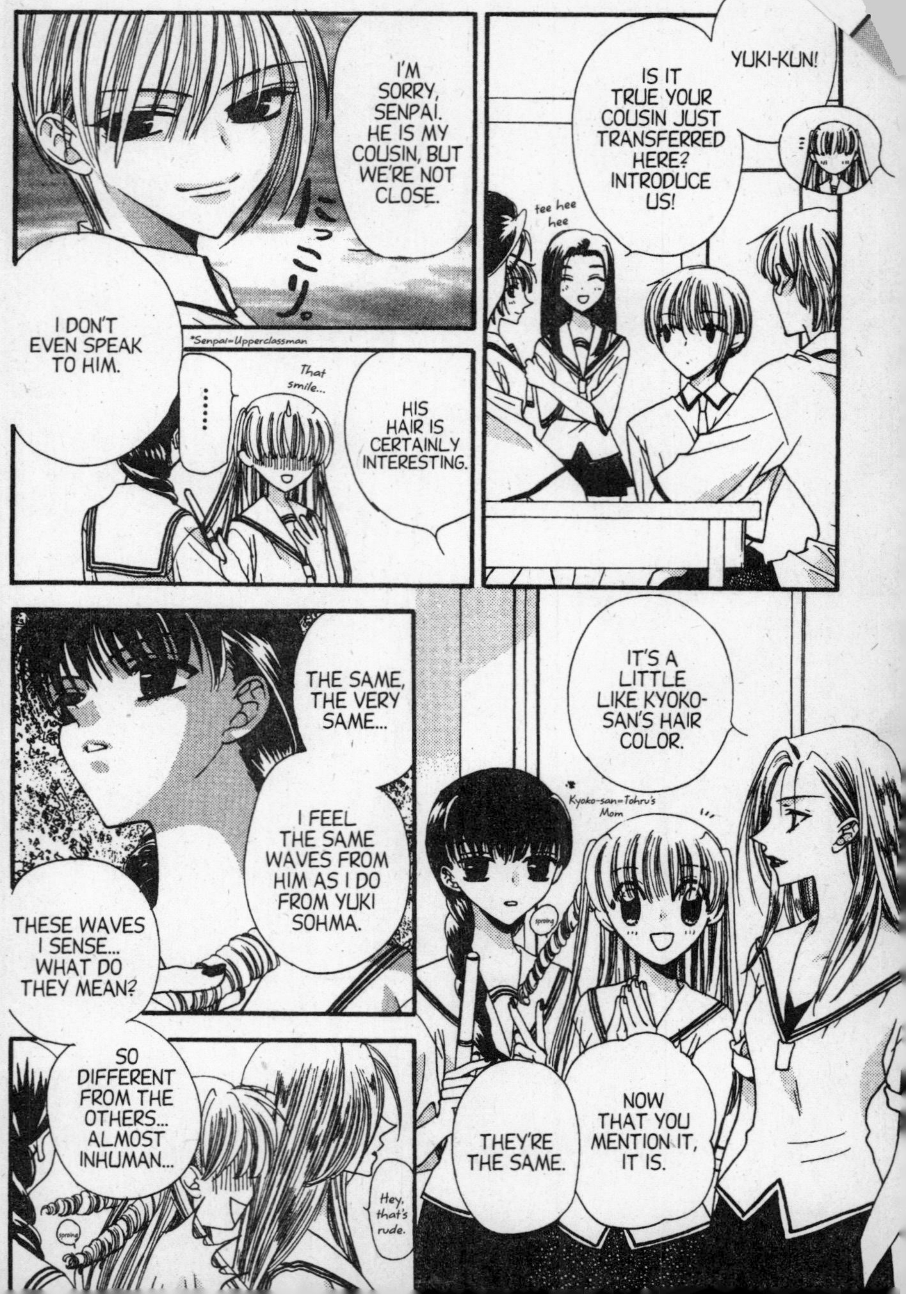
YUKI-KUN!
tee hee hee
IS IT TRUE YOUR COUSIN JUST TRANSFERRED HERE? INTRODUCE US!
I'M SORRY, SENPAI. HE IS MY COUSIN, BUT WE'RE NOT CLOSE.
にっこり
*Senpai=Upperclassman
I DON'T EVEN SPEAK TO HIM.
HIS HAIR IS CERTAINLY INTERESTING.
That smile...
......
IT'S A LITTLE LIKE KYOKO-SAN'S HAIR COLOR.
*Kyoko-san=Tohru's Mom
spring
NOW THAT YOU MENTION IT, IT IS.
THEY'RE THE SAME.
THE SAME, THE VERY SAME...
I FEEL THE SAME WAVES FROM HIM AS I DO FROM YUKI SOHMA.
THESE WAVES I SENSE... WHAT DO THEY MEAN?
SO DIFFERENT FROM THE OTHERS... ALMOST INHUMAN...
Hey, that's rude.
spring

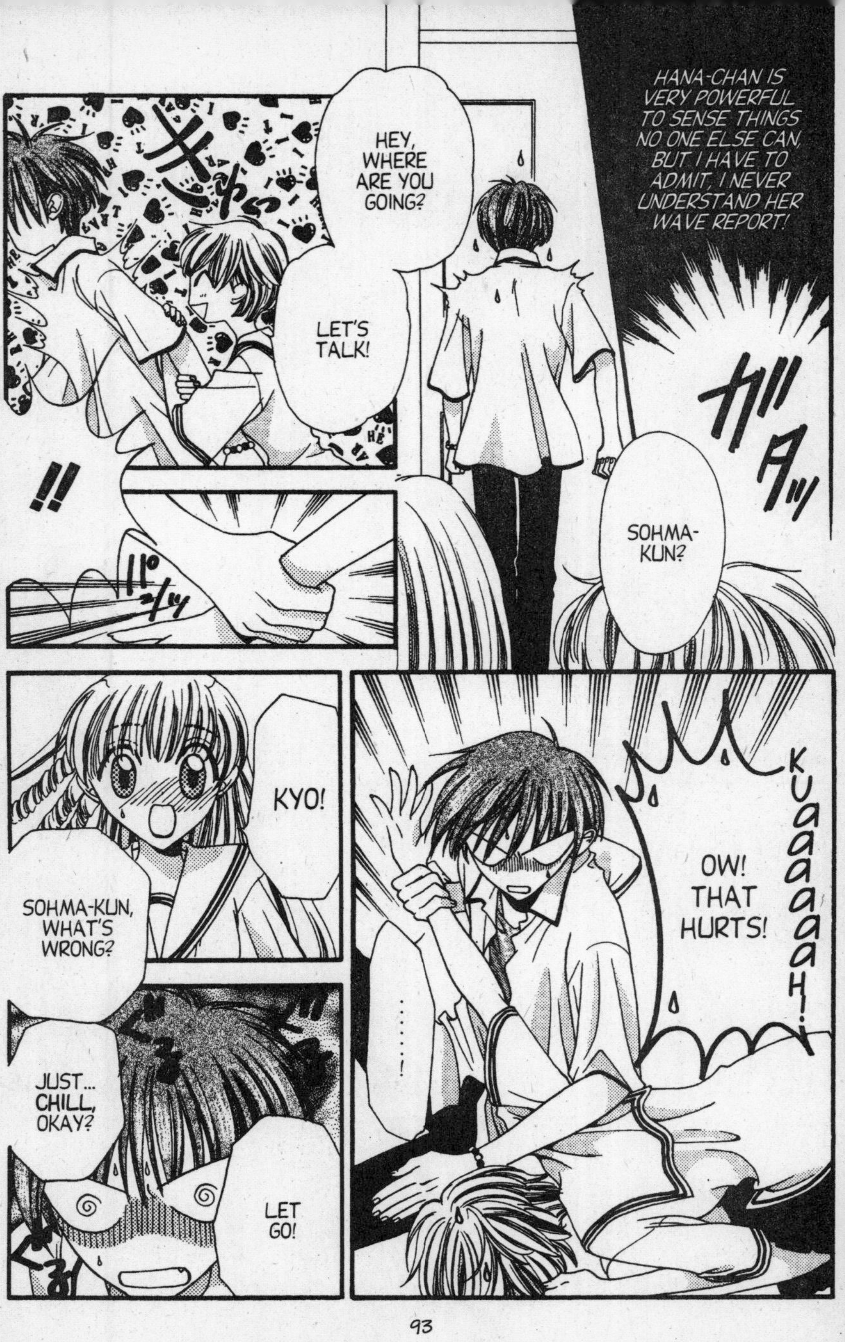

HANA-CHAN IS VERY POWERFUL TO SENSE THINGS NO ONE ELSE CAN, BUT I HAVE TO ADMIT, I NEVER UNDERSTAND HER WAVE REPORT!
HEY, WHERE ARE YOU GOING?
LET'S TALK!
SOHMA-KUN?
!!
KUAAAAAAH!!
OW! THAT HURTS!
......!
KYO!
SOHMA-KUN, WHAT'S WRONG?
JUST... CHILL, OKAY?
LET GO!

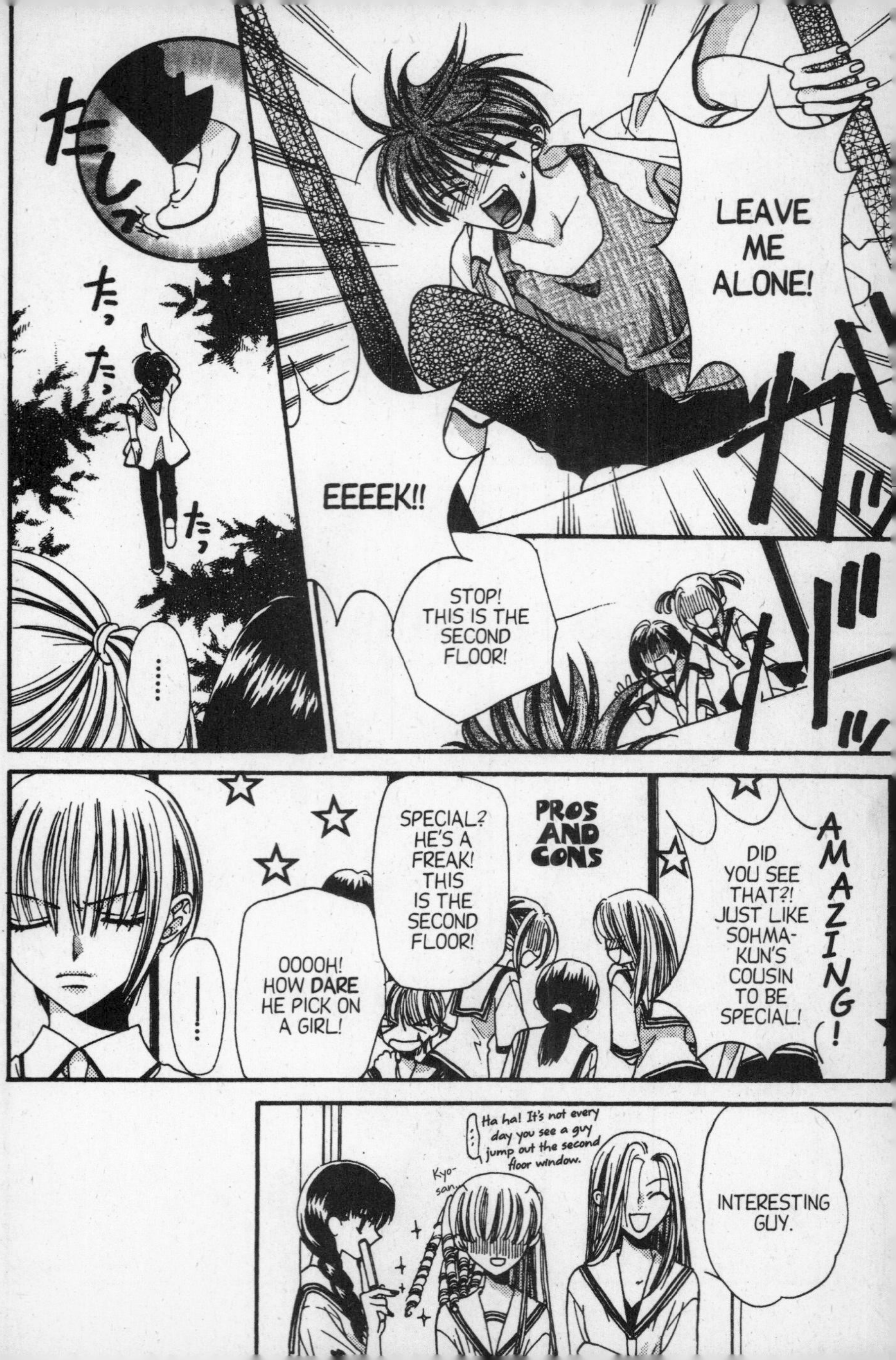
LEAVE ME ALONE!
EEEEK!!
STOP! THIS IS THE SECOND FLOOR!
たしっ
たっ
たっ
たっ
......
AMAZING!
DID YOU SEE THAT?! JUST LIKE SOHMA-KUN'S COUSIN TO BE SPECIAL!
PROS AND CONS
SPECIAL? HE'S A FREAK! THIS IS THE SECOND FLOOR!
OOOOH! HOW DARE HE PICK ON A GIRL!
...!
INTERESTING GUY.
Ha ha! It's not every day you see a guy jump out the second floor window.
Kyo-san...
...

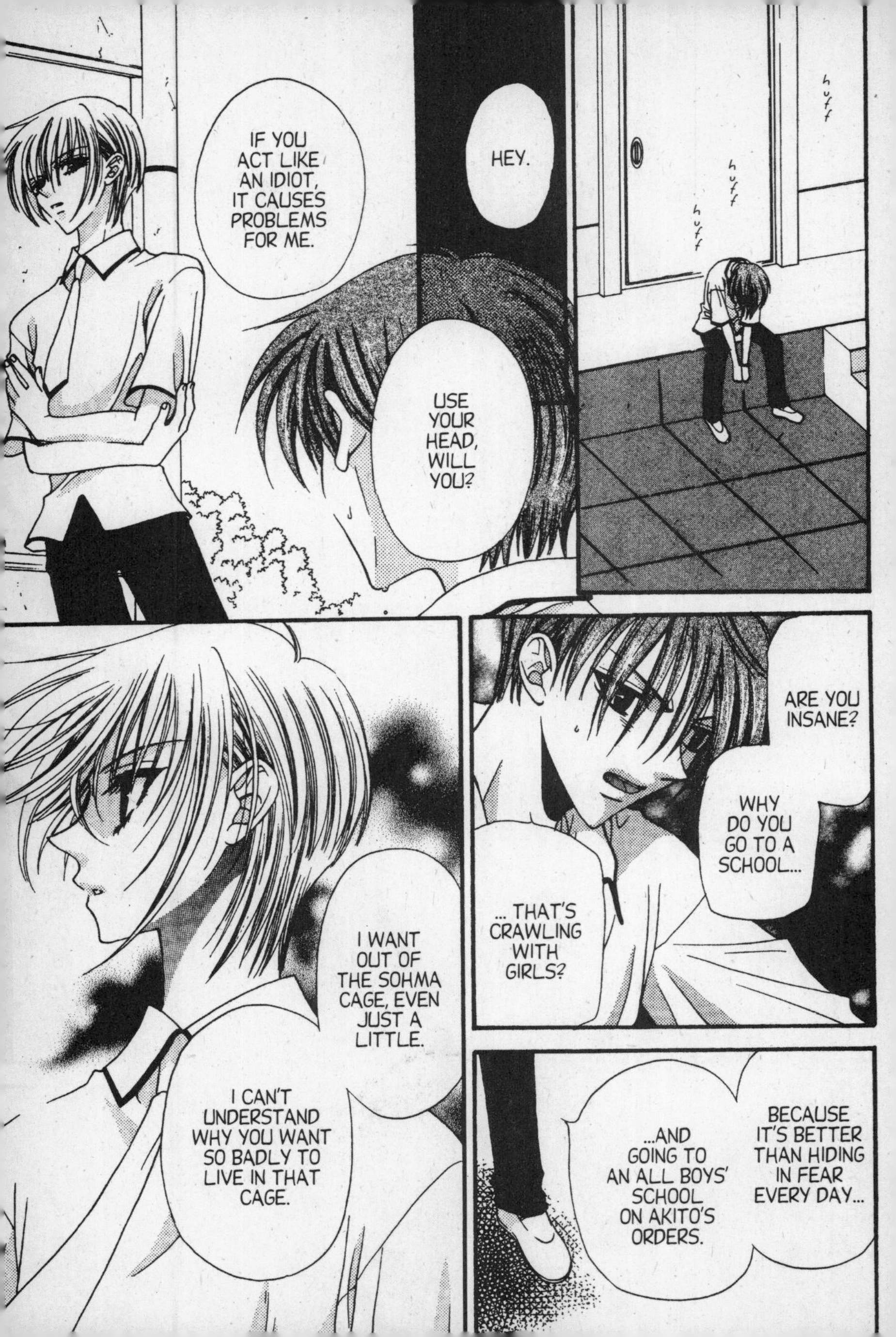
huff
huff
huff
HEY.
USE YOUR HEAD, WILL YOU?
IF YOU ACT LIKE AN IDIOT, IT CAUSES PROBLEMS FOR ME.
ARE YOU INSANE?
WHY DO YOU GO TO A SCHOOL...
... THAT'S CRAWLING WITH GIRLS?
BECAUSE IT'S BETTER THAN HIDING IN FEAR EVERY DAY...
...AND GOING TO AN ALL BOYS' SCHOOL ON AKITO'S ORDERS.
I WANT OUT OF THE SOHMA CAGE, EVEN JUST A LITTLE.
I CAN'T UNDERSTAND WHY YOU WANT SO BADLY TO LIVE IN THAT CAGE.

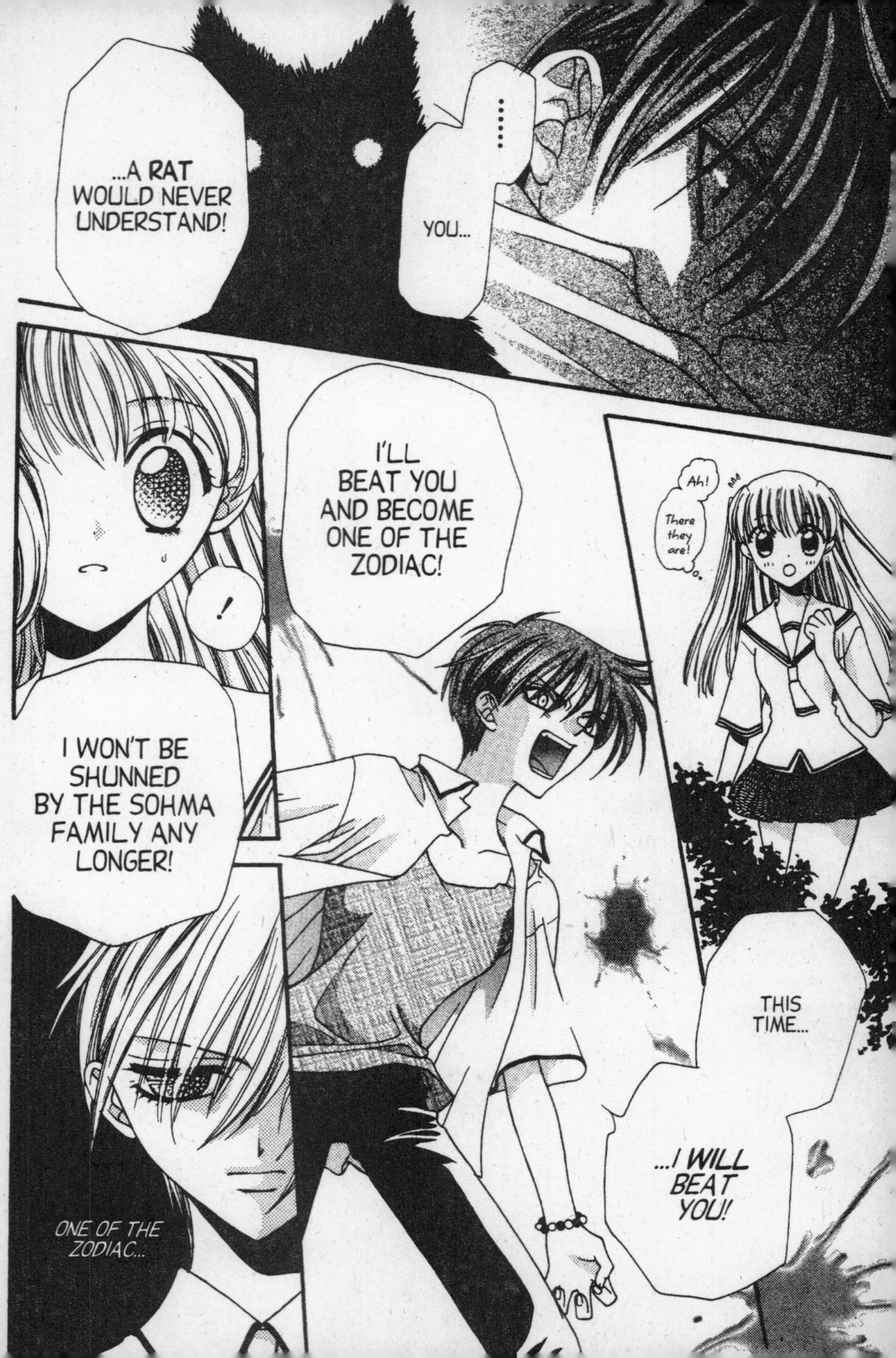
......
YOU...
...A RAT WOULD NEVER UNDERSTAND!
Ah!
There they are!
I'LL BEAT YOU AND BECOME ONE OF THE ZODIAC!
!
I WON'T BE SHUNNED BY THE SOHMA FAMILY ANY LONGER!
THIS TIME...
...I WILL BEAT YOU!
ONE OF THE ZODIAC...

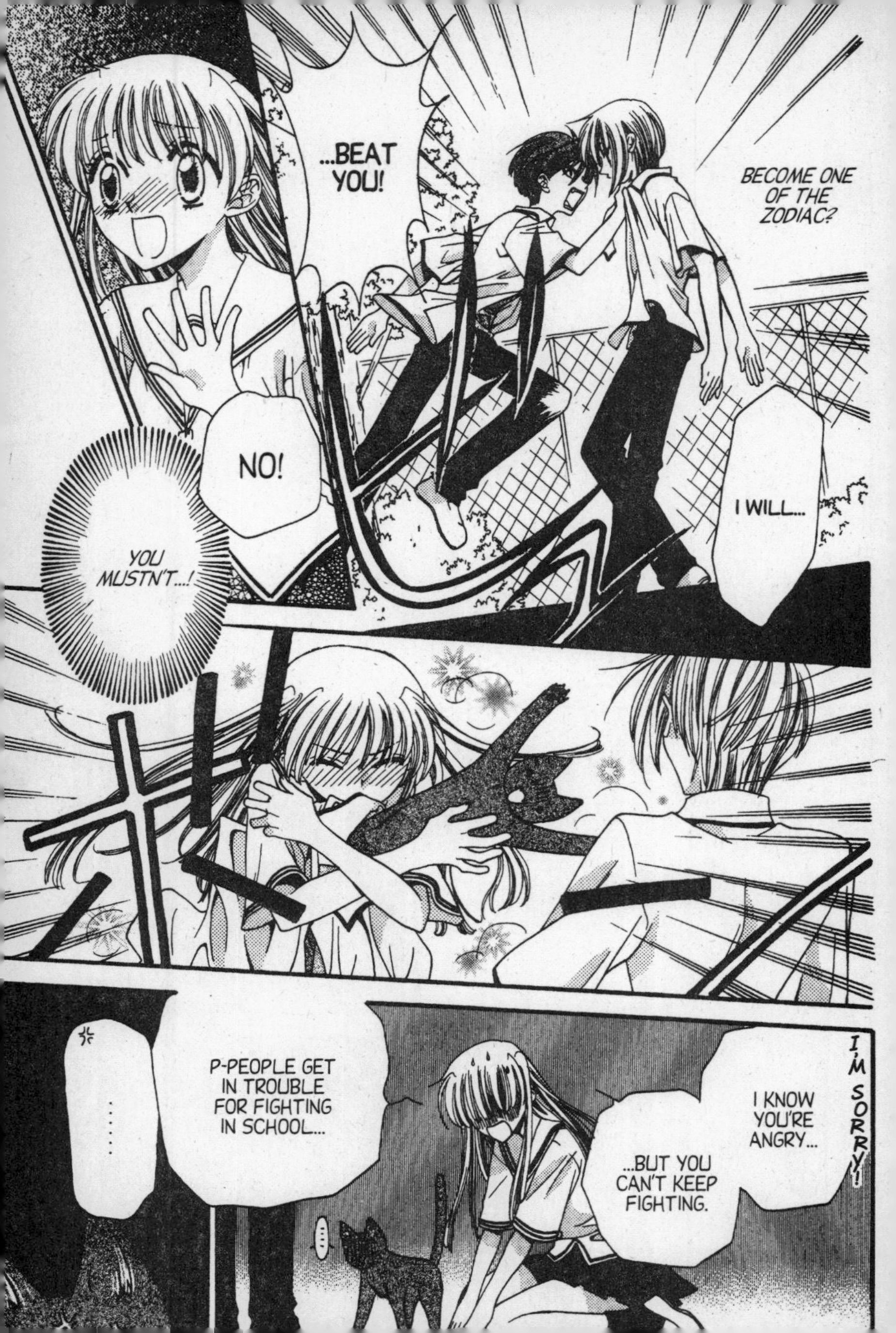
BECOME ONE OF THE ZODIAC?
I WILL...
...BEAT YOU!
NO!
YOU MUSTN'T...!
I'M SORRY!
I KNOW YOU'RE ANGRY...
...BUT YOU CAN'T KEEP FIGHTING.
P-PEOPLE GET IN TROUBLE FOR FIGHTING IN SCHOOL...
......
....

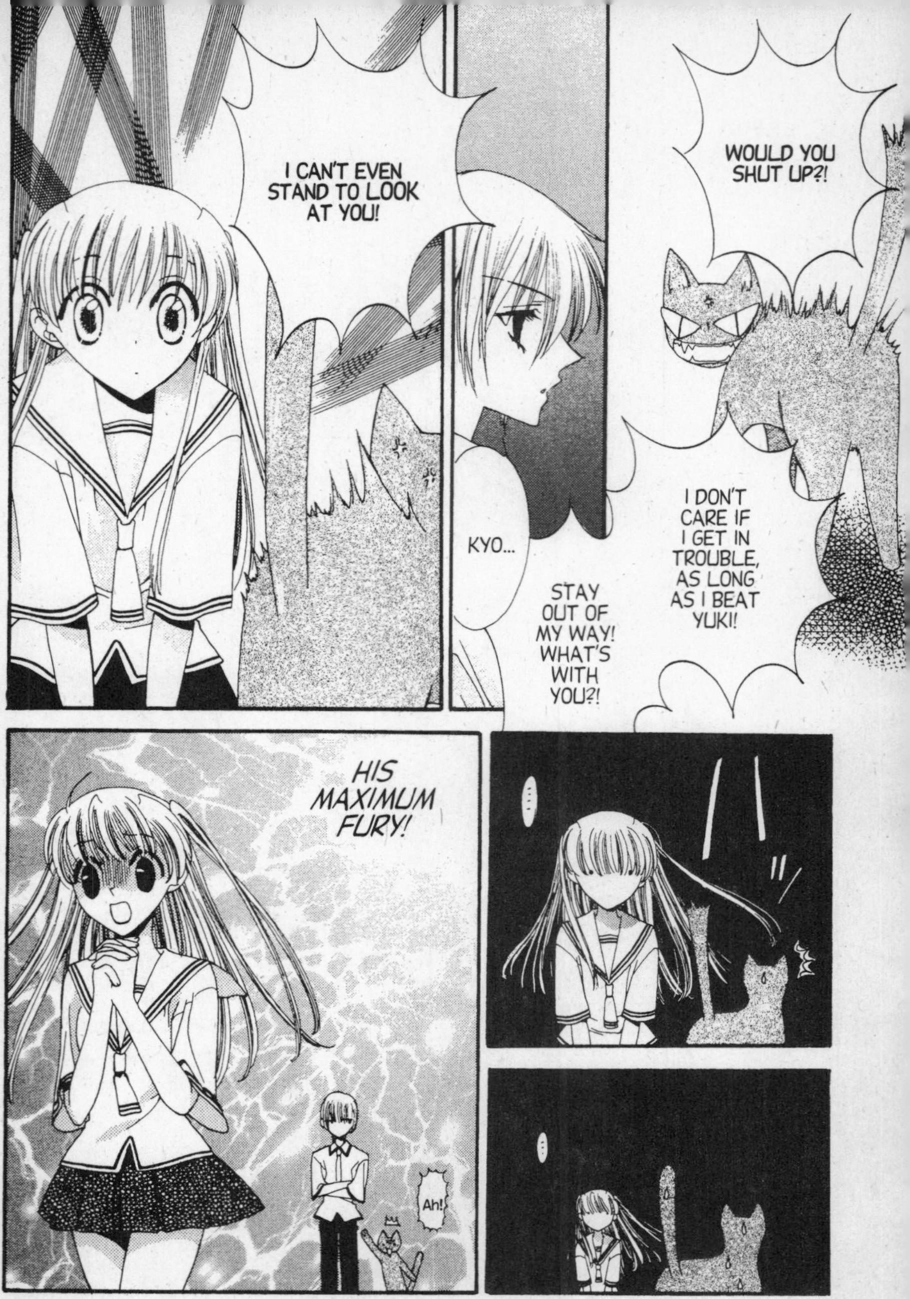
WOULD YOU SHUT UP?!
I DON'T CARE IF I GET IN TROUBLE, AS LONG AS I BEAT YUKI!
STAY OUT OF MY WAY! WHAT'S WITH YOU?!
KYO...
I CAN'T EVEN STAND TO LOOK AT YOU!
...
...
HIS MAXIMUM FURY!
Ah!

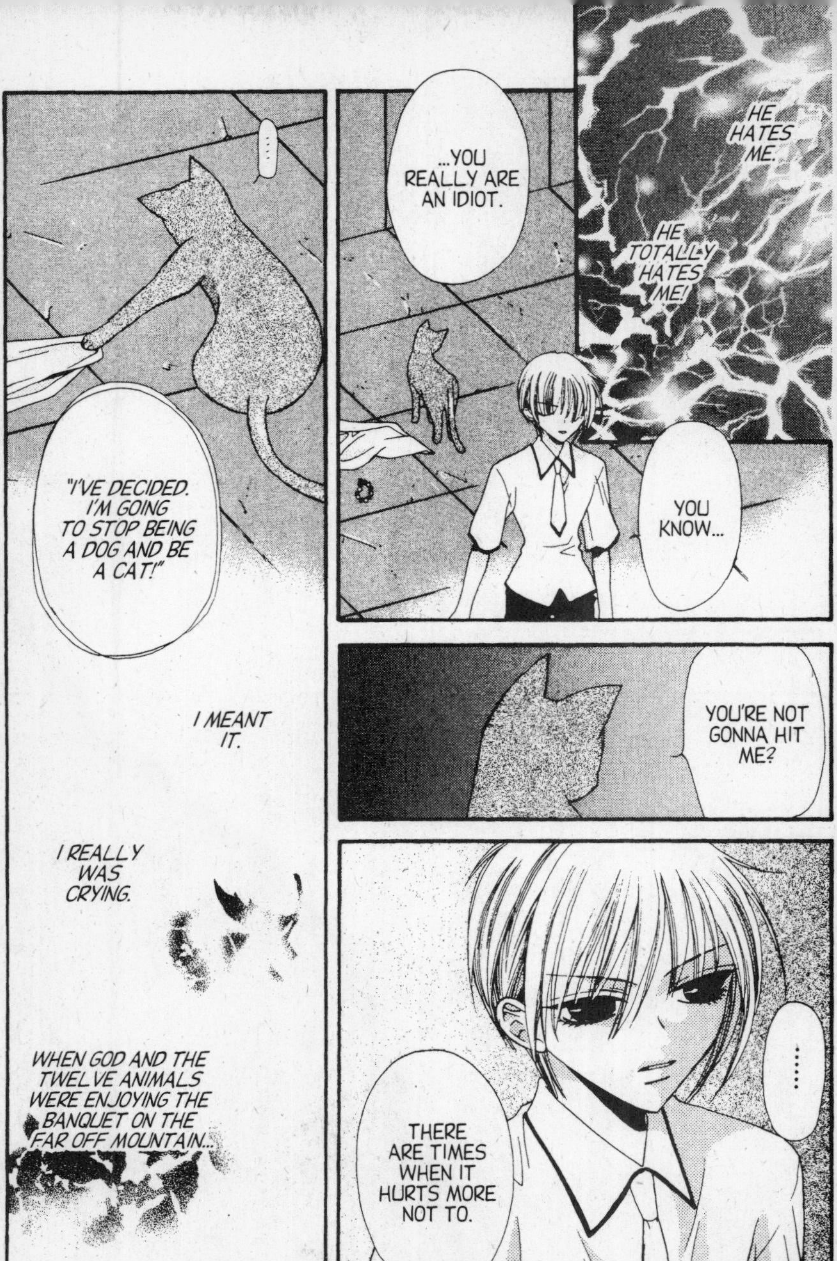
HE HATES ME.
HE TOTALLY HATES ME!
...YOU REALLY ARE AN IDIOT.
YOU KNOW...
YOU'RE NOT GONNA HIT ME?
......
THERE ARE TIMES WHEN IT HURTS MORE NOT TO.
......
"I'VE DECIDED. I'M GOING TO STOP BEING A DOG AND BE A CAT!"
I MEANT IT.
I REALLY WAS CRYING.
WHEN GOD AND THE TWELVE ANIMALS WERE ENJOYING THE BANQUET ON THE FAR OFF MOUNTAIN...

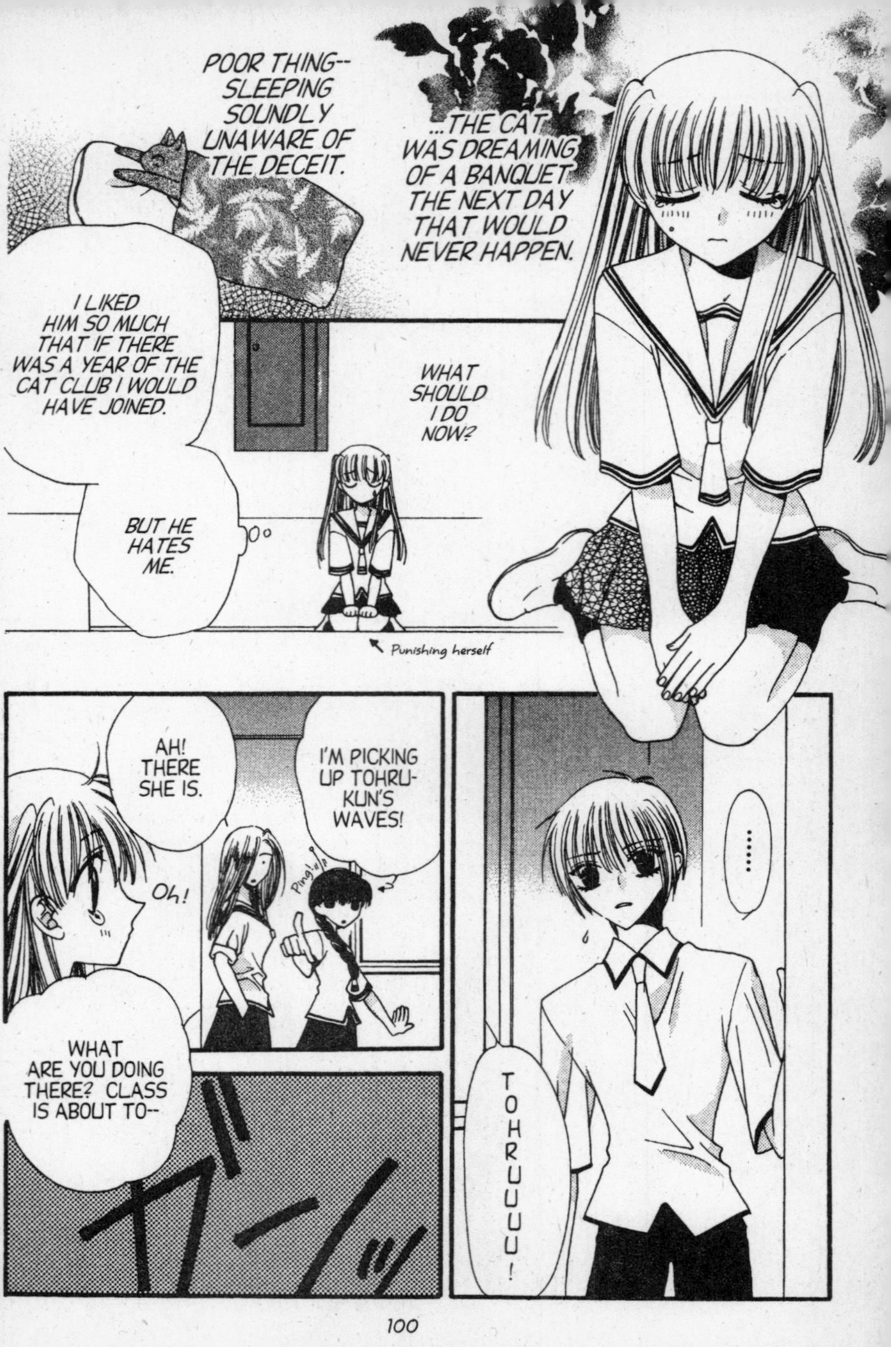
POOR THING-- SLEEPING SOUNDLY UNAWARE OF THE DECEIT.
...THE CAT WAS DREAMING OF A BANQUET THE NEXT DAY THAT WOULD NEVER HAPPEN.
I LIKED HIM SO MUCH THAT IF THERE WAS A YEAR OF THE CAT CLUB I WOULD HAVE JOINED.
BUT HE HATES ME.
WHAT SHOULD I DO NOW?
Punishing herself
......
TOHRUUUU!
I'M PICKING UP TOHRU-KUN'S WAVES!
AH! THERE SHE IS.
Ping!
Oh!
WHAT ARE YOU DOING THERE? CLASS IS ABOUT TO--

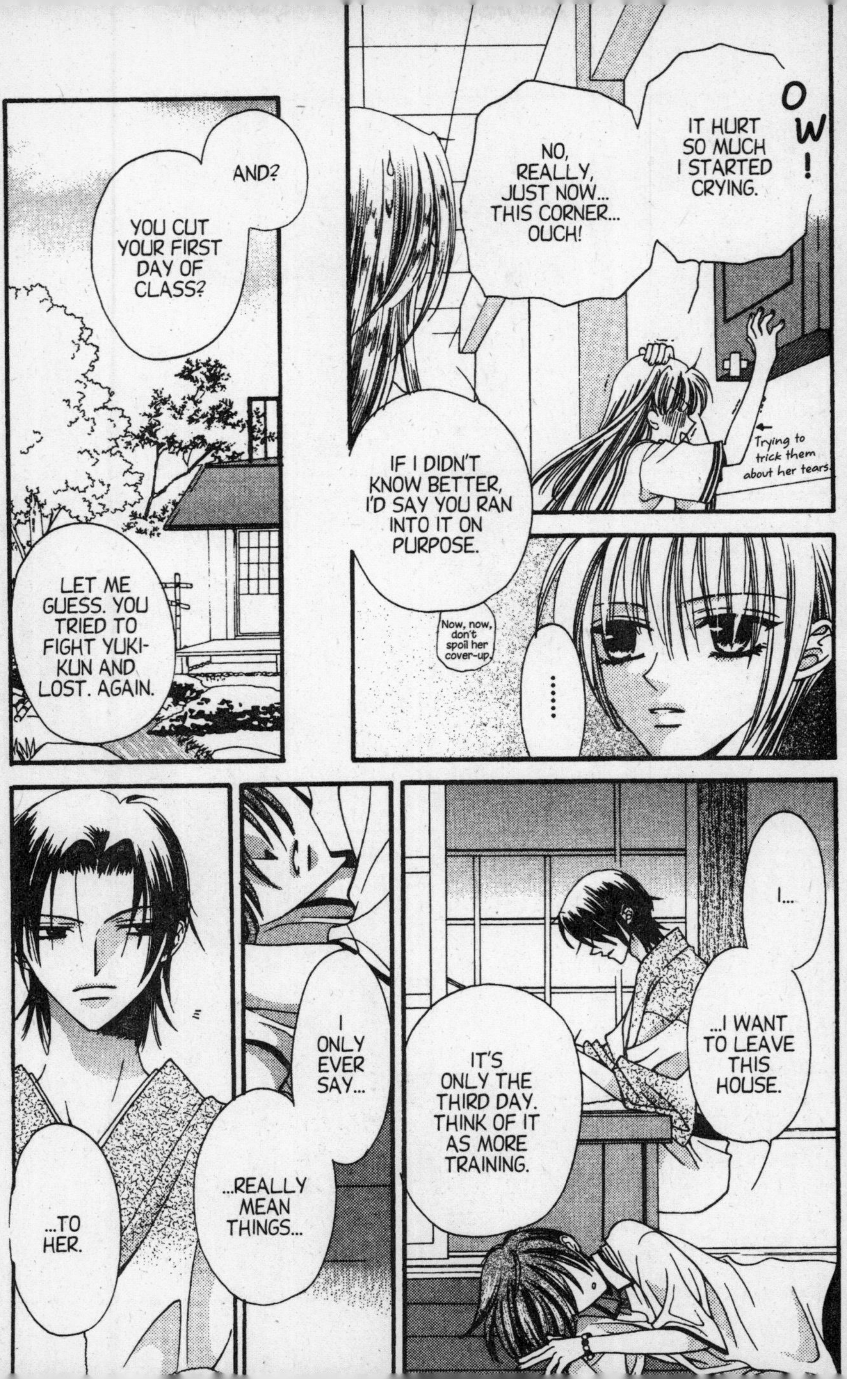
OW!
IT HURT SO MUCH I STARTED CRYING.
NO, REALLY, JUST NOW... THIS CORNER... OUCH!
Trying to trick them about her tears.
IF I DIDN'T KNOW BETTER, I'D SAY YOU RAN INTO IT ON PURPOSE.
Now, now, don't spoil her cover-up.
......
AND?
YOU CUT YOUR FIRST DAY OF CLASS?
LET ME GUESS. YOU TRIED TO FIGHT YUKI-KUN AND LOST. AGAIN.
I...
...I WANT TO LEAVE THIS HOUSE.
IT'S ONLY THE THIRD DAY. THINK OF IT AS MORE TRAINING.
I ONLY EVER SAY...
...REALLY MEAN THINGS...
...TO HER.

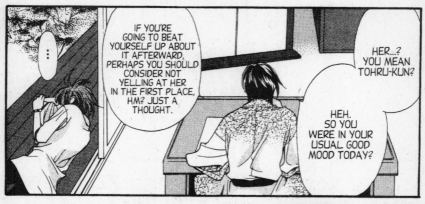

HER...? YOU MEAN TOHRU-KUN?
HEH. SO YOU WERE IN YOUR USUAL GOOD MOOD TODAY?
IF YOU'RE GOING TO BEAT YOURSELF UP ABOUT IT AFTERWARD, PERHAPS YOU SHOULD CONSIDER NOT YELLING AT HER IN THE FIRST PLACE, HM? JUST A THOUGHT.
...
I CAN'T HELP IT.
I'M...
...NOT MADE FOR INTERACTING WITH PEOPLE.
PEOPLE AREN'T BORN SOCIAL. SURE IT COMES EASIER TO SOME PEOPLE...
...BUT MOST PEOPLE, LIKE YOU, NEED TO WORK AT IT. SOME MORE THAN OTHERS. YOU'RE JUST INEXPERIENCED.
FOR EXAMPLE, AS A MARTIAL ARTIST, YOU HAVE THE STRENGTH TO BREAK THE TABLE WITH YOUR FIST.
BUT YOU ALSO HAVE THE *SELF-CONTROL* TO STOP YOUR FIST RIGHT BEFORE IT HITS THE TABLE.
YOU WEREN'T BORN WITH THAT CONTROL, WERE YOU? YOU HAD TO REFINE IT.
THAT'S THE RESULT OF FIGHTING BEARS IN THE MOUNTAINS.
I DIDN'T FIGHT BEARS!

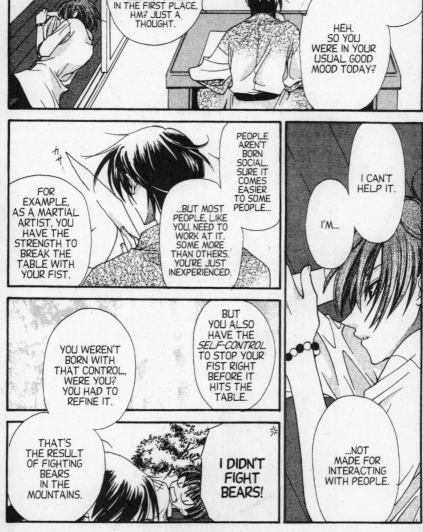

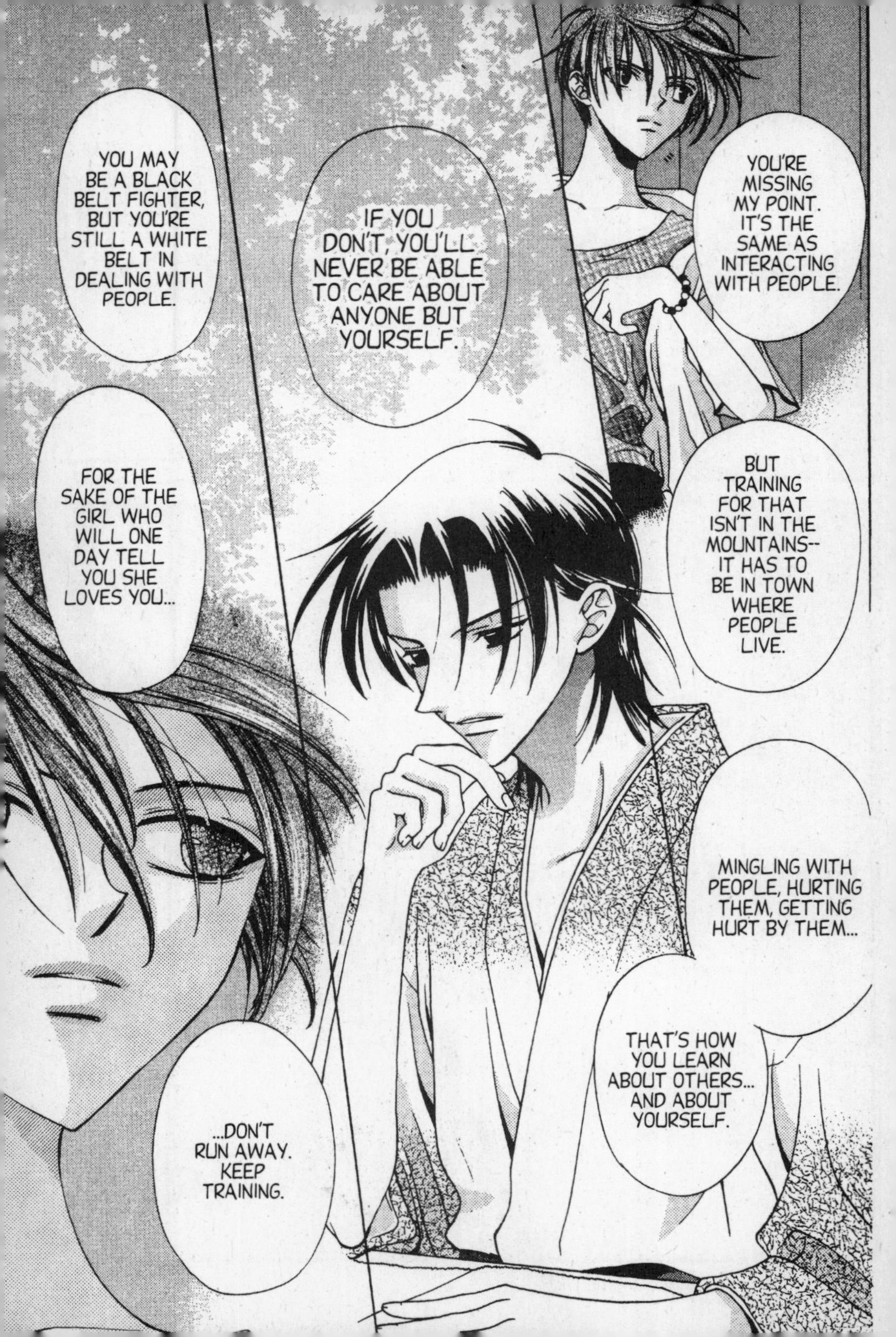

YOU'RE MISSING MY POINT. IT'S THE SAME AS INTERACTING WITH PEOPLE.
BUT TRAINING FOR THAT ISN'T IN THE MOUNTAINS-- IT HAS TO BE IN TOWN WHERE PEOPLE LIVE.
MINGLING WITH PEOPLE, HURTING THEM, GETTING HURT BY THEM...
THAT'S HOW YOU LEARN ABOUT OTHERS... AND ABOUT YOURSELF.
YOU MAY BE A BLACK BELT FIGHTER, BUT YOU'RE STILL A WHITE BELT IN DEALING WITH PEOPLE.
FOR THE SAKE OF THE GIRL WHO WILL ONE DAY TELL YOU SHE LOVES YOU...
...DON'T RUN AWAY. KEEP TRAINING.
IF YOU DON'T, YOU'LL NEVER BE ABLE TO CARE ABOUT ANYONE BUT YOURSELF.

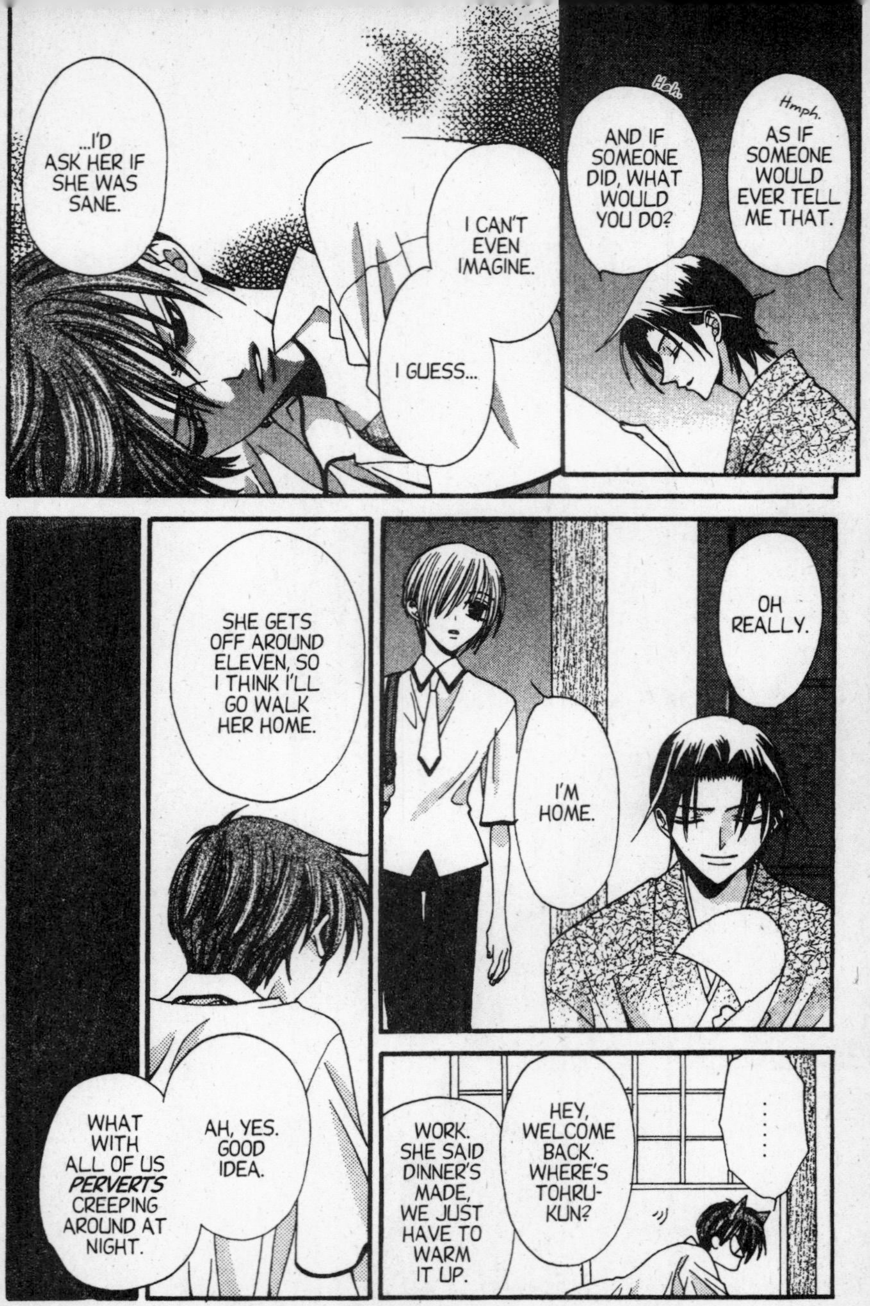
Hmph.
AS IF SOMEONE WOULD EVER TELL ME THAT.
Heh.
AND IF SOMEONE DID, WHAT WOULD YOU DO?
I CAN'T EVEN IMAGINE.
I GUESS...
...I'D ASK HER IF SHE WAS SANE.
OH REALLY.
I'M HOME.
......
HEY, WELCOME BACK. WHERE'S TOHRU-KUN?
WORK. SHE SAID DINNER'S MADE, WE JUST HAVE TO WARM IT UP.
SHE GETS OFF AROUND ELEVEN, SO I THINK I'LL GO WALK HER HOME.
AH, YES. GOOD IDEA.
WHAT WITH ALL OF US *PERVERTS* CREEPING AROUND AT NIGHT.

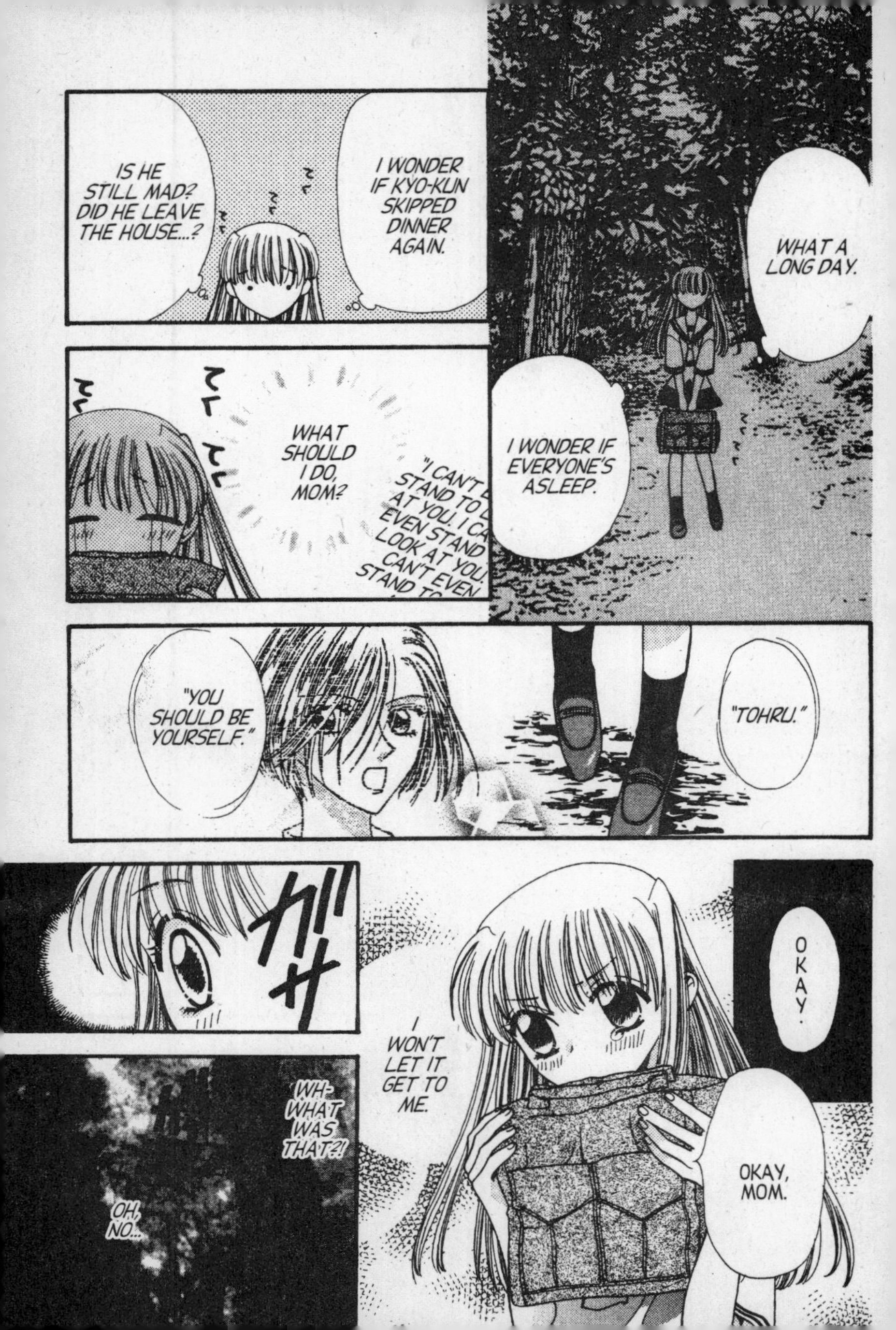
WHAT A LONG DAY.
I WONDER IF EVERYONE'S ASLEEP.
I WONDER IF KYO-KUN SKIPPED DINNER AGAIN.
IS HE STILL MAD? DID HE LEAVE THE HOUSE...?
WHAT SHOULD I DO, MOM?
"I CAN'T
STAND TO
AT YOU. I CA
EVEN STAND
LOOK AT YOU.
CAN'T EVEN
STAND TO
"TOHRU."
"YOU SHOULD BE YOURSELF."
OKAY.
OKAY, MOM.
I WON'T LET IT GET TO ME.
WH-WHAT WAS THAT?!
OH, NO...

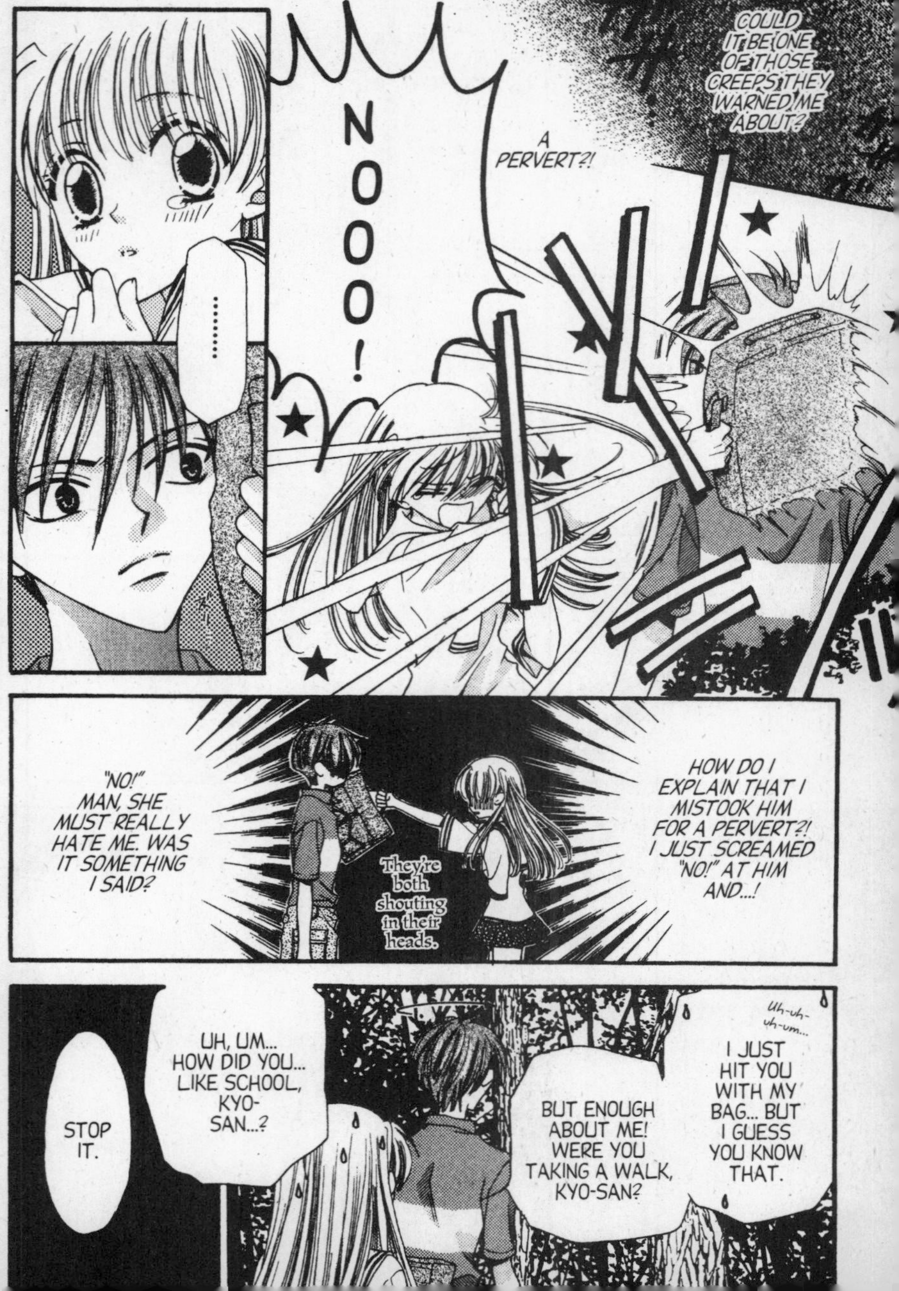
COULD IT BE ONE OF THOSE CREEPS THEY WARNED ME ABOUT?
A PERVERT?!
NOOOO!
......
HOW DO I EXPLAIN THAT I MISTOOK HIM FOR A PERVERT?! I JUST SCREAMED "NO!" AT HIM AND...!
"NO!" MAN, SHE MUST REALLY HATE ME. WAS IT SOMETHING I SAID?
They're both shouting in their heads.
Uh-uh-uh-um...
I JUST HIT YOU WITH MY BAG... BUT I GUESS YOU KNOW THAT.
BUT ENOUGH ABOUT ME! WERE YOU TAKING A WALK, KYO-SAN?
UH, UM... HOW DID YOU... LIKE SCHOOL, KYO-SAN...?
STOP IT.

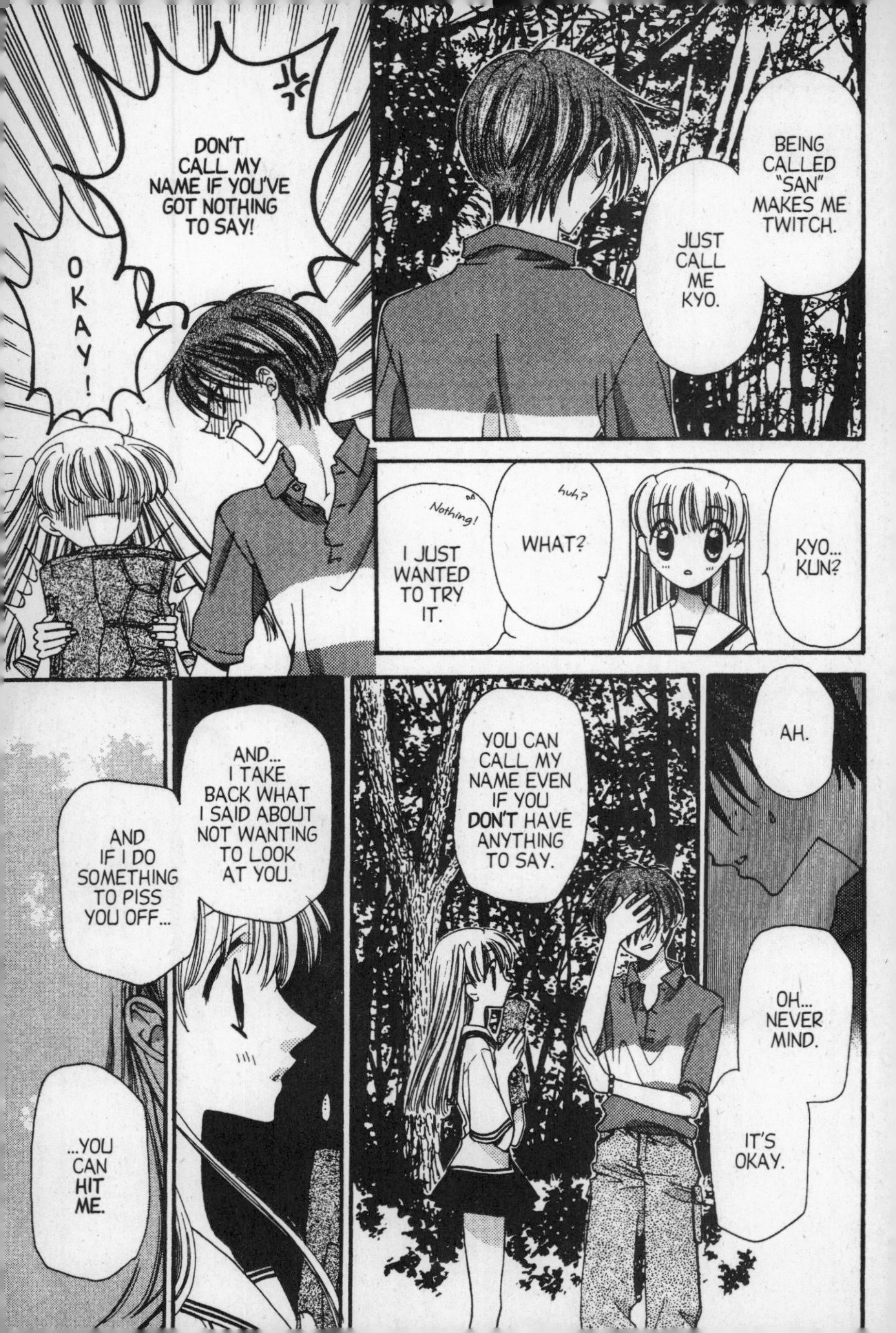
BEING CALLED "SAN" MAKES ME TWITCH.
JUST CALL ME KYO.
KYO... KUN?
WHAT?
huh?
I JUST WANTED TO TRY IT.
Nothing!
DON'T CALL MY NAME IF YOU'VE GOT NOTHING TO SAY!
OKAY!
AH.
OH... NEVER MIND.
IT'S OKAY.
YOU CAN CALL MY NAME EVEN IF YOU DON'T HAVE ANYTHING TO SAY.
AND... I TAKE BACK WHAT I SAID ABOUT NOT WANTING TO LOOK AT YOU.
AND IF I DO SOMETHING TO PISS YOU OFF...
...YOU CAN HIT ME.

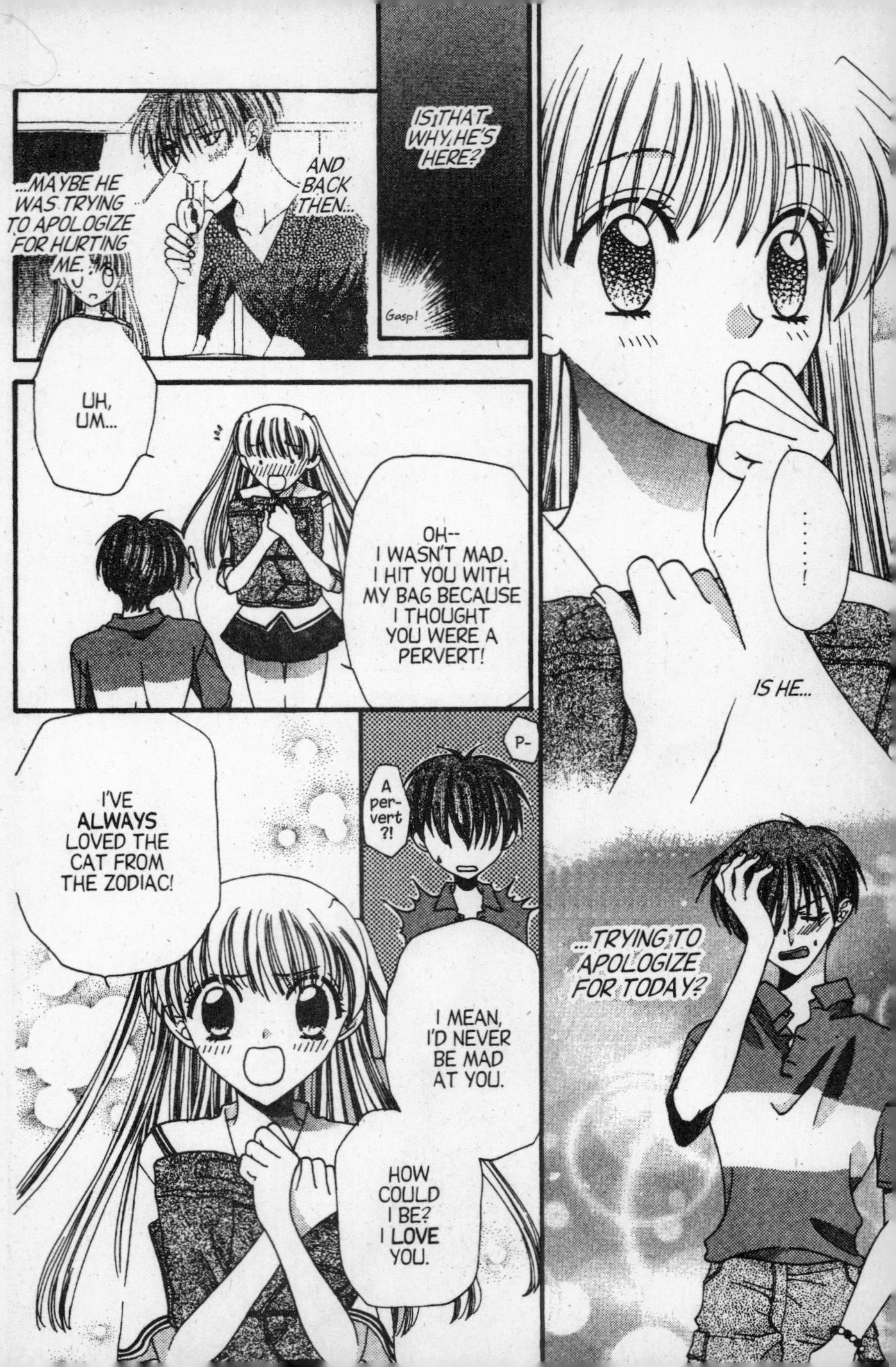
......!
IS HE...
...TRYING TO APOLOGIZE FOR TODAY?
IS THAT WHY HE'S HERE?
Gasp!
AND BACK THEN...
...MAYBE HE WAS TRYING TO APOLOGIZE FOR HURTING ME.
UH, UM...
OH-- I WASN'T MAD. I HIT YOU WITH MY BAG BECAUSE I THOUGHT YOU WERE A PERVERT!
P-
A per-vert?!
I MEAN, I'D NEVER BE MAD AT YOU.
HOW COULD I BE? I **LOVE** YOU.
I'VE **ALWAYS** LOVED THE CAT FROM THE ZODIAC!

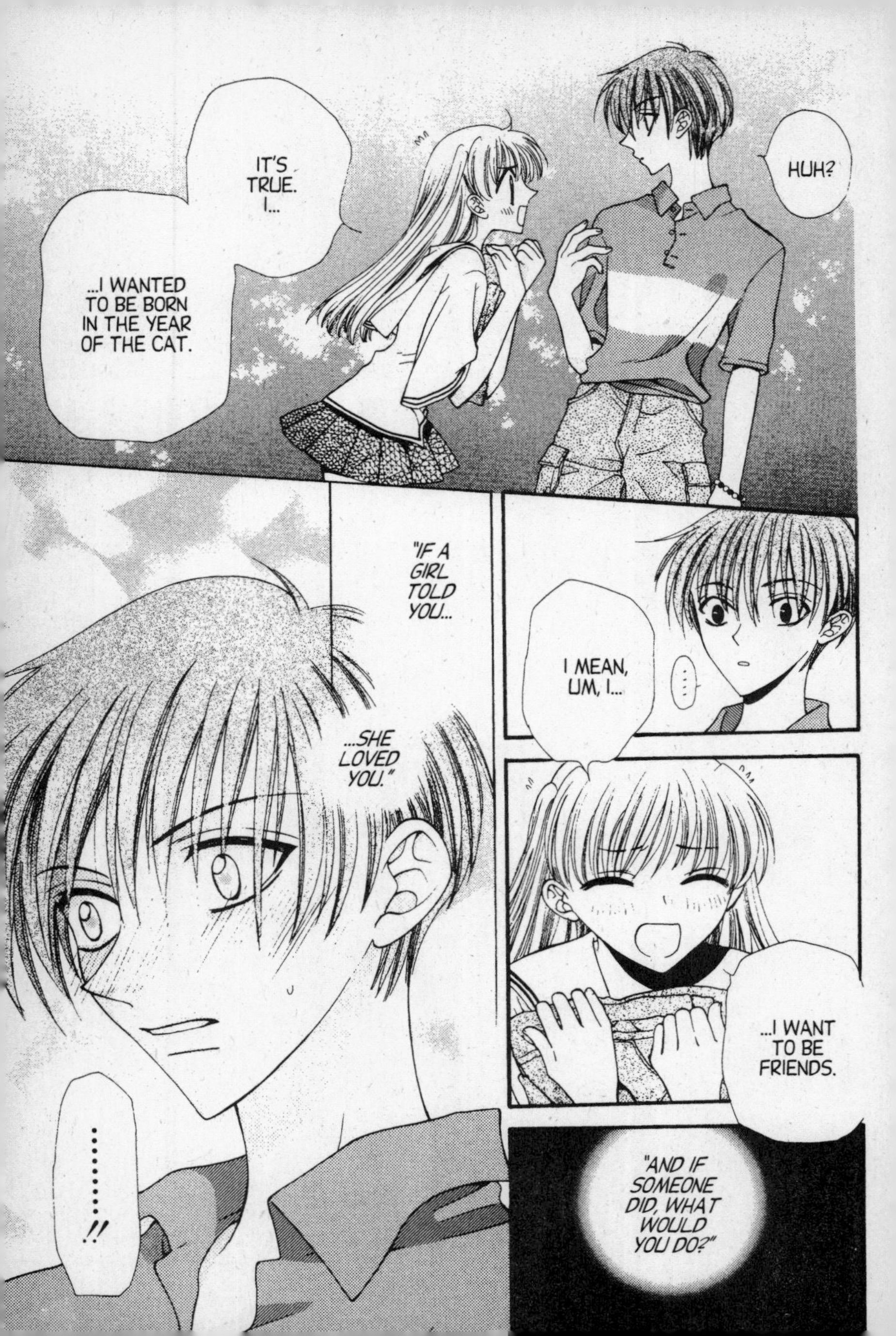
HUH?
IT'S TRUE. I...
...I WANTED TO BE BORN IN THE YEAR OF THE CAT.
I MEAN, UM, I...
...
...I WANT TO BE FRIENDS.
"AND IF SOMEONE DID, WHAT WOULD YOU DO?"
"IF A GIRL TOLD YOU...
...SHE LOVED YOU."
.......!!

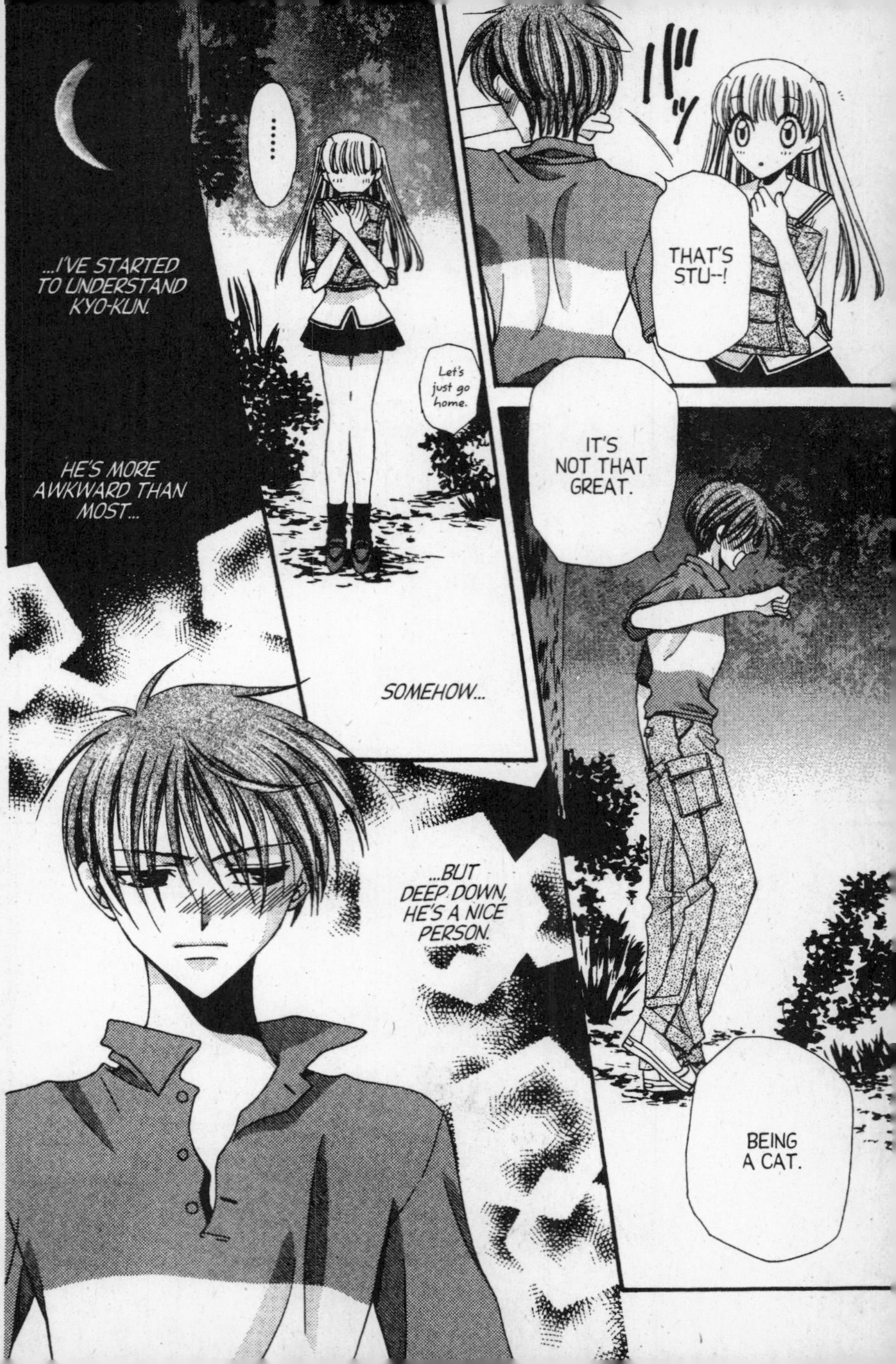
THAT'S STU--!
IT'S NOT THAT GREAT.
BEING A CAT.
......
Let's just go home.
SOMEHOW...
...I'VE STARTED TO UNDERSTAND KYO-KUN.
HE'S MORE AWKWARD THAN MOST...
...BUT DEEP DOWN, HE'S A NICE PERSON.

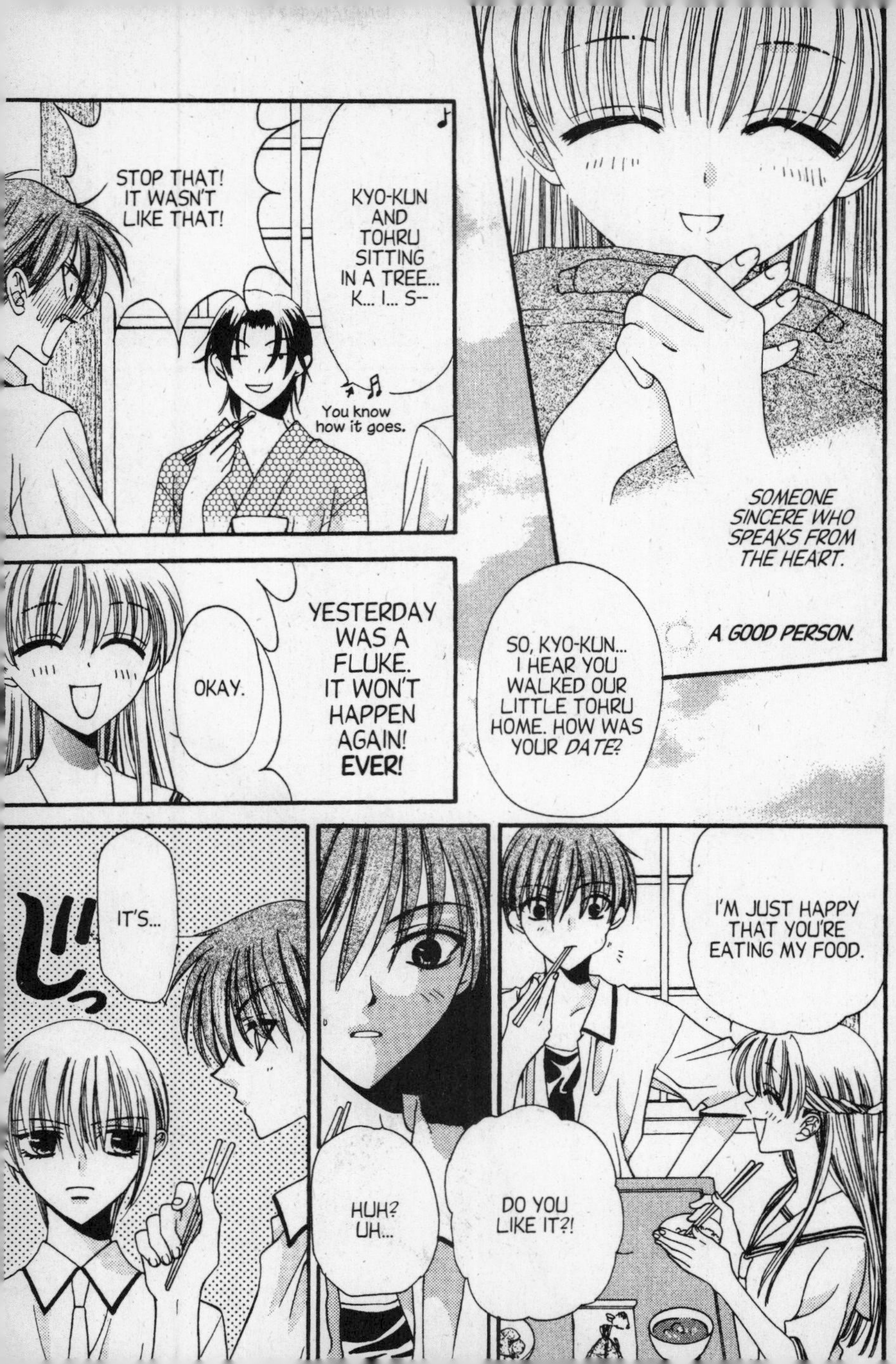

SOMEONE SINCERE WHO SPEAKS FROM THE HEART.
A GOOD PERSON.
SO, KYO-KUN... I HEAR YOU WALKED OUR LITTLE TOHRU HOME. HOW WAS YOUR *DATE*?
KYO-KUN AND TOHRU SITTING IN A TREE... K... I... S--
You know how it goes.
STOP THAT! IT WASN'T LIKE THAT!
YESTERDAY WAS A FLUKE. IT WON'T HAPPEN AGAIN! **EVER!**
OKAY.
I'M JUST HAPPY THAT YOU'RE EATING MY FOOD.
DO YOU LIKE IT?!
HUH? UH...
IT'S...
じっ

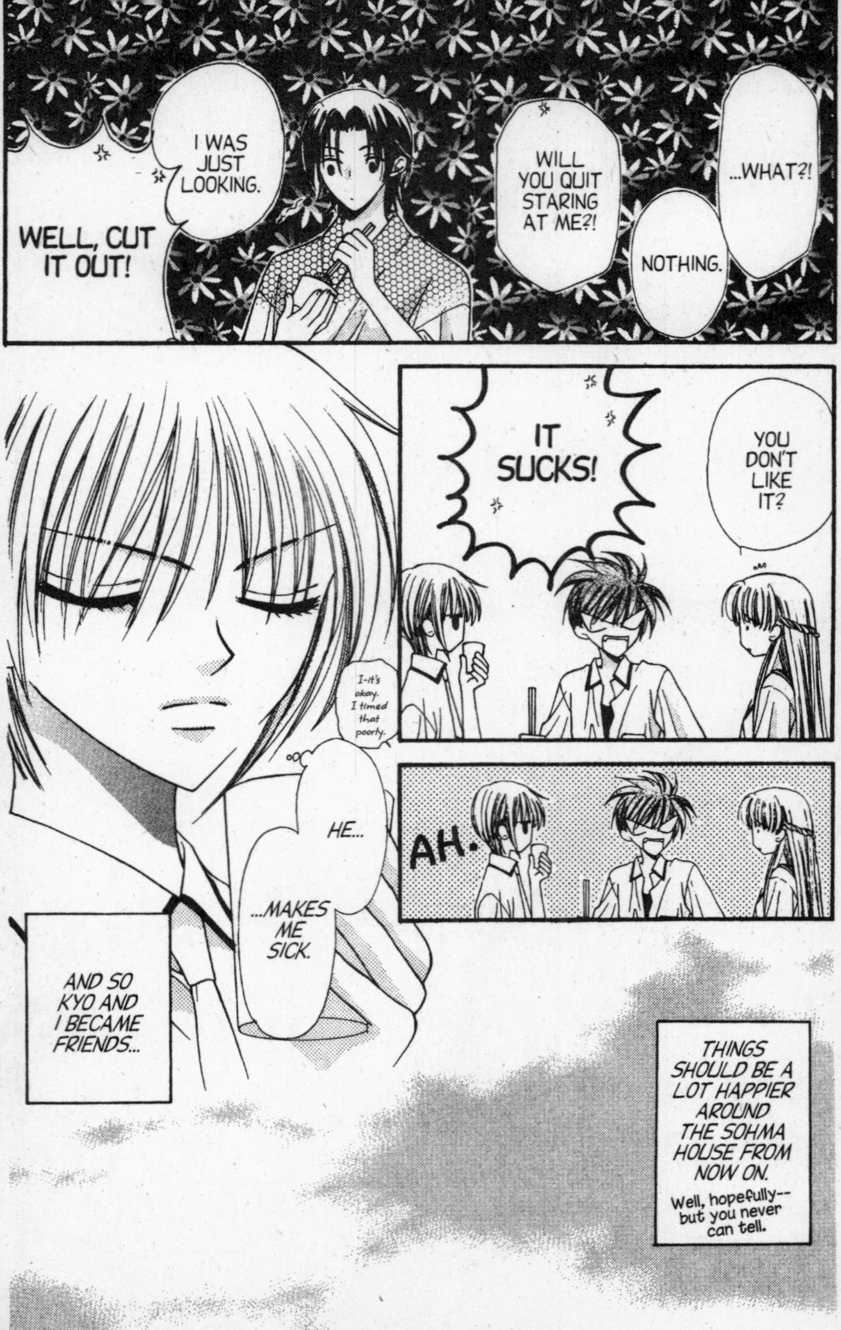
...WHAT?!
NOTHING.
WILL YOU QUIT STARING AT ME?!
I WAS JUST LOOKING.
WELL, CUT IT OUT!
YOU DON'T LIKE IT?
IT SUCKS!
I-it's okay. I timed that poorly.
AH.
HE...
...MAKES ME SICK.
AND SO KYO AND I BECAME FRIENDS...
THINGS SHOULD BE A LOT HAPPIER AROUND THE SOHMA HOUSE FROM NOW ON.
Well, hopefully--but you never can tell.

Chapter 4

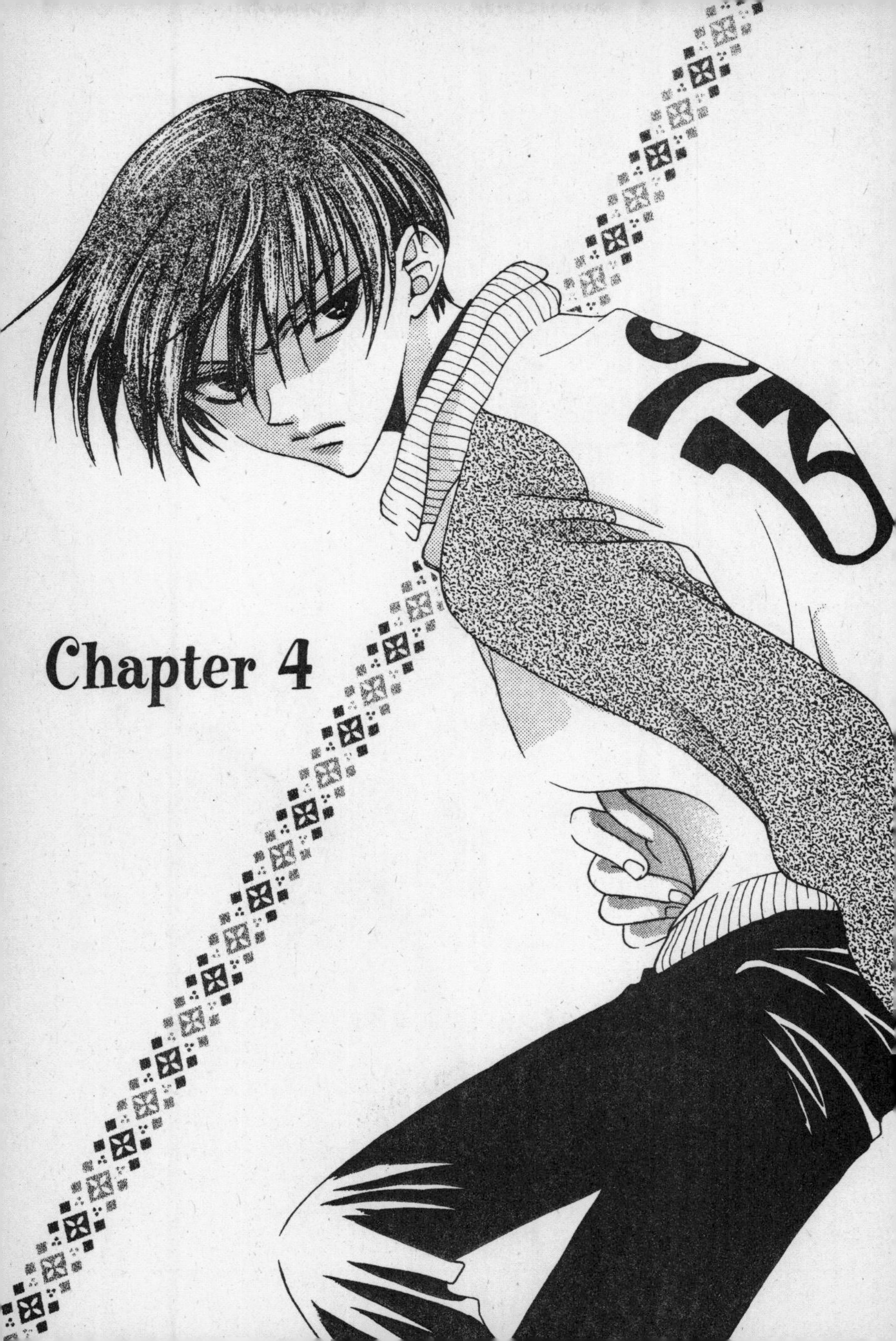

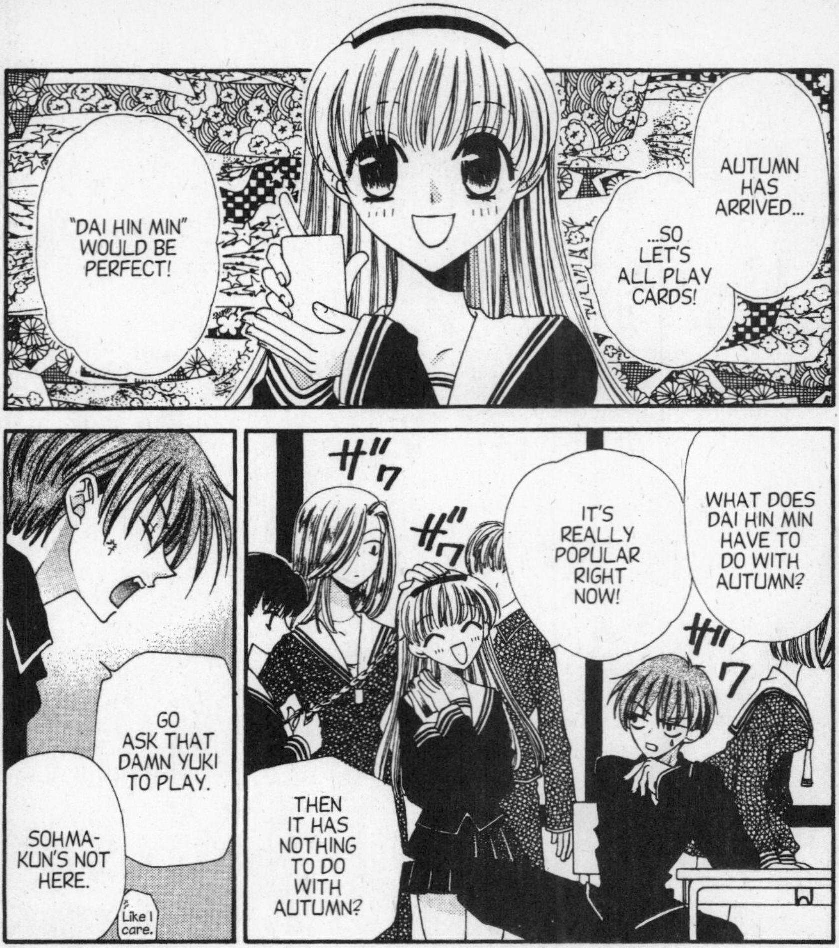
AUTUMN HAS ARRIVED...
...SO LET'S ALL PLAY CARDS!
"DAI HIN MIN" WOULD BE PERFECT!
WHAT DOES DAI HIN MIN HAVE TO DO WITH AUTUMN?
ザワ
IT'S REALLY POPULAR RIGHT NOW!
ザワ
ザワ
THEN IT HAS NOTHING TO DO WITH AUTUMN?
GO ASK THAT DAMN YUKI TO PLAY.
SOHMA-KUN'S NOT HERE.
Like I care.

ULTRA SPECIAL BLAH BLAH BLAH, NUMBER 3:

When I drew Uo-chan, people asked me, "Sensei, did you used to be a Yankee?" Well, I wasn't a Yankee, but I wasn't exactly an honor student, either. Most people don't understand about Hana-chan's "poison waves," either. Apparently there's a video game called "Pange Reef" with poison waves, but I didn't play it until after I'd started the manga.

Number 5:

"How do you name your characters in video games?" I'm asked. Well, I usually put in my own name. I stopped for a while, but then I started doing it again. Of course, I say "my own name," but Natsuki Takaya is a pen name (laugh). If it was my real name, then, yeah, I might think it was a little embarrassing. I don't think it's bad though. Because it's my game to enjoy my own way. So now, when I become friends with people in the game "Tokyo Friend," they call me "Takayan."

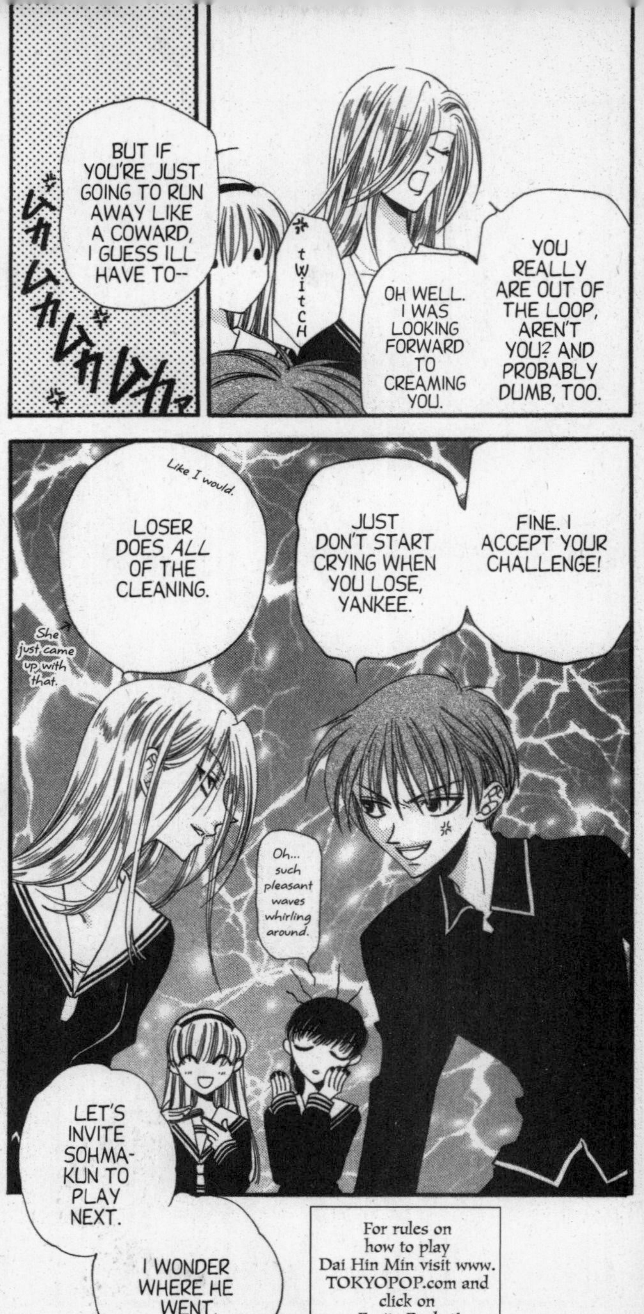
YOU REALLY ARE OUT OF THE LOOP, AREN'T YOU? AND PROBABLY DUMB, TOO.
OH WELL. I WAS LOOKING FORWARD TO CREAMING YOU.
tWitch
BUT IF YOU'RE JUST GOING TO RUN AWAY LIKE A COWARD, I GUESS ILL HAVE TO--
FINE. I ACCEPT YOUR CHALLENGE!
JUST DON'T START CRYING WHEN YOU LOSE, YANKEE.
LOSER DOES *ALL* OF THE CLEANING.
Like I would.
She just came up with that.
Oh... such pleasant waves whirling around.
LET'S INVITE SOHMA-KUN TO PLAY NEXT.
I WONDER WHERE HE WENT.

For rules on how to play Dai Hin Min visit www.TOKYOPOP.com and click on *Fruits Basket!*

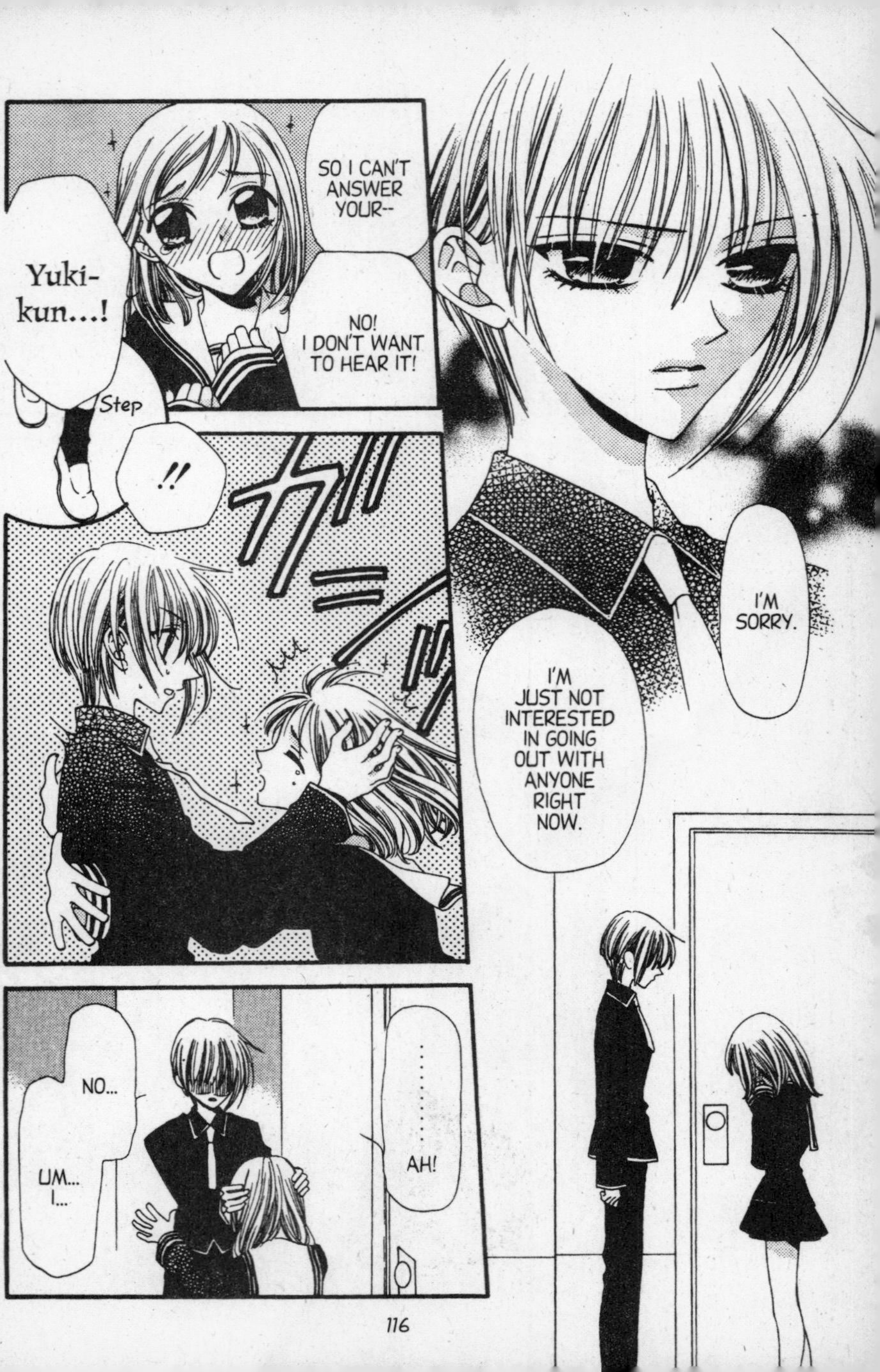
I'M SORRY.
I'M JUST NOT INTERESTED IN GOING OUT WITH ANYONE RIGHT NOW.
SO I CAN'T ANSWER YOUR--
NO! I DON'T WANT TO HEAR IT!
Yuki-kun...!
Step
!!
....
AH!
NO...
UM... I...

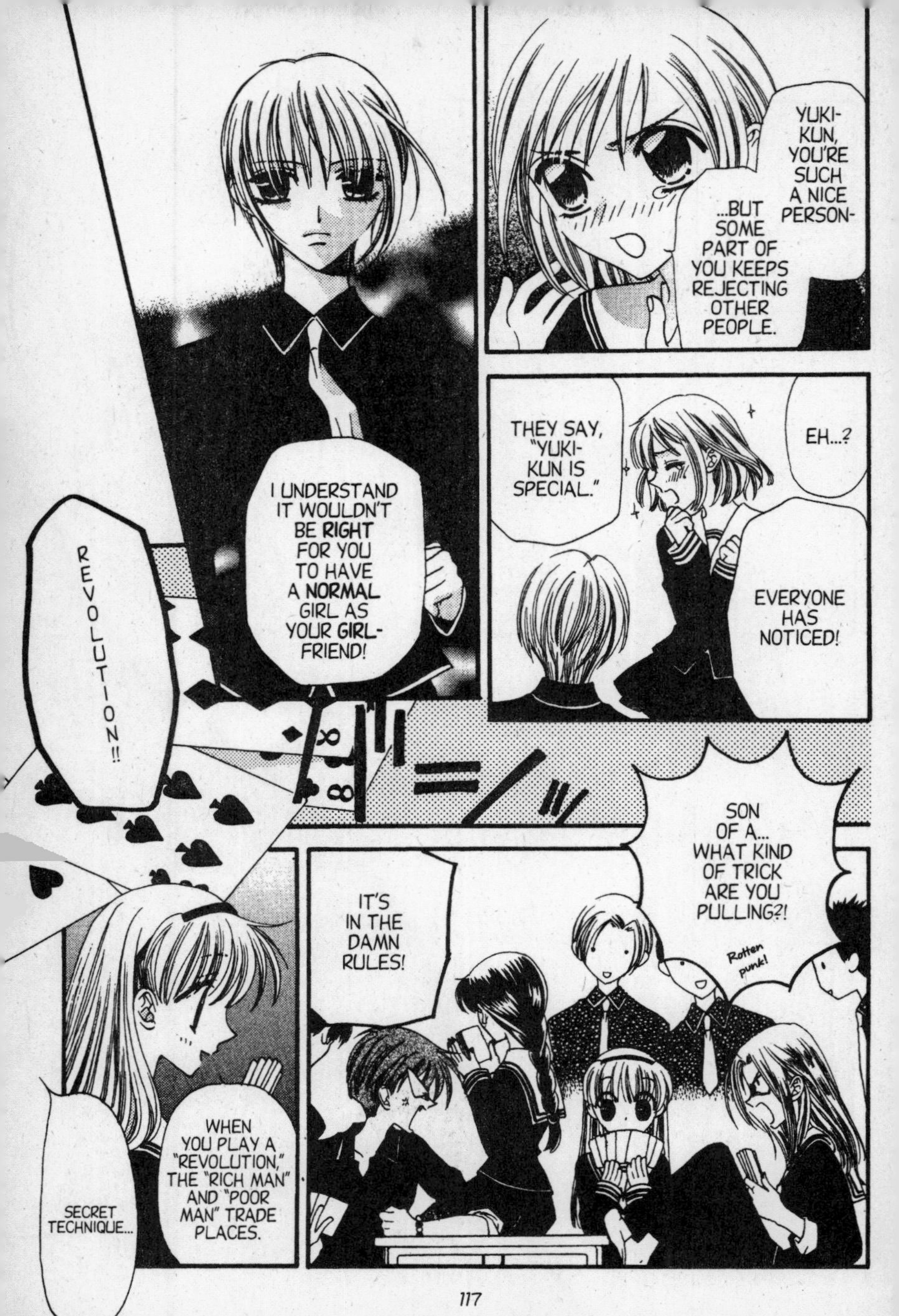
YUKI-KUN, YOU'RE SUCH A NICE PERSON-
...BUT SOME PART OF YOU KEEPS REJECTING OTHER PEOPLE.
EH...?
THEY SAY, "YUKI-KUN IS SPECIAL."
EVERYONE HAS NOTICED!
I UNDERSTAND IT WOULDN'T BE RIGHT FOR YOU TO HAVE A NORMAL GIRL AS YOUR GIRL-FRIEND!
REVOLUTION!!
SON OF A... WHAT KIND OF TRICK ARE YOU PULLING?!
Rotten punk!
IT'S IN THE DAMN RULES!
WHEN YOU PLAY A "REVOLUTION," THE "RICH MAN" AND "POOR MAN" TRADE PLACES.
SECRET TECHNIQUE...

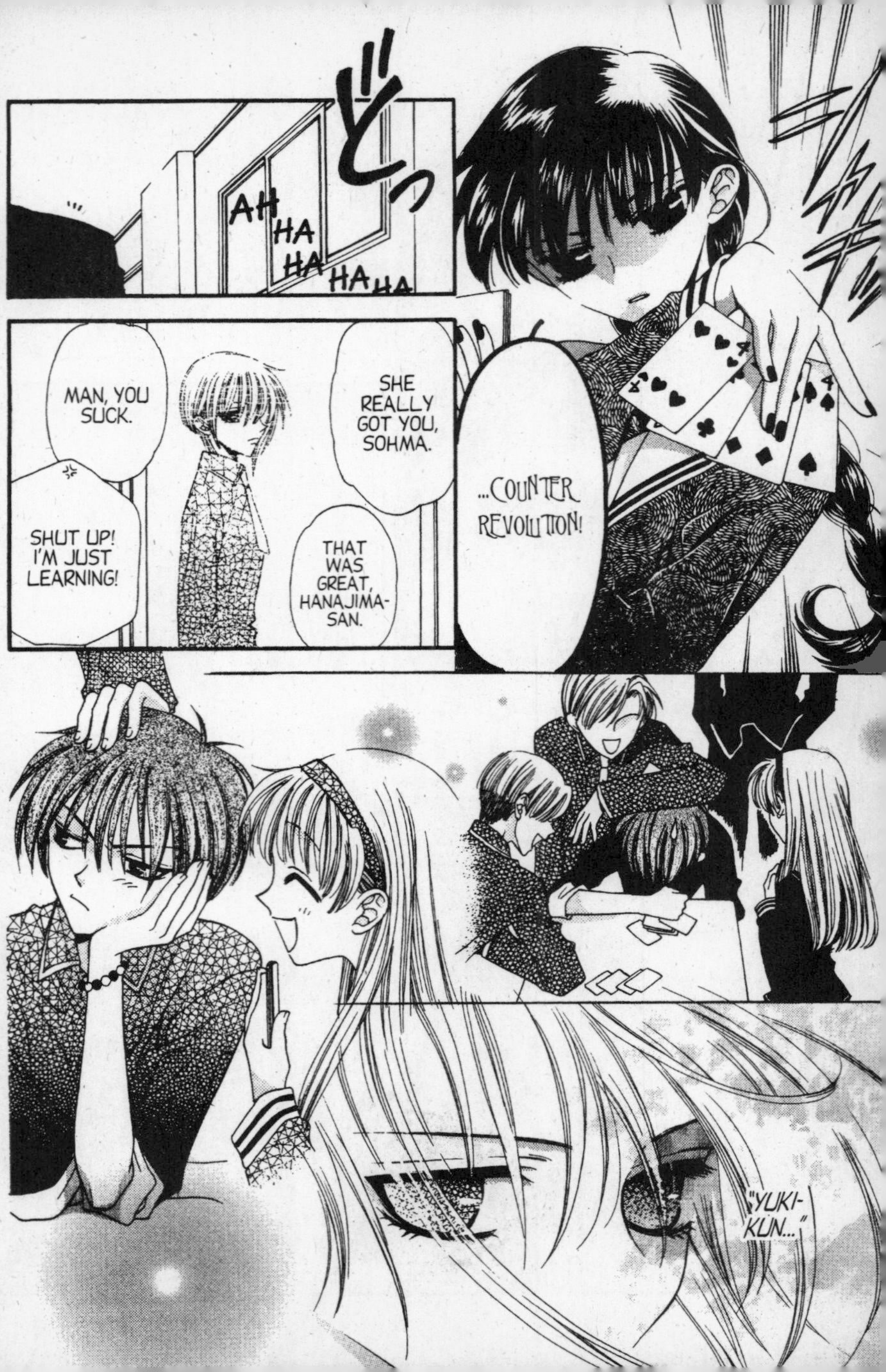
...COUNTER REVOLUTION!
どっ
AH HA HA HA HA
SHE REALLY GOT YOU, SOHMA.
THAT WAS GREAT, HANAJIMA-SAN.
MAN, YOU SUCK.
SHUT UP! I'M JUST LEARNING!
"YUKI-KUN..."

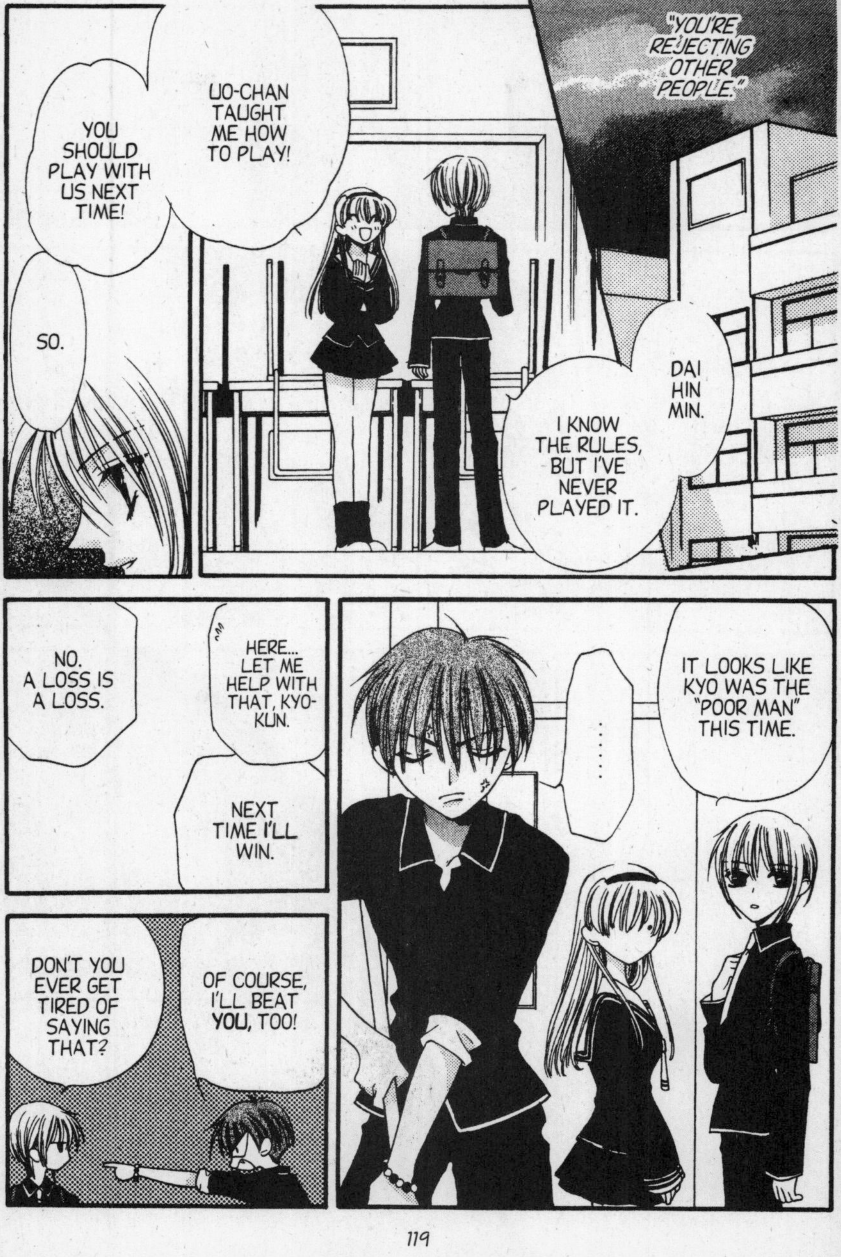
"YOU'RE REJECTING OTHER PEOPLE."
DAI HIN MIN.
I KNOW THE RULES, BUT I'VE NEVER PLAYED IT.
UO-CHAN TAUGHT ME HOW TO PLAY!
YOU SHOULD PLAY WITH US NEXT TIME!
SO.
IT LOOKS LIKE KYO WAS THE "POOR MAN" THIS TIME.
......
HERE... LET ME HELP WITH THAT, KYO-KUN.
NO. A LOSS IS A LOSS.
NEXT TIME I'LL WIN.
DON'T YOU EVER GET TIRED OF SAYING THAT?
OF COURSE, I'LL BEAT **YOU**, TOO!

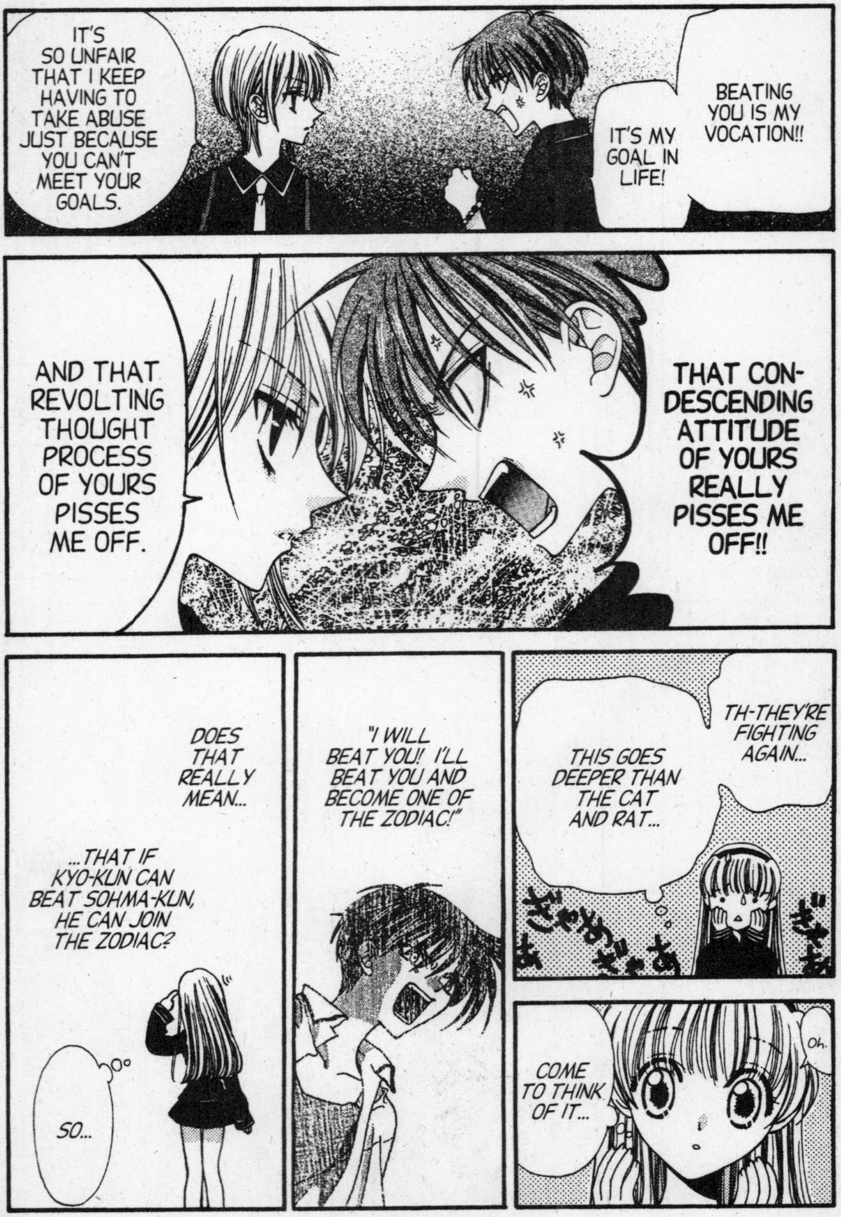
BEATING YOU IS MY VOCATION!!
IT'S MY GOAL IN LIFE!
IT'S SO UNFAIR THAT I KEEP HAVING TO TAKE ABUSE JUST BECAUSE YOU CAN'T MEET YOUR GOALS.
THAT CON-DESCENDING ATTITUDE OF YOURS REALLY PISSES ME OFF!!
AND THAT REVOLTING THOUGHT PROCESS OF YOURS PISSES ME OFF.
TH-THEY'RE FIGHTING AGAIN...
THIS GOES DEEPER THAN THE CAT AND RAT...
Oh.
COME TO THINK OF IT...
"I WILL BEAT YOU! I'LL BEAT YOU AND BECOME ONE OF THE ZODIAC!"
DOES THAT REALLY MEAN...
...THAT IF KYO-KUN CAN BEAT SOHMA-KUN, HE CAN JOIN THE ZODIAC?
SO...

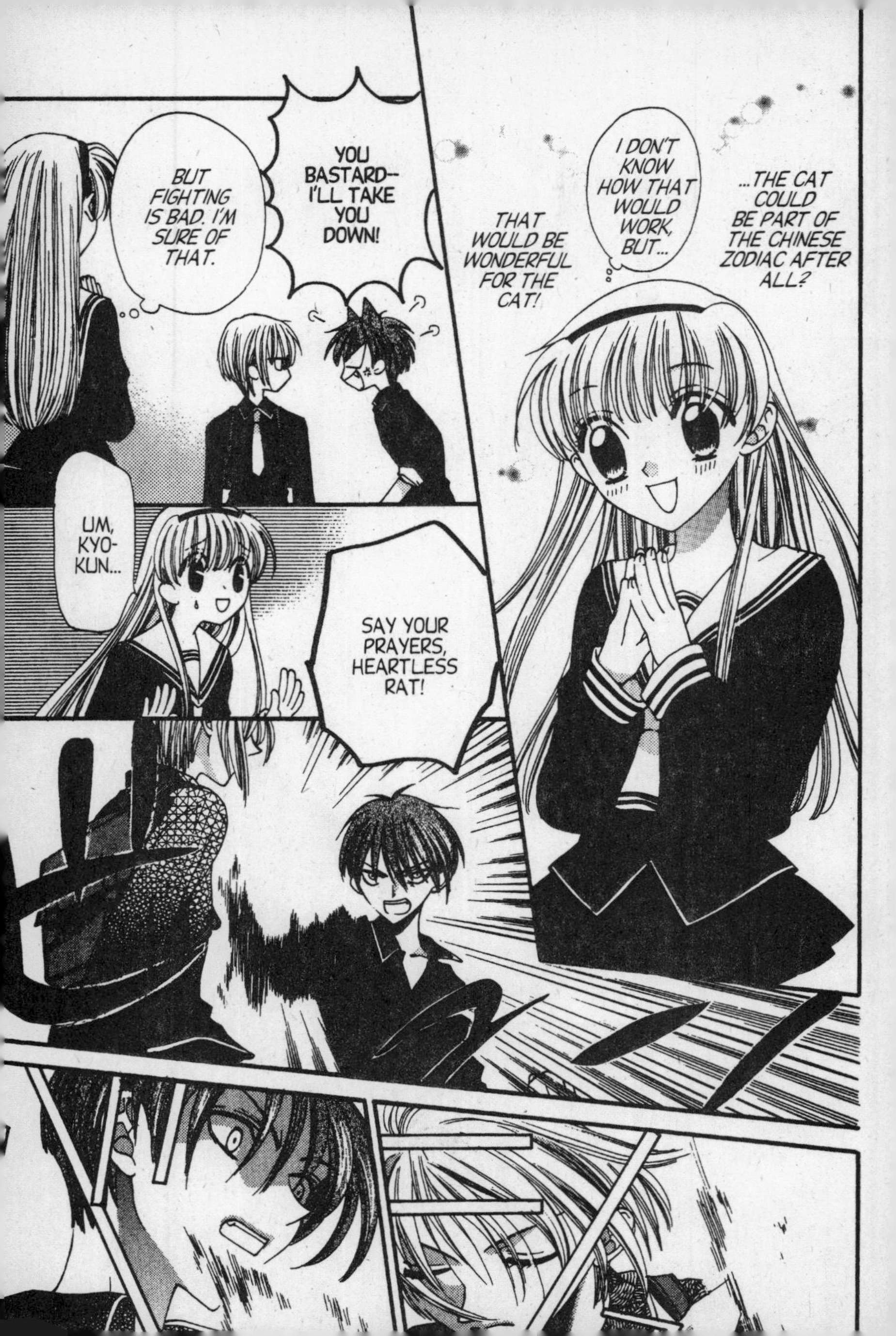
...THE CAT COULD BE PART OF THE CHINESE ZODIAC AFTER ALL?
I DON'T KNOW HOW THAT WOULD WORK, BUT...
THAT WOULD BE WONDERFUL FOR THE CAT!
YOU BASTARD— I'LL TAKE YOU DOWN!
BUT FIGHTING IS BAD. I'M SURE OF THAT.
SAY YOUR PRAYERS, HEARTLESS RAT!
UM, KYO-KUN...

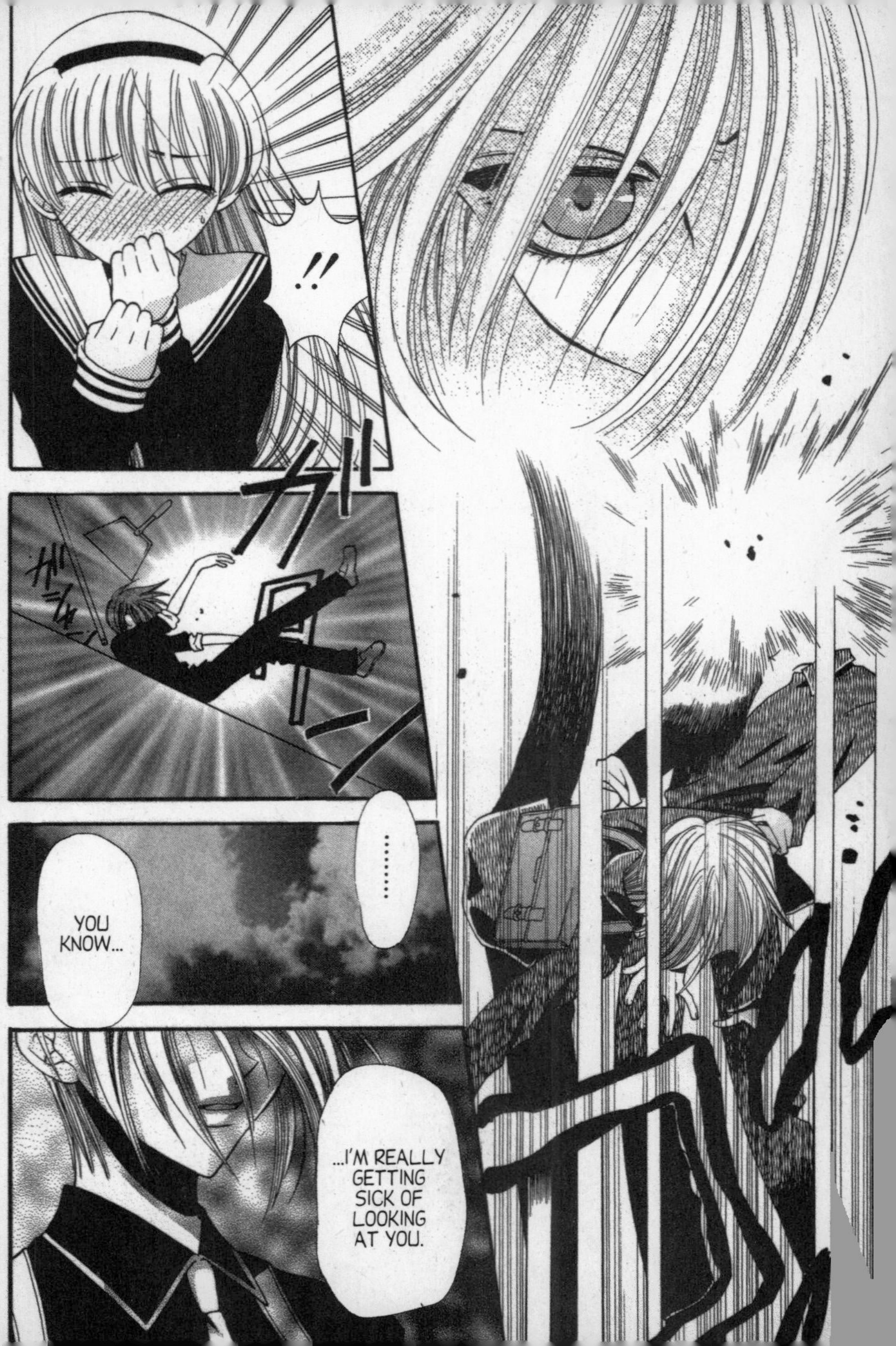
!!
......
YOU KNOW...
...I'M REALLY GETTING SICK OF LOOKING AT YOU.

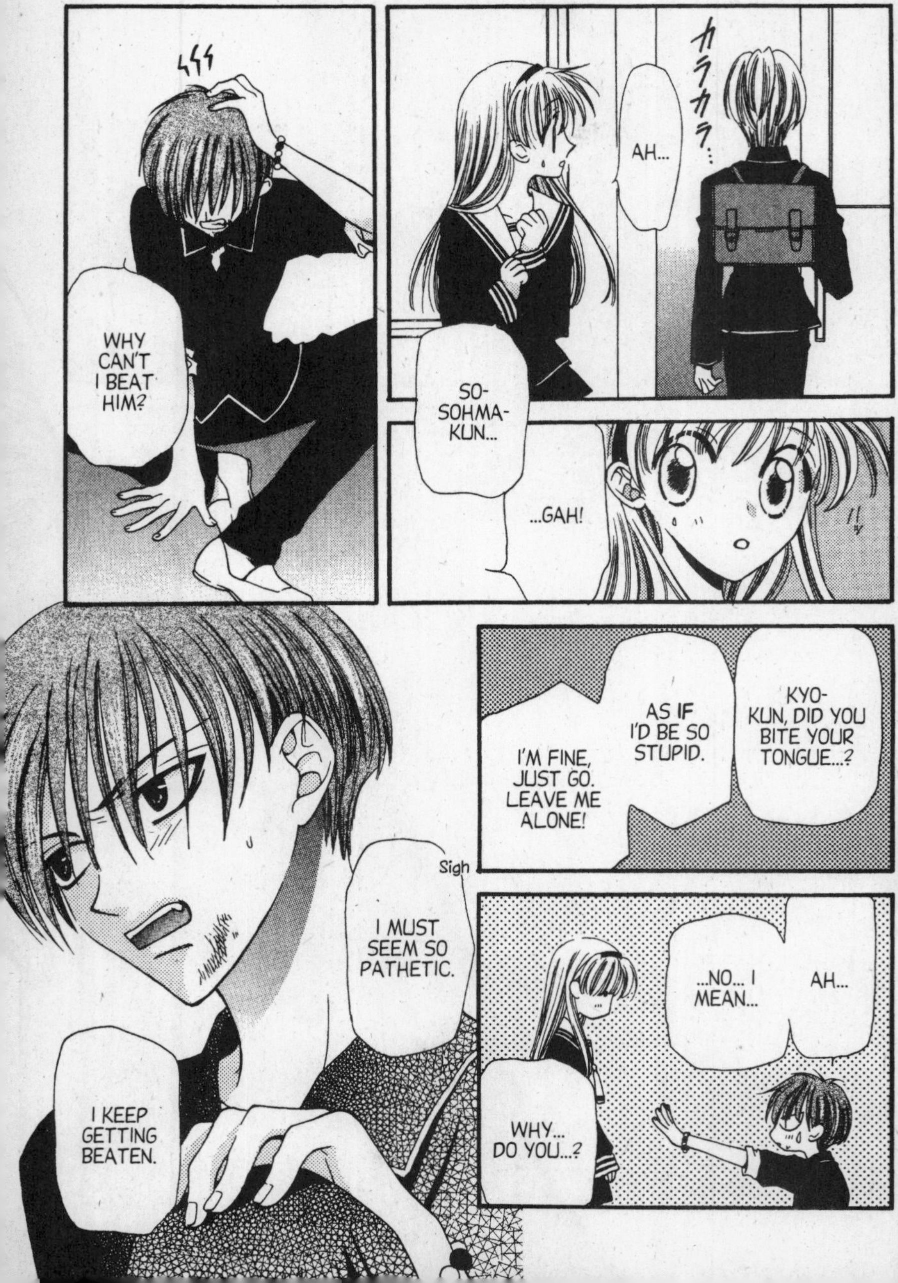
カラカラ...
AH...
SO-SOHMA-KUN...
...GAH!
WHY CAN'T I BEAT HIM?
KYO-KUN, DID YOU BITE YOUR TONGUE...?
AS IF I'D BE SO STUPID.
I'M FINE, JUST GO. LEAVE ME ALONE!
AH...
...NO... I MEAN...
WHY... DO YOU...?
Sigh
I MUST SEEM SO PATHETIC.
I KEEP GETTING BEATEN.

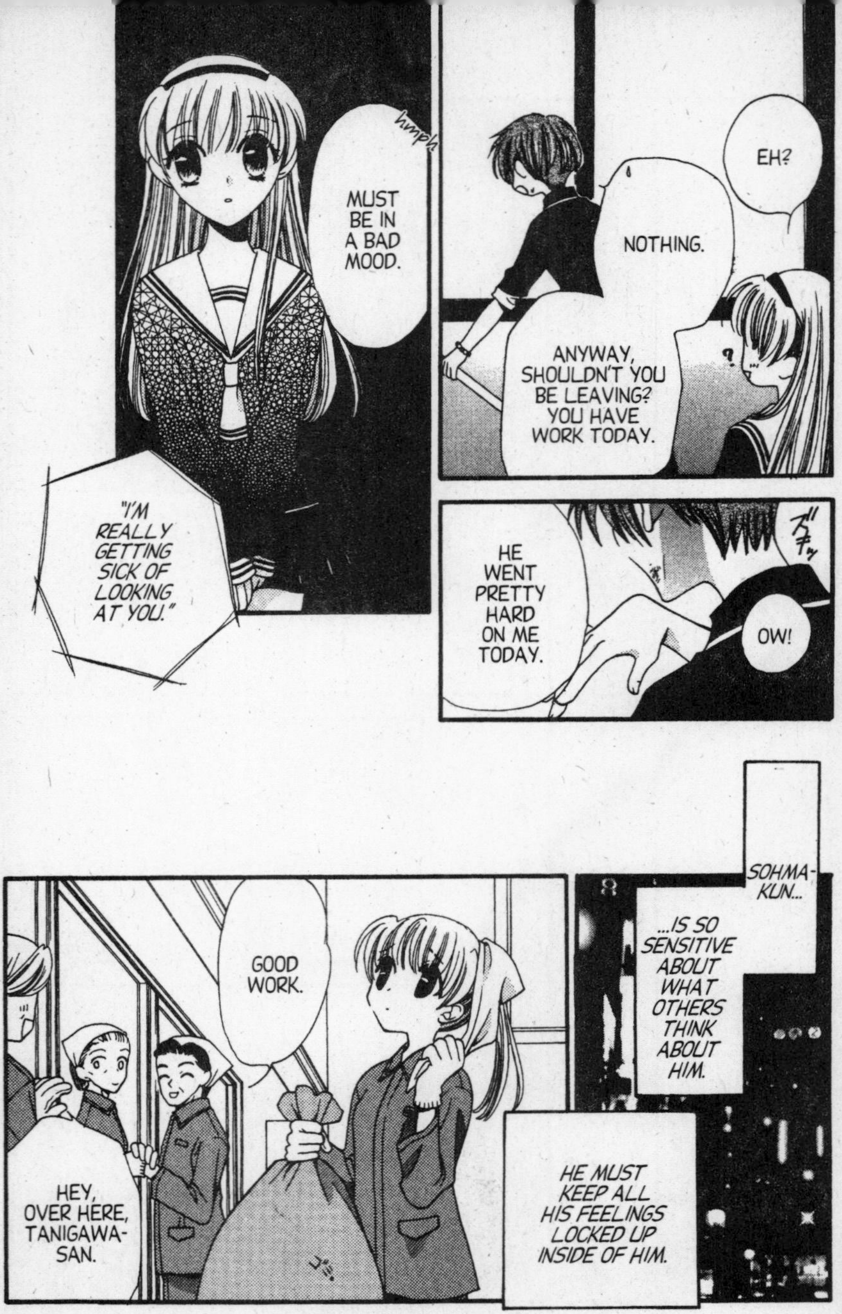
EH?
NOTHING.
ANYWAY, SHOULDN'T YOU BE LEAVING? YOU HAVE WORK TODAY.
HE WENT PRETTY HARD ON ME TODAY.
OW!
hmph
MUST BE IN A BAD MOOD.
"I'M REALLY GETTING SICK OF LOOKING AT YOU."
SOHMA-KUN...
...IS SO SENSITIVE ABOUT WHAT OTHERS THINK ABOUT HIM.
HE MUST KEEP ALL HIS FEELINGS LOCKED UP INSIDE OF HIM.
GOOD WORK.
HEY, OVER HERE, TANIGAWA-SAN.

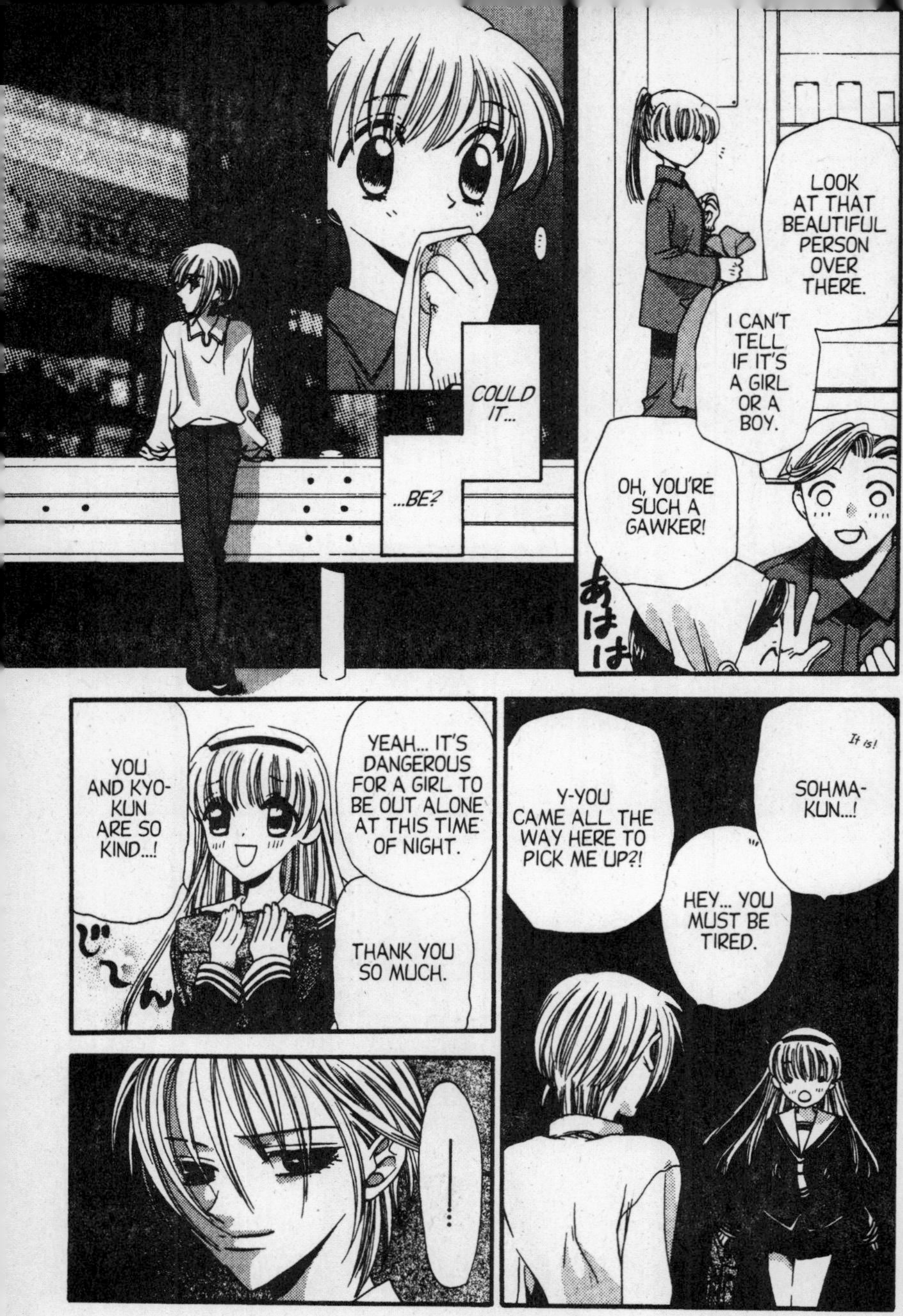
LOOK AT THAT BEAUTIFUL PERSON OVER THERE.
I CAN'T TELL IF IT'S A GIRL OR A BOY.
OH, YOU'RE SUCH A GAWKER!
あはは
...
COULD IT...
...BE?
It is!
SOHMA-KUN...!
Y-YOU CAME ALL THE WAY HERE TO PICK ME UP?!
HEY... YOU MUST BE TIRED.
YEAH... IT'S DANGEROUS FOR A GIRL TO BE OUT ALONE AT THIS TIME OF NIGHT.
YOU AND KYO-KUN ARE SO KIND...!
THANK YOU SO MUCH.
じ〜ん
......!

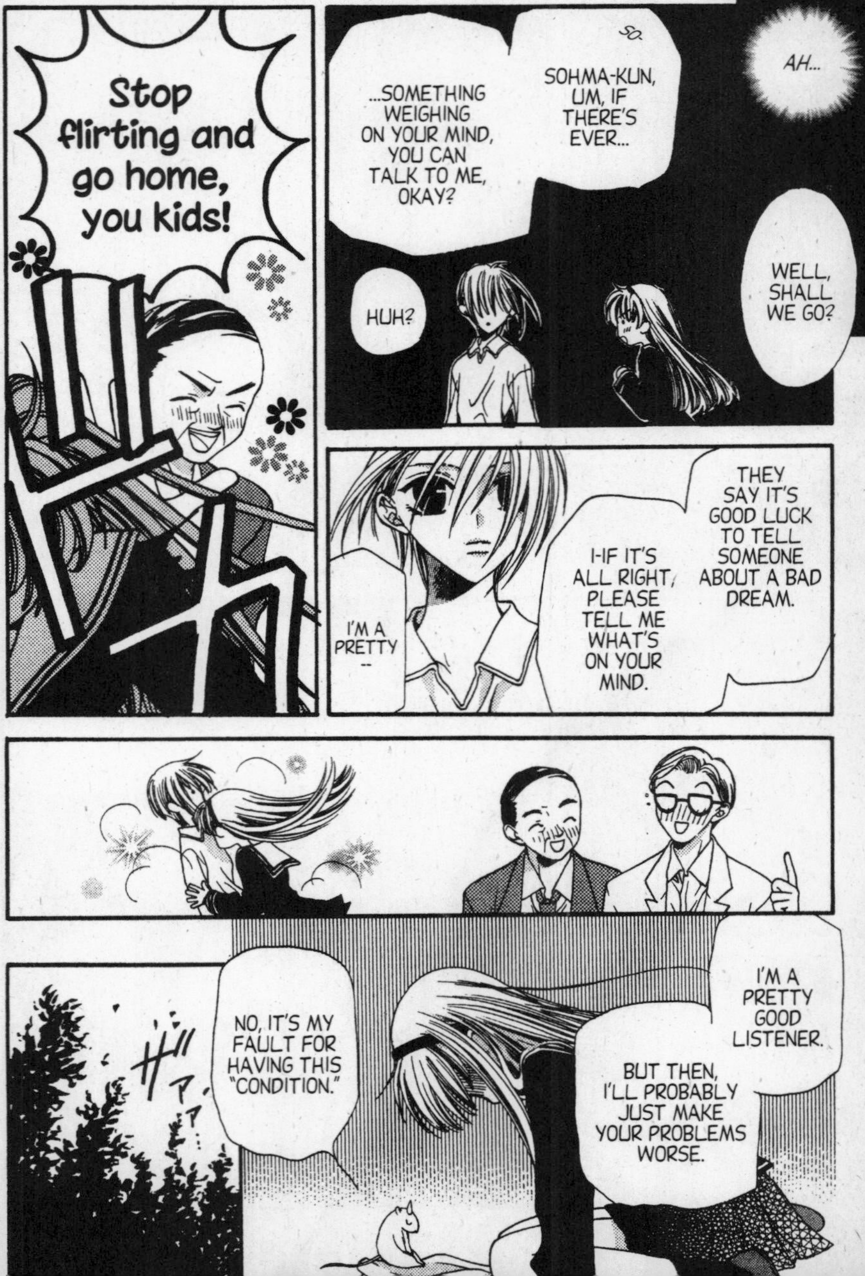
AH...
SO.
SOHMA-KUN, UM, IF THERE'S EVER...
...SOMETHING WEIGHING ON YOUR MIND, YOU CAN TALK TO ME, OKAY?
WELL, SHALL WE GO?
HUH?
THEY SAY IT'S GOOD LUCK TO TELL SOMEONE ABOUT A BAD DREAM.
I-IF IT'S ALL RIGHT, PLEASE TELL ME WHAT'S ON YOUR MIND.
I'M A PRETTY --
Stop flirting and go home, you kids!
I'M A PRETTY GOOD LISTENER.
BUT THEN, I'LL PROBABLY JUST MAKE YOUR PROBLEMS WORSE.
NO, IT'S MY FAULT FOR HAVING THIS "CONDITION."
ザアア…

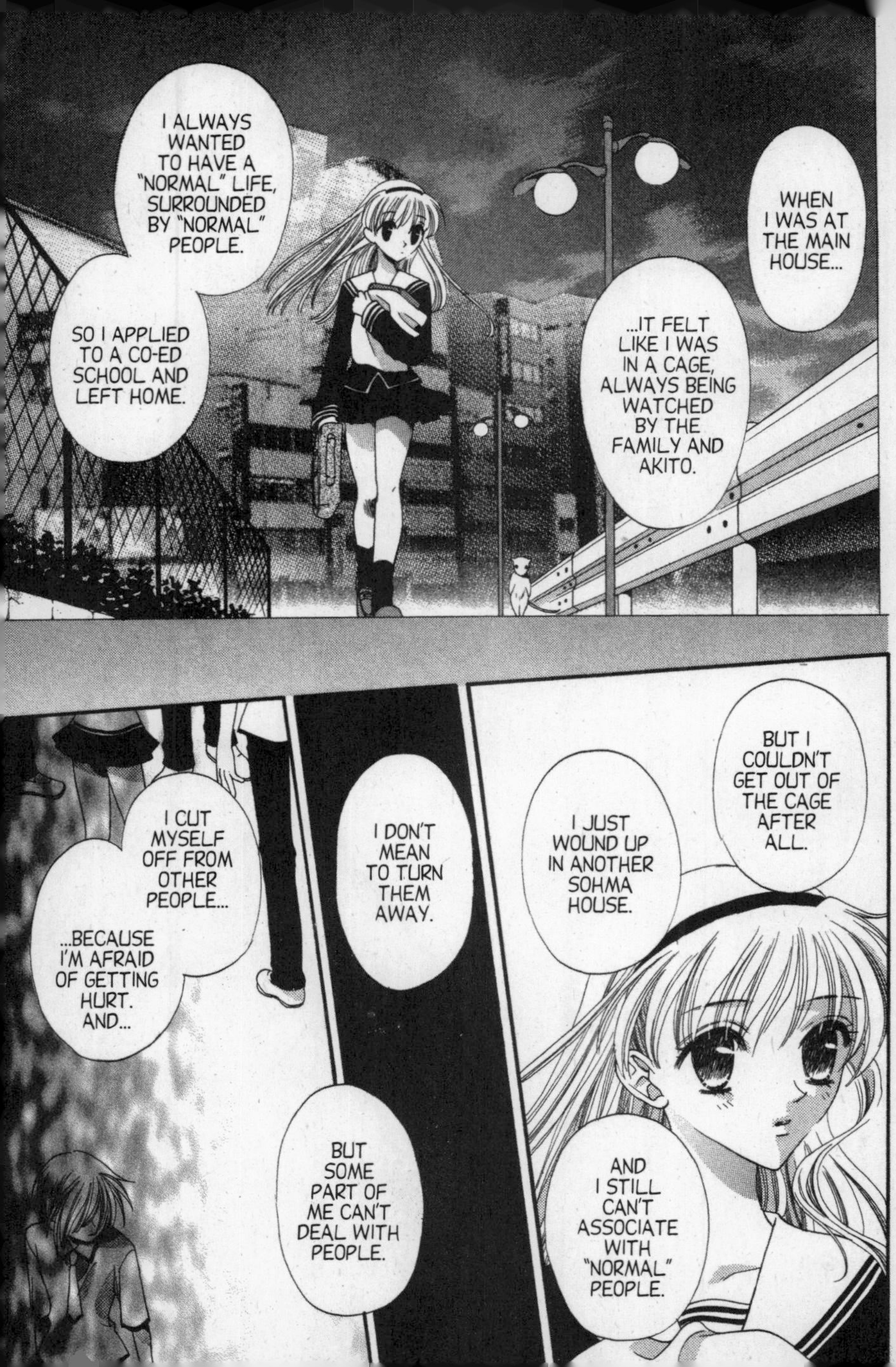
WHEN I WAS AT THE MAIN HOUSE...
...IT FELT LIKE I WAS IN A CAGE, ALWAYS BEING WATCHED BY THE FAMILY AND AKITO.
I ALWAYS WANTED TO HAVE A "NORMAL" LIFE, SURROUNDED BY "NORMAL" PEOPLE.
SO I APPLIED TO A CO-ED SCHOOL AND LEFT HOME.
BUT I COULDN'T GET OUT OF THE CAGE AFTER ALL.
I JUST WOUND UP IN ANOTHER SOHMA HOUSE.
AND I STILL CAN'T ASSOCIATE WITH "NORMAL" PEOPLE.
I DON'T MEAN TO TURN THEM AWAY.
BUT SOME PART OF ME CAN'T DEAL WITH PEOPLE.
I CUT MYSELF OFF FROM OTHER PEOPLE...
...BECAUSE I'M AFRAID OF GETTING HURT. AND...

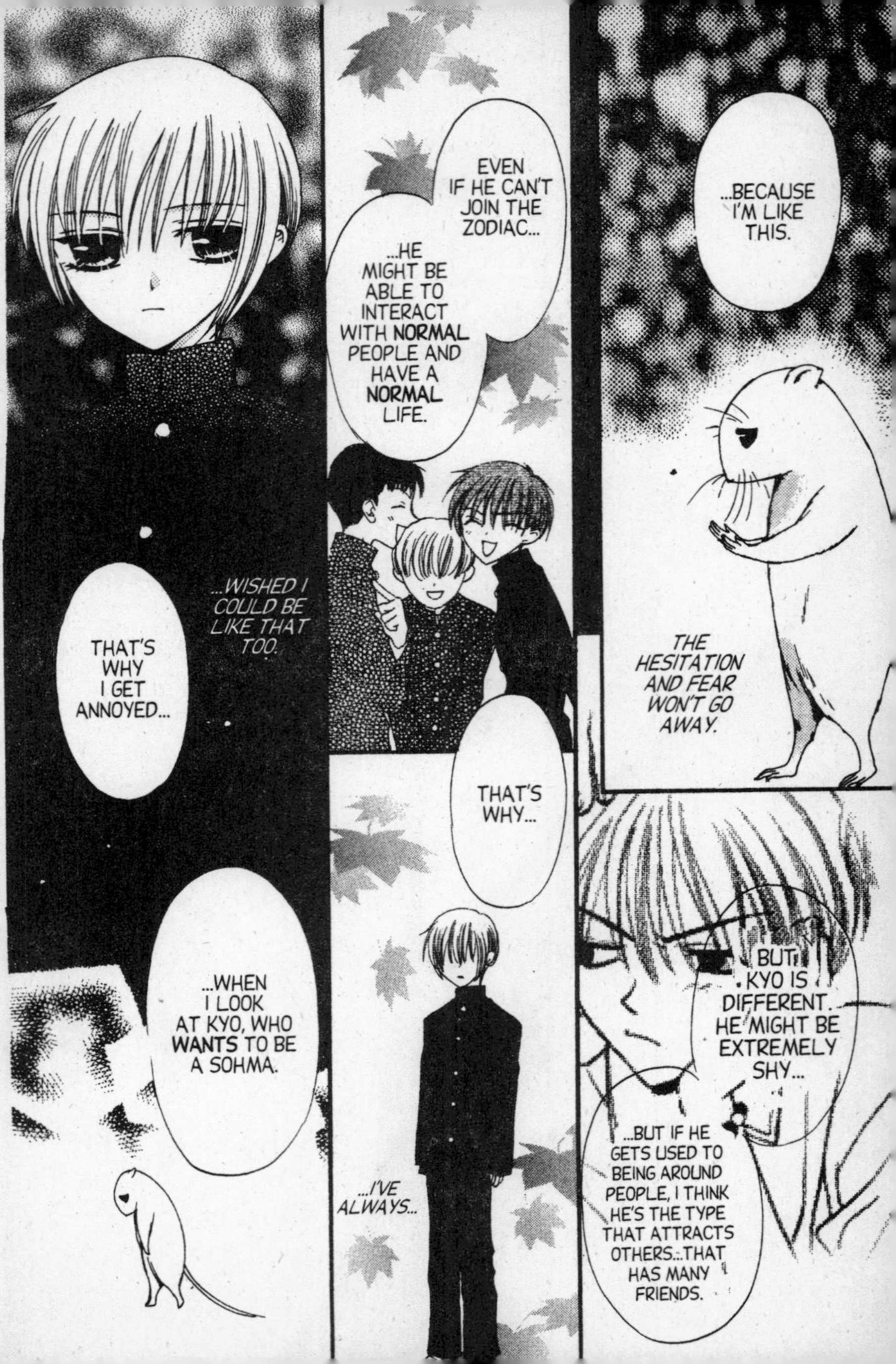
...BECAUSE I'M LIKE THIS.
THE HESITATION AND FEAR WON'T GO AWAY.
BUT KYO IS DIFFERENT. HE MIGHT BE EXTREMELY SHY...
...BUT IF HE GETS USED TO BEING AROUND PEOPLE, I THINK HE'S THE TYPE THAT ATTRACTS OTHERS...THAT HAS MANY FRIENDS.
EVEN IF HE CAN'T JOIN THE ZODIAC...
...HE MIGHT BE ABLE TO INTERACT WITH NORMAL PEOPLE AND HAVE A NORMAL LIFE.
THAT'S WHY...
...I'VE ALWAYS...
...WISHED I COULD BE LIKE THAT TOO.
THAT'S WHY I GET ANNOYED...
...WHEN I LOOK AT KYO, WHO WANTS TO BE A SOHMA.

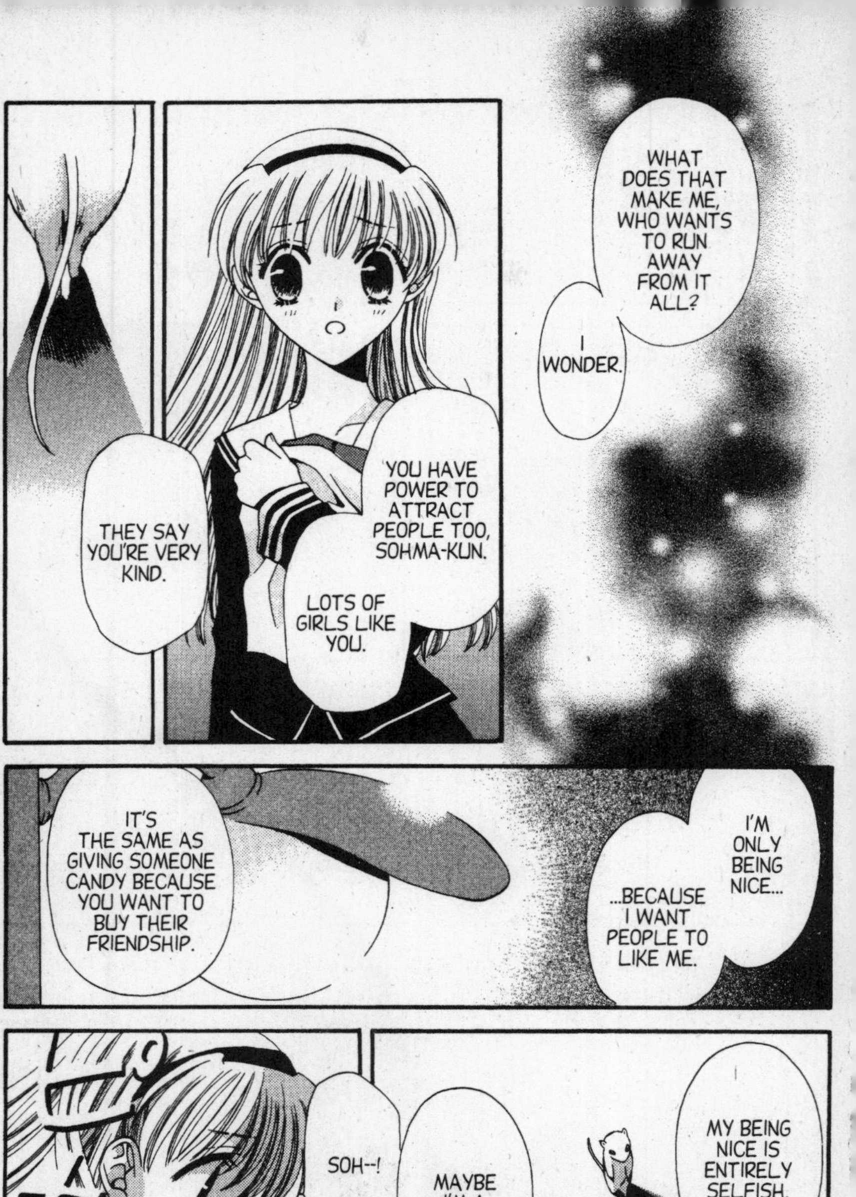
WHAT DOES THAT MAKE ME, WHO WANTS TO RUN AWAY FROM IT ALL?
I WONDER.
YOU HAVE POWER TO ATTRACT PEOPLE TOO, SOHMA-KUN.
LOTS OF GIRLS LIKE YOU.
THEY SAY YOU'RE VERY KIND.
I'M ONLY BEING NICE...
...BECAUSE I WANT PEOPLE TO LIKE ME.
IT'S THE SAME AS GIVING SOMEONE CANDY BECAUSE YOU WANT TO BUY THEIR FRIENDSHIP.
MY BEING NICE IS ENTIRELY SELFISH.
MAYBE I'M A HYPOCRITE.
SOH--!

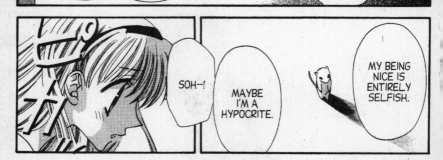

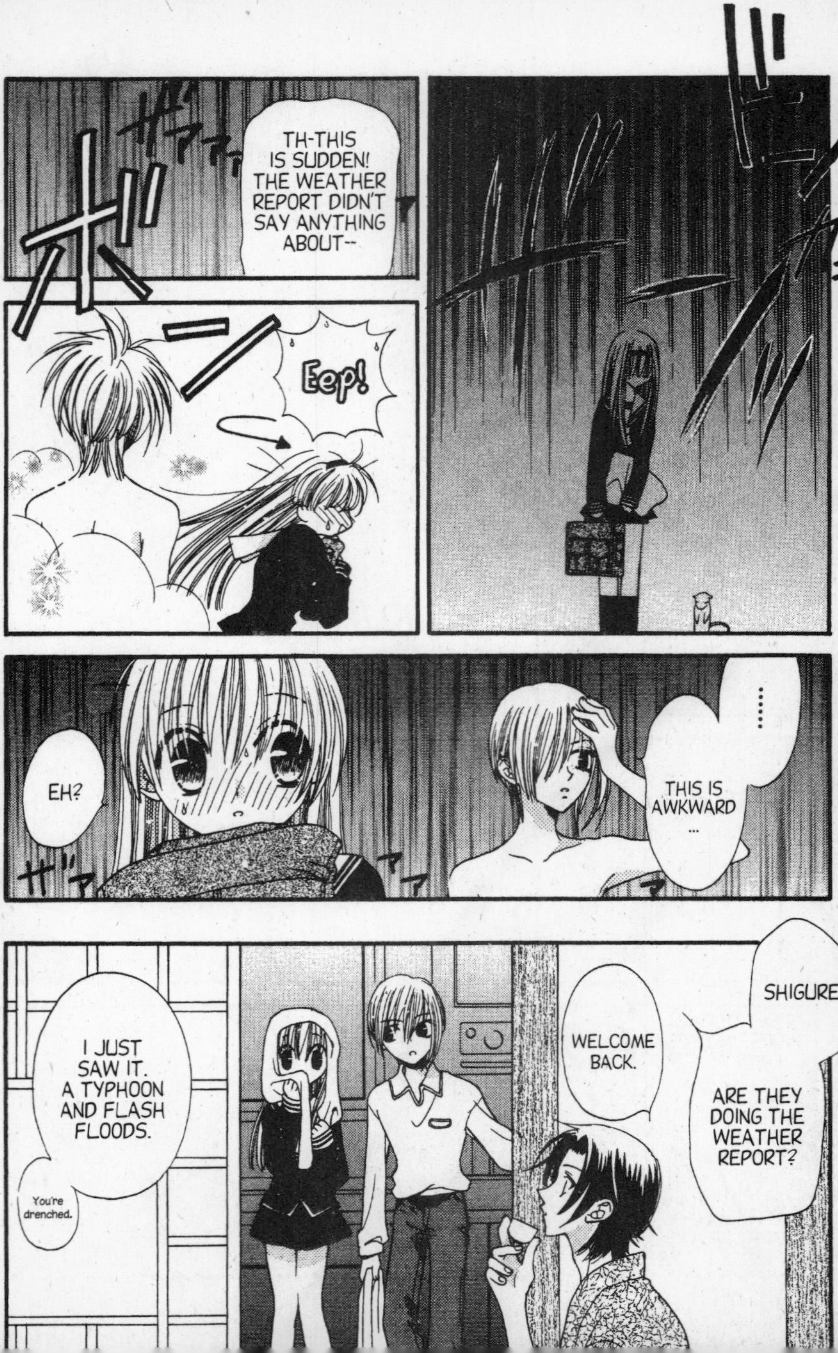
TH-THIS IS SUDDEN! THE WEATHER REPORT DIDN'T SAY ANYTHING ABOUT--
Eep!
......
THIS IS AWKWARD ...
EH?
SHIGURE!
WELCOME BACK.
ARE THEY DOING THE WEATHER REPORT?
I JUST SAW IT. A TYPHOON AND FLASH FLOODS.
You're drenched.

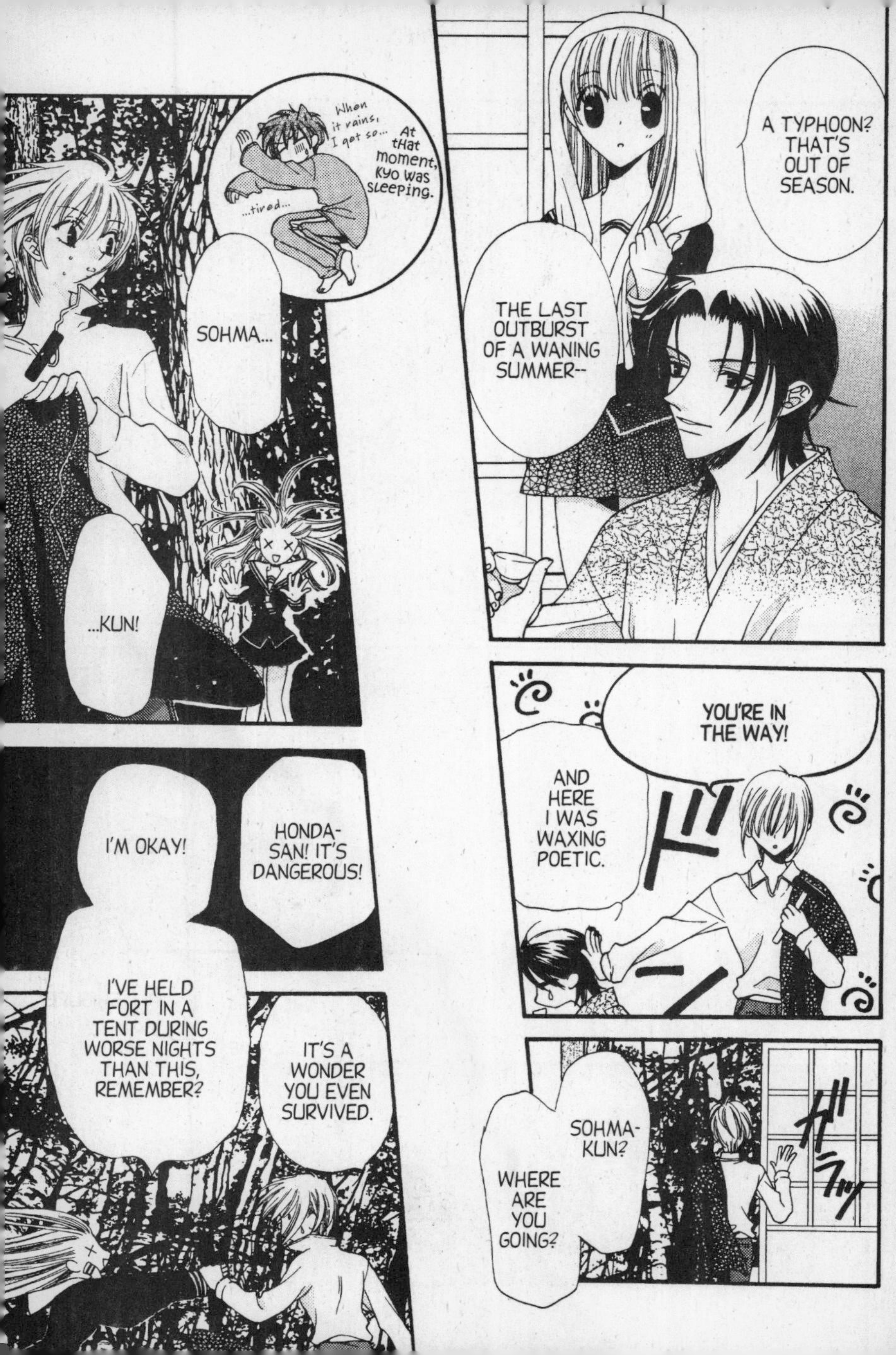
A TYPHOON? THAT'S OUT OF SEASON.
THE LAST OUTBURST OF A WANING SUMMER--
YOU'RE IN THE WAY!
AND HERE I WAS WAXING POETIC.
SOHMA-KUN?
WHERE ARE YOU GOING?
When it rains, I get so... ...tired...
At that moment, Kyo was sleeping.
SOHMA...
...KUN!
HONDA-SAN! IT'S DANGEROUS!
I'M OKAY!
I'VE HELD FORT IN A TENT DURING WORSE NIGHTS THAN THIS, REMEMBER?
IT'S A WONDER YOU EVEN SURVIVED.

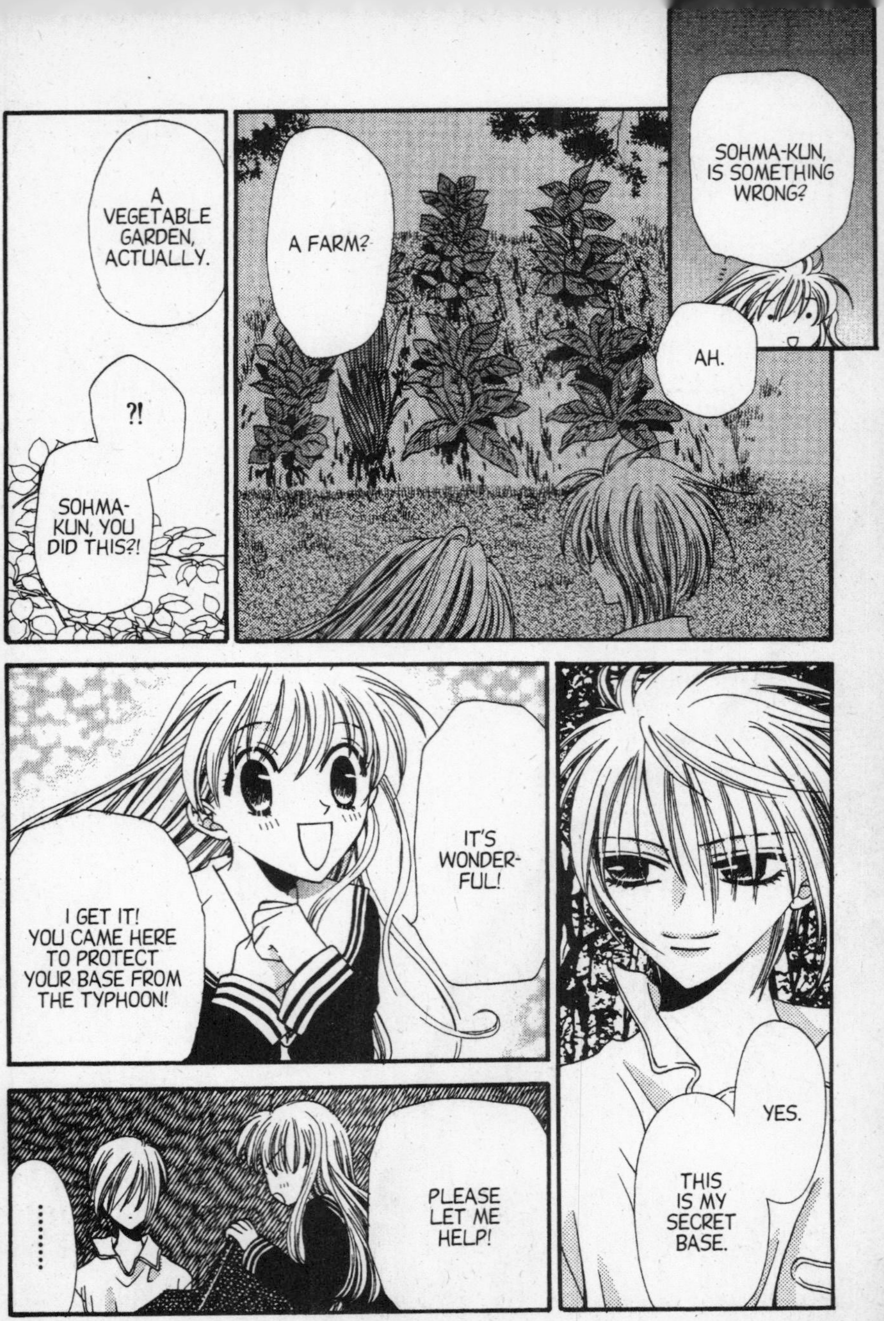
SOHMA-KUN, IS SOMETHING WRONG?
AH.
A FARM?
A VEGETABLE GARDEN, ACTUALLY.
?!
SOHMA-KUN, YOU DID THIS?!
YES.
THIS IS MY SECRET BASE.
IT'S WONDERFUL!
I GET IT! YOU CAME HERE TO PROTECT YOUR BASE FROM THE TYPHOON!
PLEASE LET ME HELP!
....

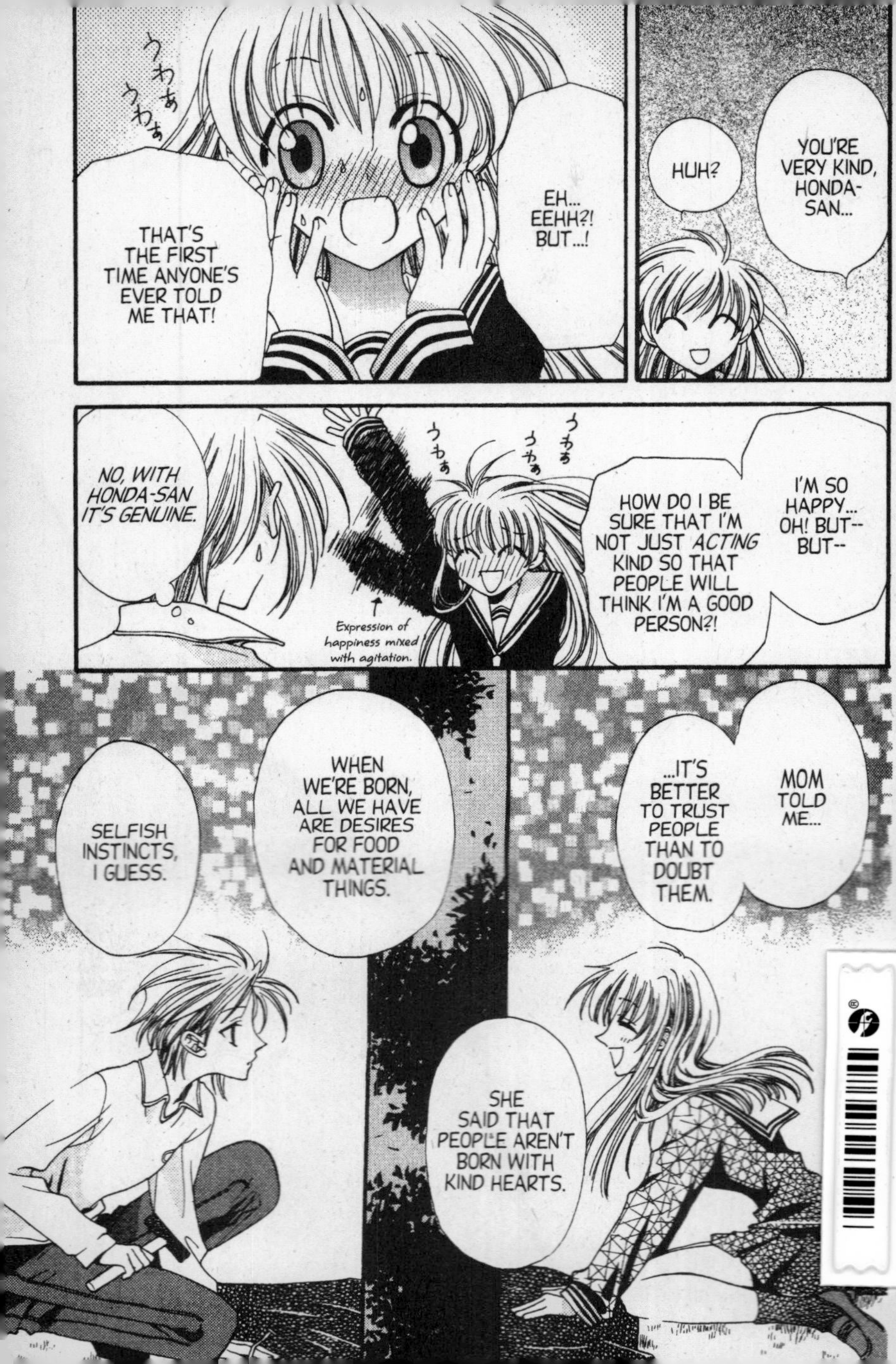
YOU'RE VERY KIND, HONDA-SAN...
HUH?
EH... EEHH?! BUT...!
THAT'S THE FIRST TIME ANYONE'S EVER TOLD ME THAT!
うわぁ うわぁ
I'M SO HAPPY... OH! BUT-- BUT--
HOW DO I BE SURE THAT I'M NOT JUST *ACTING* KIND SO THAT PEOPLE WILL THINK I'M A GOOD PERSON?!
うわぁ うわぁ うわぁ
NO, WITH HONDA-SAN IT'S GENUINE.
Expression of happiness mixed with agitation.
MOM TOLD ME...
...IT'S BETTER TO TRUST PEOPLE THAN TO DOUBT THEM.
SHE SAID THAT PEOPLE AREN'T BORN WITH KIND HEARTS.
WHEN WE'RE BORN, ALL WE HAVE ARE DESIRES FOR FOOD AND MATERIAL THINGS.
SELFISH INSTINCTS, I GUESS.

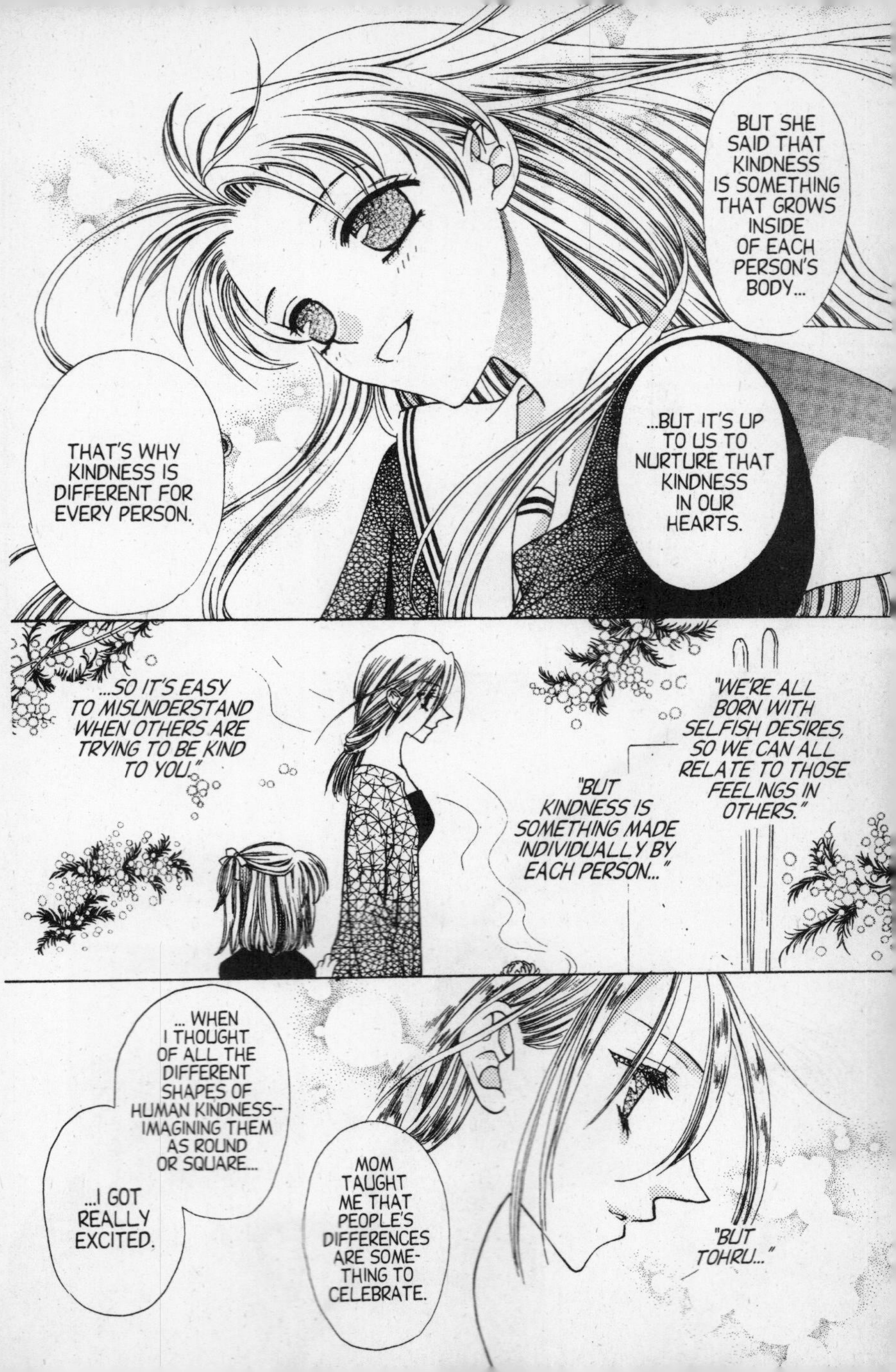
BUT SHE SAID THAT KINDNESS IS SOMETHING THAT GROWS INSIDE OF EACH PERSON'S BODY...
...BUT IT'S UP TO US TO NURTURE THAT KINDNESS IN OUR HEARTS.
THAT'S WHY KINDNESS IS DIFFERENT FOR EVERY PERSON.
"WE'RE ALL BORN WITH SELFISH DESIRES, SO WE CAN ALL RELATE TO THOSE FEELINGS IN OTHERS."
"BUT KINDNESS IS SOMETHING MADE INDIVIDUALLY BY EACH PERSON..."
...SO IT'S EASY TO MISUNDERSTAND WHEN OTHERS ARE TRYING TO BE KIND TO YOU."
"BUT TOHRU..."
MOM TAUGHT ME THAT PEOPLE'S DIFFERENCES ARE SOME-THING TO CELEBRATE.
... WHEN I THOUGHT OF ALL THE DIFFERENT SHAPES OF HUMAN KINDNESS--IMAGINING THEM AS ROUND OR SQUARE...
...I GOT REALLY EXCITED.

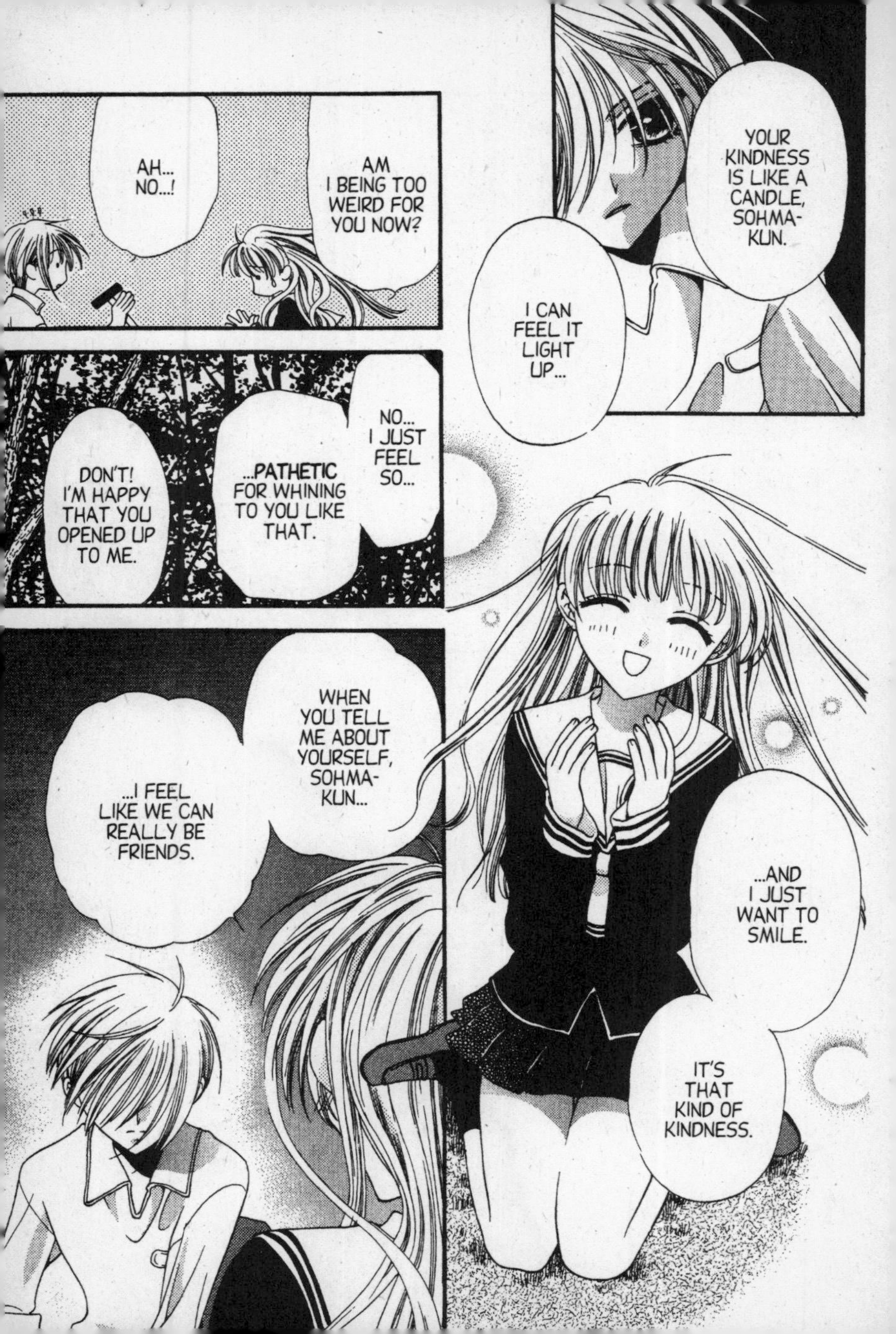
YOUR KINDNESS IS LIKE A CANDLE, SOHMA-KUN.
I CAN FEEL IT LIGHT UP...
AM I BEING TOO WEIRD FOR YOU NOW?
AH... NO...!
NO... I JUST FEEL SO...
...**PATHETIC** FOR WHINING TO YOU LIKE THAT.
DON'T! I'M HAPPY THAT YOU OPENED UP TO ME.
WHEN YOU TELL ME ABOUT YOURSELF, SOHMA-KUN...
...I FEEL LIKE WE CAN REALLY BE FRIENDS.
...AND I JUST WANT TO SMILE.
IT'S THAT KIND OF KINDNESS.

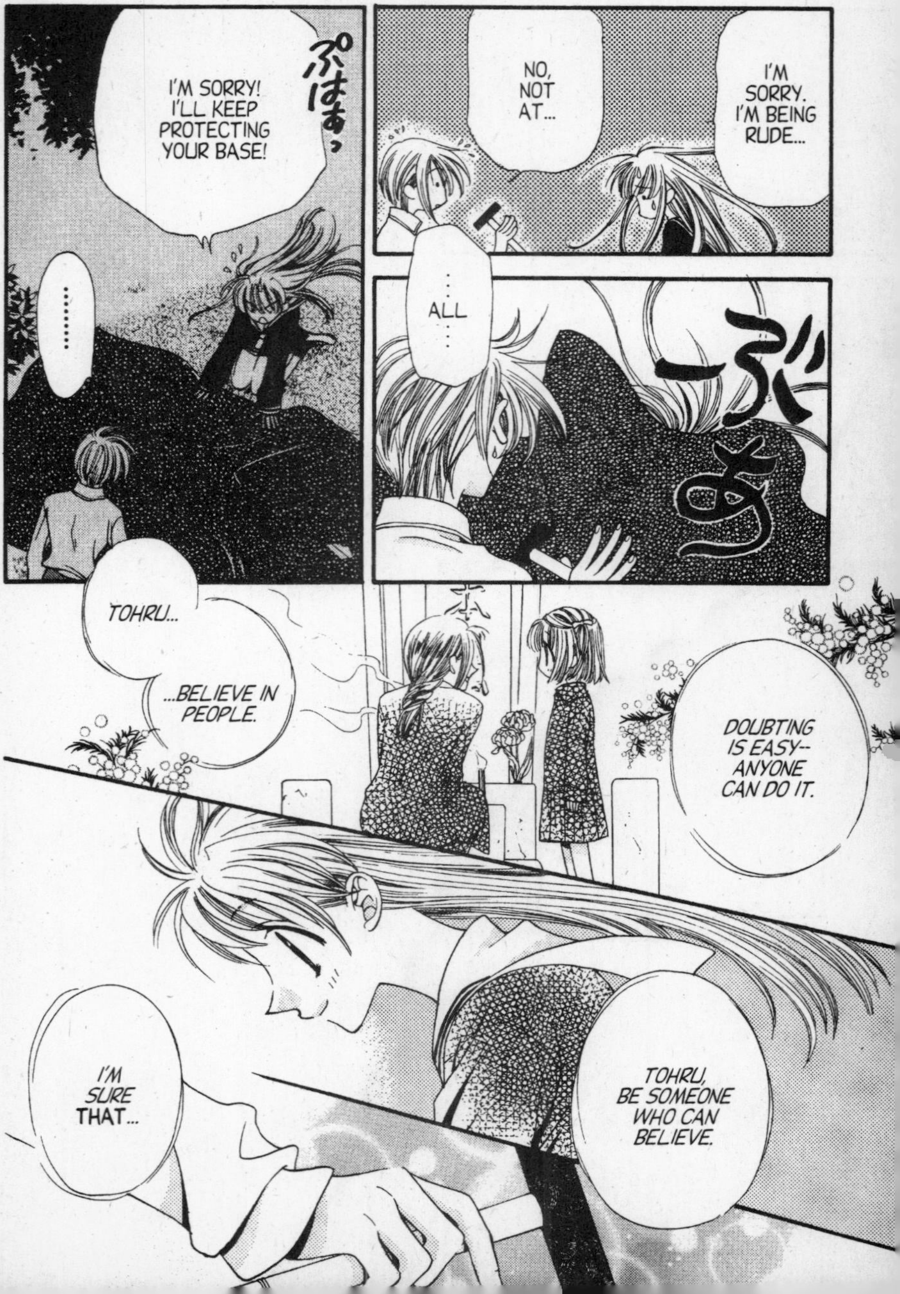
I'M SORRY. I'M BEING RUDE...
NO, NOT AT...
...ALL...
I'M SORRY! I'LL KEEP PROTECTING YOUR BASE!
ぷはぁっ
......
DOUBTING IS EASY-- ANYONE CAN DO IT.
TOHRU...
...BELIEVE IN PEOPLE.
TOHRU, BE SOMEONE WHO CAN BELIEVE.
I'M SURE THAT...

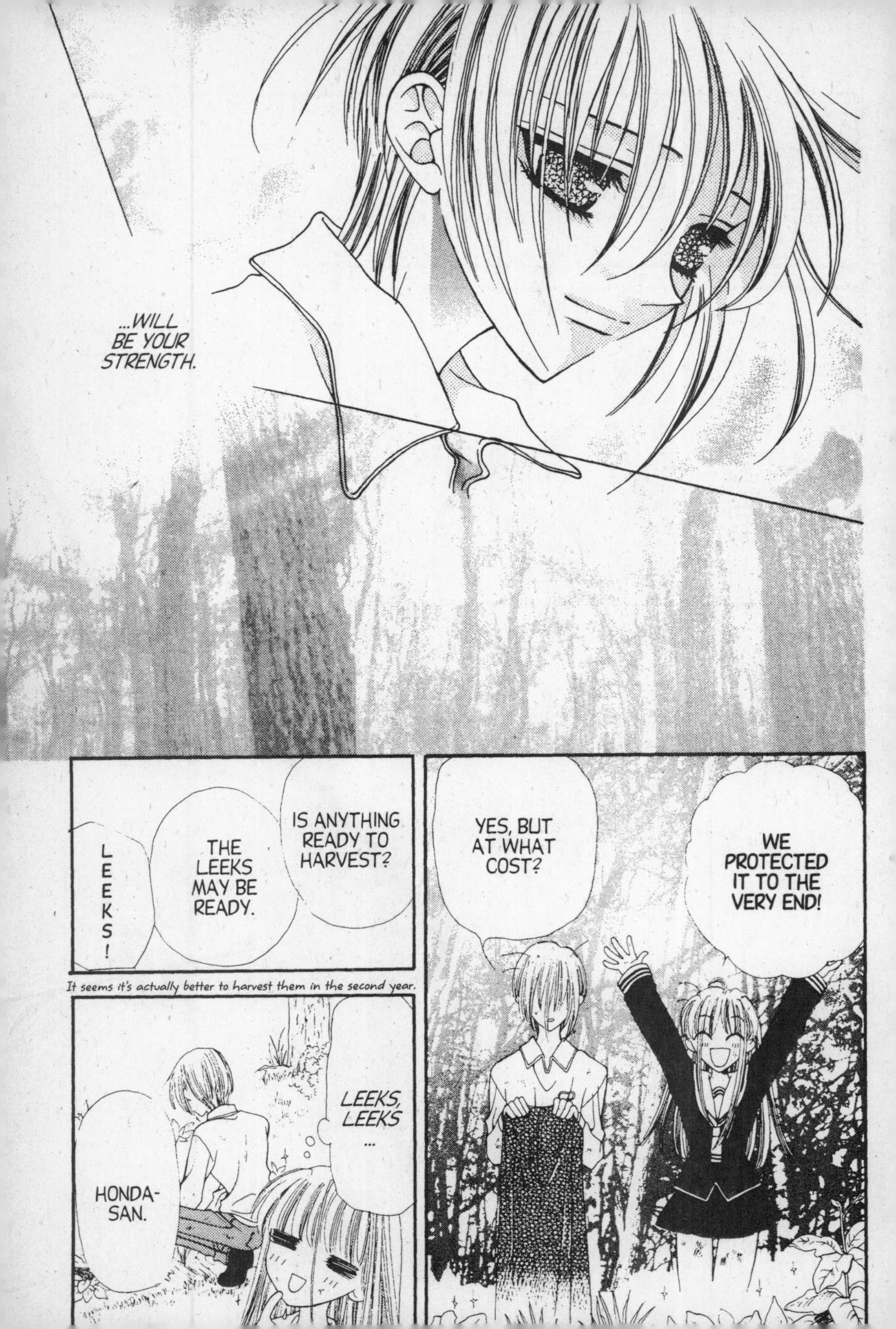
...WILL BE YOUR STRENGTH.
WE PROTECTED IT TO THE VERY END!
YES, BUT AT WHAT COST?
IS ANYTHING READY TO HARVEST?
THE LEEKS MAY BE READY.
LEEKS!
LEEKS, LEEKS ...
HONDA-SAN.
It seems it's actually better to harvest them in the second year.

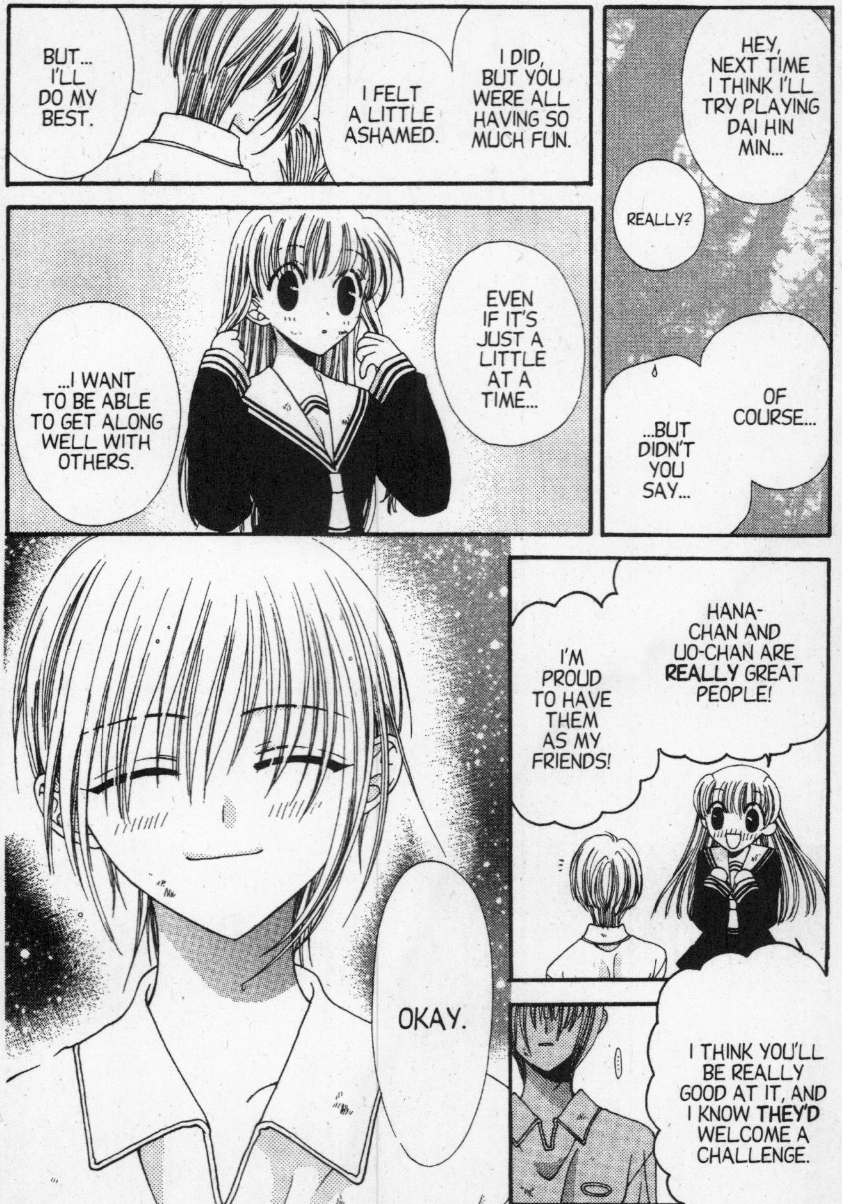
HEY, NEXT TIME I THINK I'LL TRY PLAYING DAI HIN MIN...
REALLY?
OF COURSE...
...BUT DIDN'T YOU SAY...
I DID, BUT YOU WERE ALL HAVING SO MUCH FUN.
I FELT A LITTLE ASHAMED.
BUT... I'LL DO MY BEST.
EVEN IF IT'S JUST A LITTLE AT A TIME...
...I WANT TO BE ABLE TO GET ALONG WELL WITH OTHERS.
HANA-CHAN AND UO-CHAN ARE **REALLY** GREAT PEOPLE!
I'M PROUD TO HAVE THEM AS MY FRIENDS!
I THINK YOU'LL BE REALLY GOOD AT IT, AND I KNOW **THEY'D** WELCOME A CHALLENGE.
OKAY.

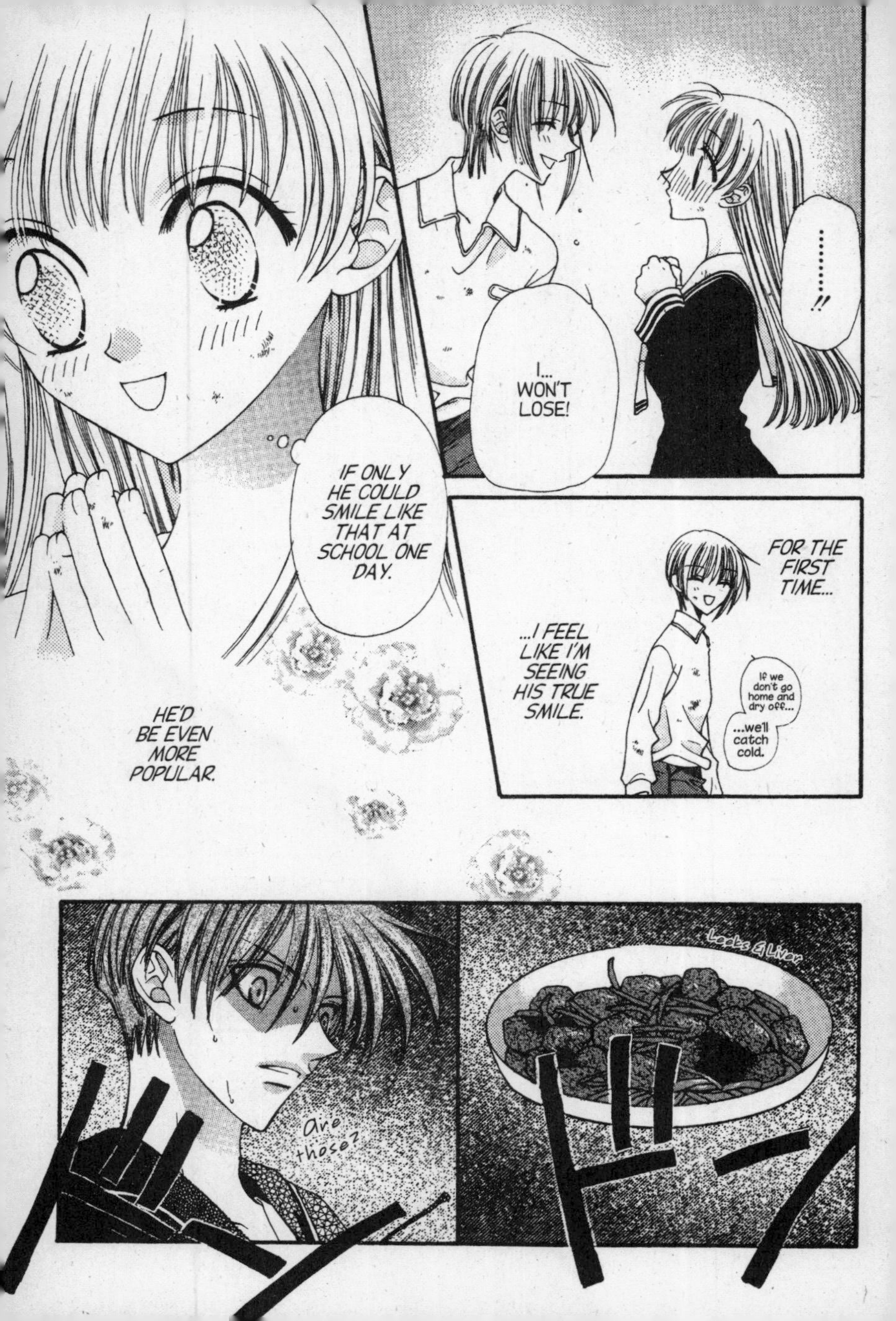

......!!
I... WON'T LOSE!
FOR THE FIRST TIME...
...I FEEL LIKE I'M SEEING HIS TRUE SMILE.
If we don't go home and dry off...
...we'll catch cold.
IF ONLY HE COULD SMILE LIKE THAT AT SCHOOL ONE DAY.
HE'D BE EVEN MORE POPULAR.
Leeks & Liver
Are those?

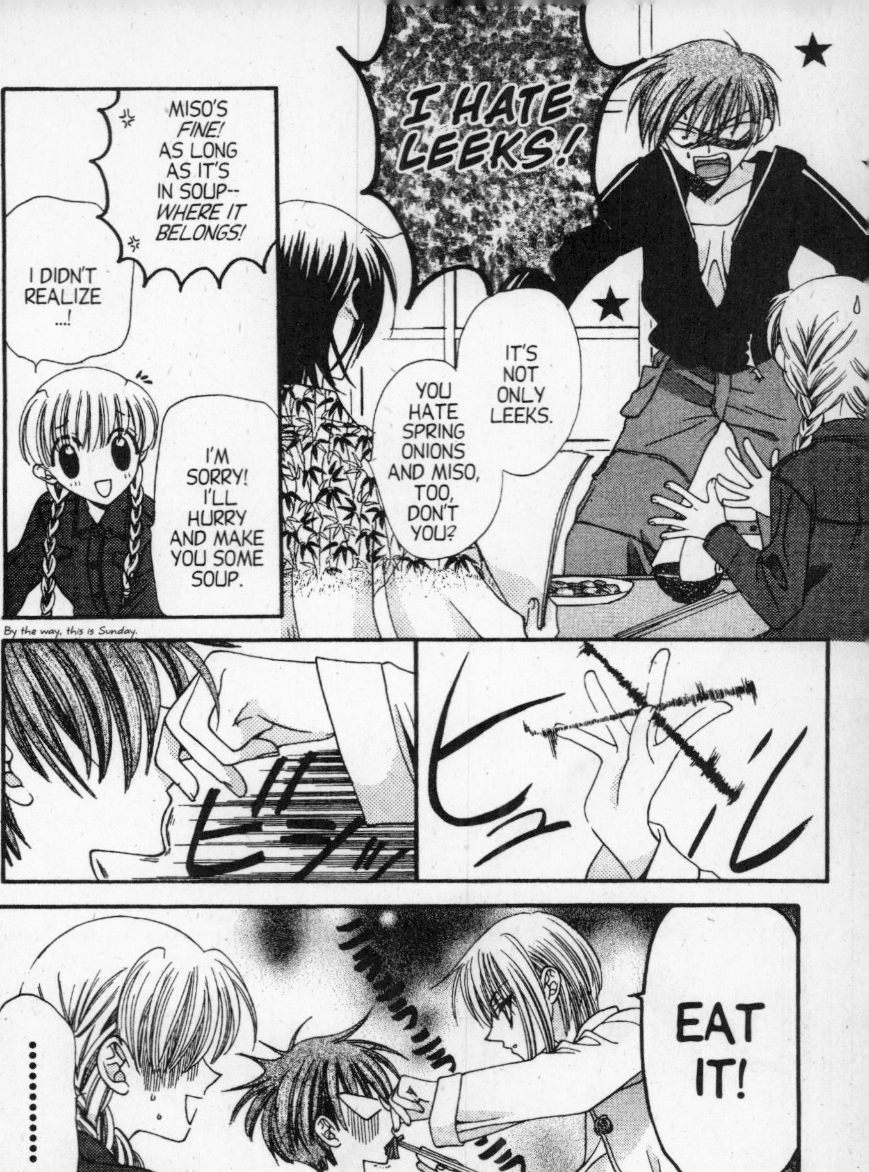
I HATE LEEKS!
IT'S NOT ONLY LEEKS.
YOU HATE SPRING ONIONS AND MISO, TOO, DON'T YOU?
MISO'S FINE! AS LONG AS IT'S IN SOUP-- WHERE IT BELONGS!
I DIDN'T REALIZE ...!
I'M SORRY! I'LL HURRY AND MAKE YOU SOME SOUP.
By the way, this is Sunday.
EAT IT!
....

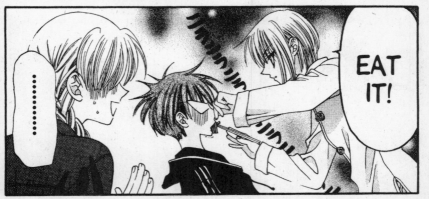

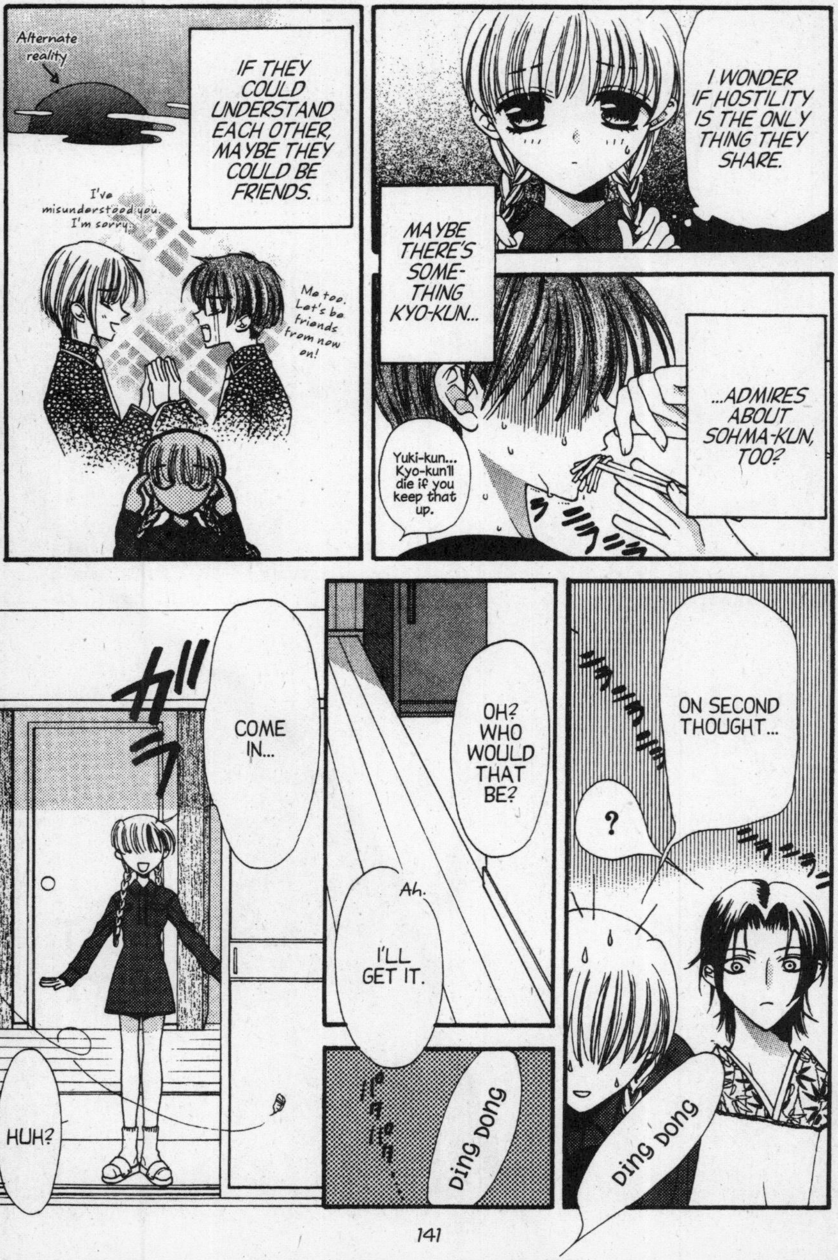
I WONDER IF HOSTILITY IS THE ONLY THING THEY SHARE.
MAYBE THERE'S SOME-THING KYO-KUN...
...ADMIRES ABOUT SOHMA-KUN, TOO?
Yuki-kun... Kyo-kun'll die if you keep that up.
IF THEY COULD UNDERSTAND EACH OTHER, MAYBE THEY COULD BE FRIENDS.
Alternate reality
I've misunderstood you. I'm sorry.
Me too. Let's be friends from now on!
ON SECOND THOUGHT...
?
DING DONG
OH? WHO WOULD THAT BE?
Ah.
I'LL GET IT.
DING DONG
COME IN...
HUH?

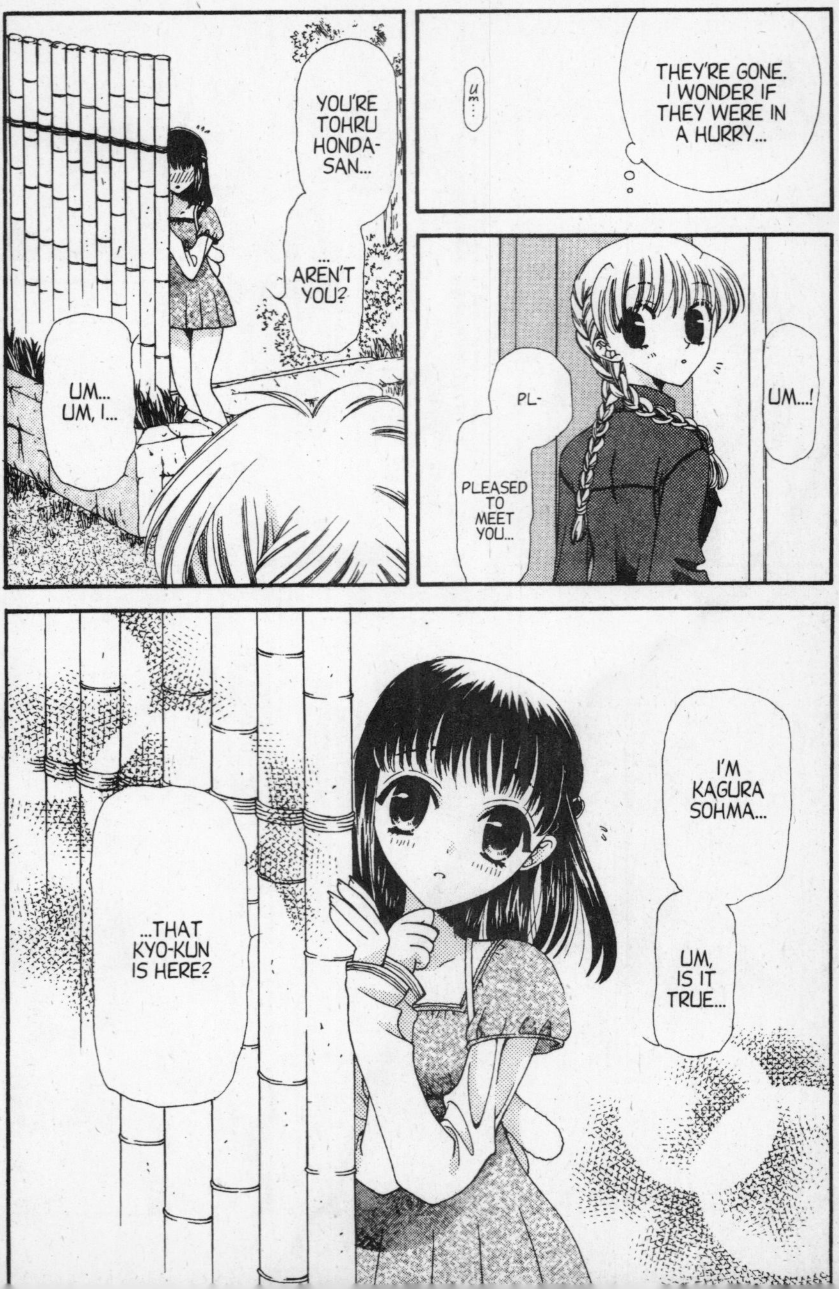
THEY'RE GONE. I WONDER IF THEY WERE IN A HURRY...
um...
UM...!
PL-
PLEASED TO MEET YOU...
YOU'RE TOHRU HONDA-SAN...
...AREN'T YOU?
UM... UM, I...
I'M KAGURA SOHMA...
UM, IS IT TRUE...
...THAT KYO-KUN IS HERE?

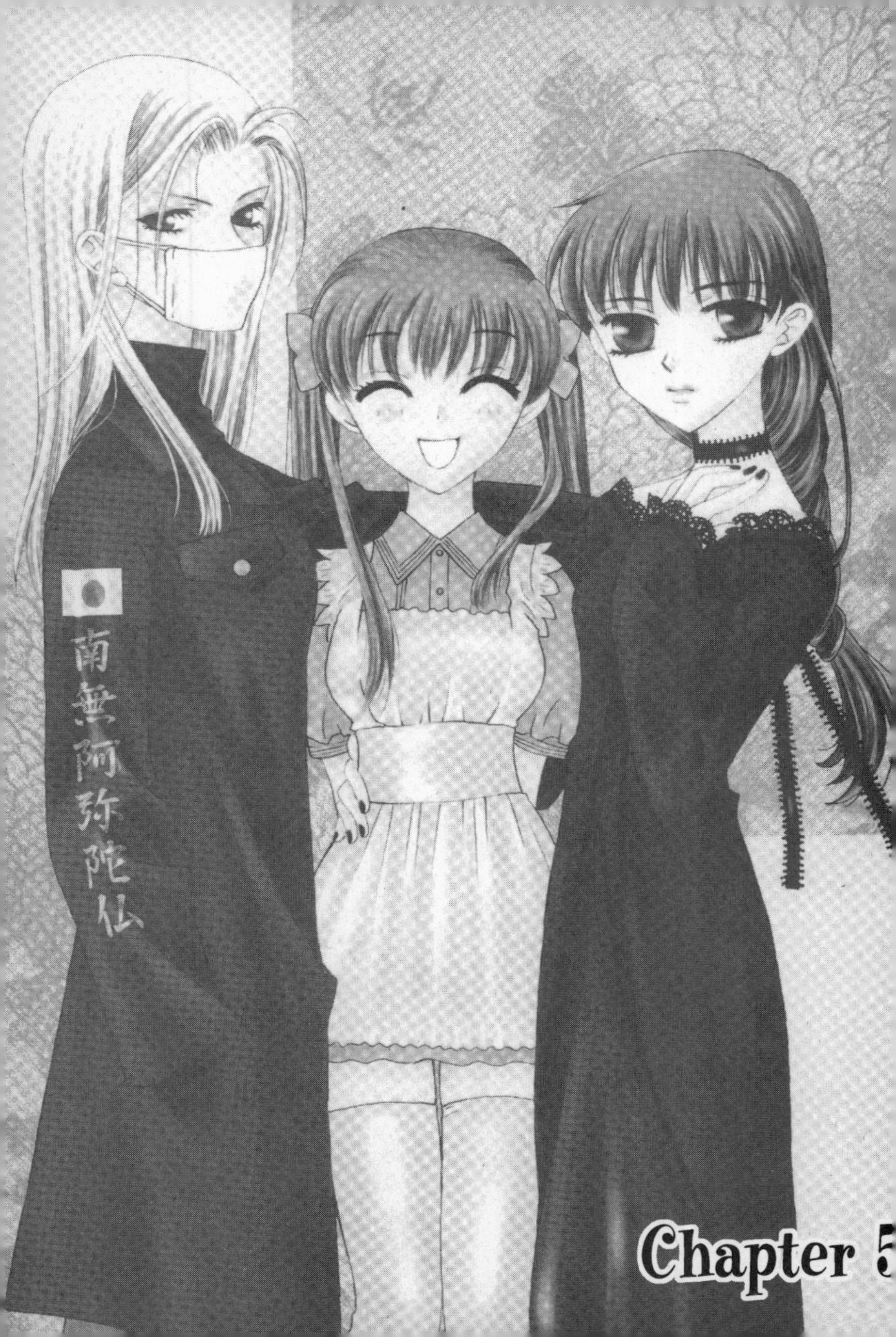
南無阿弥陀仏
Chapter 5

Omake Theater 3: Are you kidding or are you serious?

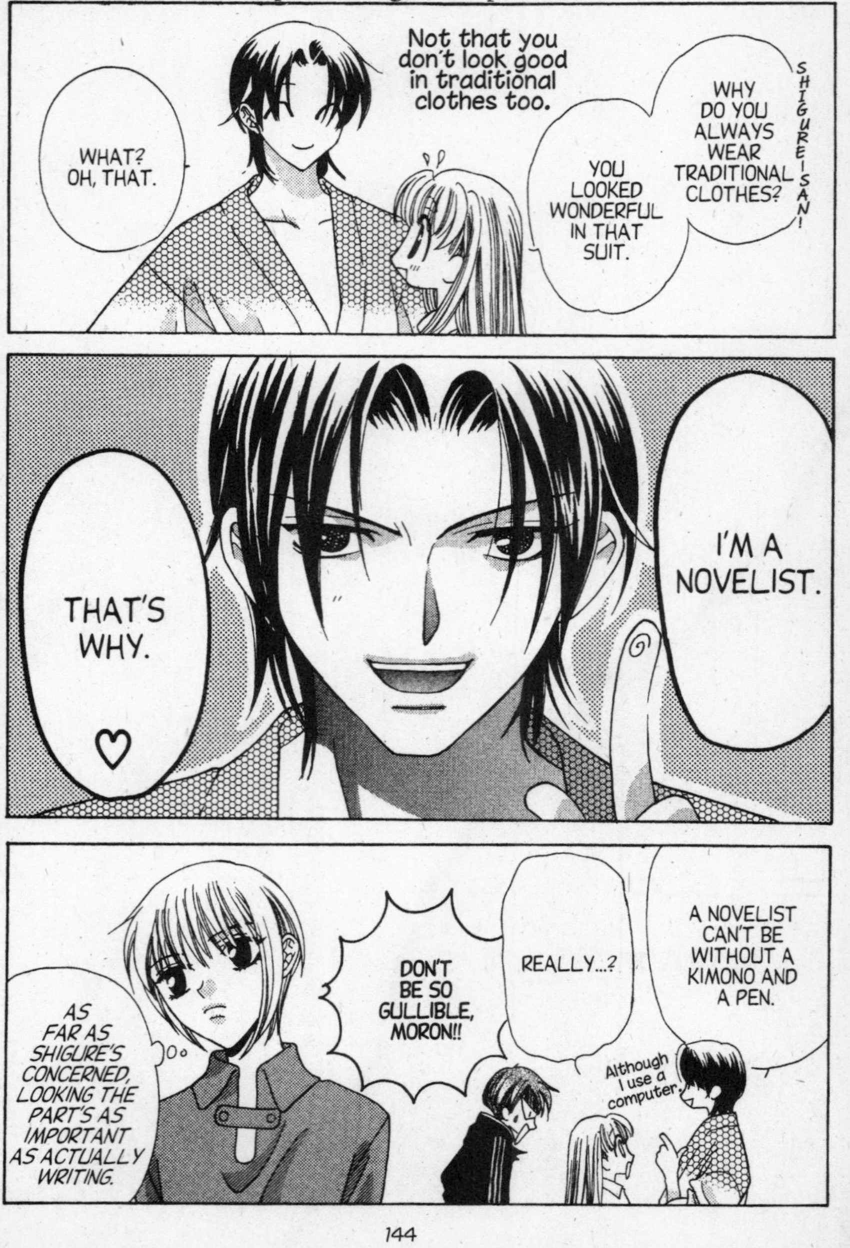
SHIGURE-SAN!
WHY DO YOU ALWAYS WEAR TRADITIONAL CLOTHES?
YOU LOOKED WONDERFUL IN THAT SUIT.
Not that you don't look good in traditional clothes too.
WHAT? OH, THAT.
I'M A NOVELIST.
THAT'S WHY. ♡
A NOVELIST CAN'T BE WITHOUT A KIMONO AND A PEN.
Although I use a computer.
REALLY...?
DON'T BE SO GULLIBLE, MORON!!
AS FAR AS SHIGURE'S CONCERNED, LOOKING THE PART'S AS IMPORTANT AS ACTUALLY WRITING.

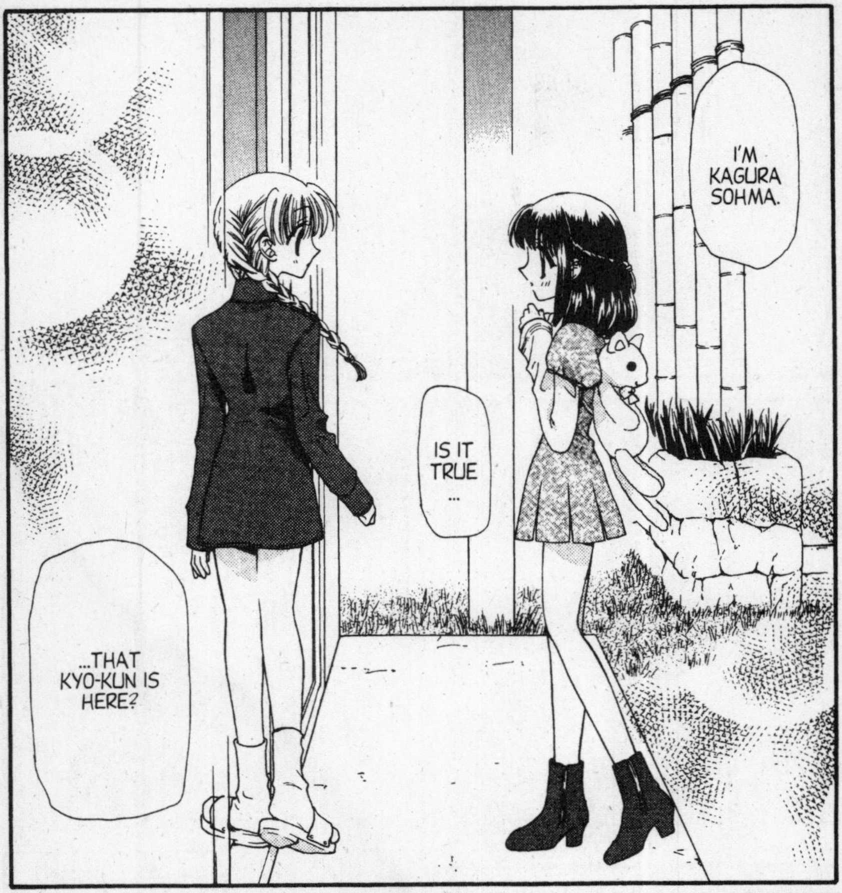
I'M KAGURA SOHMA.
IS IT TRUE ...
...THAT KYO-KUN IS HERE?

ULTRA SPECIAL BLAH BLAH BLAH, NUMBER 4.

I couldn't help wanting to draw a girl like Kagura. So I'm pleased (ha ha). I thought the opinions on her would be divided between, "She's hilarious!" and "Why does she hit him? That's so mean!" and I was right. She hits him because she loves him. It's the ultimate expression of love (ha ha).

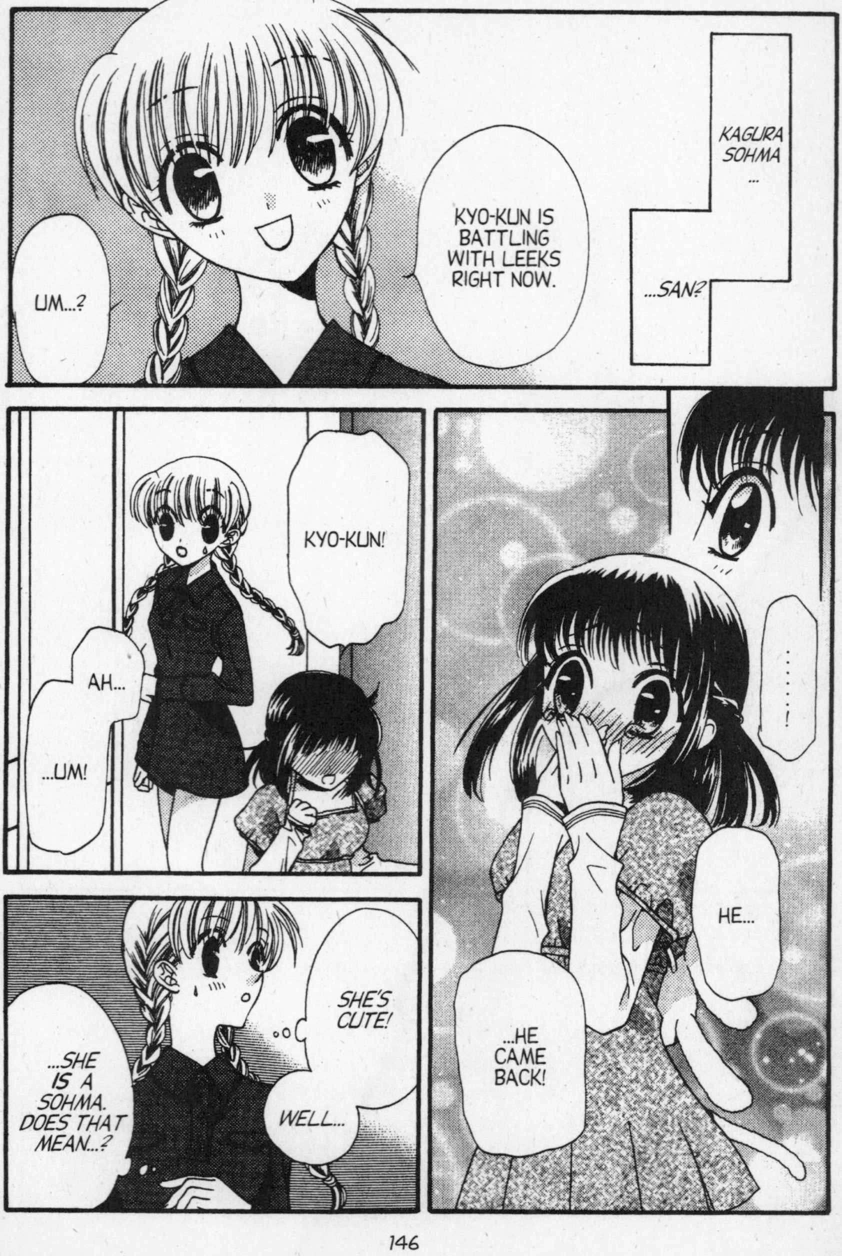
KAGURA SOHMA ...
...SAN?
KYO-KUN IS BATTLING WITH LEEKS RIGHT NOW.
UM...?
......!
HE...
...HE CAME BACK!
KYO-KUN!
AH...
...UM!
SHE'S CUTE!
WELL...
...SHE IS A SOHMA. DOES THAT MEAN...?

Number 6:

I have the Internet now. I feel weird about the Internet. I think it's a world that's there but not, and fake but real; I don't know what to call it (ha ha). It reminds me of "Soul Hackers." Yeah! I'm about half way through that game right now. Oh, no... I'm bubbling again- stay on target! I'm really getting into surfing around and checking out people's home pages. Home pages, huh...? I think I'd like to make one of my own, but I don't know how. If someone started one for me...? (ha ha) My home page would probably just talk about video games all the time!

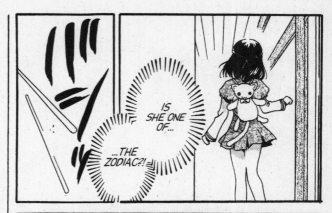

IS SHE ONE OF...
...THE ZODIAC?!
CUT THAT OUT!
IF I SAID I'M NOT GONNA EAT LEEKS, I'M NOT GONNA EAT THEM!
IF YOU HAVE A PROBLEM WITH IT, GET OUT.
YOU DON'T HAVE TO CONVINCE ME TO GET OUT OF THIS HOUSE!
THEY FIGHT LIKE A MARRIED COUPLE.
NOW, NOW... YUKI-KUN, KYO-KUN...

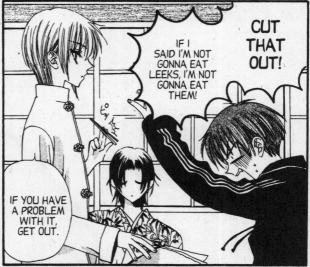

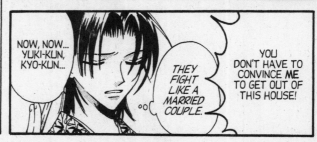

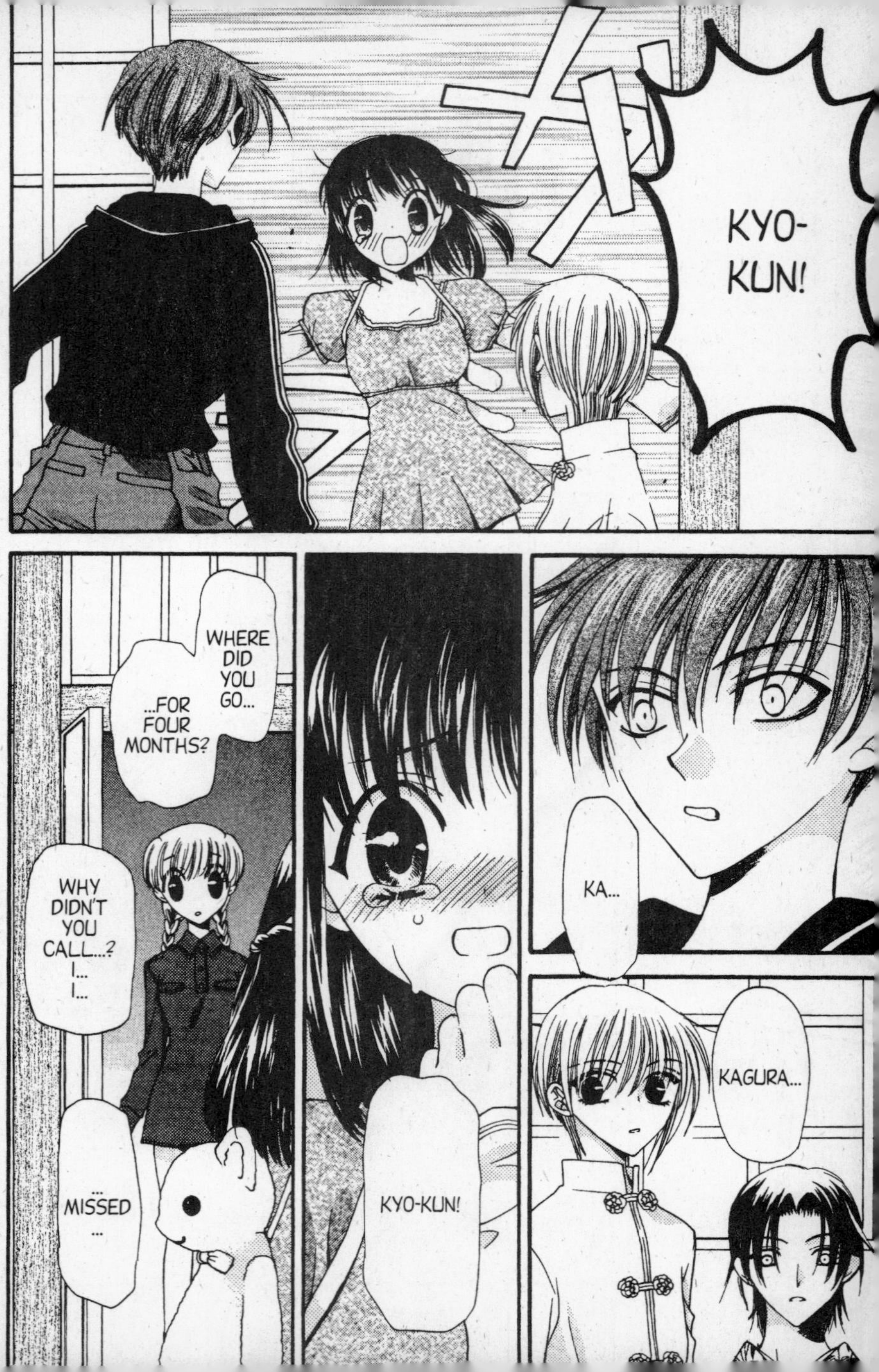
KYO-KUN!
KA...
KAGURA...
KYO-KUN!
WHERE DID YOU GO...
...FOR FOUR MONTHS?
WHY DIDN'T YOU CALL...? I... I...
... MISSED ...

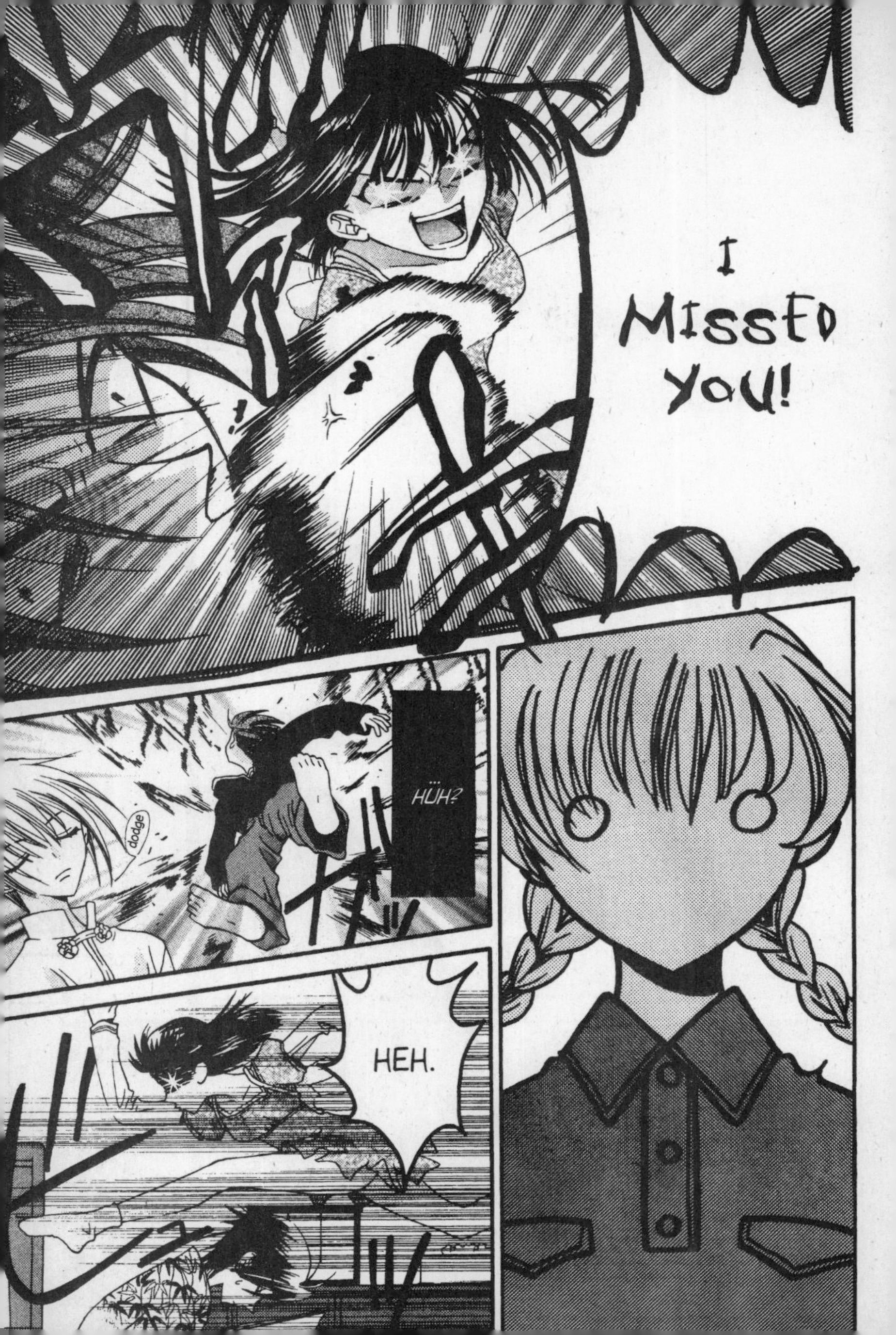
I MISSED YOU!
HÜH?
dodge
HEH.

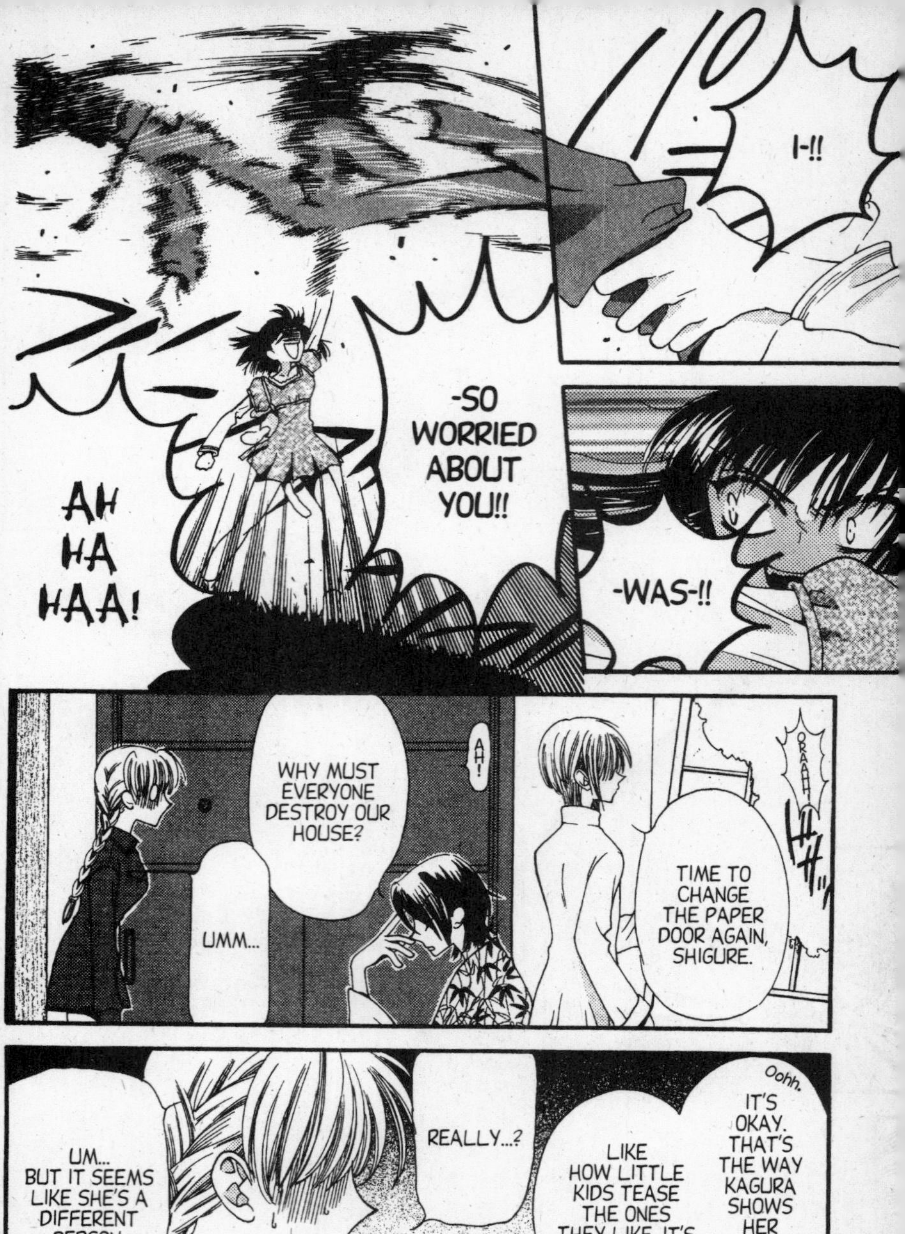
I-!!
-WAS-!!
-SO WORRIED ABOUT YOU!!
AH HA HAA!
ORAAAH
TIME TO CHANGE THE PAPER DOOR AGAIN, SHIGURE.
AH!
WHY MUST EVERYONE DESTROY OUR HOUSE?
UMM...
Oohh.
IT'S OKAY. THAT'S THE WAY KAGURA SHOWS HER LOVE.
LIKE HOW LITTLE KIDS TEASE THE ONES THEY LIKE. IT'S LIKE THAT.
REALLY...?
UM... BUT IT SEEMS LIKE SHE'S A DIFFERENT PERSON.

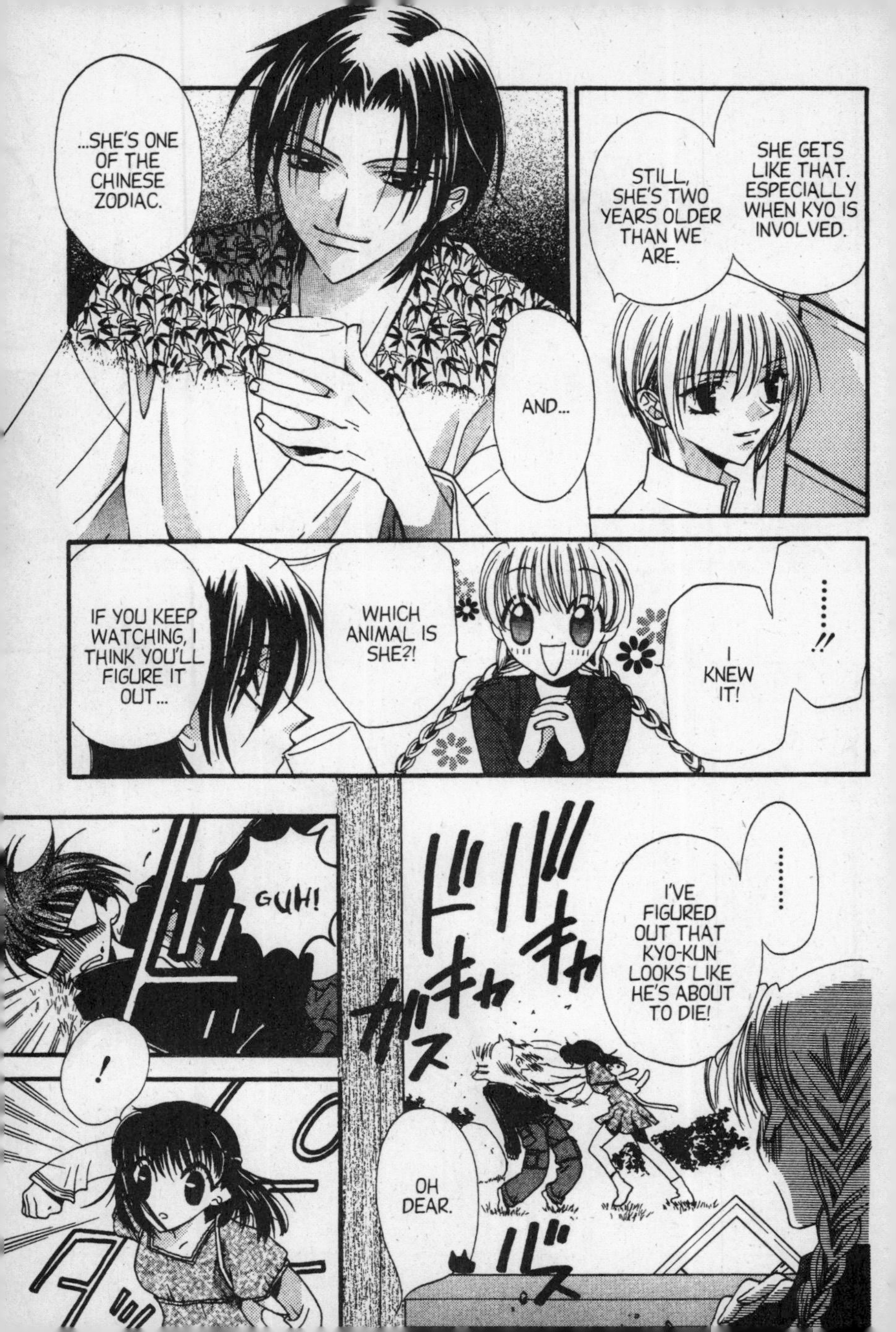
SHE GETS LIKE THAT. ESPECIALLY WHEN KYO IS INVOLVED.
STILL, SHE'S TWO YEARS OLDER THAN WE ARE.
AND...
...SHE'S ONE OF THE CHINESE ZODIAC.
......!!
I KNEW IT!
WHICH ANIMAL IS SHE?!
IF YOU KEEP WATCHING, I THINK YOU'LL FIGURE IT OUT...
......
I'VE FIGURED OUT THAT KYO-KUN LOOKS LIKE HE'S ABOUT TO DIE!
ドド
キャキャ
ガス
OH DEAR.
ドス
GUH!
!

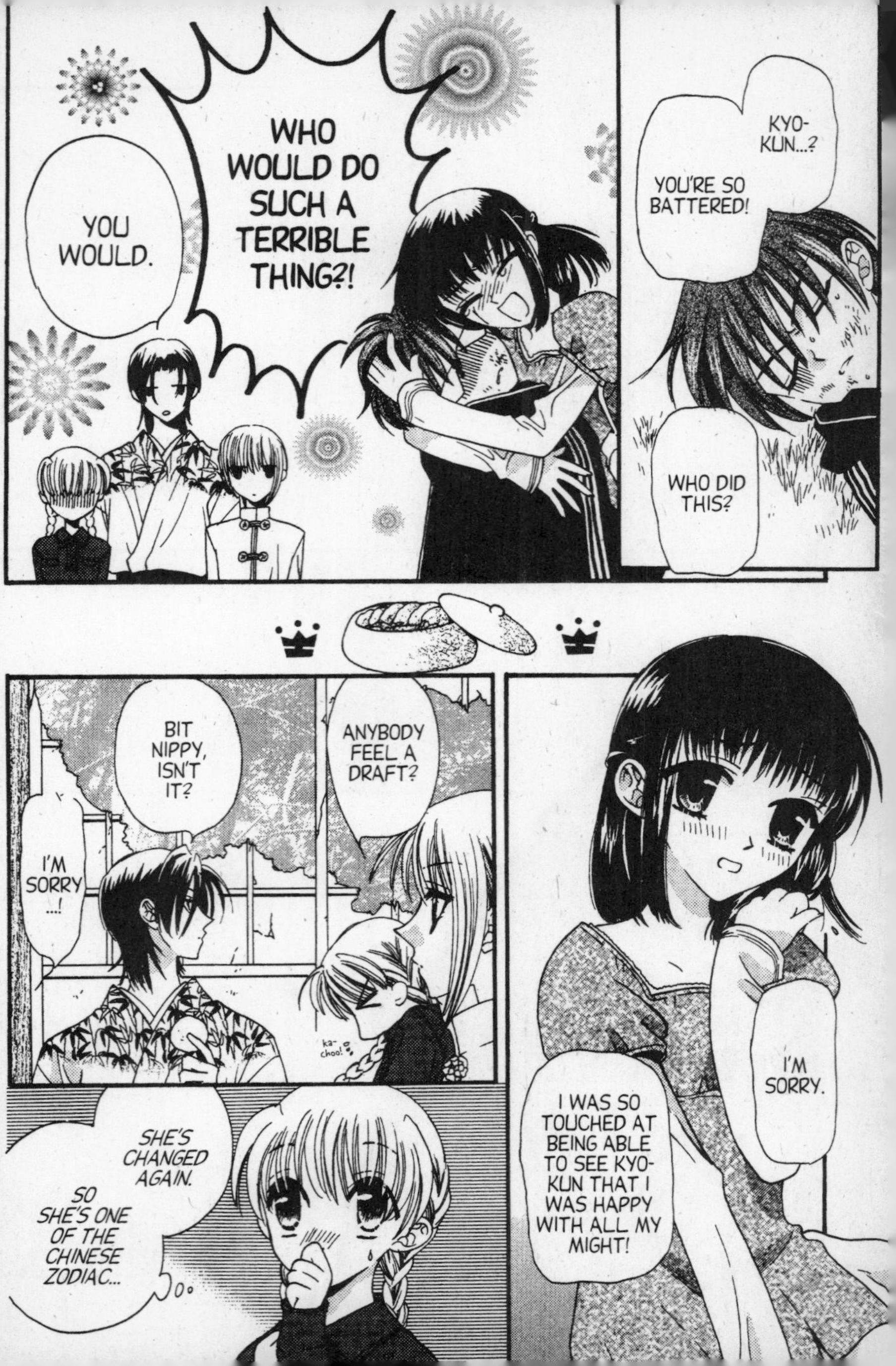
KYO-KUN...?
YOU'RE SO BATTERED!
WHO DID THIS?
WHO WOULD DO SUCH A TERRIBLE THING?!
YOU WOULD.
I'M SORRY.
I WAS SO TOUCHED AT BEING ABLE TO SEE KYO-KUN THAT I WAS HAPPY WITH ALL MY MIGHT!
ANYBODY FEEL A DRAFT?
BIT NIPPY, ISN'T IT?
I'M SORRY...!
ka-choo!
SHE'S CHANGED AGAIN.
SO SHE'S ONE OF THE CHINESE ZODIAC...

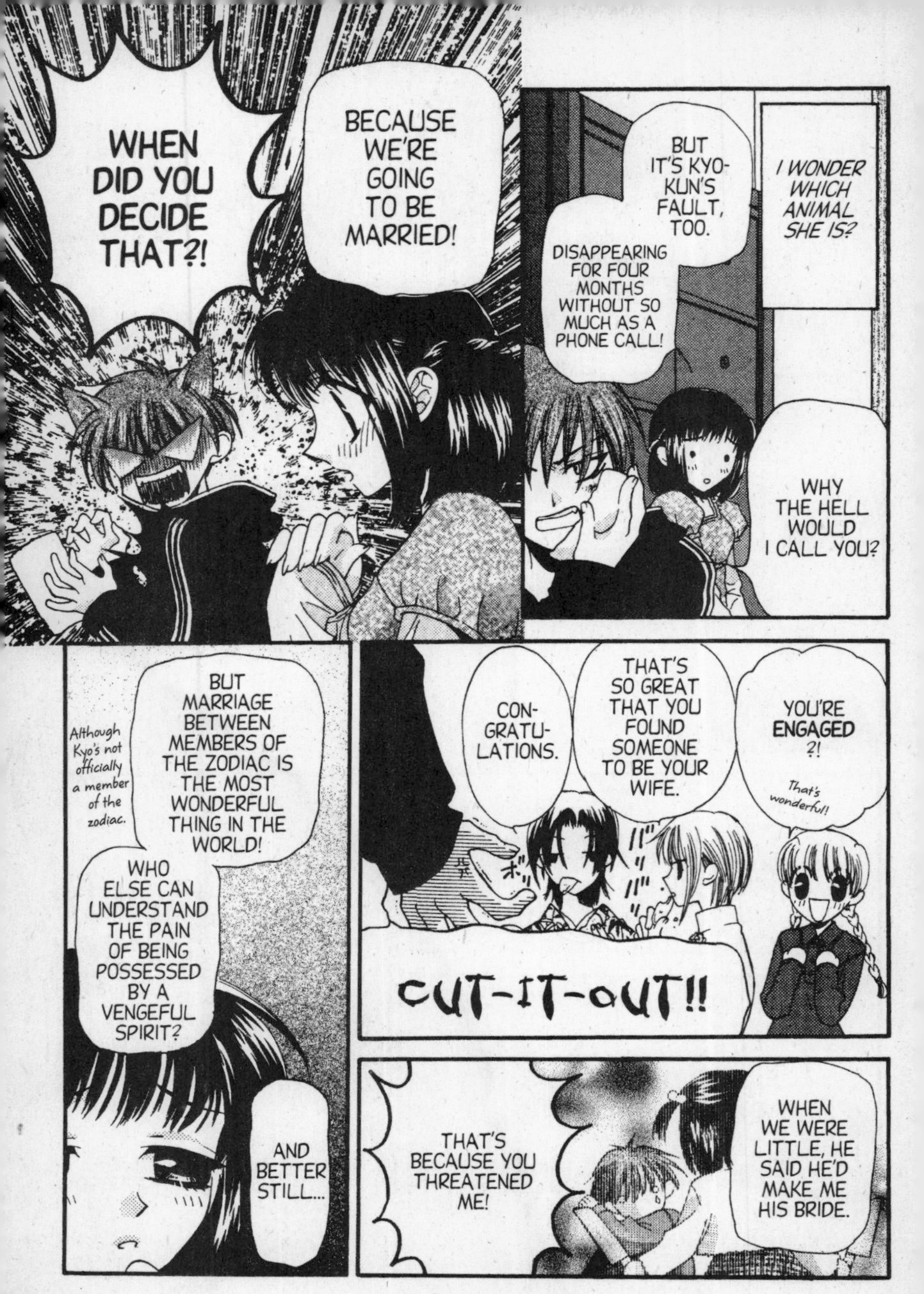
I WONDER WHICH ANIMAL SHE IS?
BUT IT'S KYO-KUN'S FAULT, TOO.
DISAPPEARING FOR FOUR MONTHS WITHOUT SO MUCH AS A PHONE CALL!
WHY THE HELL WOULD I CALL YOU?
BECAUSE WE'RE GOING TO BE MARRIED!
WHEN DID YOU DECIDE THAT?!
YOU'RE ENGAGED?!
That's wonderful!
THAT'S SO GREAT THAT YOU FOUND SOMEONE TO BE YOUR WIFE.
CON-GRATU-LATIONS.
CUT-IT-OUT!!
WHEN WE WERE LITTLE, HE SAID HE'D MAKE ME HIS BRIDE.
THAT'S BECAUSE YOU THREATENED ME!
BUT MARRIAGE BETWEEN MEMBERS OF THE ZODIAC IS THE MOST WONDERFUL THING IN THE WORLD!
Although Kyo's not officially a member of the zodiac.
WHO ELSE CAN UNDERSTAND THE PAIN OF BEING POSSESSED BY A VENGEFUL SPIRIT?
AND BETTER STILL...

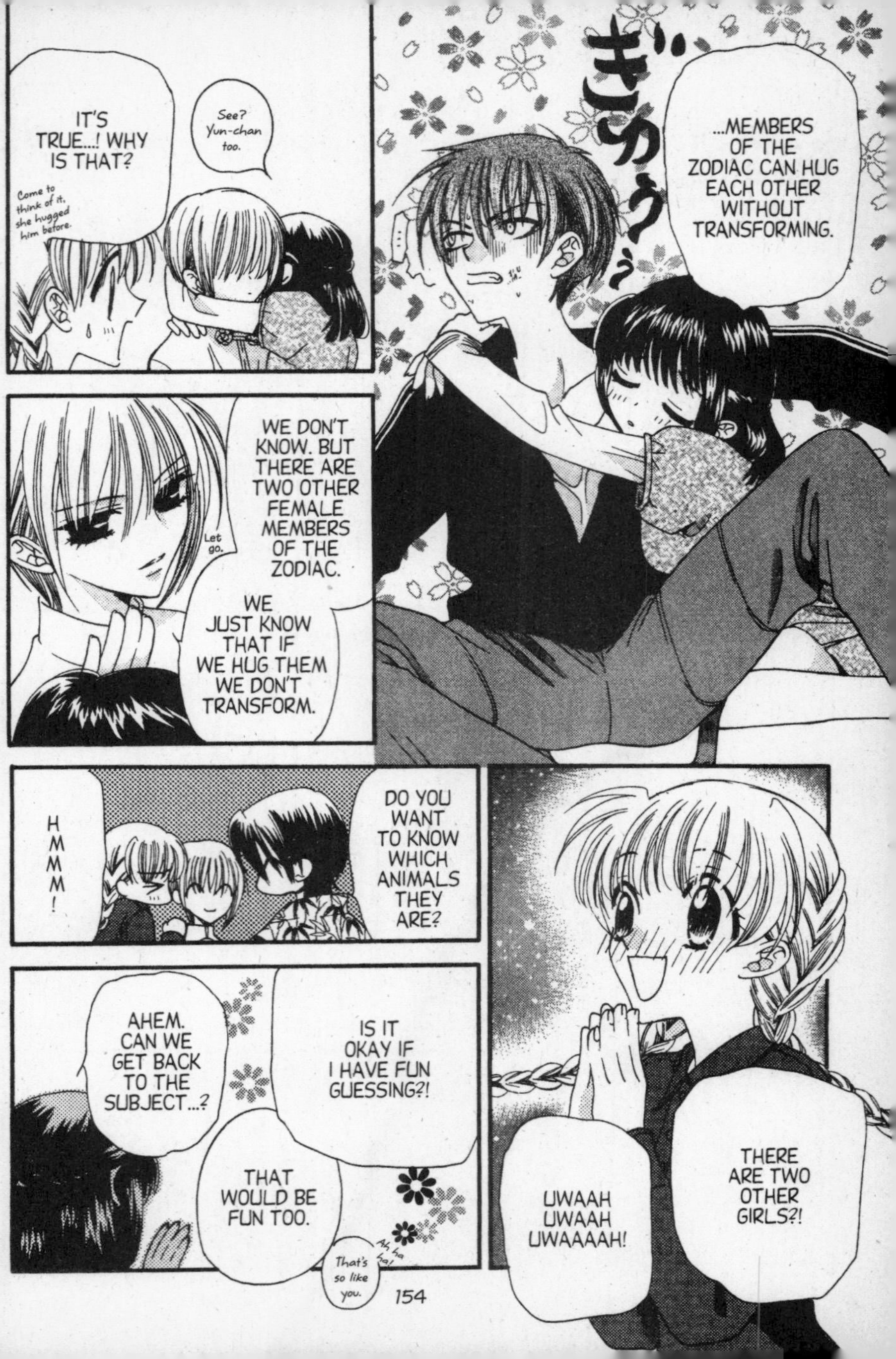
ぎゅう〜
...MEMBERS OF THE ZODIAC CAN HUG EACH OTHER WITHOUT TRANSFORMING.
See? Yun-chan too.
IT'S TRUE...! WHY IS THAT?
Come to think of it, she hugged him before.
WE DON'T KNOW. BUT THERE ARE TWO OTHER FEMALE MEMBERS OF THE ZODIAC.
Let go.
WE JUST KNOW THAT IF WE HUG THEM WE DON'T TRANSFORM.
THERE ARE TWO OTHER GIRLS?!
UWAAH UWAAH UWAAAAH!
DO YOU WANT TO KNOW WHICH ANIMALS THEY ARE?
HMMM!
IS IT OKAY IF I HAVE FUN GUESSING?!
AHEM. CAN WE GET BACK TO THE SUBJECT...?
THAT WOULD BE FUN TOO.
Ah ha ha!
That's so like you.

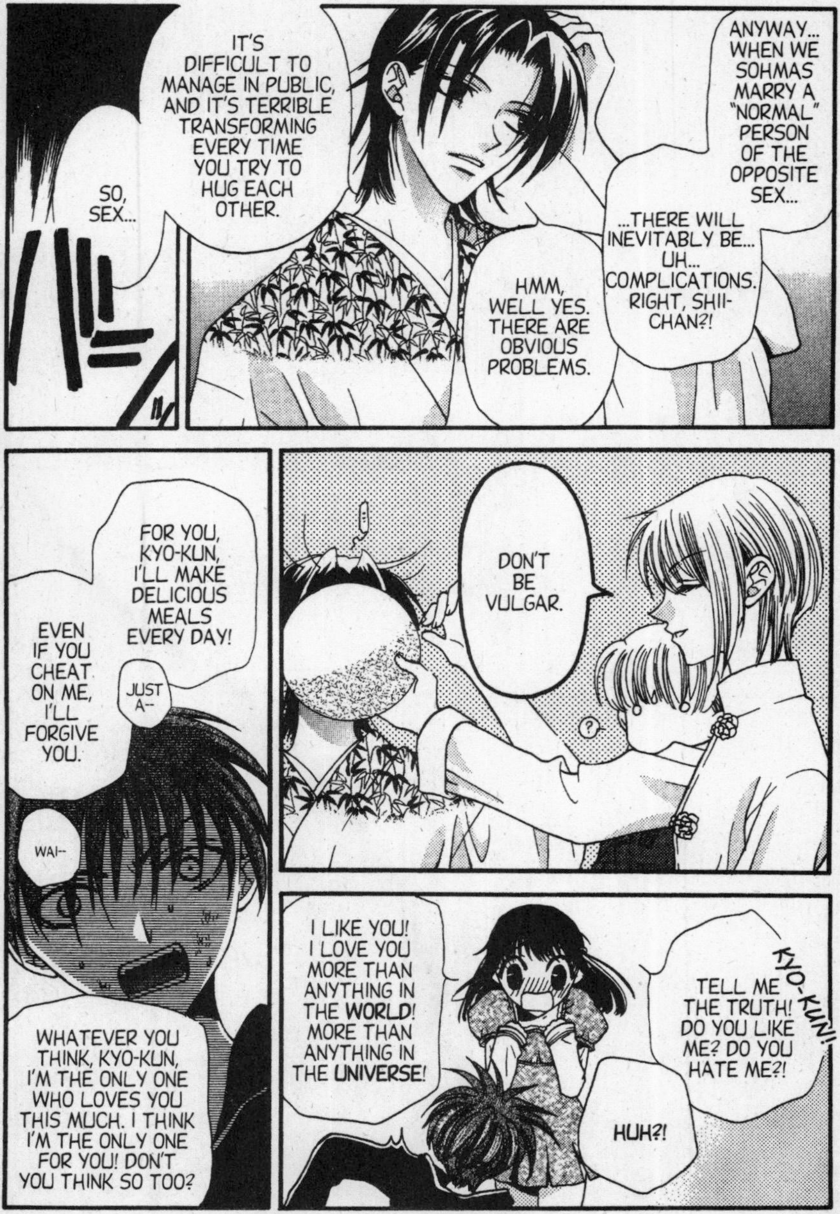
ANYWAY... WHEN WE SOHMAS MARRY A "NORMAL" PERSON OF THE OPPOSITE SEX...
...THERE WILL INEVITABLY BE... UH... COMPLICATIONS. RIGHT, SHII-CHAN?!
HMM, WELL YES. THERE ARE OBVIOUS PROBLEMS.
IT'S DIFFICULT TO MANAGE IN PUBLIC, AND IT'S TERRIBLE TRANSFORMING EVERY TIME YOU TRY TO HUG EACH OTHER.
SO, SEX...
...
DON'T BE VULGAR.
?
KYO-KUN!!
TELL ME THE TRUTH! DO YOU LIKE ME? DO YOU HATE ME?!
HUH?!
I LIKE YOU! I LOVE YOU MORE THAN ANYTHING IN THE **WORLD**! MORE THAN ANYTHING IN THE **UNIVERSE**!
FOR YOU, KYO-KUN, I'LL MAKE DELICIOUS MEALS EVERY DAY!
EVEN IF YOU CHEAT ON ME, I'LL FORGIVE YOU.
JUST A--
WAI--
WHATEVER YOU THINK, KYO-KUN, I'M THE ONLY ONE WHO LOVES YOU THIS MUCH. I THINK I'M THE ONLY ONE FOR YOU! DON'T YOU THINK SO TOO?

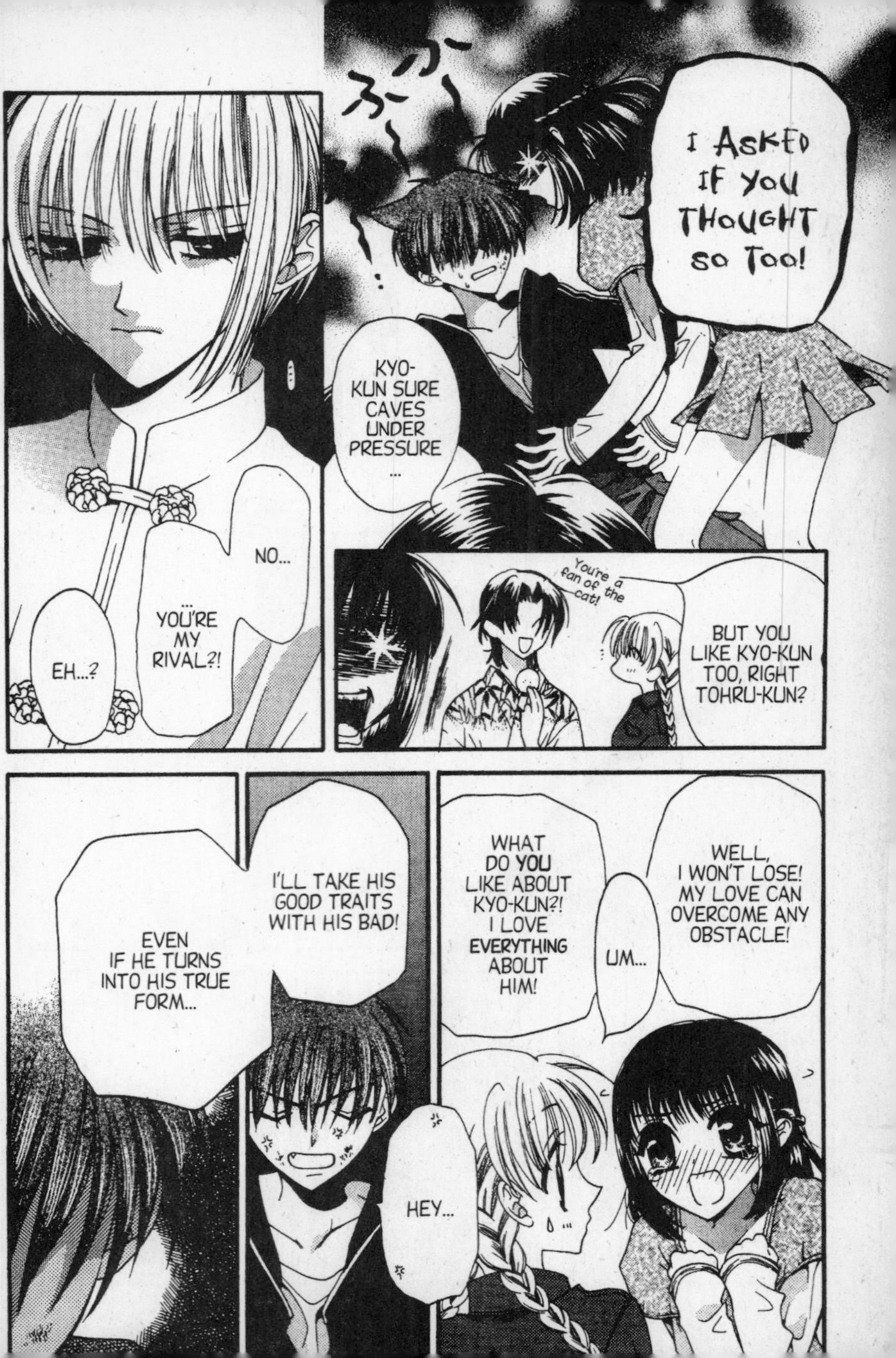
ふ～ ふ～
I ASKED IF YOU THOUGHT SO TOO!
KYO-KUN SURE CAVES UNDER PRESSURE ...
BUT YOU LIKE KYO-KUN TOO, RIGHT TOHRU-KUN?
You're a fan of the cat!
NO...
... YOU'RE MY RIVAL?!
EH...?
WELL, I WON'T LOSE! MY LOVE CAN OVERCOME ANY OBSTACLE!
UM...
WHAT DO YOU LIKE ABOUT KYO-KUN?! I LOVE EVERYTHING ABOUT HIM!
HEY...
I'LL TAKE HIS GOOD TRAITS WITH HIS BAD!
EVEN IF HE TURNS INTO HIS TRUE FORM...

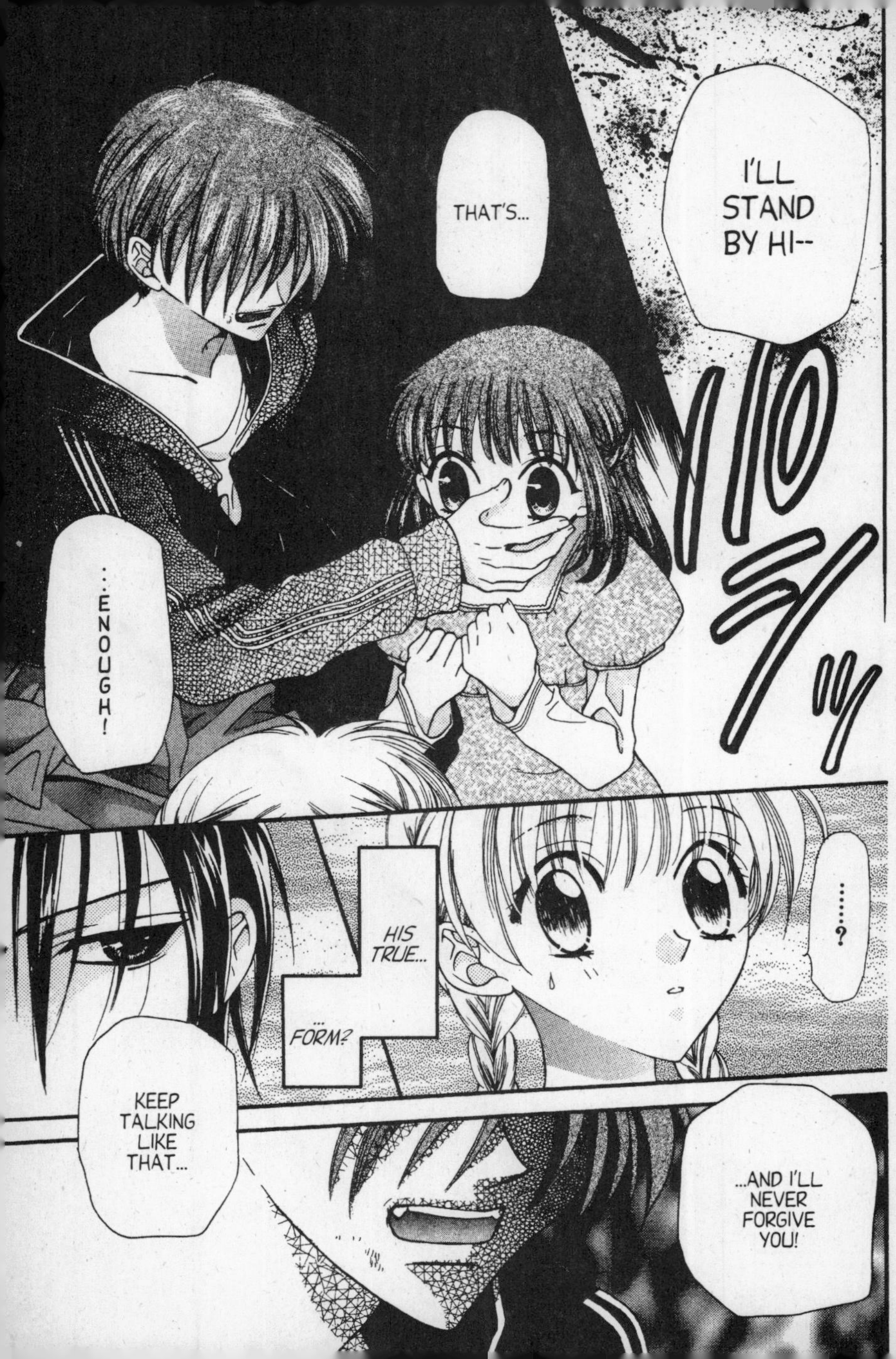
I'LL STAND BY HI--
THAT'S...
...ENOUGH!
......?
HIS TRUE...
...FORM?
KEEP TALKING LIKE THAT...
...AND I'LL NEVER FORGIVE YOU!

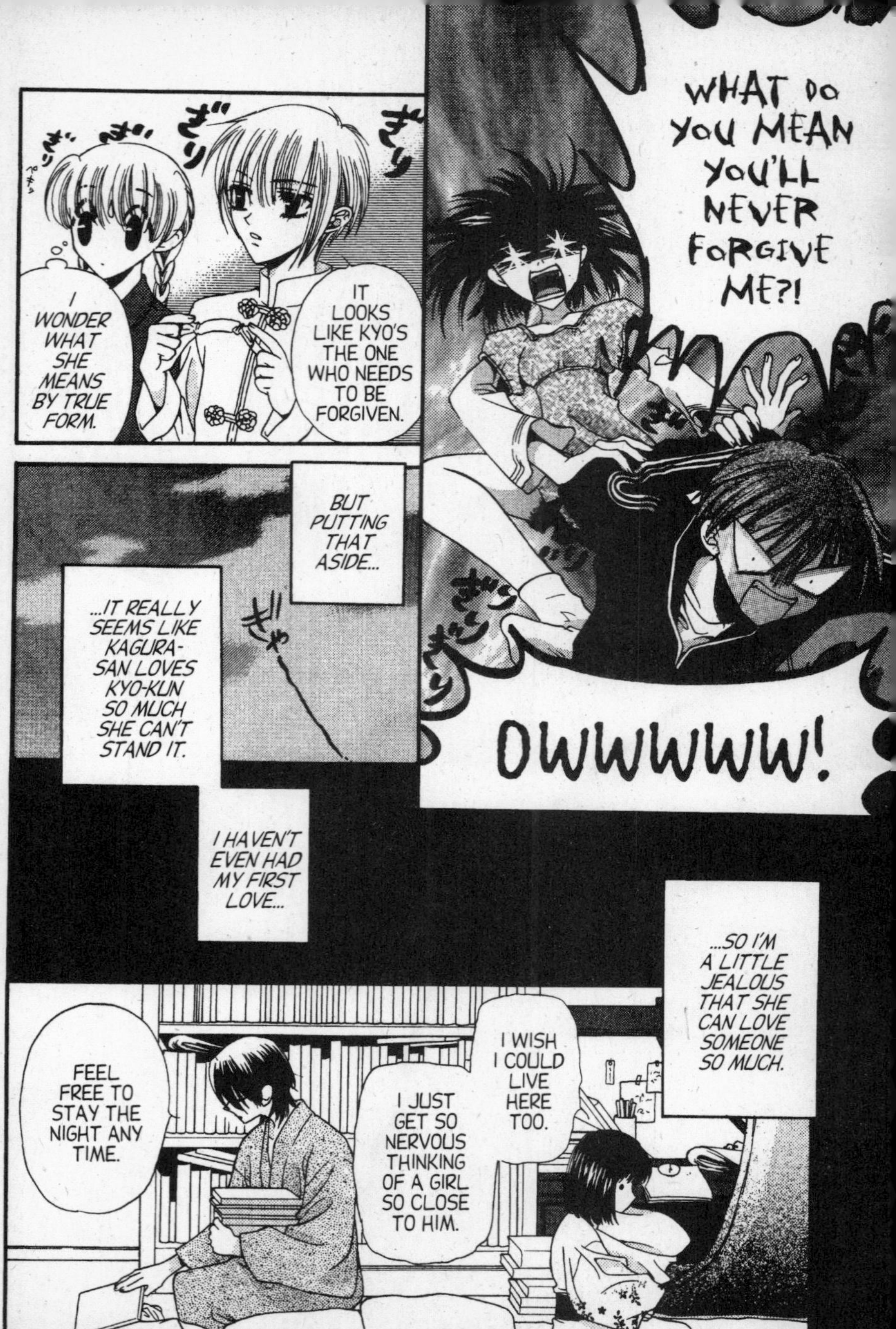
WHAT DO YOU MEAN YOU'LL NEVER FORGIVE ME?!
OWWWWWW!
IT LOOKS LIKE KYO'S THE ONE WHO NEEDS TO BE FORGIVEN.
I WONDER WHAT SHE MEANS BY TRUE FORM.
BUT PUTTING THAT ASIDE...
...IT REALLY SEEMS LIKE KAGURA-SAN LOVES KYO-KUN SO MUCH SHE CAN'T STAND IT.
I HAVEN'T EVEN HAD MY FIRST LOVE...
...SO I'M A LITTLE JEALOUS THAT SHE CAN LOVE SOMEONE SO MUCH.
I WISH I COULD LIVE HERE TOO.
I JUST GET SO NERVOUS THINKING OF A GIRL SO CLOSE TO HIM.
FEEL FREE TO STAY THE NIGHT ANY TIME.

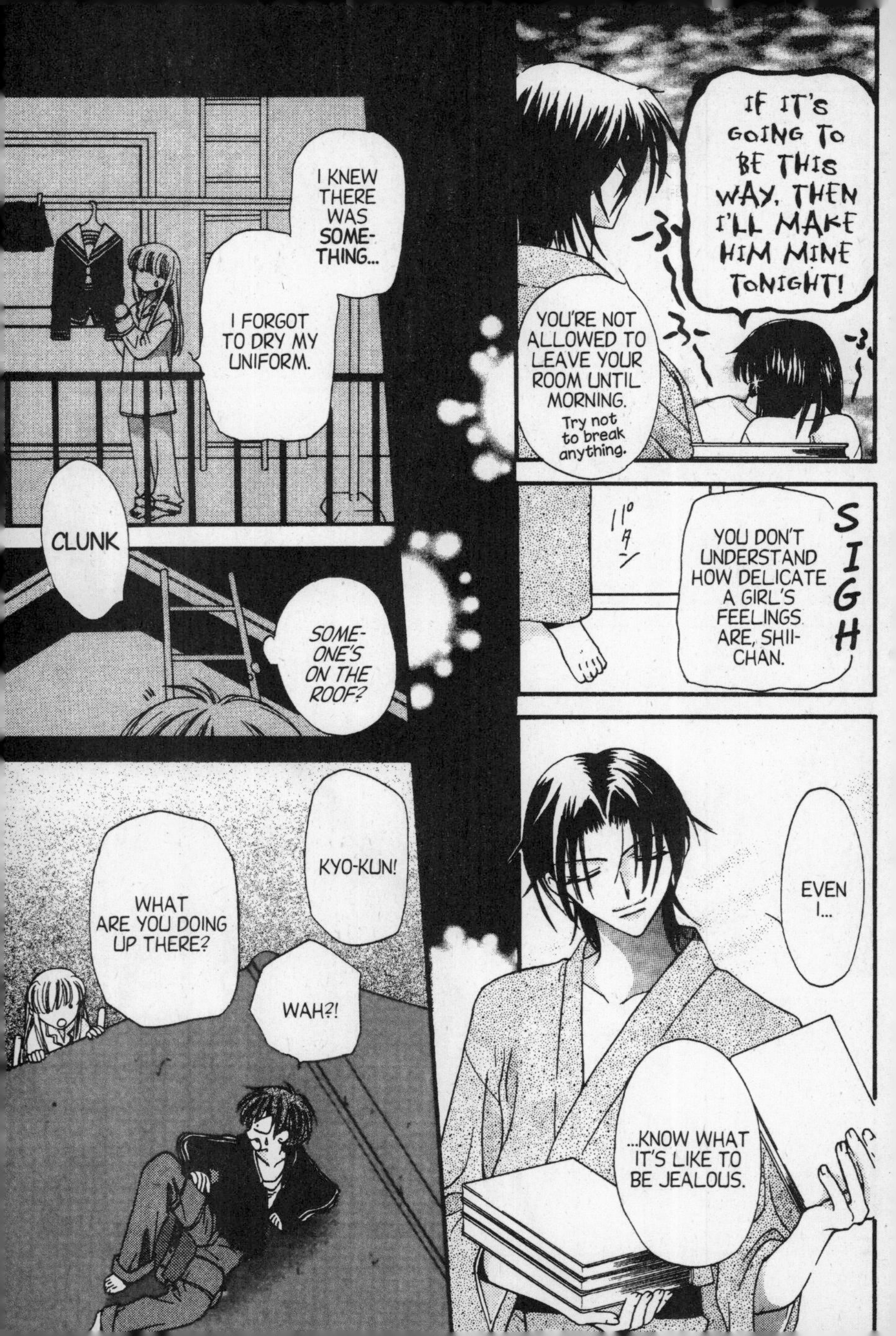
IF IT'S GOING TO BE THIS WAY, THEN I'LL MAKE HIM MINE TONIGHT!
YOU'RE NOT ALLOWED TO LEAVE YOUR ROOM UNTIL MORNING. Try not to break anything.
YOU DON'T UNDERSTAND HOW DELICATE A GIRL'S FEELINGS ARE, SHII-CHAN.
SIGH
EVEN I...
...KNOW WHAT IT'S LIKE TO BE JEALOUS.
I KNEW THERE WAS SOME-THING...
I FORGOT TO DRY MY UNIFORM.
CLUNK
SOME-ONE'S ON THE ROOF?
KYO-KUN!
WHAT ARE YOU DOING UP THERE?
WAH?!

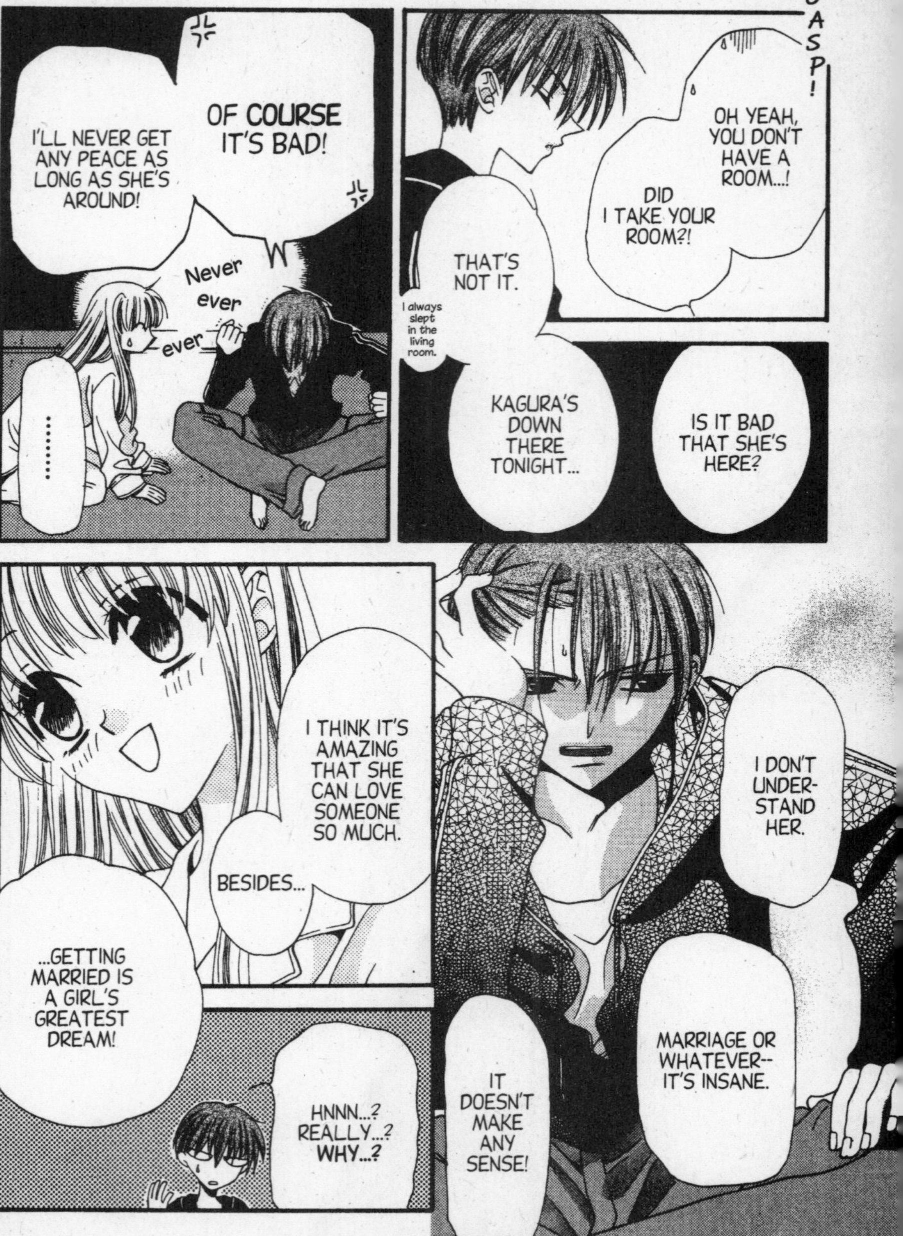
GASP!
OH YEAH, YOU DON'T HAVE A ROOM...!
DID I TAKE YOUR ROOM?!
THAT'S NOT IT.
I always slept in the living room.
KAGURA'S DOWN THERE TONIGHT...
IS IT BAD THAT SHE'S HERE?
OF COURSE IT'S BAD!
I'LL NEVER GET ANY PEACE AS LONG AS SHE'S AROUND!
Never ever ever
....
I DON'T UNDER-STAND HER.
MARRIAGE OR WHATEVER-- IT'S INSANE.
IT DOESN'T MAKE ANY SENSE!
I THINK IT'S AMAZING THAT SHE CAN LOVE SOMEONE SO MUCH.
BESIDES...
...GETTING MARRIED IS A GIRL'S GREATEST DREAM!
HNNN...? REALLY...? WHY...?

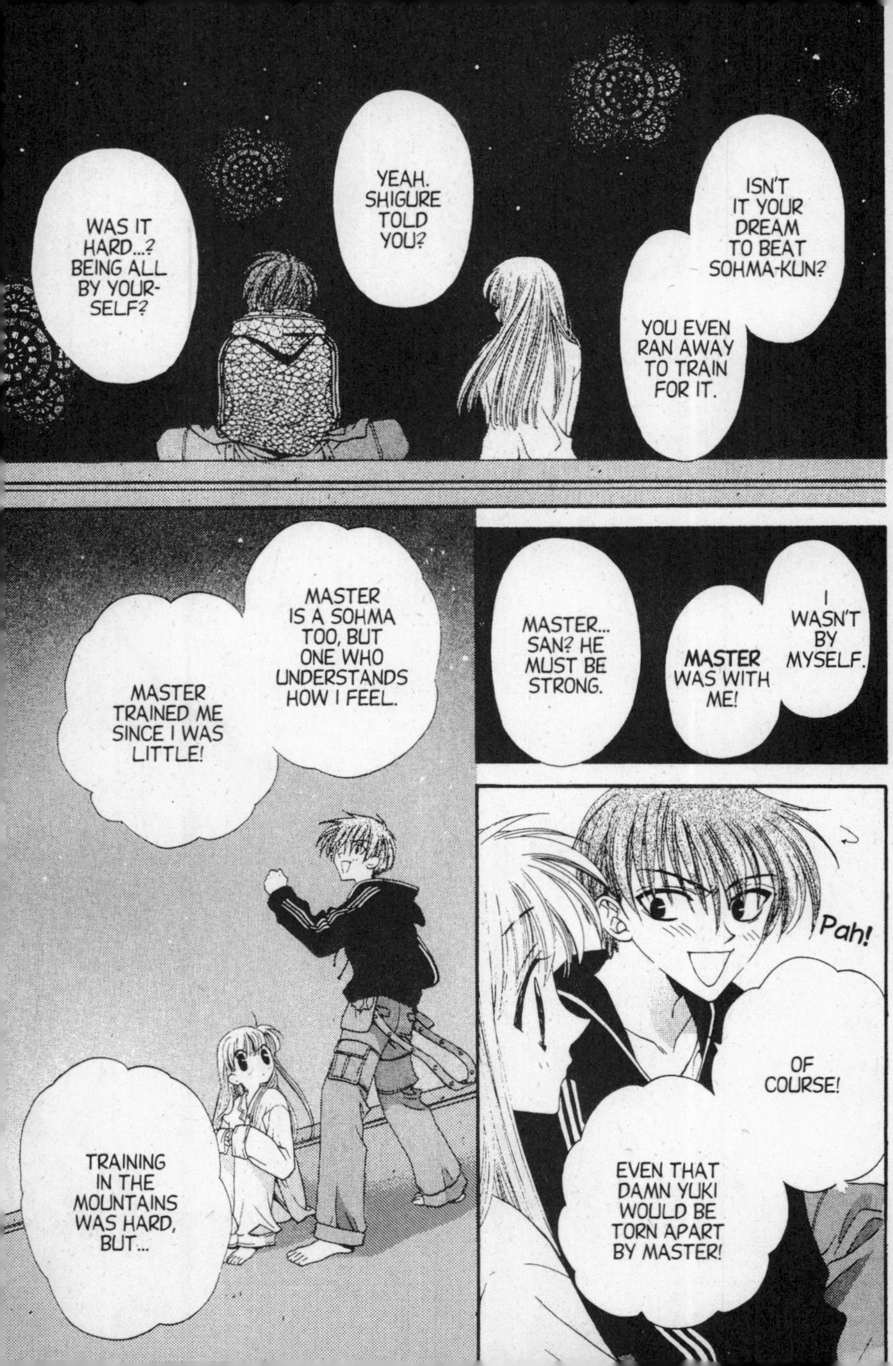

ISN'T IT YOUR DREAM TO BEAT SOHMA-KUN?
YOU EVEN RAN AWAY TO TRAIN FOR IT.
YEAH. SHIGURE TOLD YOU?
WAS IT HARD...? BEING ALL BY YOUR-SELF?
I WASN'T BY MYSELF.
MASTER WAS WITH ME!
MASTER... SAN? HE MUST BE STRONG.
Pah!
OF COURSE!
EVEN THAT DAMN YUKI WOULD BE TORN APART BY MASTER!
MASTER IS A SOHMA TOO, BUT ONE WHO UNDERSTANDS HOW I FEEL.
MASTER TRAINED ME SINCE I WAS LITTLE!
TRAINING IN THE MOUNTAINS WAS HARD, BUT...

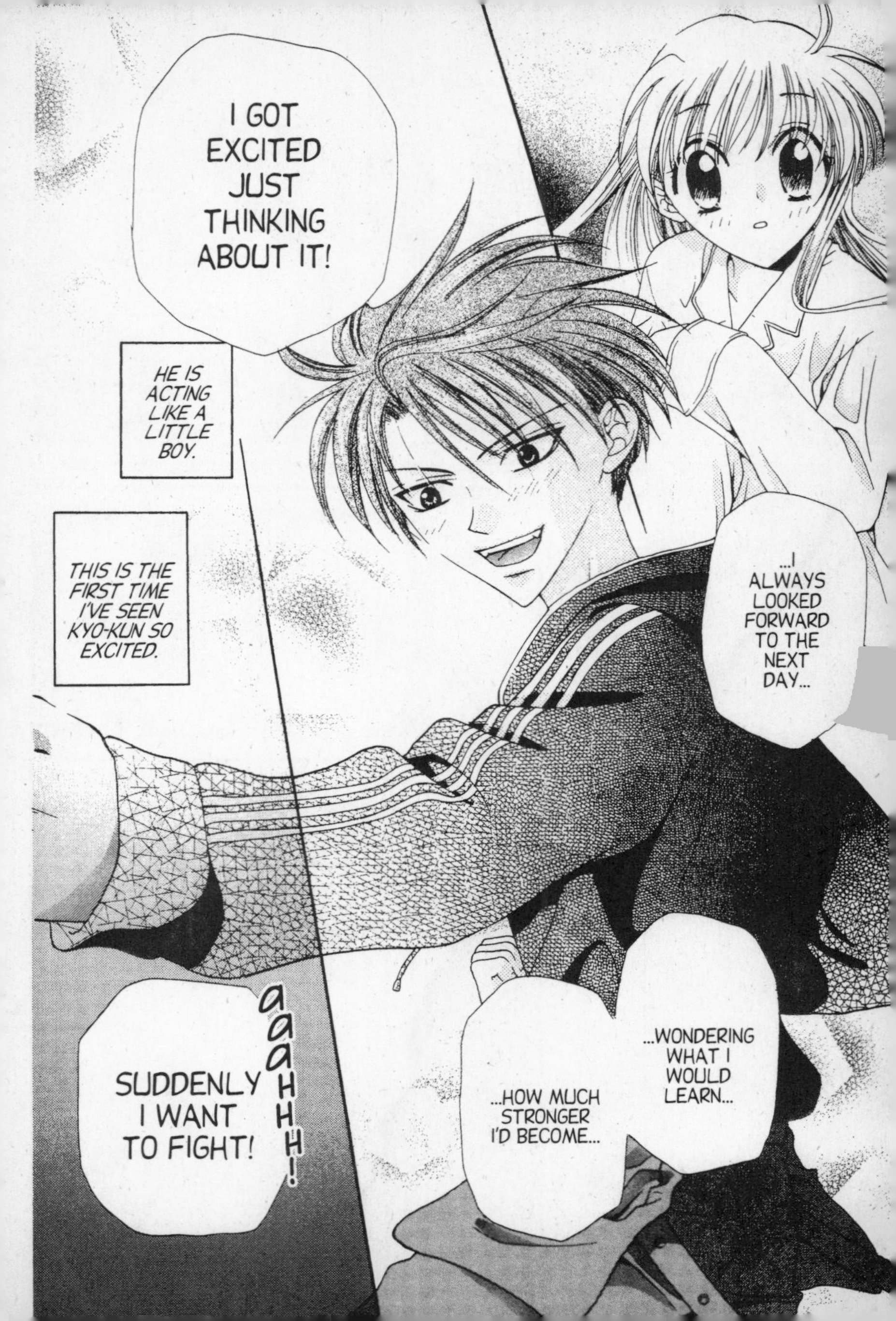

...I ALWAYS LOOKED FORWARD TO THE NEXT DAY...
...WONDERING WHAT I WOULD LEARN...
...HOW MUCH STRONGER I'D BECOME...
I GOT EXCITED JUST THINKING ABOUT IT!
HE IS ACTING LIKE A LITTLE BOY.
THIS IS THE FIRST TIME I'VE SEEN KYO-KUN SO EXCITED.
SUDDENLY I WANT TO FIGHT!
aaaHHH!

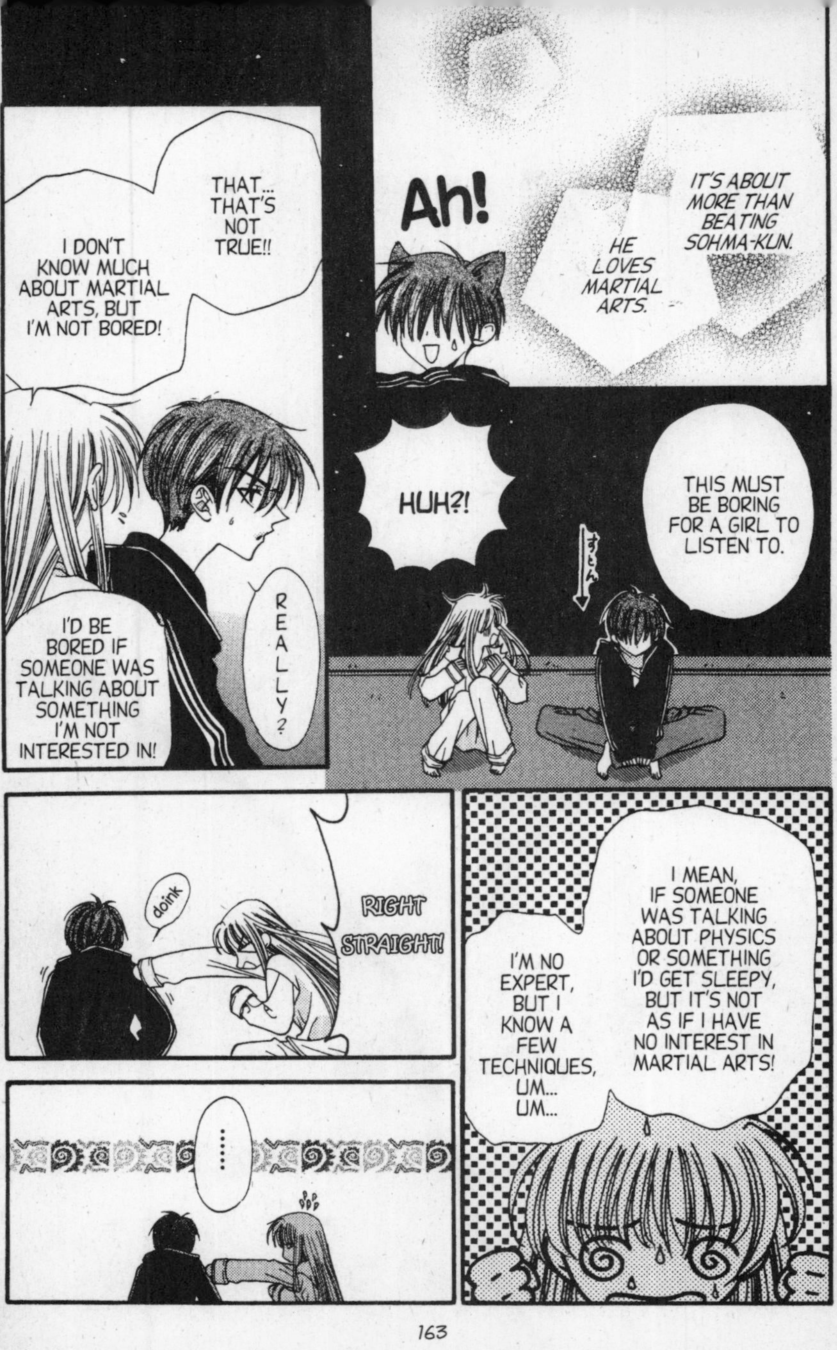
IT'S ABOUT MORE THAN BEATING SOHMA-KUN.
HE LOVES MARTIAL ARTS.
Ah!
THIS MUST BE BORING FOR A GIRL TO LISTEN TO.
すとん
HUH?!
THAT... THAT'S NOT TRUE!!
I DON'T KNOW MUCH ABOUT MARTIAL ARTS, BUT I'M NOT BORED!
REALLY?
I'D BE BORED IF SOMEONE WAS TALKING ABOUT SOMETHING I'M NOT INTERESTED IN!
I MEAN, IF SOMEONE WAS TALKING ABOUT PHYSICS OR SOMETHING I'D GET SLEEPY, BUT IT'S NOT AS IF I HAVE NO INTEREST IN MARTIAL ARTS!
I'M NO EXPERT, BUT I KNOW A FEW TECHNIQUES, UM... UM...
RIGHT STRAIGHT!
doink
......

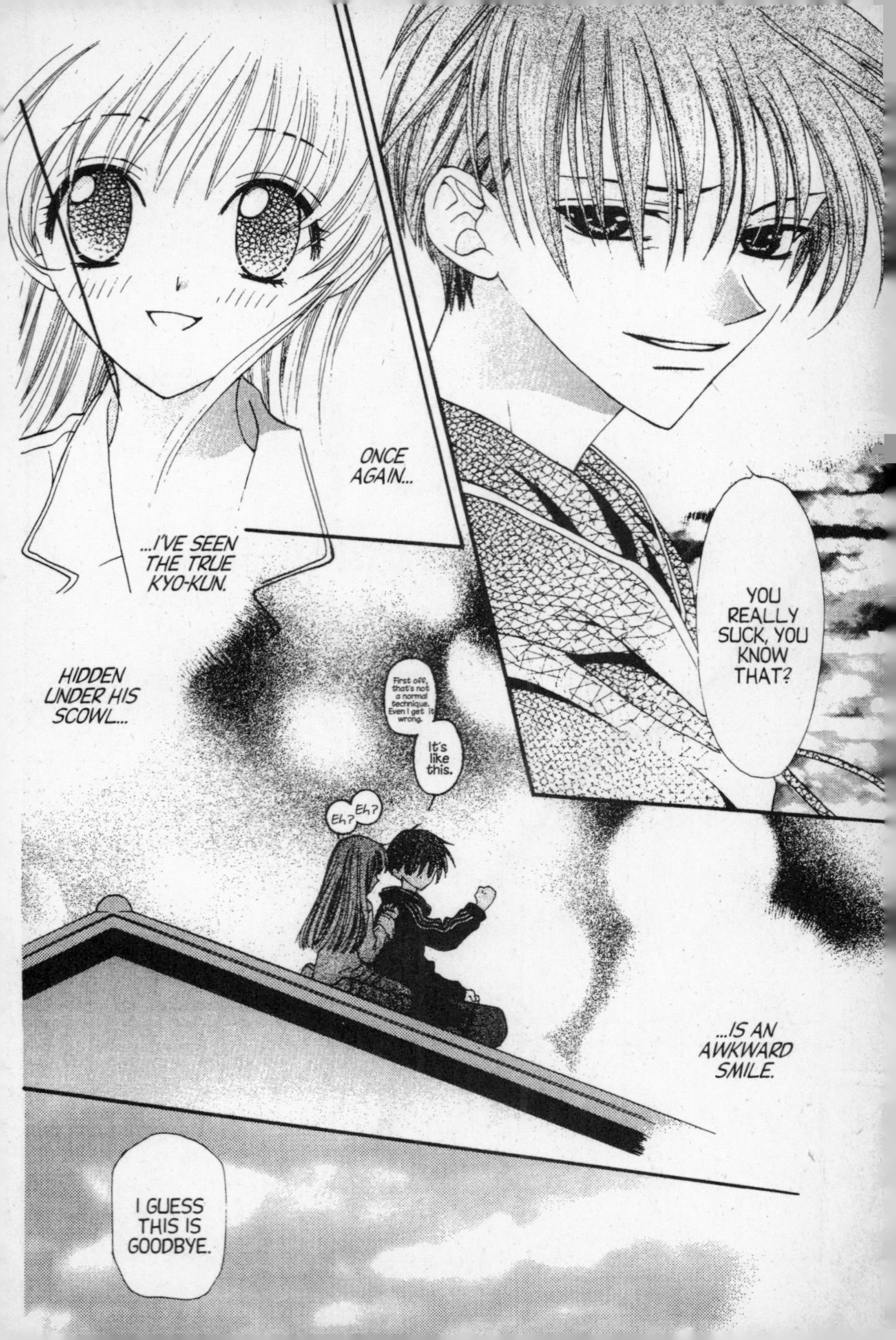
YOU REALLY SUCK, YOU KNOW THAT?
ONCE AGAIN...
...I'VE SEEN THE TRUE KYO-KUN.
HIDDEN UNDER HIS SCOWL...
...IS AN AWKWARD SMILE.
First off, that's not a normal technique. Even I get it wrong.
It's like this.
Eh?
Eh?
I GUESS THIS IS GOODBYE.

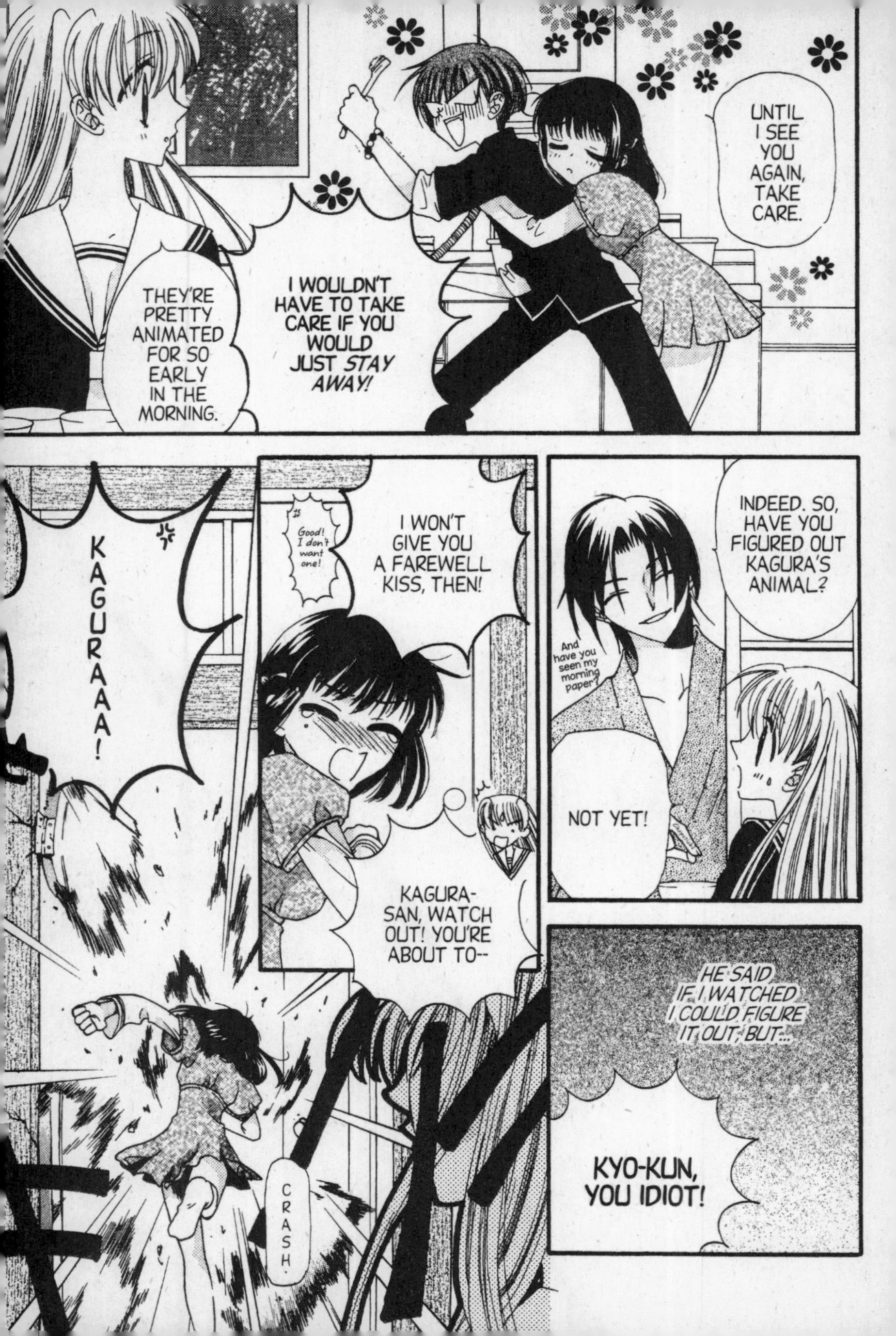
UNTIL I SEE YOU AGAIN, TAKE CARE.
I WOULDN'T HAVE TO TAKE CARE IF YOU WOULD JUST *STAY AWAY!*
THEY'RE PRETTY ANIMATED FOR SO EARLY IN THE MORNING.
INDEED. SO, HAVE YOU FIGURED OUT KAGURA'S ANIMAL?
And have you seen my morning paper?
NOT YET!
I WON'T GIVE YOU A FAREWELL KISS, THEN!
Good! I don't want one!
KAGURA-SAN, WATCH OUT! YOU'RE ABOUT TO--
KAGURAAAA!
CRASH
HE SAID IF I WATCHED I COULD FIGURE IT OUT, BUT...
KYO-KUN, YOU IDIOT!

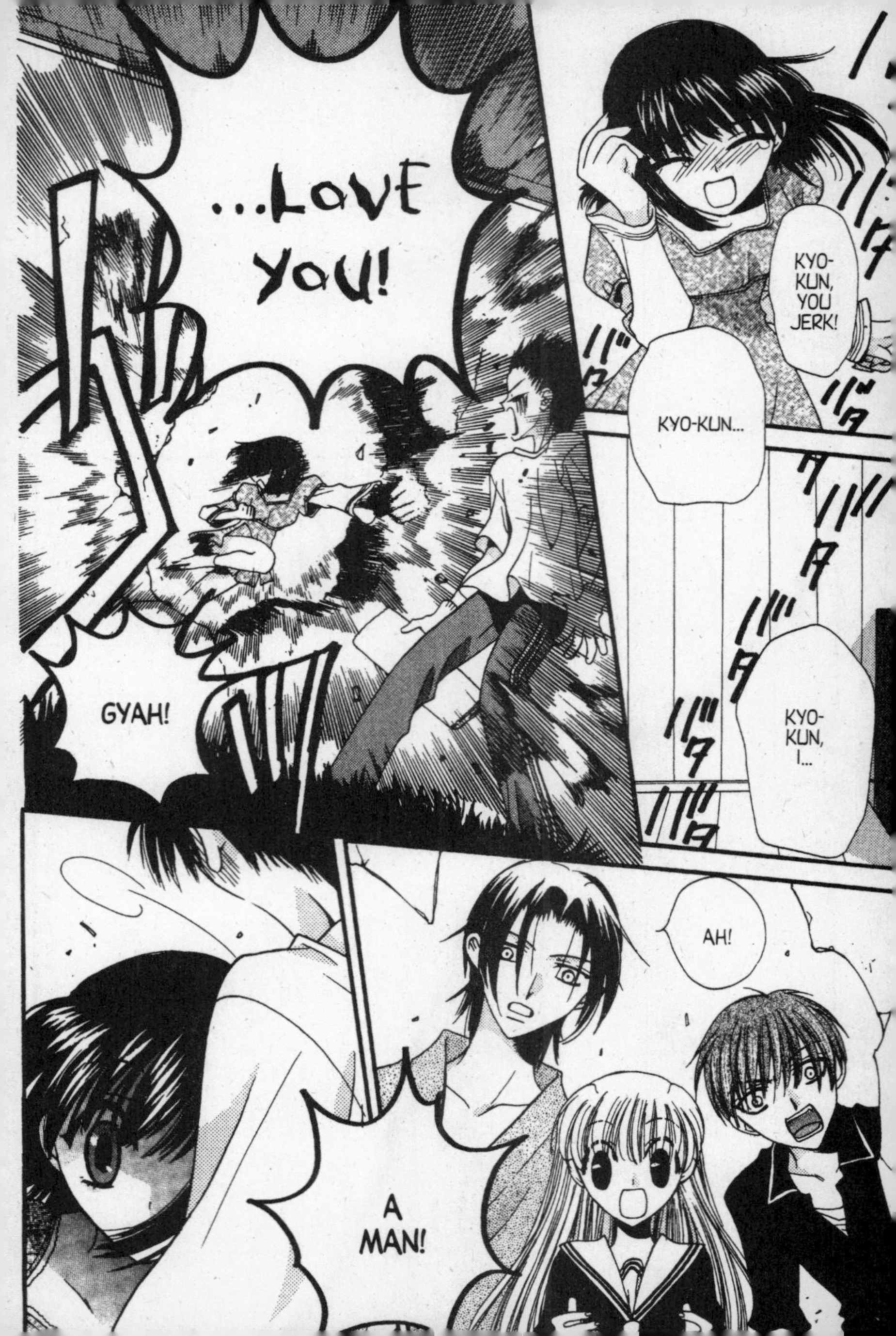
KYO-KUN, YOU JERK!
KYO-KUN...
KYO-KUN, I...
...LOVE YOU!
GYAH!
AH!
A MAN!

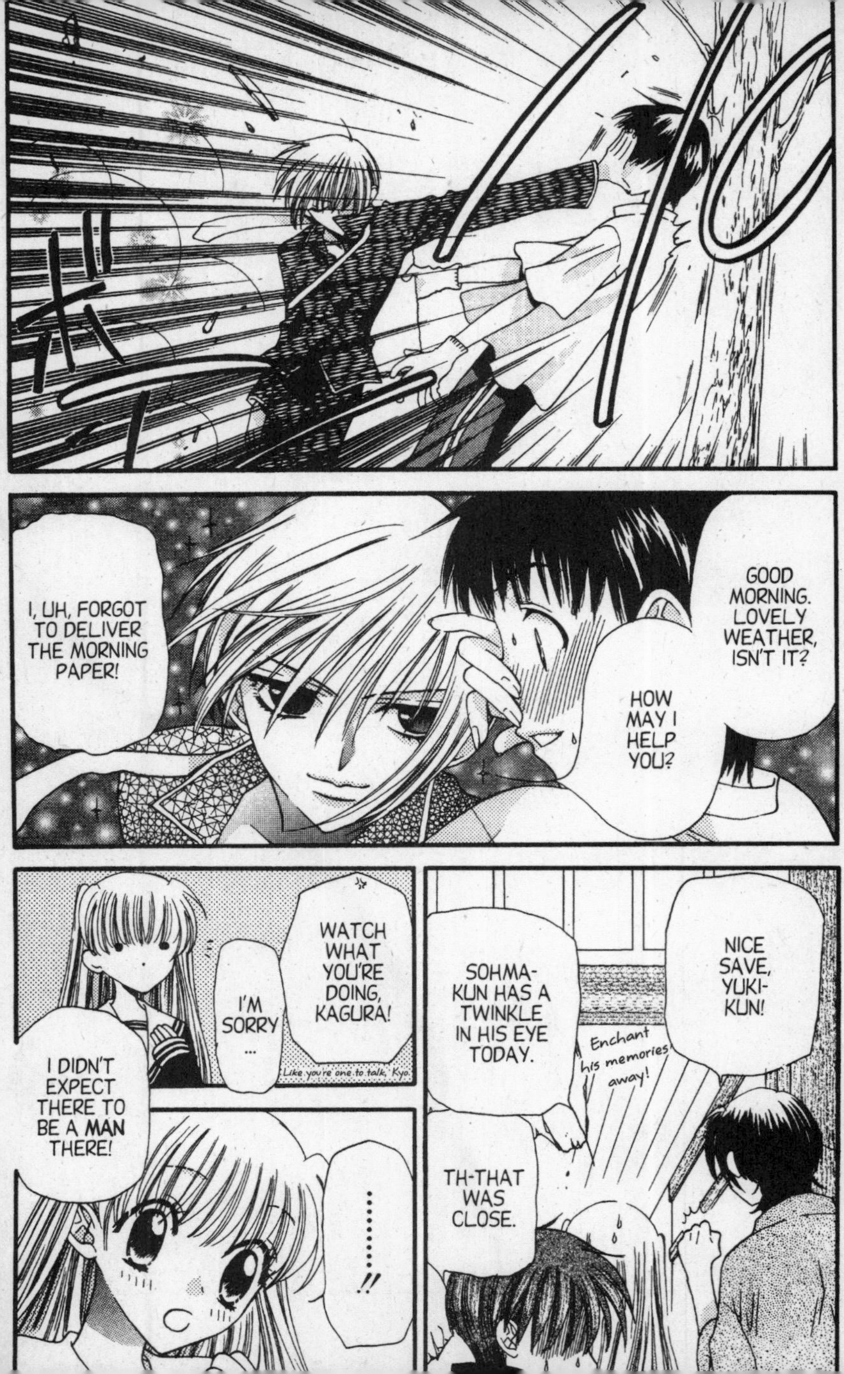
GOOD MORNING. LOVELY WEATHER, ISN'T IT?
HOW MAY I HELP YOU?
I, UH, FORGOT TO DELIVER THE MORNING PAPER!
NICE SAVE, YUKI-KUN!
SOHMA-KUN HAS A TWINKLE IN HIS EYE TODAY.
Enchant his memories away!
TH-THAT WAS CLOSE.
WATCH WHAT YOU'RE DOING, KAGURA!
I'M SORRY ...
Like you're one to talk, Kyo.
I DIDN'T EXPECT THERE TO BE A MAN THERE!
......!!

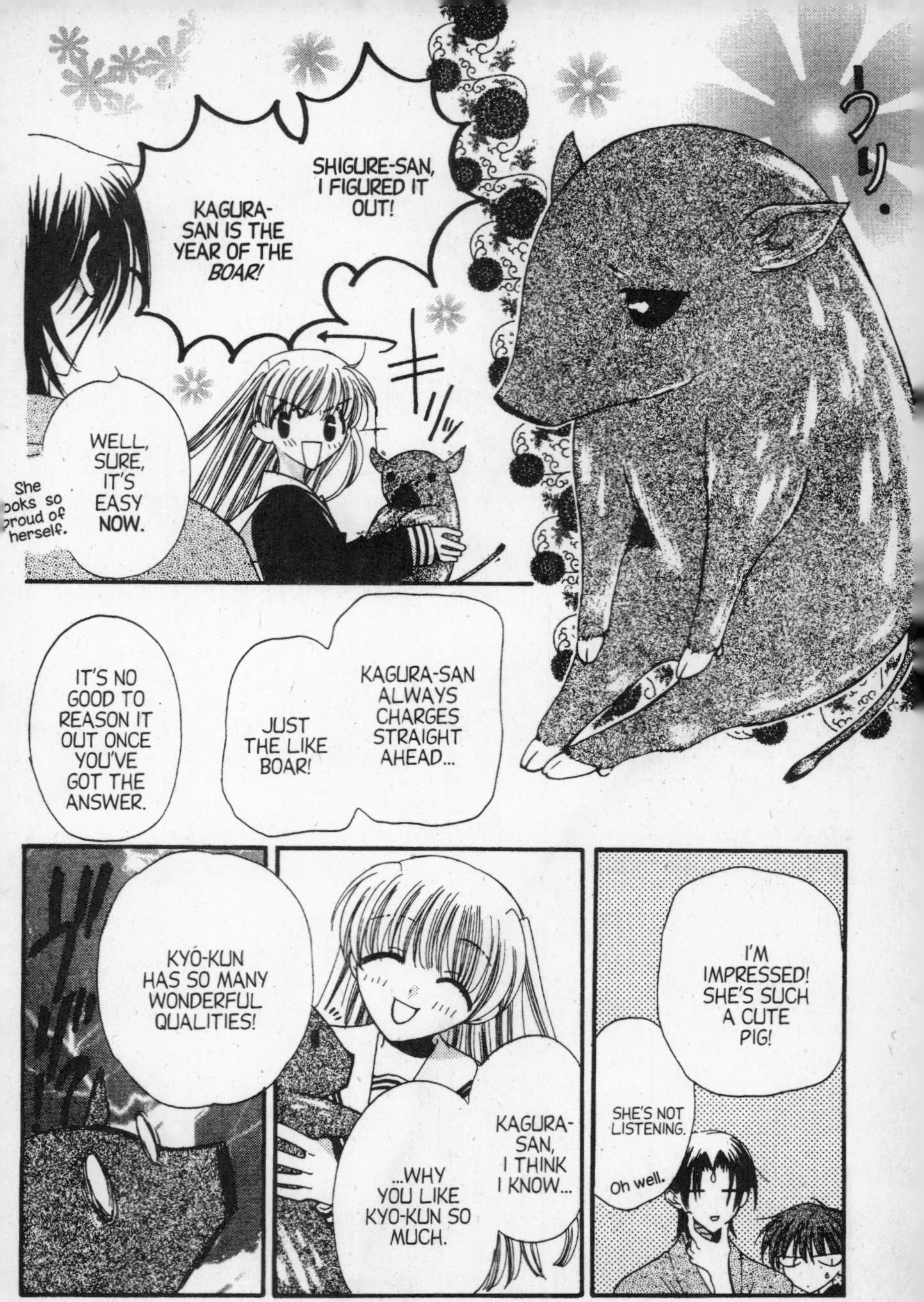
ウリ・
SHIGURE-SAN, I FIGURED IT OUT!
KAGURA-SAN IS THE YEAR OF THE *BOAR!*
WELL, SURE, IT'S EASY NOW.
She ooks so proud of herself.
KAGURA-SAN ALWAYS CHARGES STRAIGHT AHEAD...
JUST THE LIKE BOAR!
IT'S NO GOOD TO REASON IT OUT ONCE YOU'VE GOT THE ANSWER.
I'M IMPRESSED! SHE'S SUCH A CUTE PIG!
SHE'S NOT LISTENING.
Oh well.
KAGURA-SAN, I THINK I KNOW...
...WHY YOU LIKE KYO-KUN SO MUCH.
KYO-KUN HAS SO MANY WONDERFUL QUALITIES!

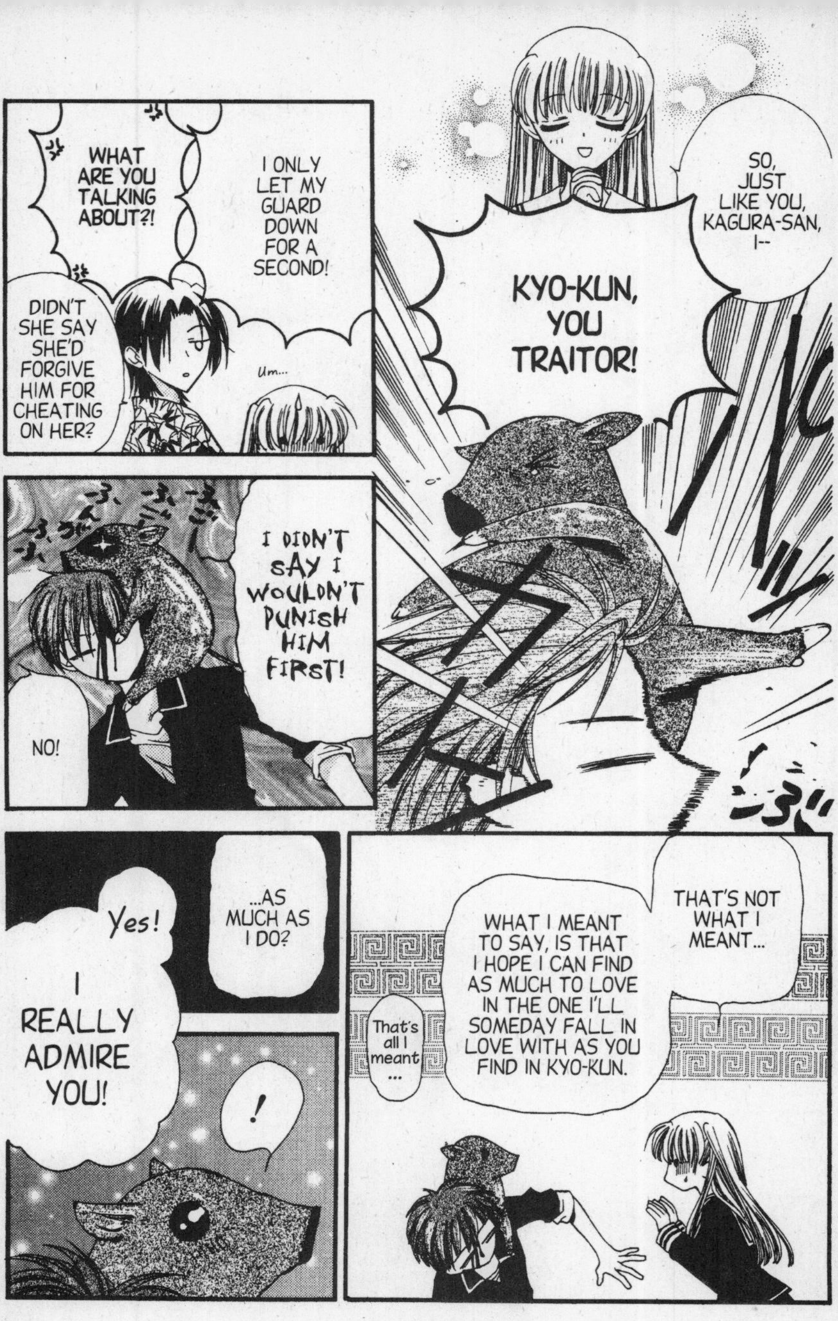
SO, JUST LIKE YOU, KAGURA-SAN, I--
KYO-KUN, YOU TRAITOR!
WHAT ARE YOU TALKING ABOUT?!
I ONLY LET MY GUARD DOWN FOR A SECOND!
Um...
DIDN'T SHE SAY SHE'D FORGIVE HIM FOR CHEATING ON HER?
I DIDN'T SAY I WOULDN'T PUNISH HIM FIRST!
NO!
THAT'S NOT WHAT I MEANT...
WHAT I MEANT TO SAY, IS THAT I HOPE I CAN FIND AS MUCH TO LOVE IN THE ONE I'LL SOMEDAY FALL IN LOVE WITH AS YOU FIND IN KYO-KUN.
That's all I meant...
...AS MUCH AS I DO?
Yes!
I REALLY ADMIRE YOU!
!

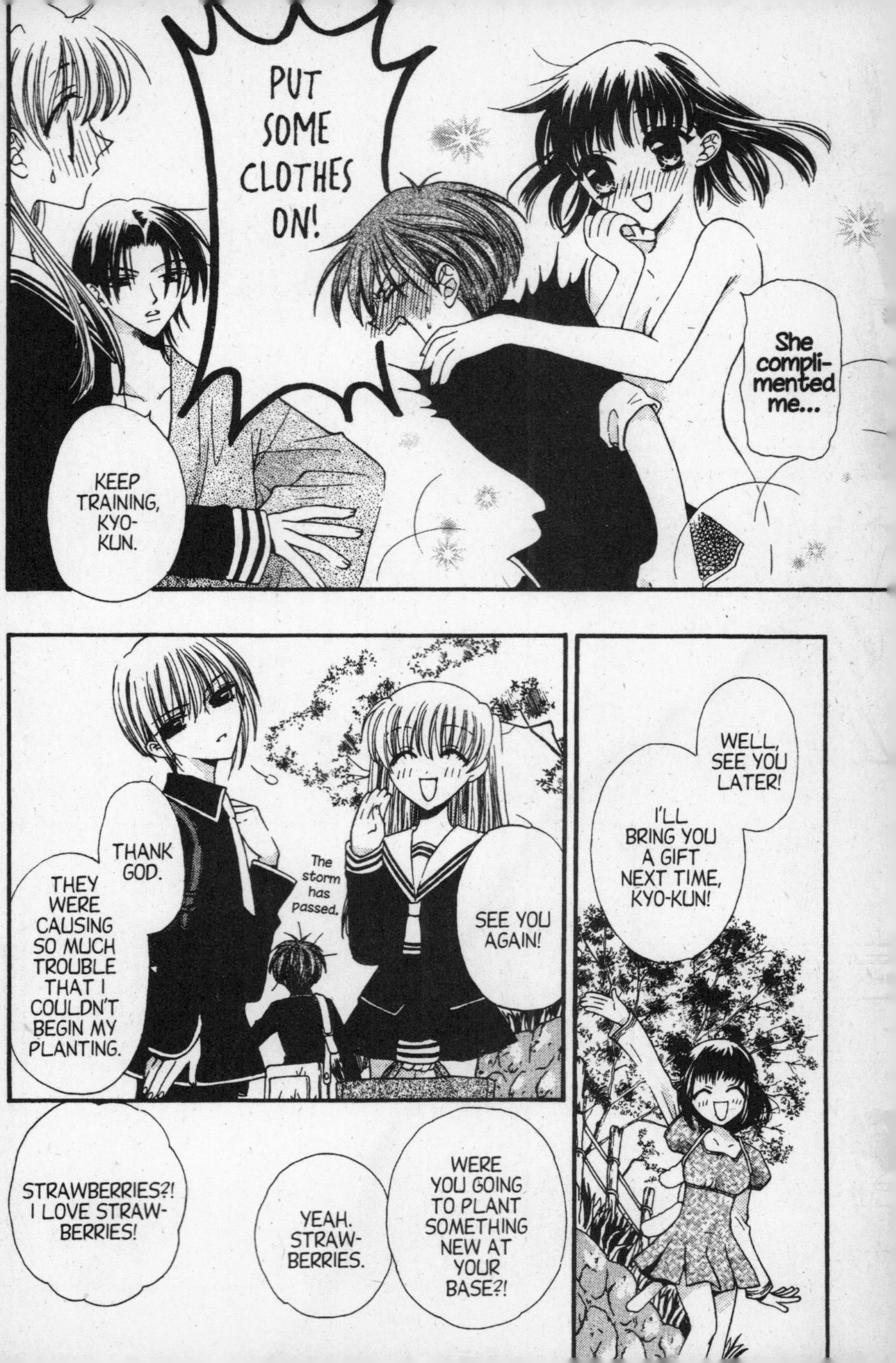
She compli-mented me...
PUT SOME CLOTHES ON!
KEEP TRAINING, KYO-KUN.
WELL, SEE YOU LATER!
I'LL BRING YOU A GIFT NEXT TIME, KYO-KUN!
SEE YOU AGAIN!
The storm has passed.
THANK GOD.
THEY WERE CAUSING SO MUCH TROUBLE THAT I COULDN'T BEGIN MY PLANTING.
WERE YOU GOING TO PLANT SOMETHING NEW AT YOUR BASE?!
YEAH. STRAW-BERRIES.
STRAWBERRIES?! I LOVE STRAW-BERRIES!

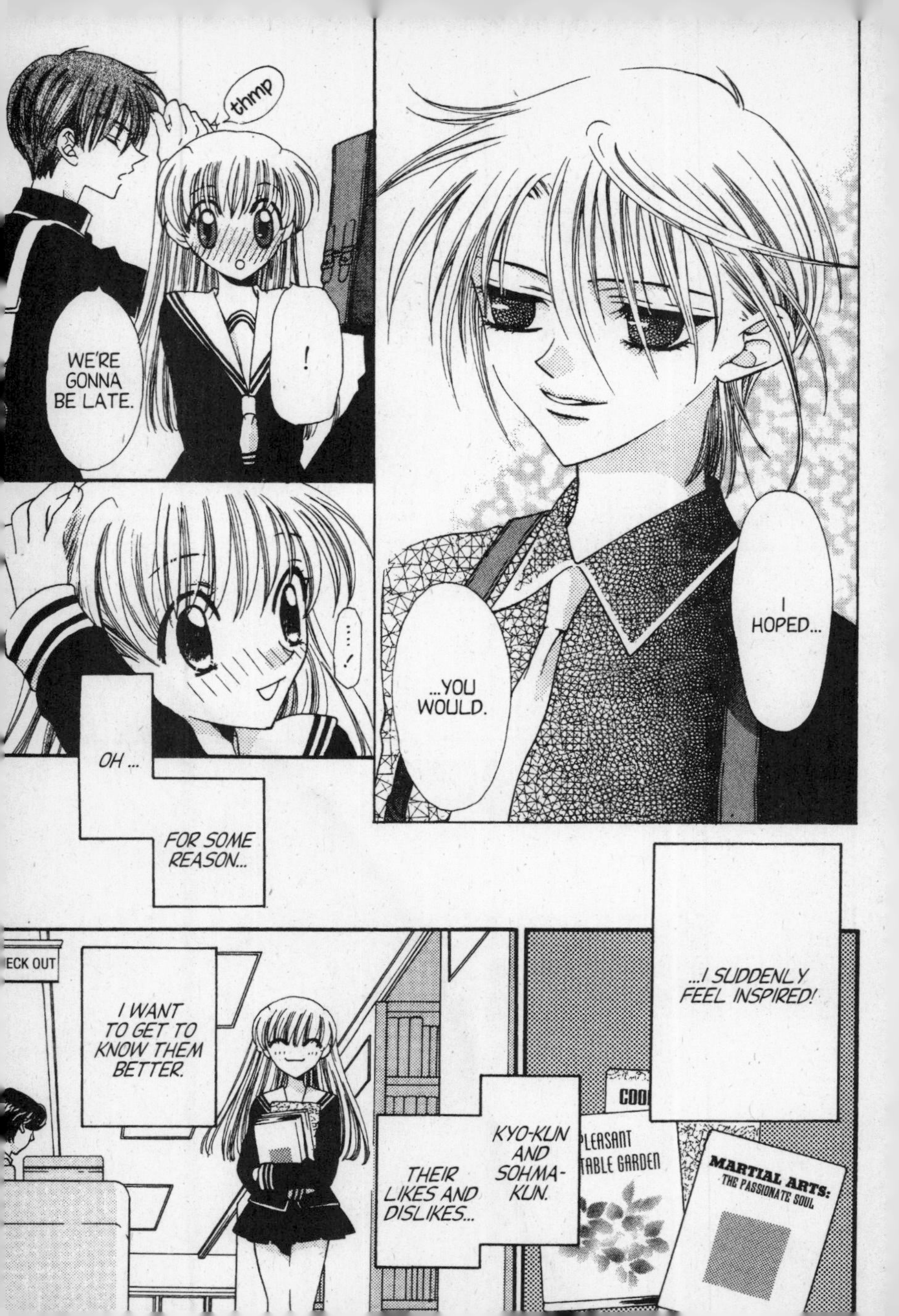
I HOPED...
...YOU WOULD.
thmp
!
WE'RE GONNA BE LATE.
...!
OH ...
FOR SOME REASON...
...I SUDDENLY FEEL INSPIRED!
MARTIAL ARTS: THE PASSIONATE SOUL
PLEASANT
TABLE GARDEN
COO
KYO-KUN AND SOHMA-KUN.
THEIR LIKES AND DISLIKES...
I WANT TO GET TO KNOW THEM BETTER.
ECK OUT

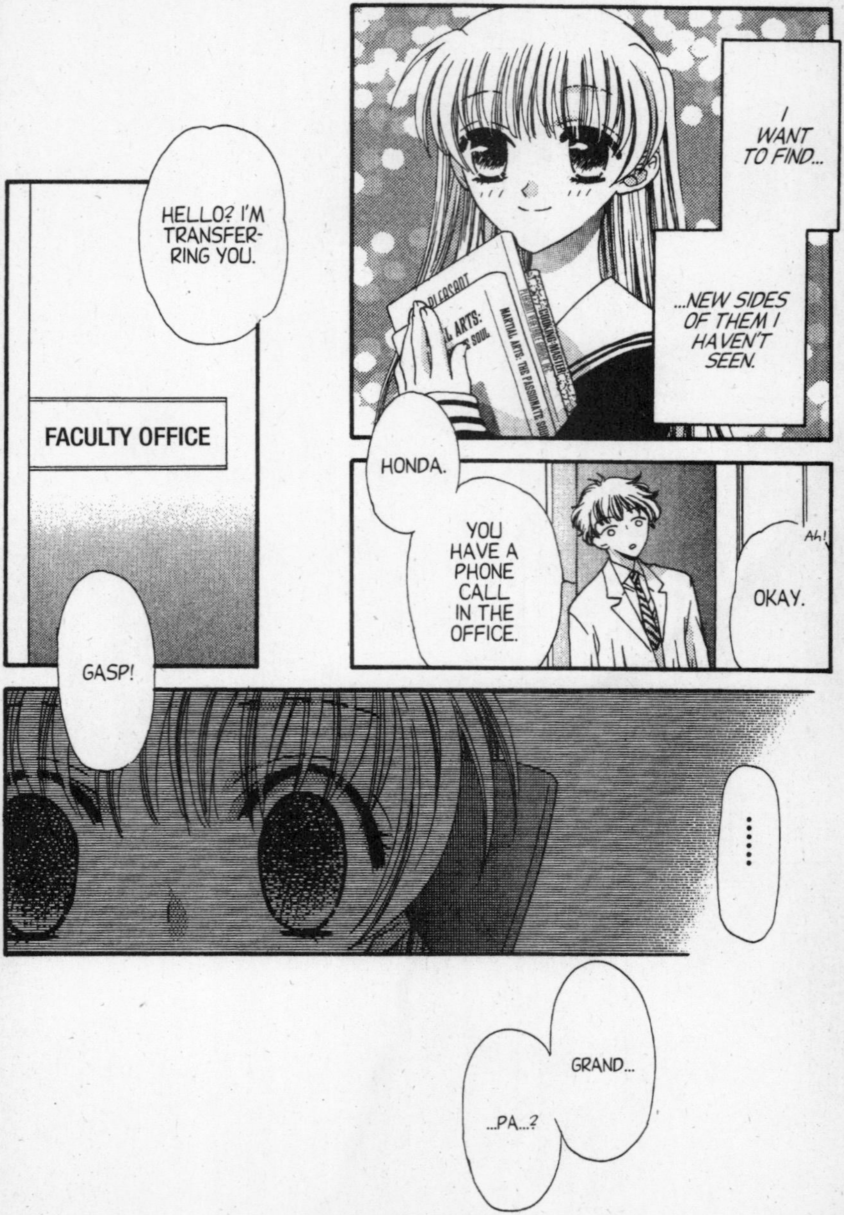
I WANT TO FIND...
...NEW SIDES OF THEM I HAVEN'T SEEN.
MARTIAL ARTS: THE PASSIONATE SOUL
HONDA.
YOU HAVE A PHONE CALL IN THE OFFICE.
Ah!
OKAY.
HELLO? I'M TRANSFER-RING YOU.
FACULTY OFFICE
GASP!
......
GRAND...
...PA...?

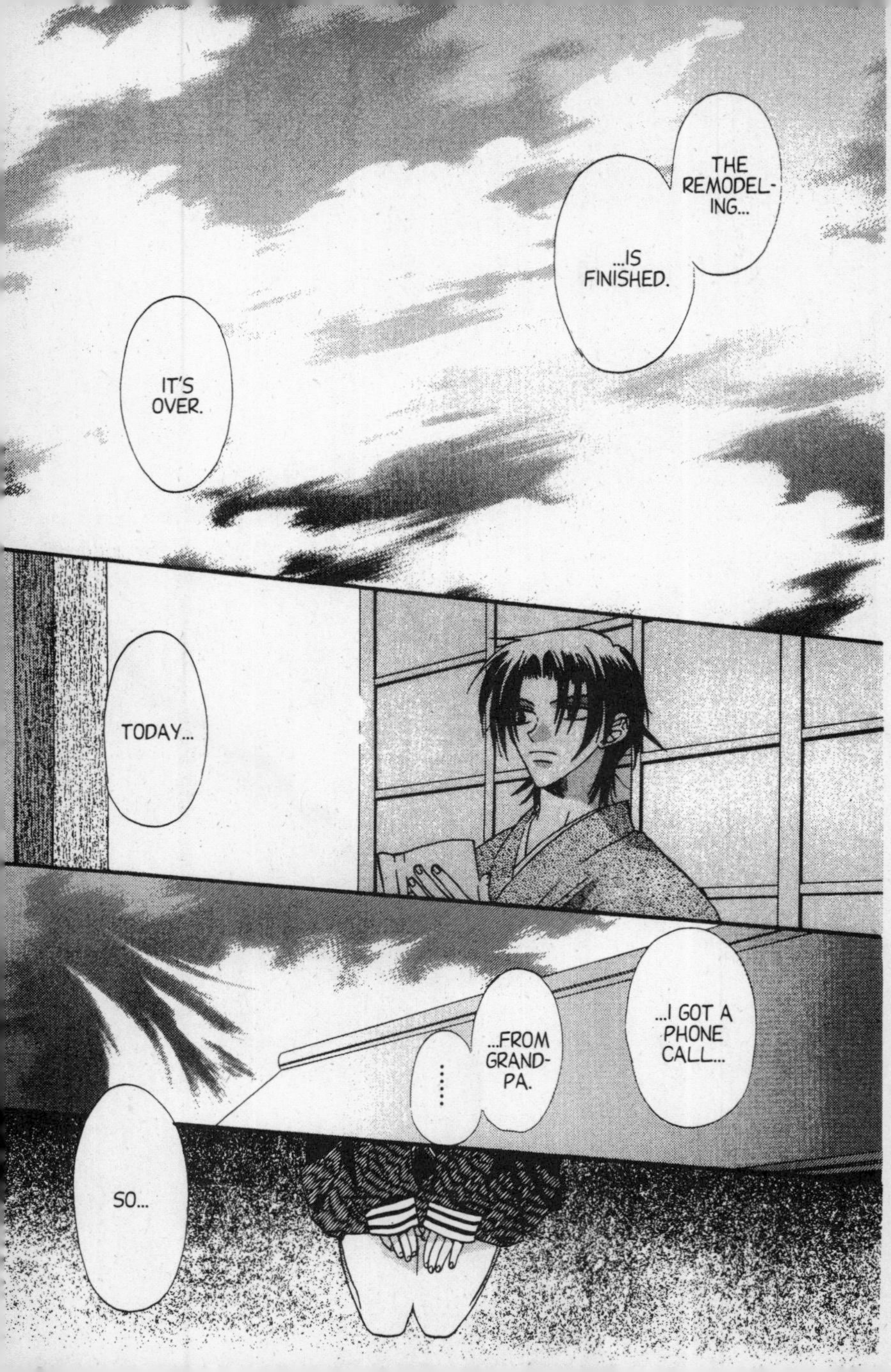

THE REMODEL-ING...
...IS FINISHED.
IT'S OVER.
TODAY...
...I GOT A PHONE CALL...
...FROM GRAND-PA.
......
SO...

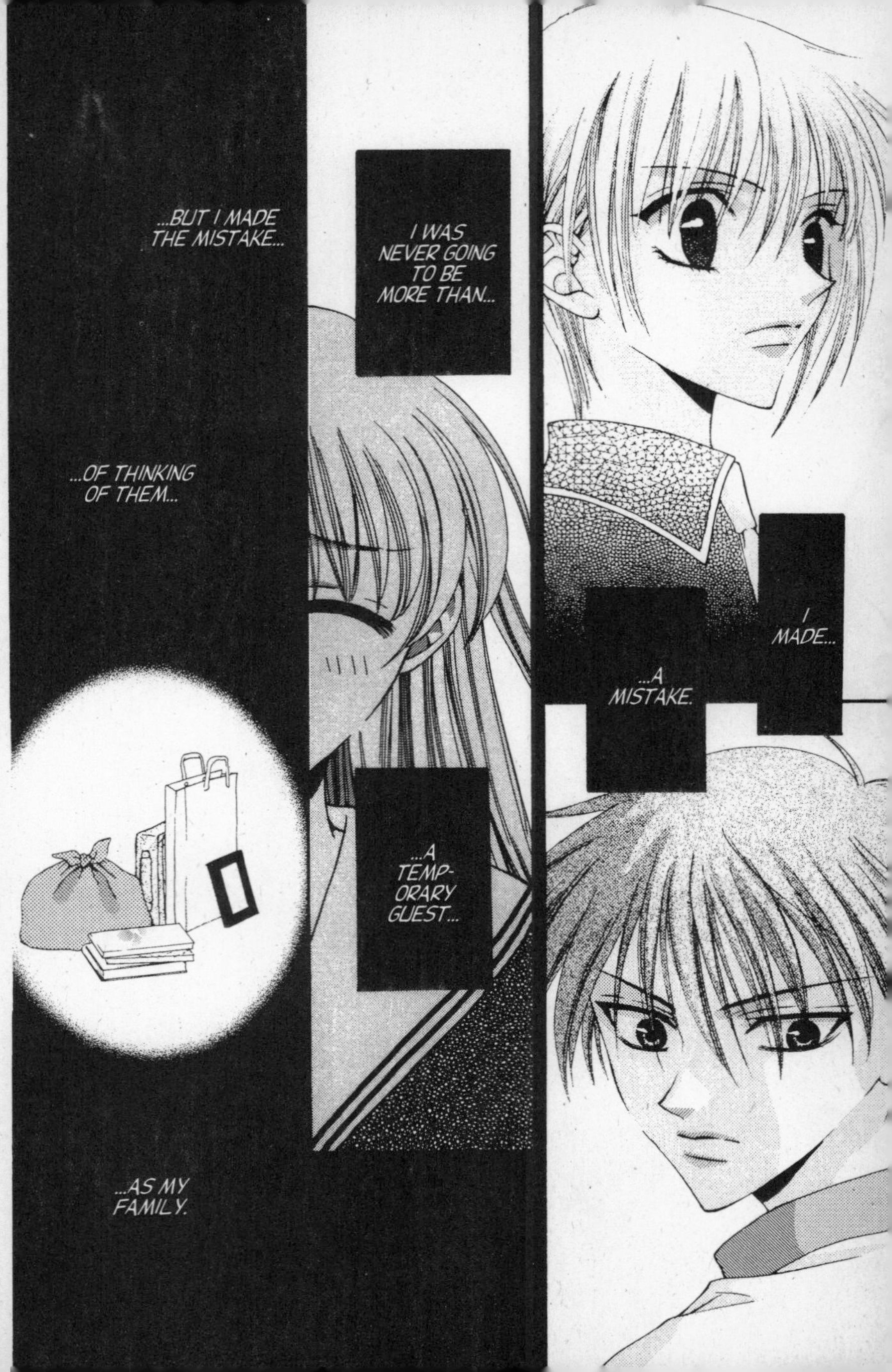
I MADE...
...A MISTAKE.
I WAS NEVER GOING TO BE MORE THAN...
...A TEMP-ORARY GUEST...
...BUT I MADE THE MISTAKE...
...OF THINKING OF THEM...
...AS MY FAMILY.

Chapter 6

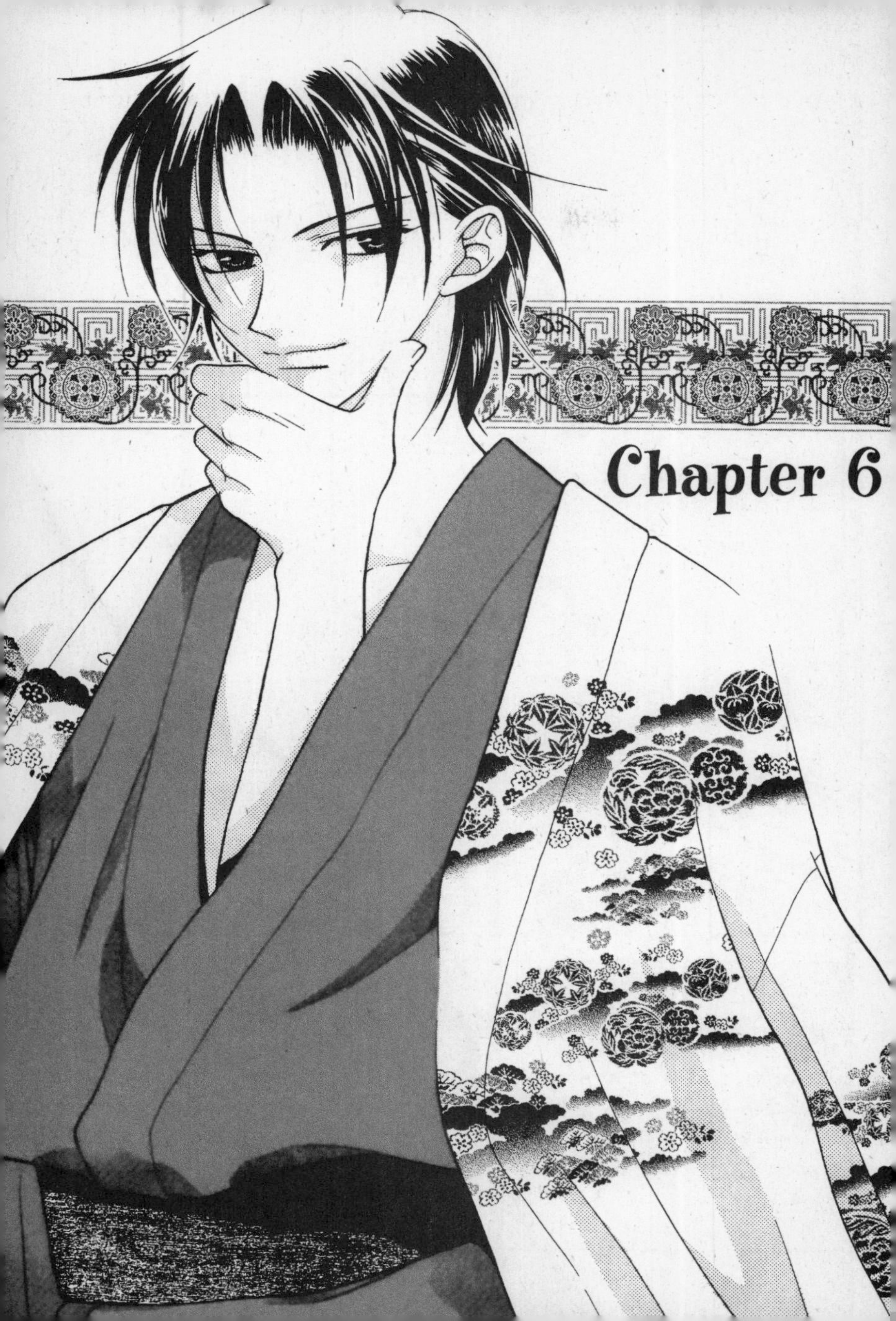

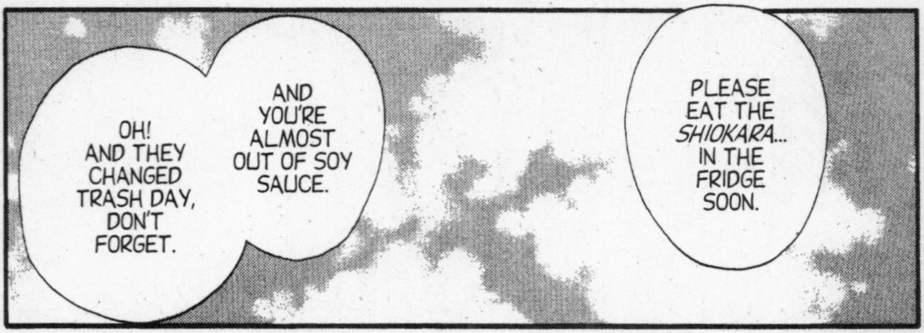
PLEASE EAT THE *SHIOKARA*... IN THE FRIDGE SOON.
AND YOU'RE ALMOST OUT OF SOY SAUCE.
OH! AND THEY CHANGED TRASH DAY, DON'T FORGET.

*Salted fish guts

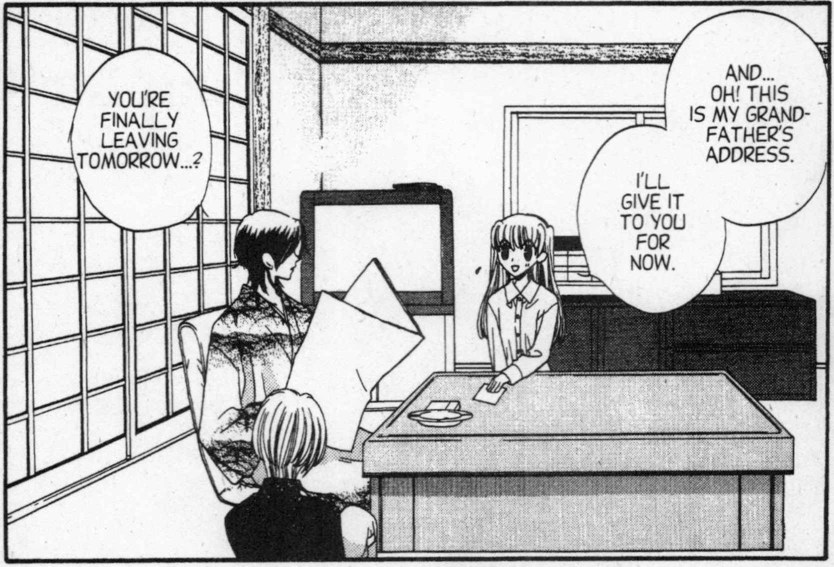
AND... OH! THIS IS MY GRAND-FATHER'S ADDRESS.
I'LL GIVE IT TO YOU FOR NOW.
YOU'RE FINALLY LEAVING TOMORROW...?

ULTRA SPECIAL BLAH BLAH BLAH, NUMBER 5:

This series is kind of turning into a sitcom, but I don't really think of it as a comedy when I draw it. I mean -- it is funny (Of course I don't mind if people call it a comedy. I love comedies. Especially dry humor). I just kind of feel like, "Oh. Is it?" I have no idea what I'm trying to say.

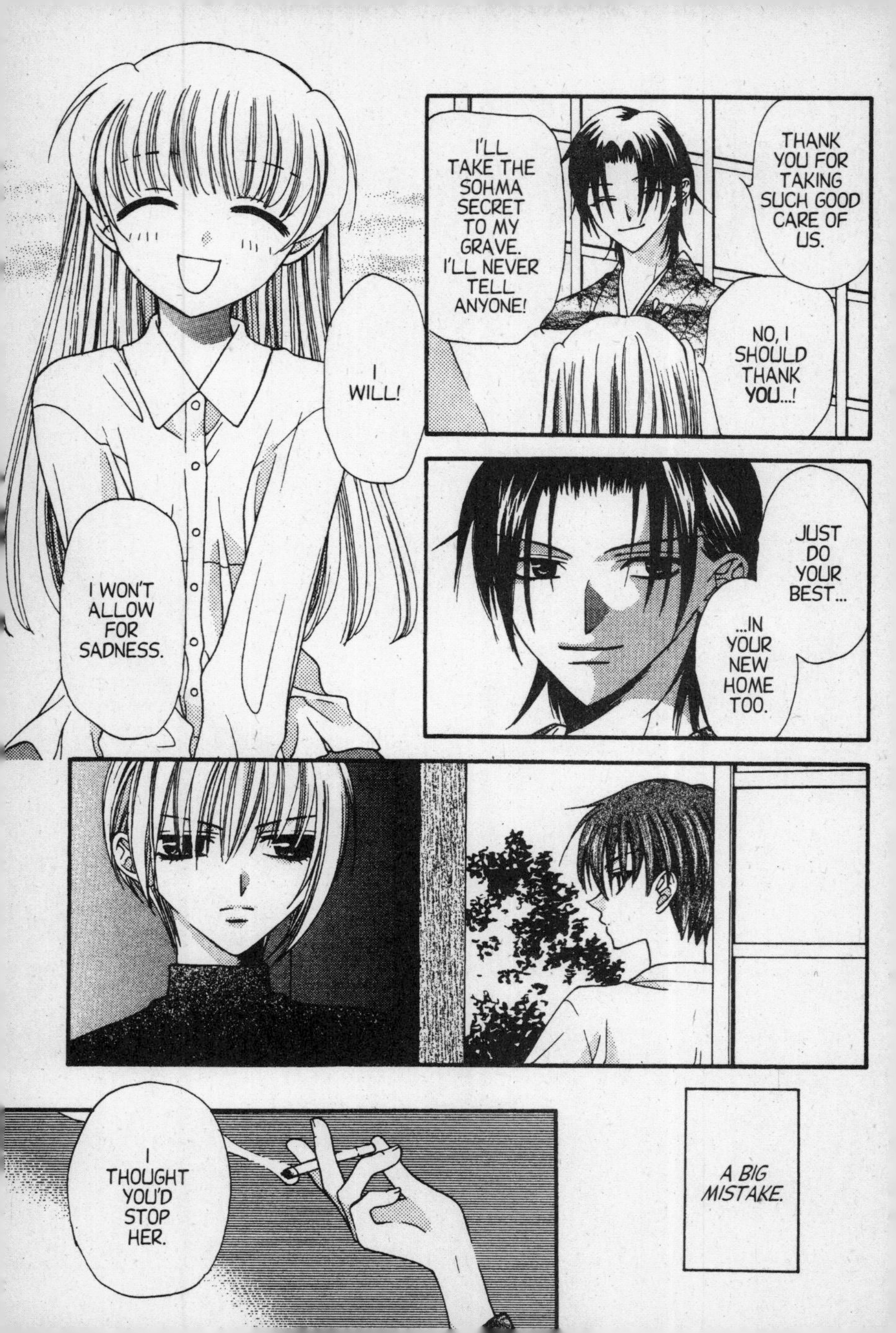
THANK YOU FOR TAKING SUCH GOOD CARE OF US.
I'LL TAKE THE SOHMA SECRET TO MY GRAVE. I'LL NEVER TELL ANYONE!
NO, I SHOULD THANK **YOU**...!
JUST DO YOUR BEST...
...IN YOUR NEW HOME TOO.
I WILL!
I WON'T ALLOW FOR SADNESS.
A BIG MISTAKE.
I THOUGHT YOU'D STOP HER.

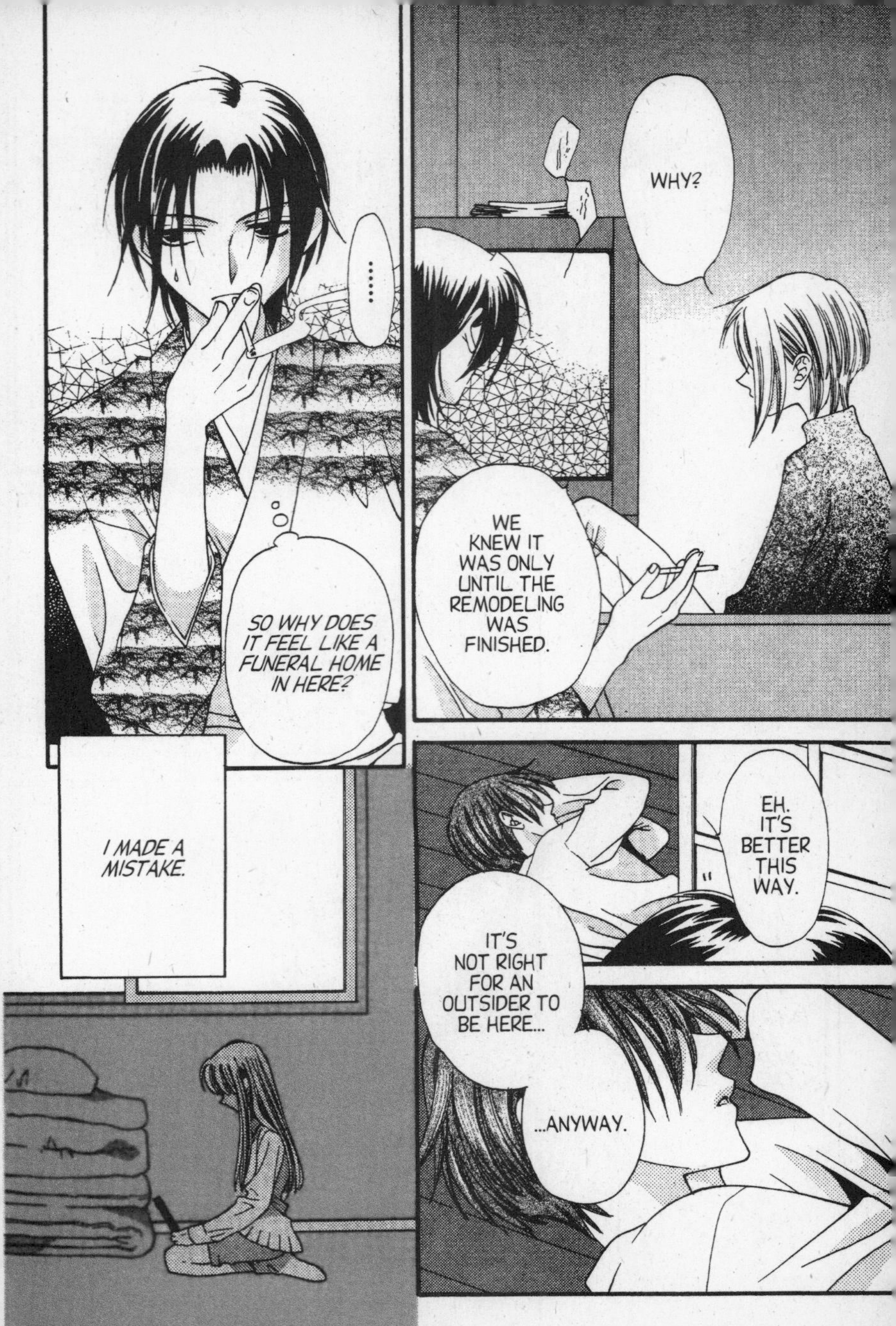
WHY?
WE KNEW IT WAS ONLY UNTIL THE REMODELING WAS FINISHED.
......
SO WHY DOES IT FEEL LIKE A FUNERAL HOME IN HERE?
EH. IT'S BETTER THIS WAY.
IT'S NOT RIGHT FOR AN OUTSIDER TO BE HERE...
...ANYWAY.
I MADE A MISTAKE.

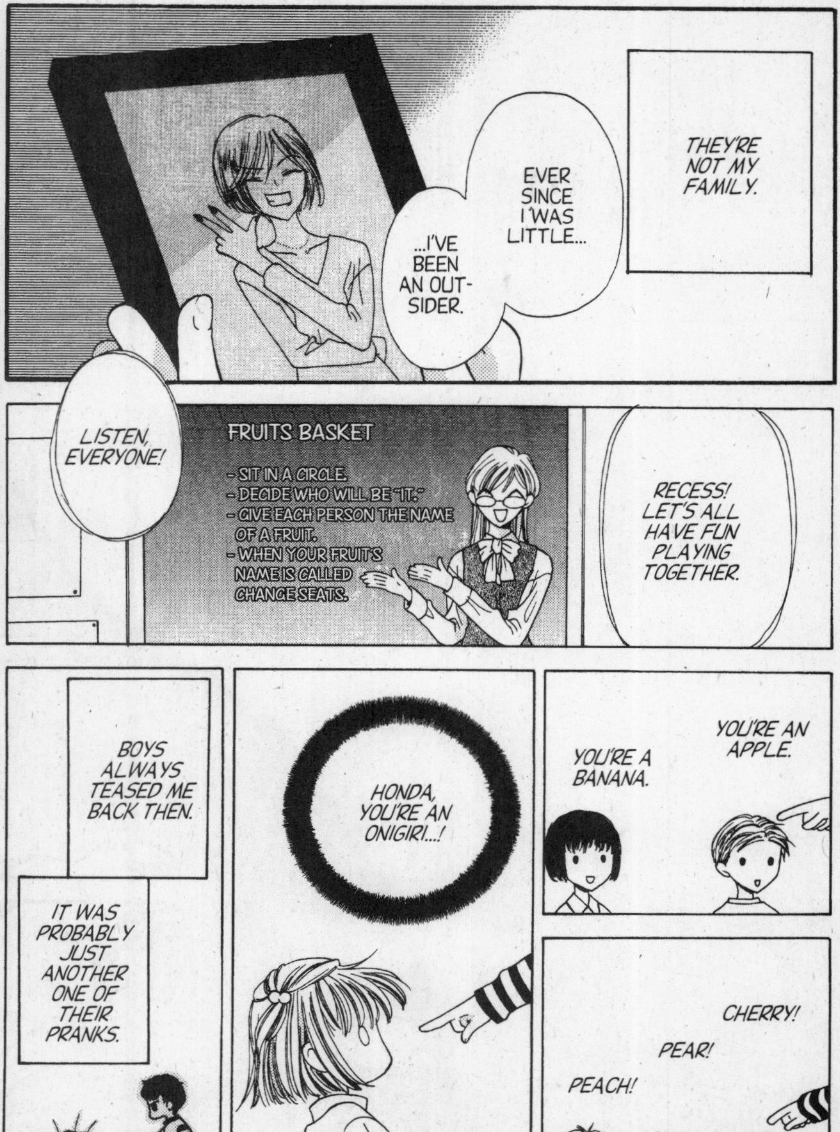
THEY'RE NOT MY FAMILY.
EVER SINCE I WAS LITTLE...
...I'VE BEEN AN OUT-SIDER.
RECESS! LET'S ALL HAVE FUN PLAYING TOGETHER.
FRUITS BASKET
- SIT IN A CIRCLE.
- DECIDE WHO WILL BE "IT."
- GIVE EACH PERSON THE NAME OF A FRUIT.
- WHEN YOUR FRUIT'S NAME IS CALLED CHANGE SEATS.
LISTEN, EVERYONE!
YOU'RE AN APPLE.
YOU'RE A BANANA.
CHERRY!
PEAR!
PEACH!
HONDA, YOU'RE AN ONIGIRI...!
*Onigiri = rice ball
BOYS ALWAYS TEASED ME BACK THEN.
IT WAS PROBABLY JUST ANOTHER ONE OF THEIR PRANKS.

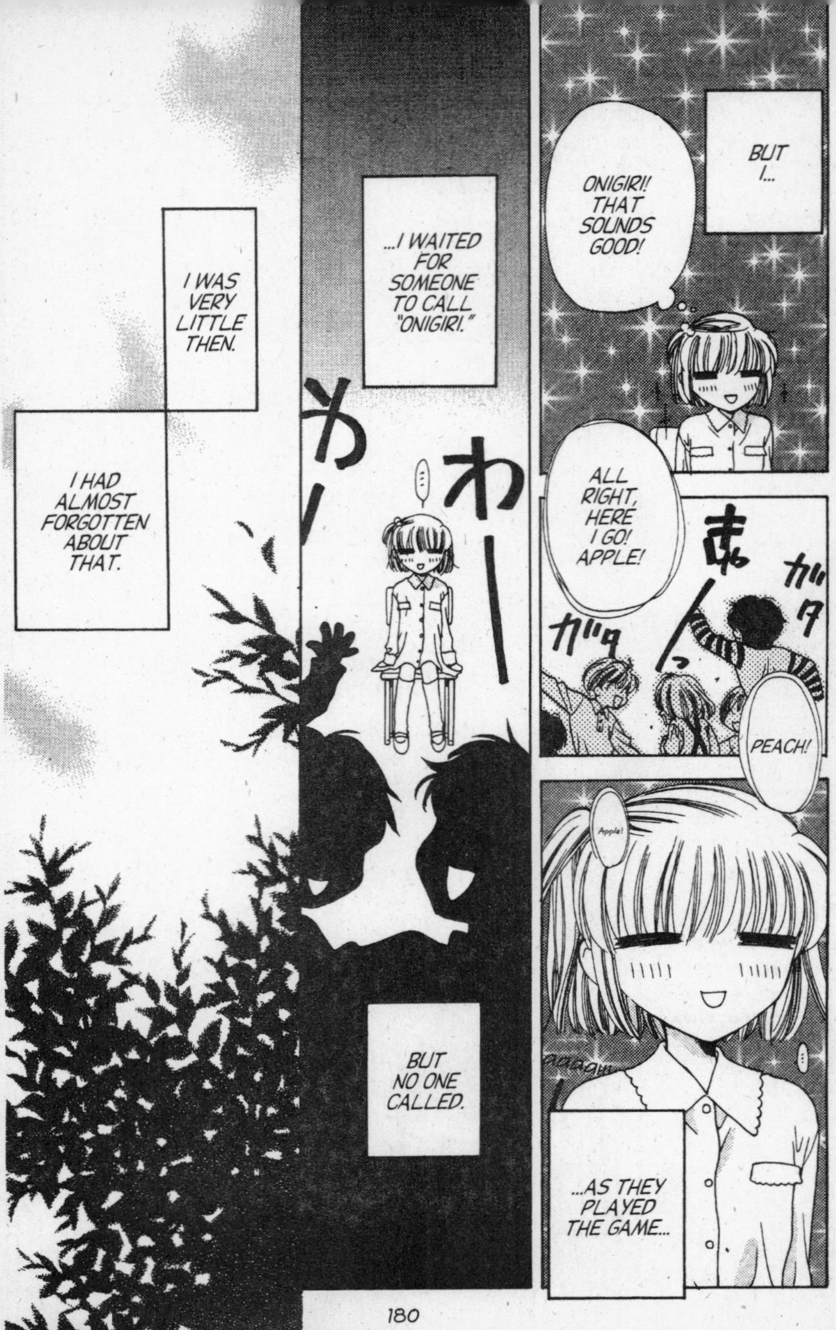
BUT I...
ONIGIRI! THAT SOUNDS GOOD!
ALL RIGHT, HERE I GO! APPLE!
PEACH!
Apple!
...AS THEY PLAYED THE GAME...
...I WAITED FOR SOMEONE TO CALL "ONIGIRI."
BUT NO ONE CALLED.
I WAS VERY LITTLE THEN.
I HAD ALMOST FORGOTTEN ABOUT THAT.

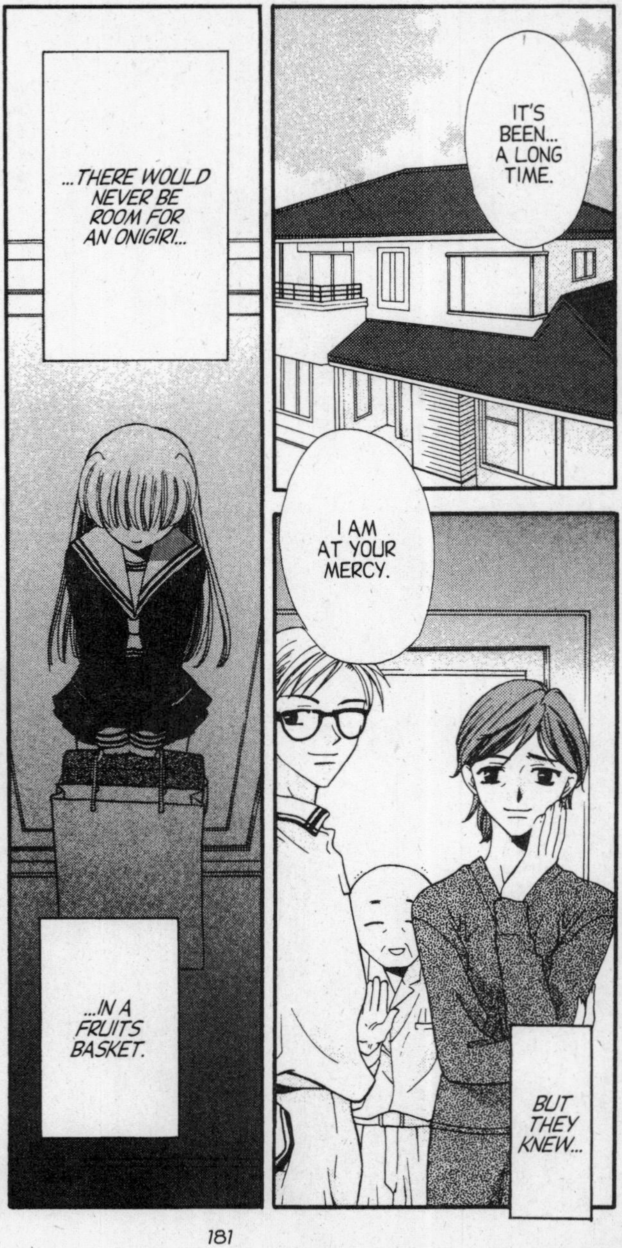
IT'S BEEN... A LONG TIME.
I AM AT YOUR MERCY.
BUT THEY KNEW...
...THERE WOULD NEVER BE ROOM FOR AN ONIGIRI...
...IN A FRUITS BASKET.

Number 7: When "Furuba" started in "Hana to Yume Magazine," there was a popularity contest. Here are the results:
First place... Yuki.
Second place... Tohru.
Third place... Kyo.
Fourth place... Shigure.
Fifth place... Hana.
Sixth place... Uo.
Seventh place... Mama.
If we do it now, we might have different results. Like, Kyo had only been around for one chapter. No one had a chance to fall in love with him yet!
Oh, and remember when Shigure teases Kyo with a song? The original words were "kyo-o-kun no su-ke-be." (Kyo-kun is a pervert). Can you guess the tune? Don't worry about it. I don't think anyone would really know it anyway. It'll just be my secret!

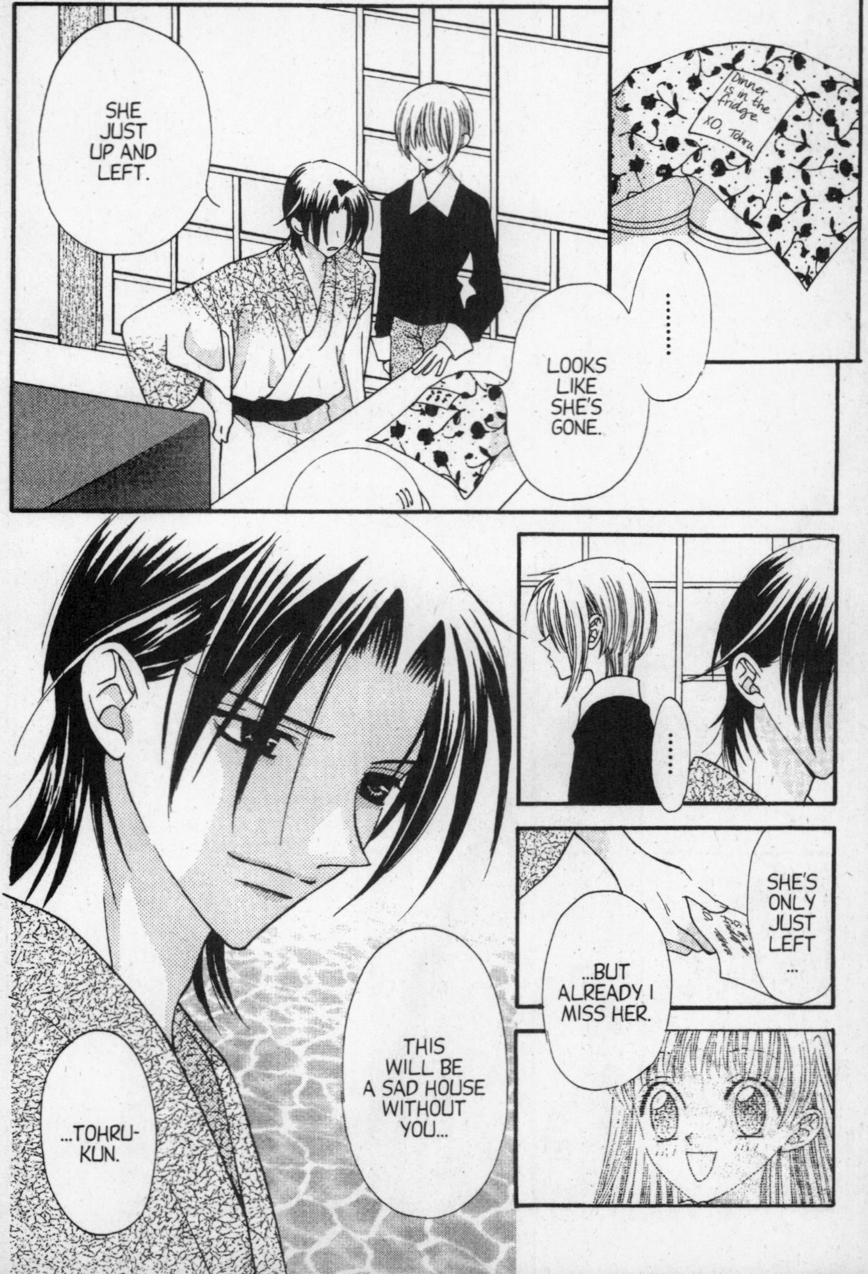

Dinner is in the fridge. XO, Tohru
……
LOOKS LIKE SHE'S GONE.
SHE JUST UP AND LEFT.
……
SHE'S ONLY JUST LEFT ...
...BUT ALREADY I MISS HER.
THIS WILL BE A SAD HOUSE WITHOUT YOU...
...TOHRU-KUN.

"I LOVE STRAW-BERRIES!"

"STRAW-BERRIES!"

"IF MY MEMORIES ARE ERASED..."

"...PLEASE..."

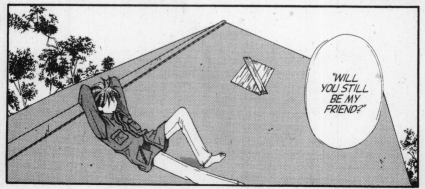

"WILL YOU STILL BE MY FRIEND?"

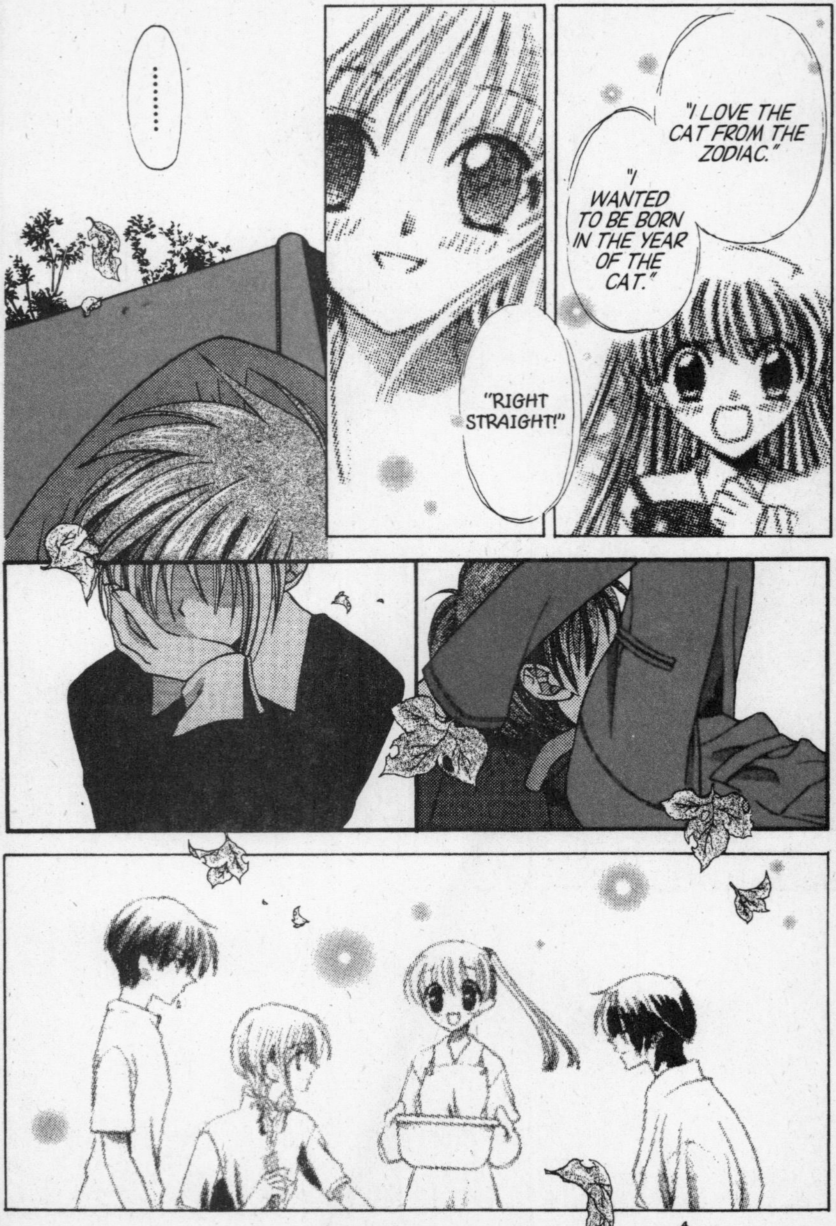
"I LOVE THE CAT FROM THE ZODIAC."
"I WANTED TO BE BORN IN THE YEAR OF THE CAT."
"RIGHT STRAIGHT!"
....

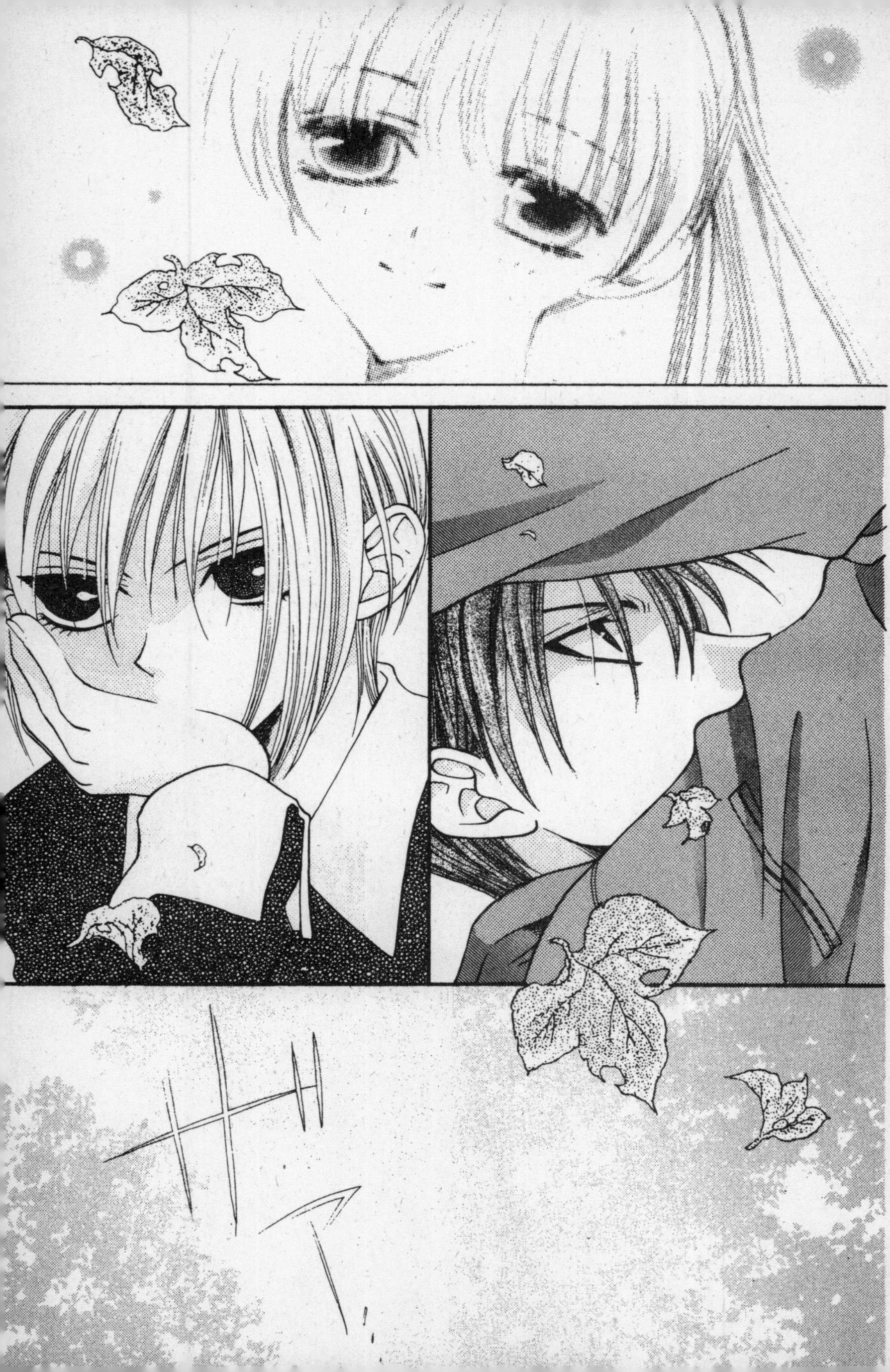

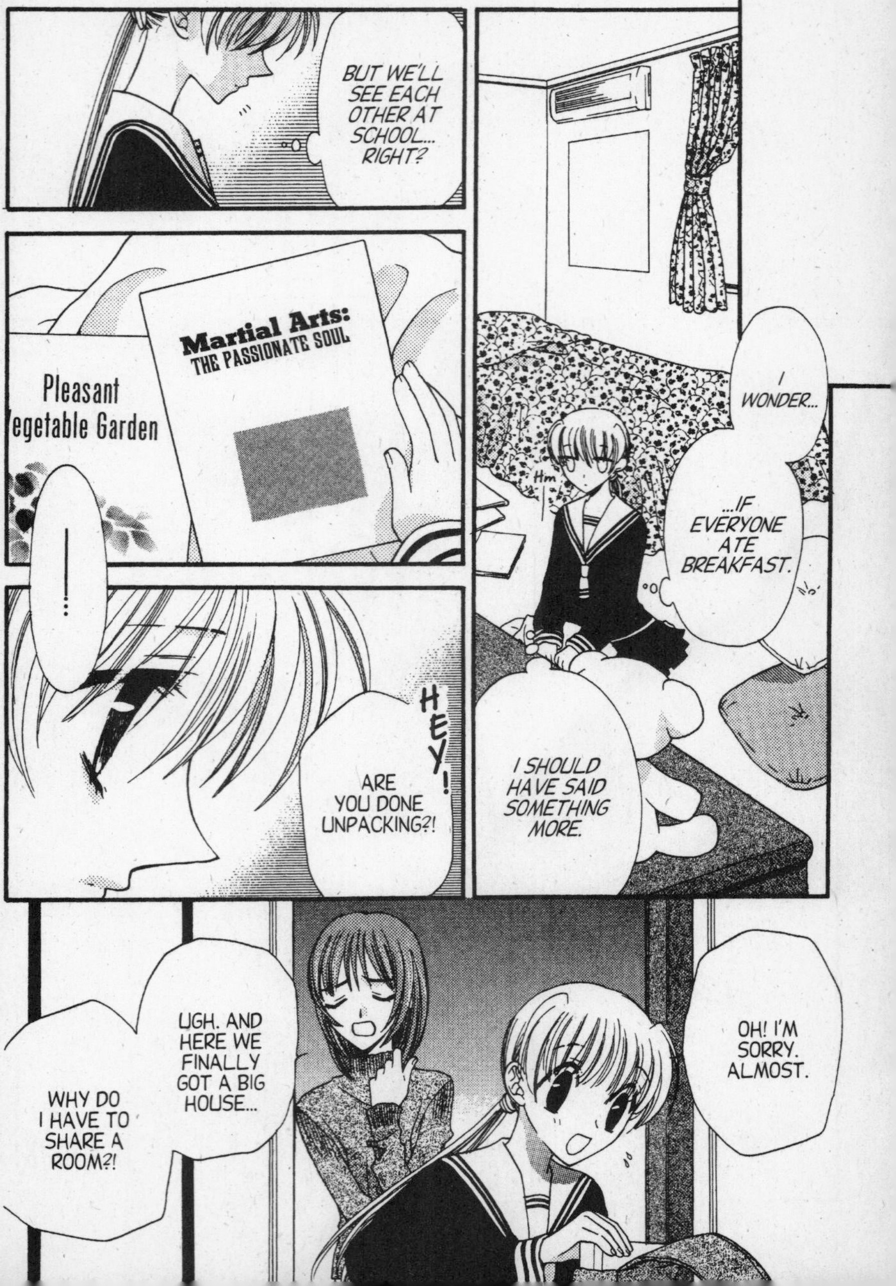
I WONDER...
...IF EVERYONE ATE BREAKFAST.
Hm
I SHOULD HAVE SAID SOMETHING MORE.
BUT WE'LL SEE EACH OTHER AT SCHOOL... RIGHT?
Martial Arts: THE PASSIONATE SOUL
Pleasant
egetable Garden
...!
HEY!
ARE YOU DONE UNPACKING?!
OH! I'M SORRY. ALMOST.
UGH. AND HERE WE FINALLY GOT A BIG HOUSE...
WHY DO I HAVE TO SHARE A ROOM?!

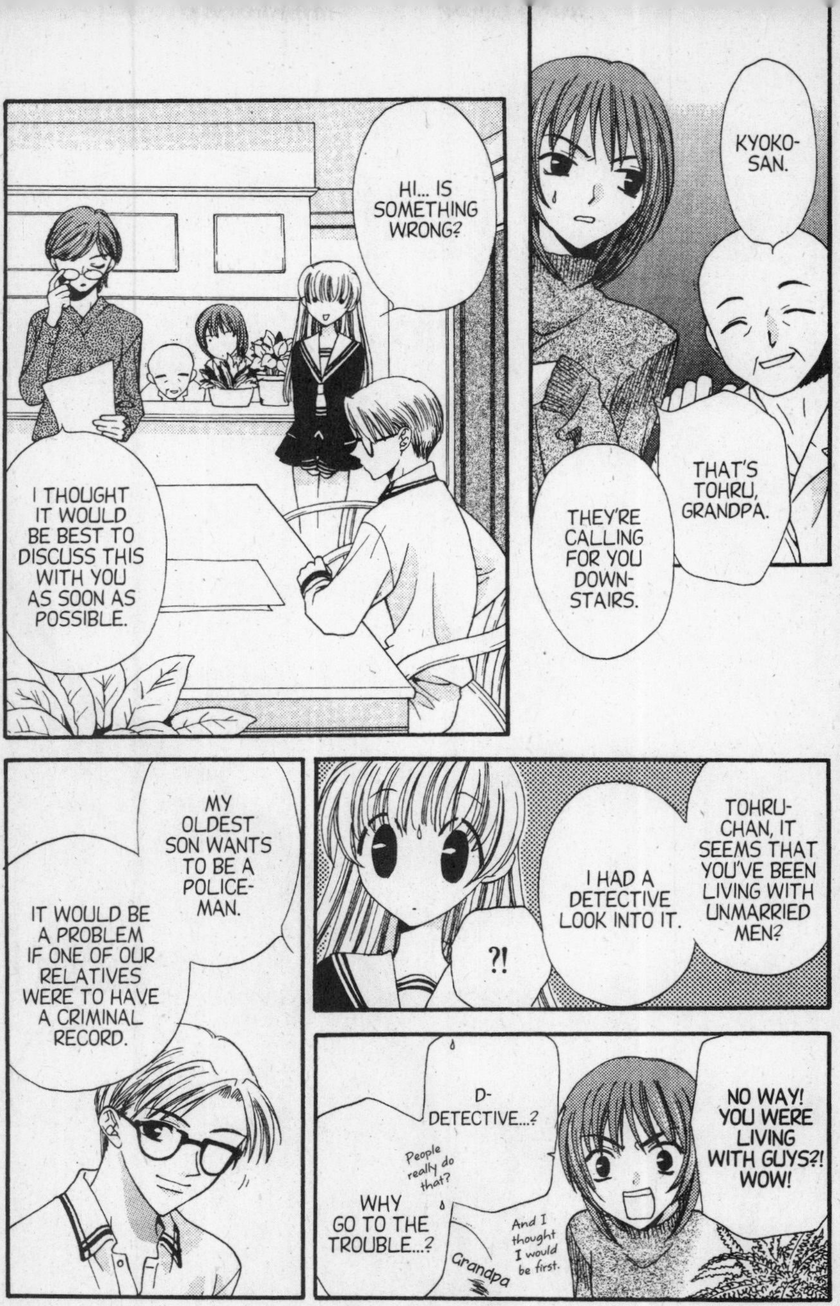
KYOKO-SAN.
THAT'S TOHRU, GRANDPA.
THEY'RE CALLING FOR YOU DOWNSTAIRS.
HI... IS SOMETHING WRONG?
I THOUGHT IT WOULD BE BEST TO DISCUSS THIS WITH YOU AS SOON AS POSSIBLE.
TOHRU-CHAN, IT SEEMS THAT YOU'VE BEEN LIVING WITH UNMARRIED MEN?
I HAD A DETECTIVE LOOK INTO IT.
?!
NO WAY! YOU WERE LIVING WITH GUYS?! WOW!
And I thought I would be first.
D-DETECTIVE...?
People really do that?
WHY GO TO THE TROUBLE...?
Grandpa
MY OLDEST SON WANTS TO BE A POLICEMAN.
IT WOULD BE A PROBLEM IF ONE OF OUR RELATIVES WERE TO HAVE A CRIMINAL RECORD.

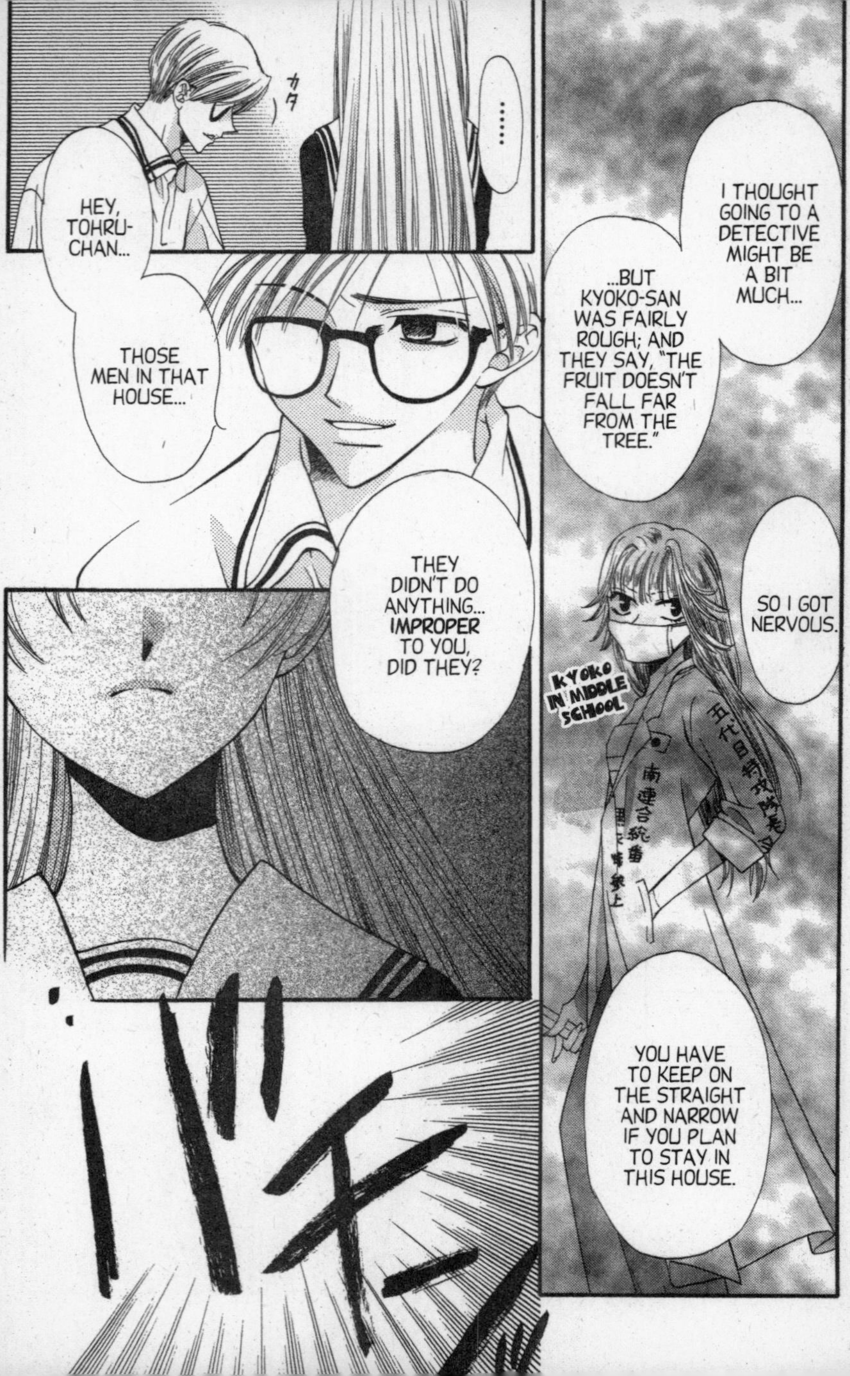
I THOUGHT GOING TO A DETECTIVE MIGHT BE A BIT MUCH...
...BUT KYOKO-SAN WAS FAIRLY ROUGH; AND THEY SAY, "THE FRUIT DOESN'T FALL FAR FROM THE TREE."
SO I GOT NERVOUS.
KYOKO IN MIDDLE SCHOOL
YOU HAVE TO KEEP ON THE STRAIGHT AND NARROW IF YOU PLAN TO STAY IN THIS HOUSE.
カタ
......
HEY, TOHRU-CHAN...
THOSE MEN IN THAT HOUSE...
THEY DIDN'T DO ANYTHING... **IMPROPER** TO YOU, DID THEY?

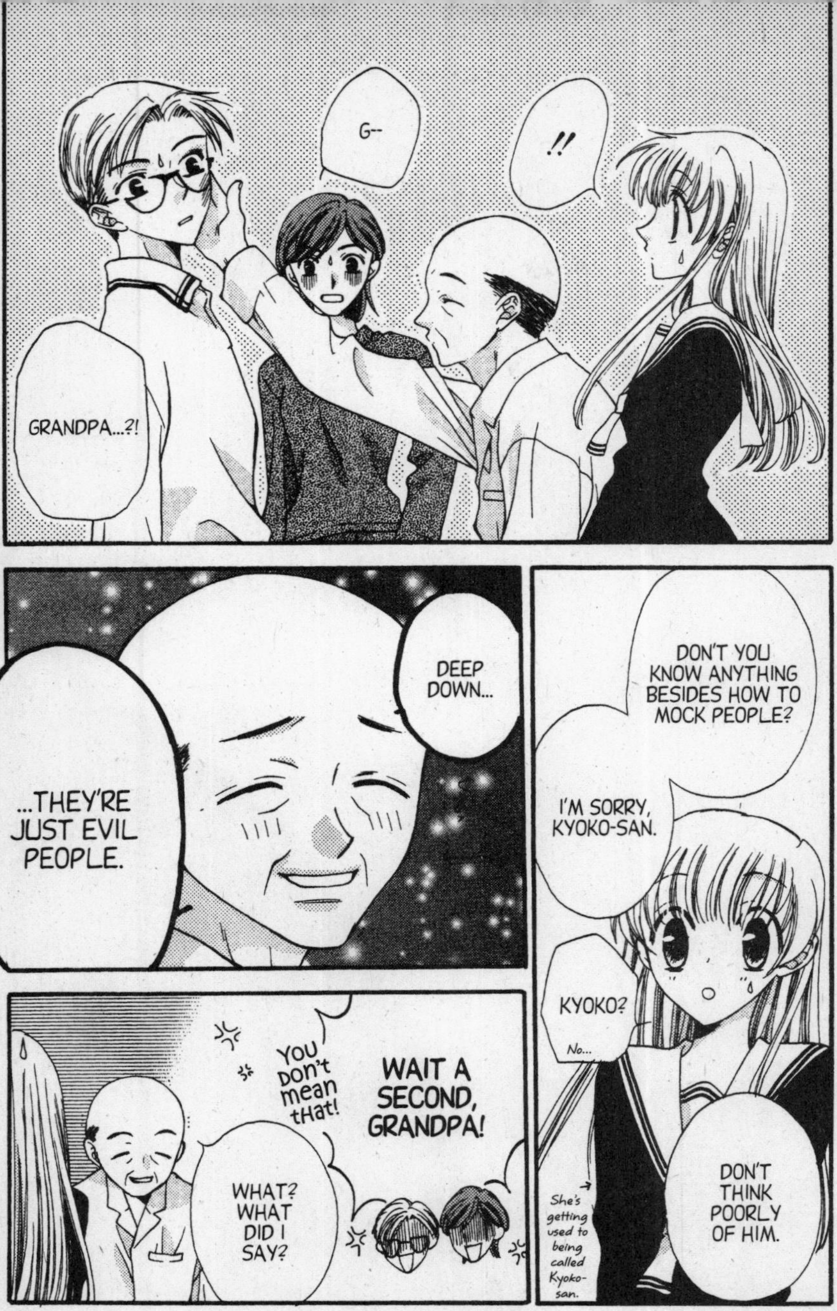
!!
G--
GRANDPA...?!
DON'T YOU KNOW ANYTHING BESIDES HOW TO MOCK PEOPLE?
I'M SORRY, KYOKO-SAN.
KYOKO?
No...
DON'T THINK POORLY OF HIM.
She's getting used to being called Kyoko-san.
DEEP DOWN...
...THEY'RE JUST EVIL PEOPLE.
WAIT A SECOND, GRANDPA!
You don't mean that!
WHAT? WHAT DID I SAY?

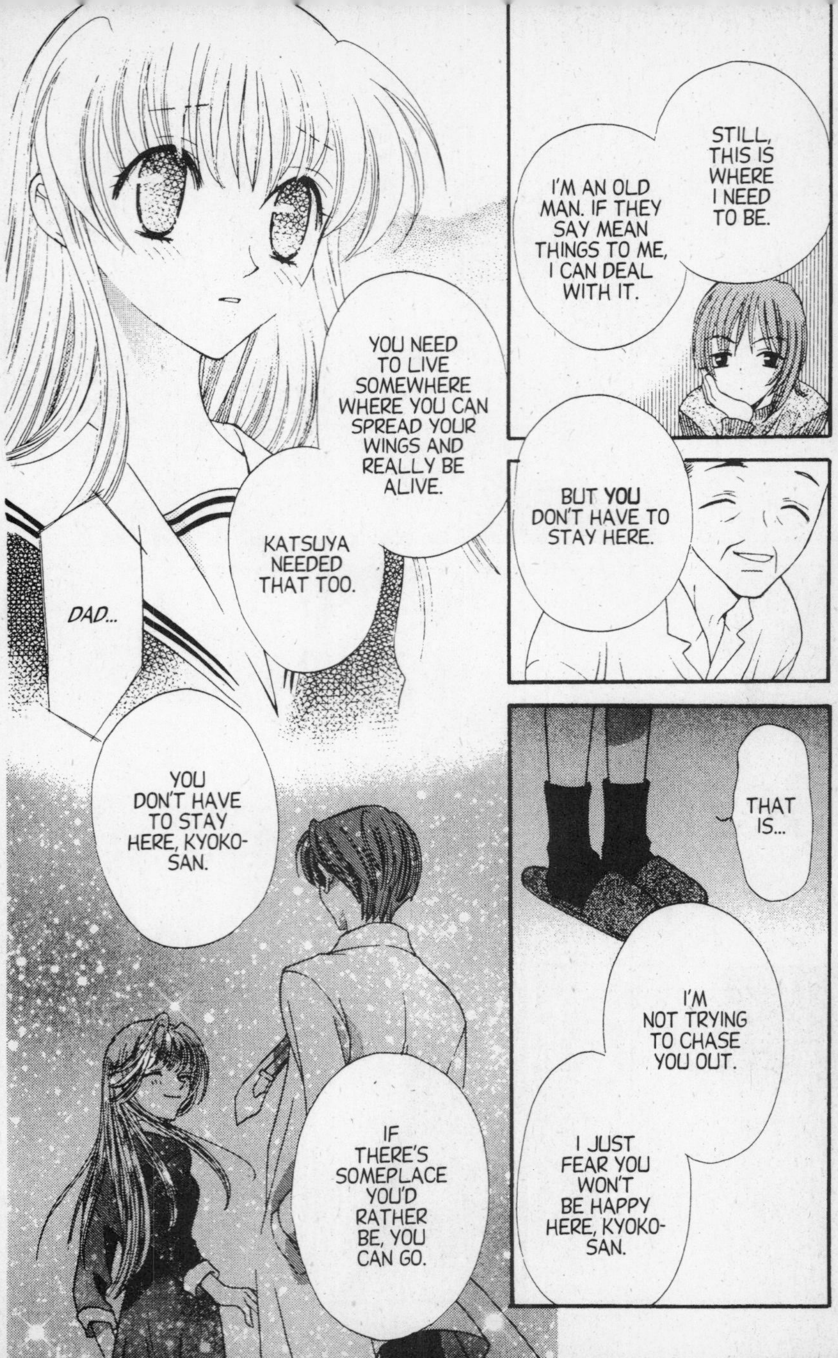
STILL, THIS IS WHERE I NEED TO BE.
I'M AN OLD MAN. IF THEY SAY MEAN THINGS TO ME, I CAN DEAL WITH IT.
BUT YOU DON'T HAVE TO STAY HERE.
THAT IS...
I'M NOT TRYING TO CHASE YOU OUT.
I JUST FEAR YOU WON'T BE HAPPY HERE, KYOKO-SAN.
YOU NEED TO LIVE SOMEWHERE WHERE YOU CAN SPREAD YOUR WINGS AND REALLY BE ALIVE.
KATSUYA NEEDED THAT TOO.
DAD...
YOU DON'T HAVE TO STAY HERE, KYOKO-SAN.
IF THERE'S SOMEPLACE YOU'D RATHER BE, YOU CAN GO.

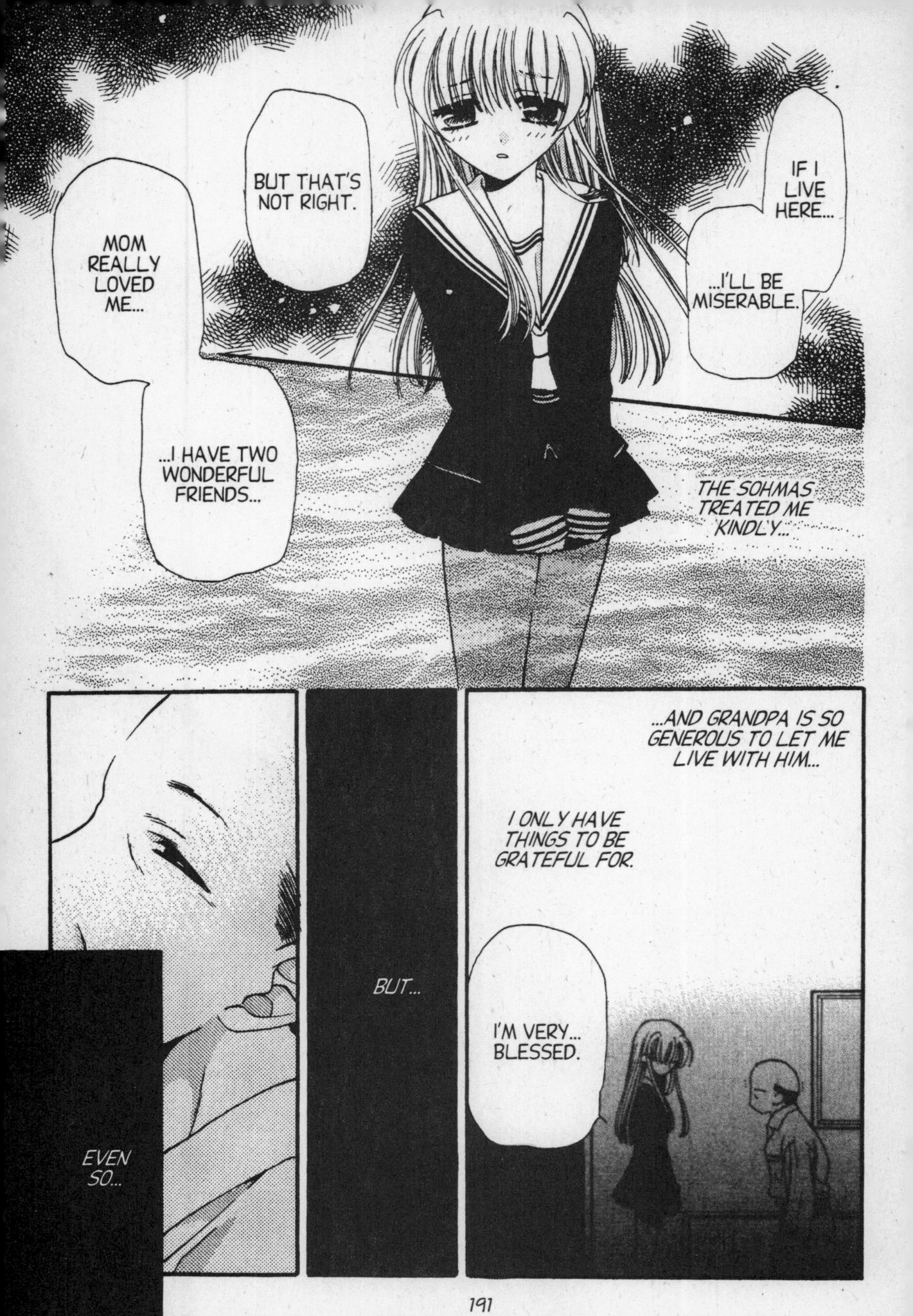
IF I LIVE HERE...
...I'LL BE MISERABLE.
BUT THAT'S NOT RIGHT.
MOM REALLY LOVED ME...
...I HAVE TWO WONDERFUL FRIENDS...
THE SOHMAS TREATED ME KINDLY...
...AND GRANDPA IS SO GENEROUS TO LET ME LIVE WITH HIM...
I ONLY HAVE THINGS TO BE GRATEFUL FOR.
I'M VERY... BLESSED.
BUT...
EVEN SO...

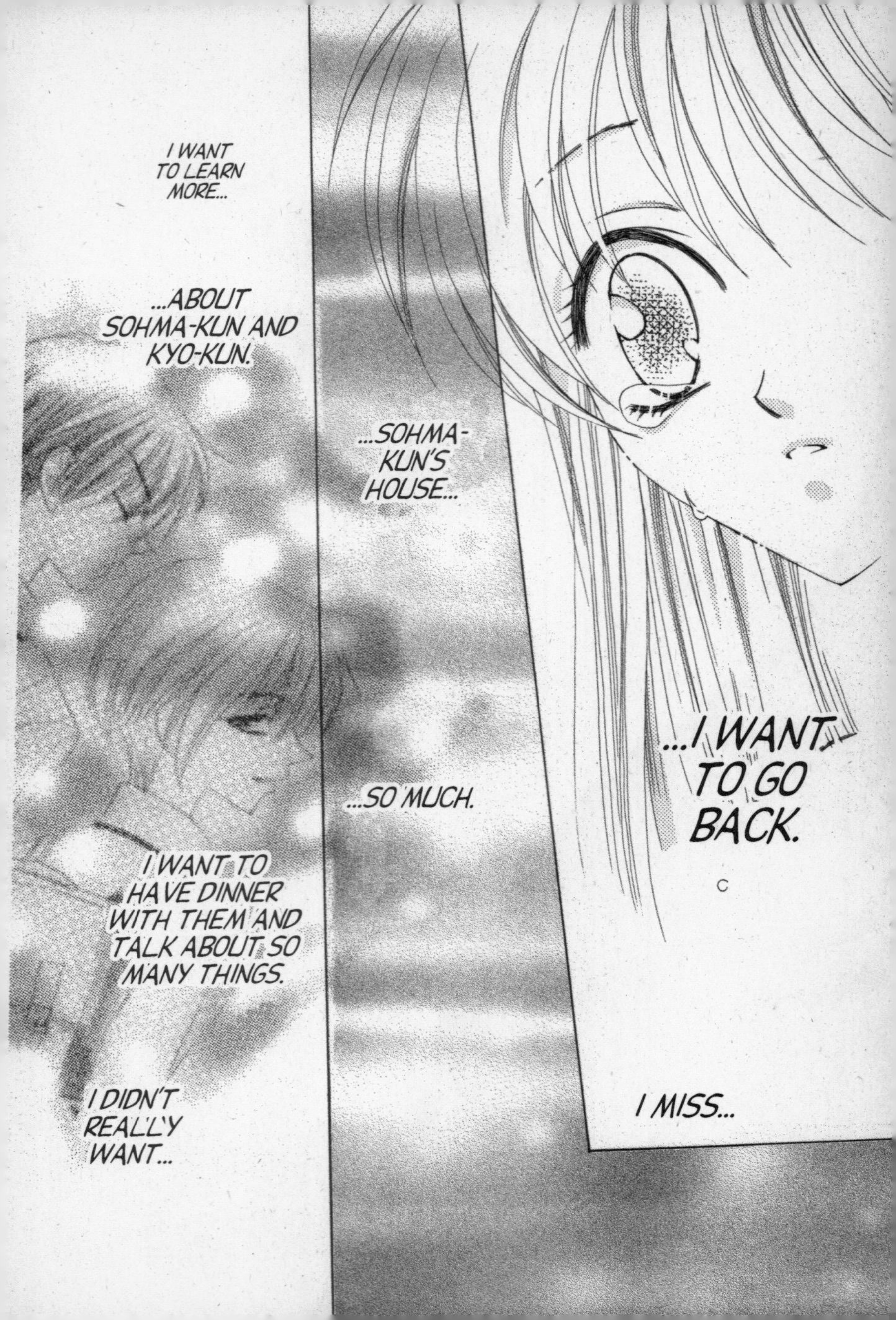
...I WANT TO GO BACK.
I MISS...
...SOHMA-KUN'S HOUSE...
...SO MUCH.
I WANT TO LEARN MORE...
...ABOUT SOHMA-KUN AND KYO-KUN.
I WANT TO HAVE DINNER WITH THEM AND TALK ABOUT SO MANY THINGS.
I DIDN'T REALLY WANT...

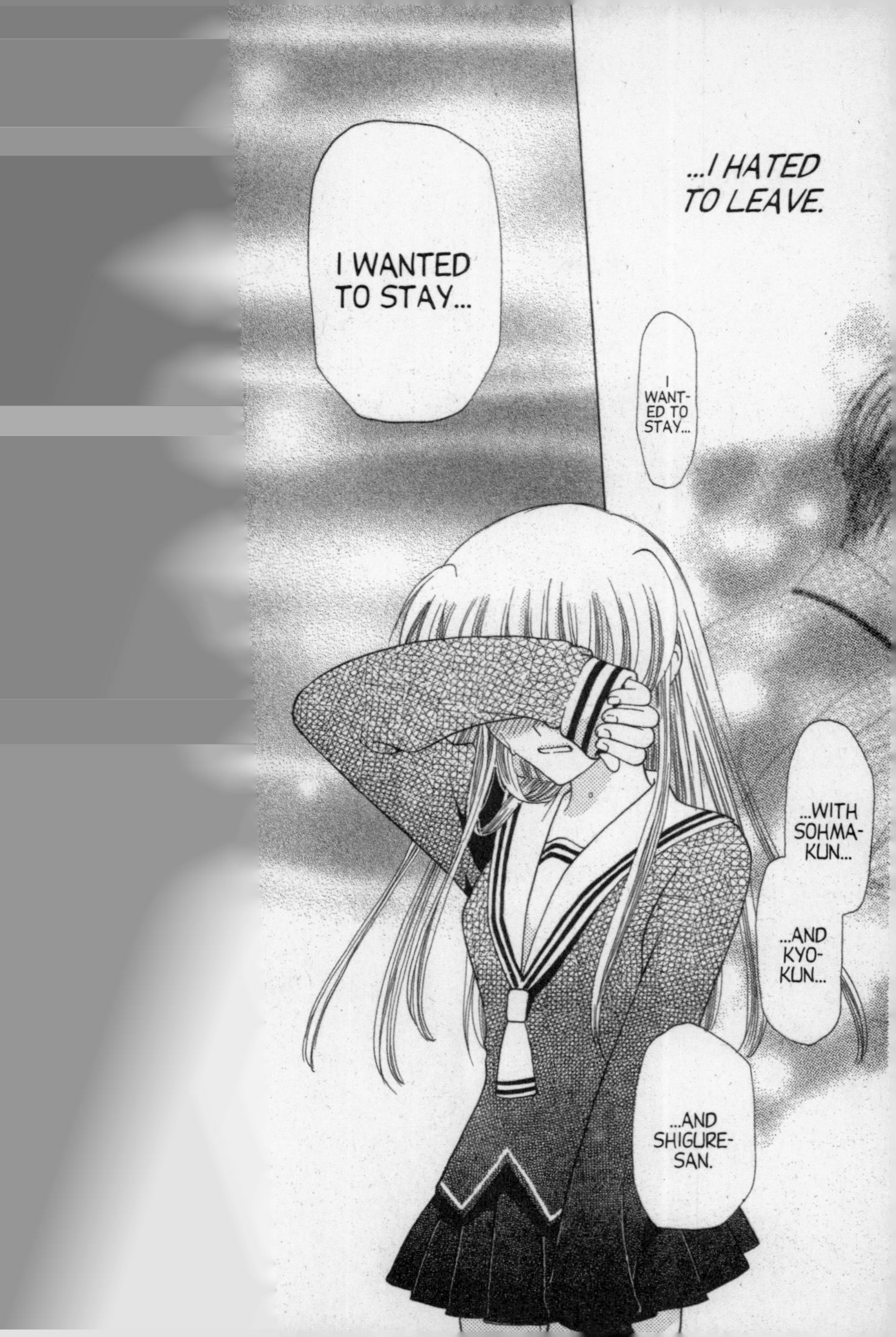
...I HATED TO LEAVE.
I WANTED TO STAY...
I WANTED TO STAY...
...WITH SOHMA-KUN...
...AND KYO-KUN...
...AND SHIGURE-SAN.

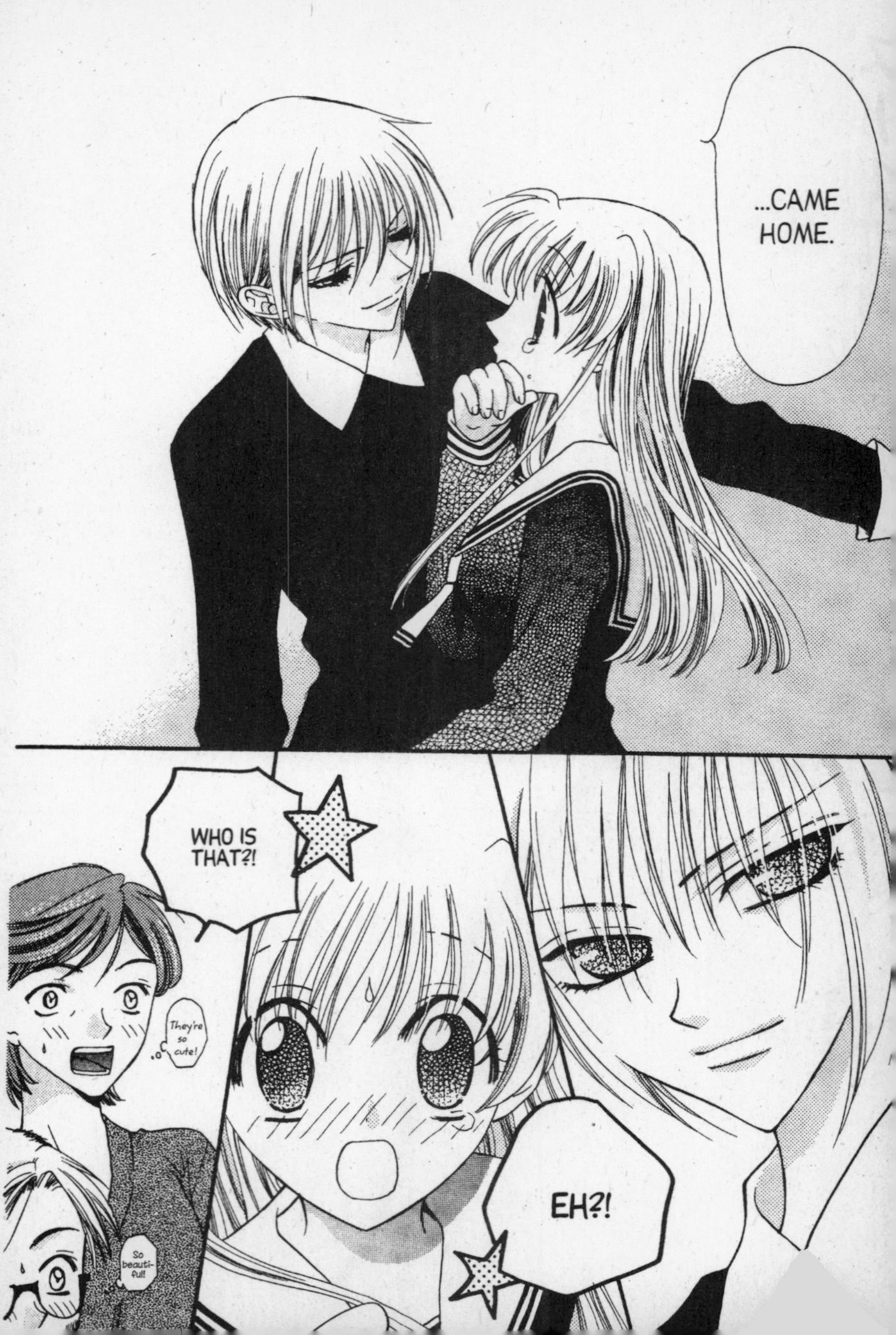
...CAME HOME.
EH?!
WHO IS THAT?!
They're so cute!
So beauti-ful!

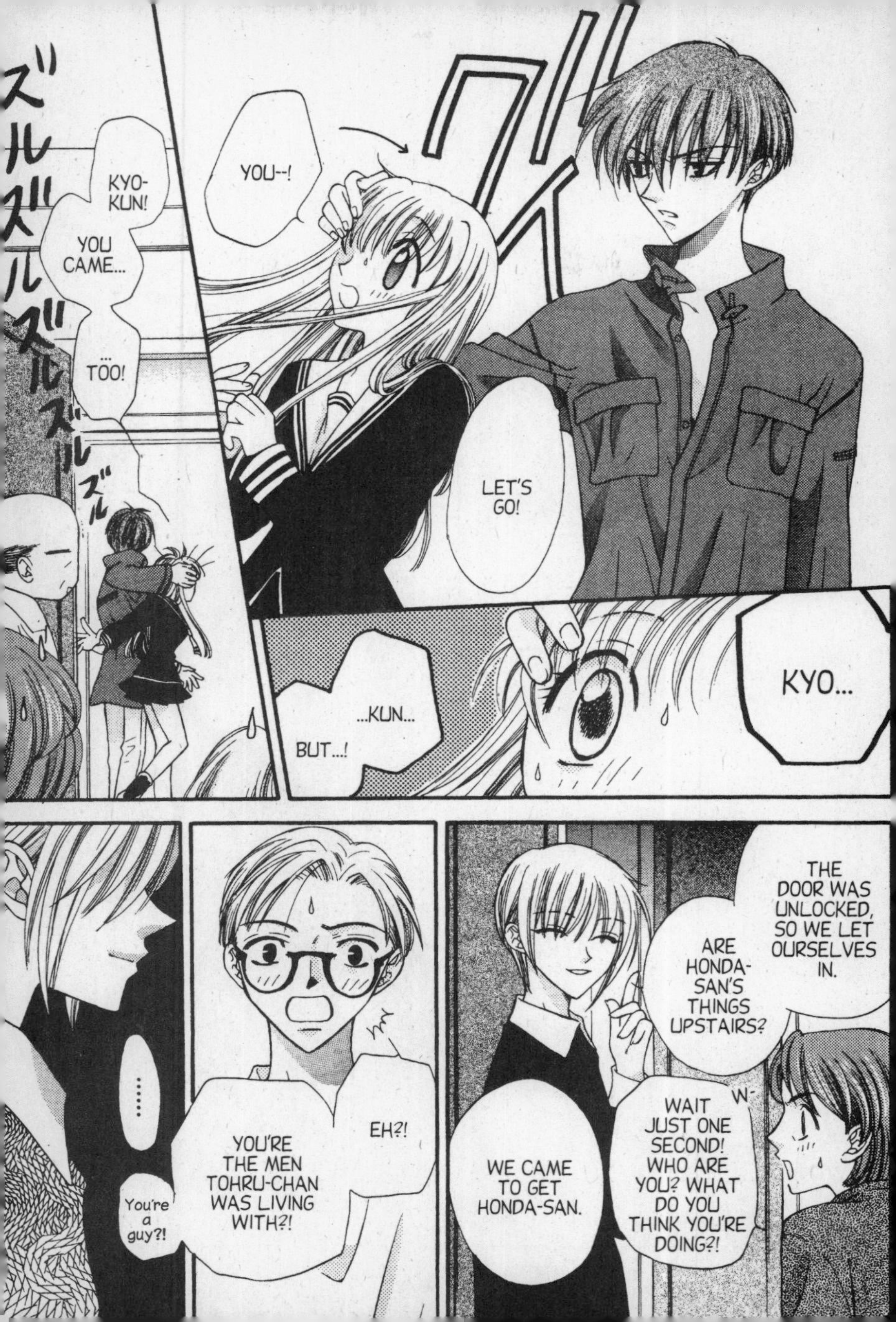
YOU--!
LET'S GO!
KYO...
...KUN...
BUT...!
KYO-KUN!
YOU CAME...
...TOO!
THE DOOR WAS UNLOCKED, SO WE LET OURSELVES IN.
ARE HONDA-SAN'S THINGS UPSTAIRS?
W-WAIT JUST ONE SECOND! WHO ARE YOU? WHAT DO YOU THINK YOU'RE DOING?!
WE CAME TO GET HONDA-SAN.
EH?!
YOU'RE THE MEN TOHRU-CHAN WAS LIVING WITH?!
......
You're a guy?!

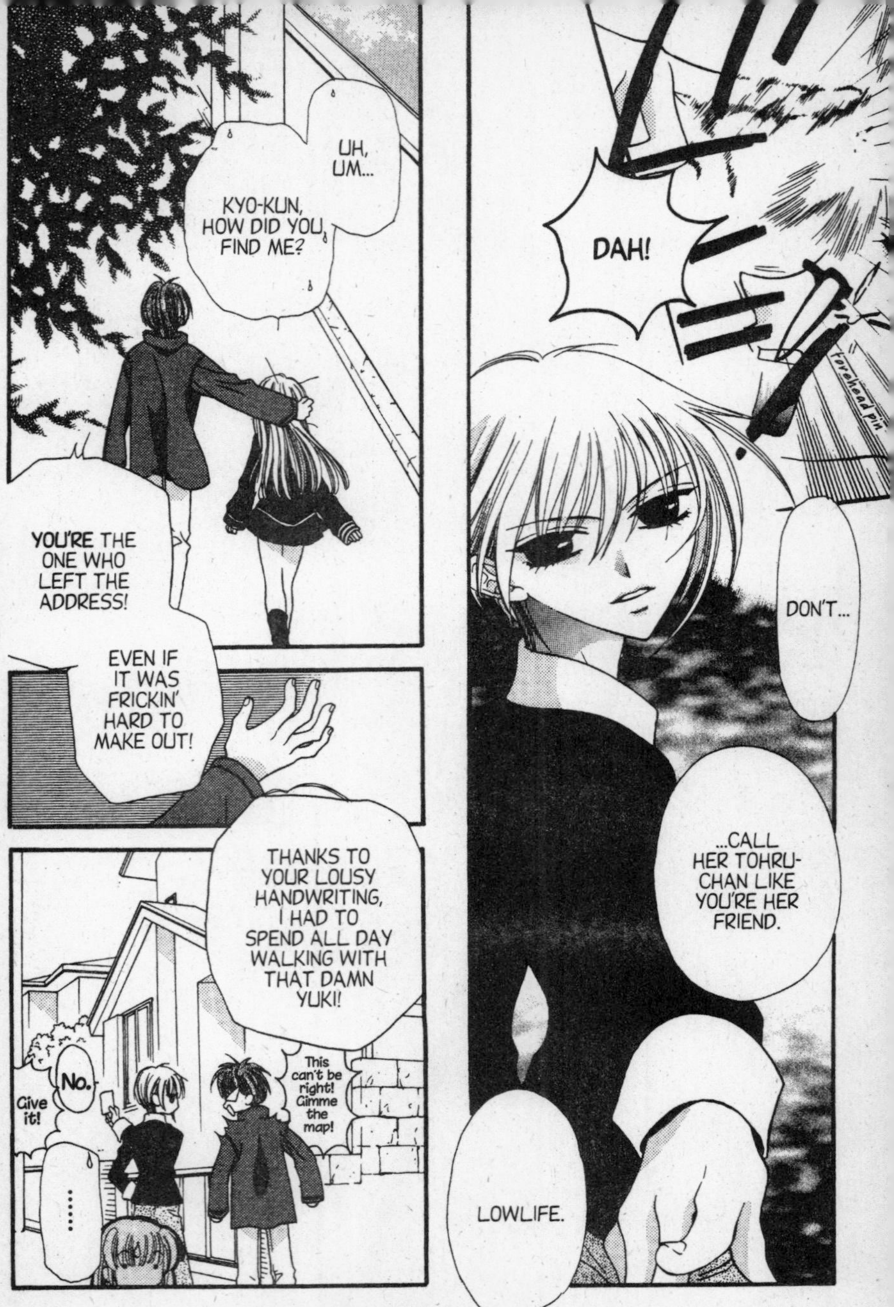
DAH!
forehead pin
DON'T...
...CALL HER TOHRU-CHAN LIKE YOU'RE HER FRIEND.
LOWLIFE.
UH, UM...
KYO-KUN, HOW DID YOU FIND ME?
YOU'RE THE ONE WHO LEFT THE ADDRESS!
EVEN IF IT WAS FRICKIN' HARD TO MAKE OUT!
THANKS TO YOUR LOUSY HANDWRITING, I HAD TO SPEND ALL DAY WALKING WITH THAT DAMN YUKI!
This can't be right! Gimme the map!
No.
Give it!
......

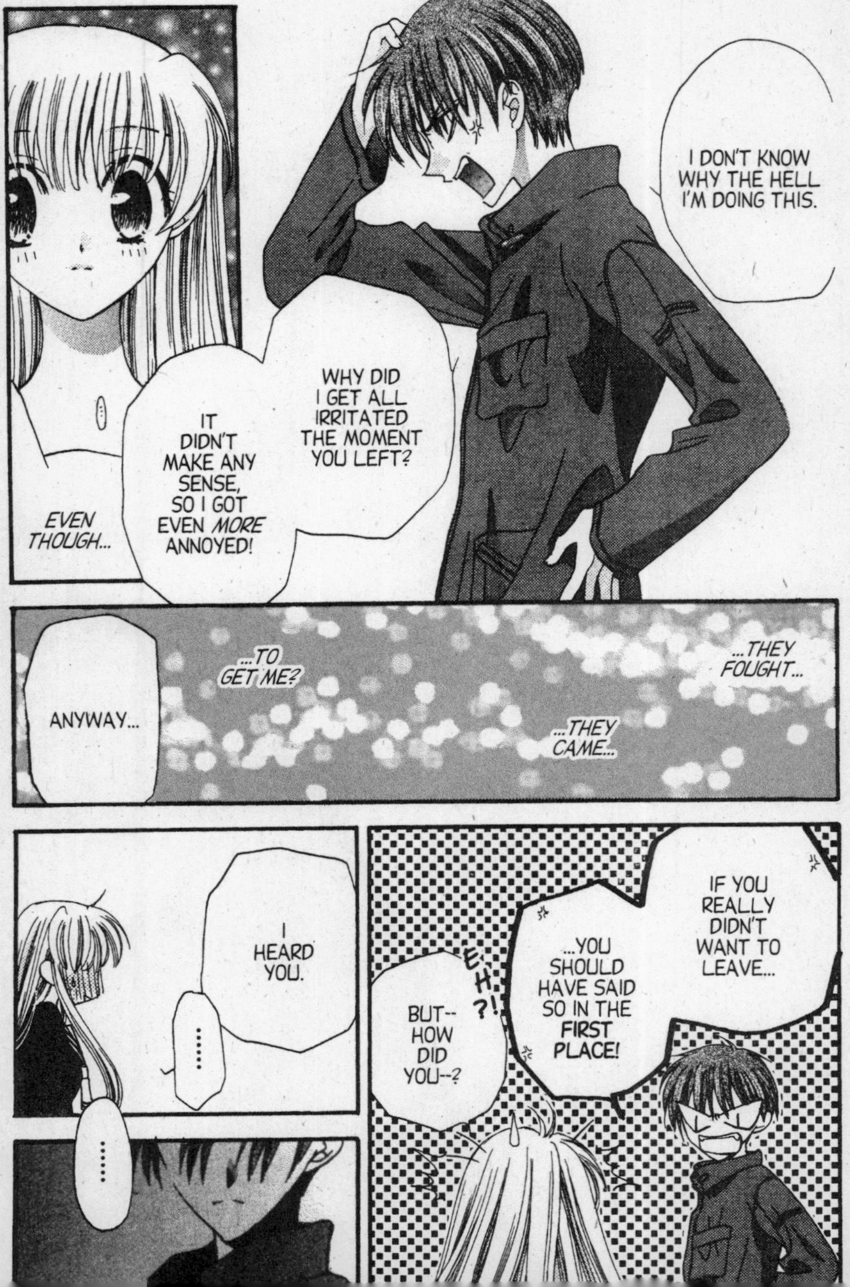

I DON'T KNOW WHY THE HELL I'M DOING THIS.
WHY DID I GET ALL IRRITATED THE MOMENT YOU LEFT?
IT DIDN'T MAKE ANY SENSE, SO I GOT EVEN *MORE* ANNOYED!
EVEN THOUGH...
...THEY FOUGHT...
...THEY CAME...
...TO GET ME?
ANYWAY...
IF YOU REALLY DIDN'T WANT TO LEAVE...
...YOU SHOULD HAVE SAID SO IN THE **FIRST PLACE!**
EH?!
BUT--HOW DID YOU--?
I HEARD YOU.
......
......

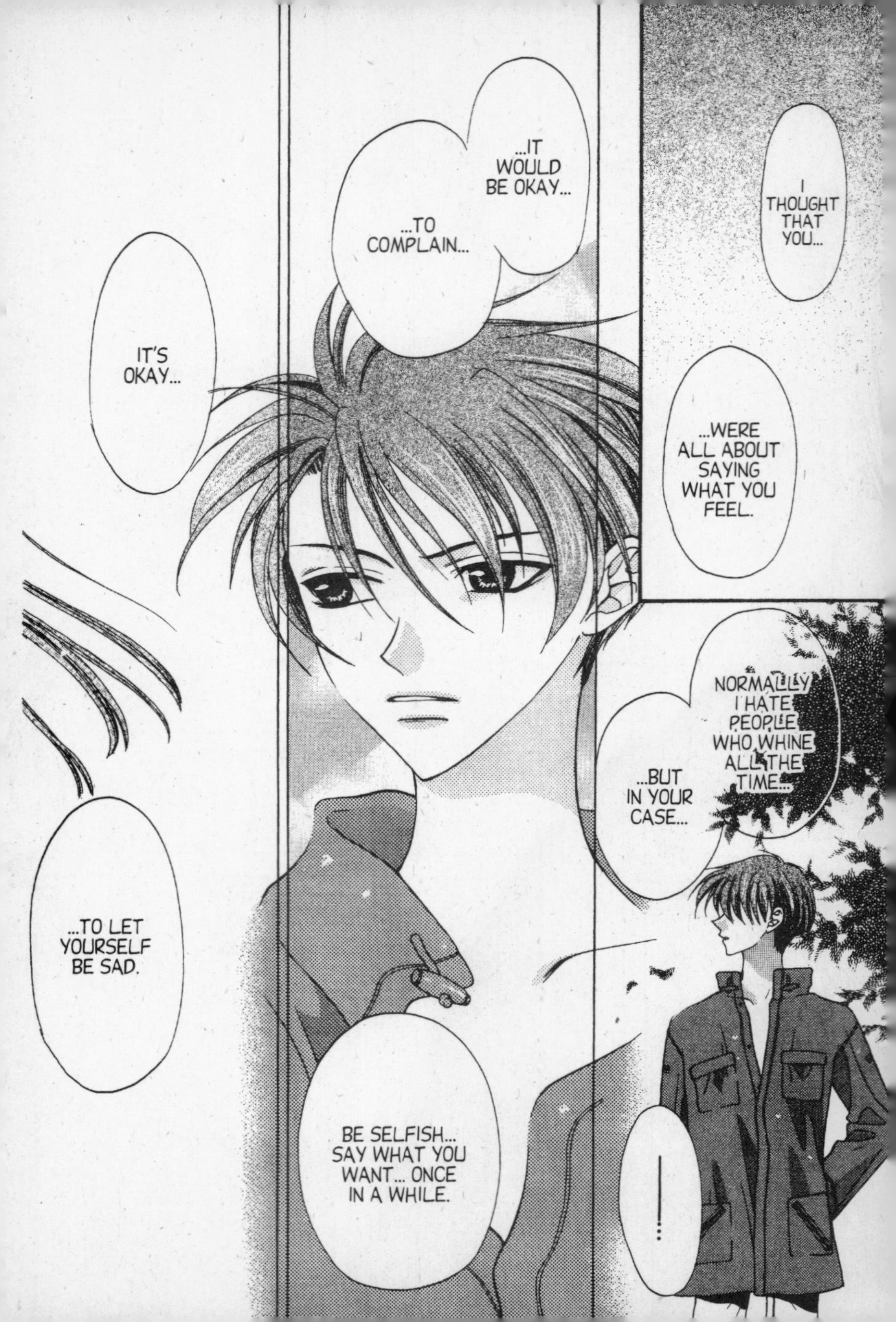
I THOUGHT THAT YOU...
...WERE ALL ABOUT SAYING WHAT YOU FEEL.
NORMALLY I HATE PEOPLE WHO WHINE ALL THE TIME...
...BUT IN YOUR CASE...
—...!
...IT WOULD BE OKAY...
...TO COMPLAIN...
BE SELFISH... SAY WHAT YOU WANT... ONCE IN A WHILE.
IT'S OKAY...
...TO LET YOURSELF BE SAD.

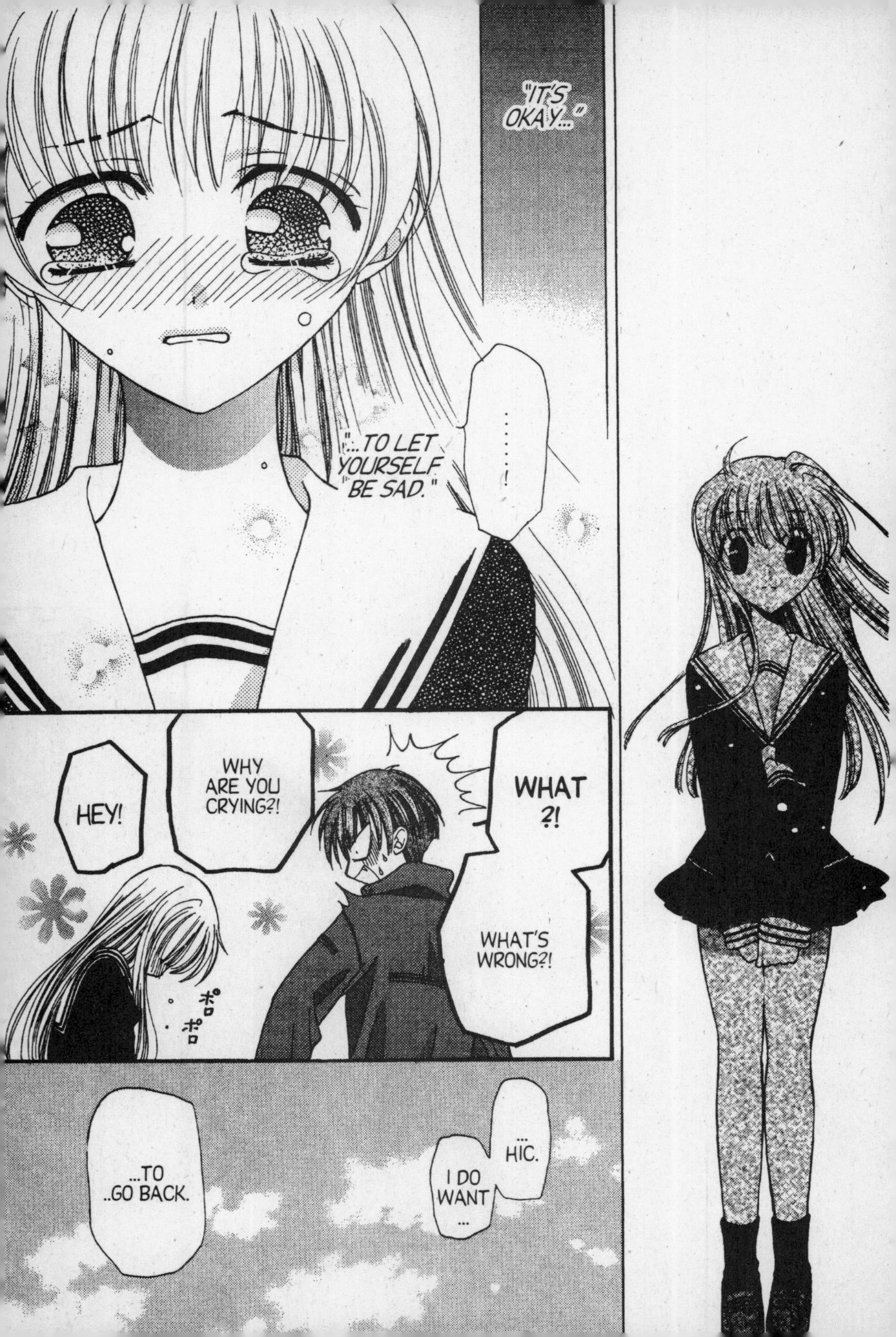
"IT'S OKAY..."
"...TO LET YOURSELF BE SAD."
......!
WHAT ?!
WHAT'S WRONG?!
WHY ARE YOU CRYING?!
HEY!
ポロ ポロ
...HIC.
I DO WANT ...
...TO ..GO BACK.

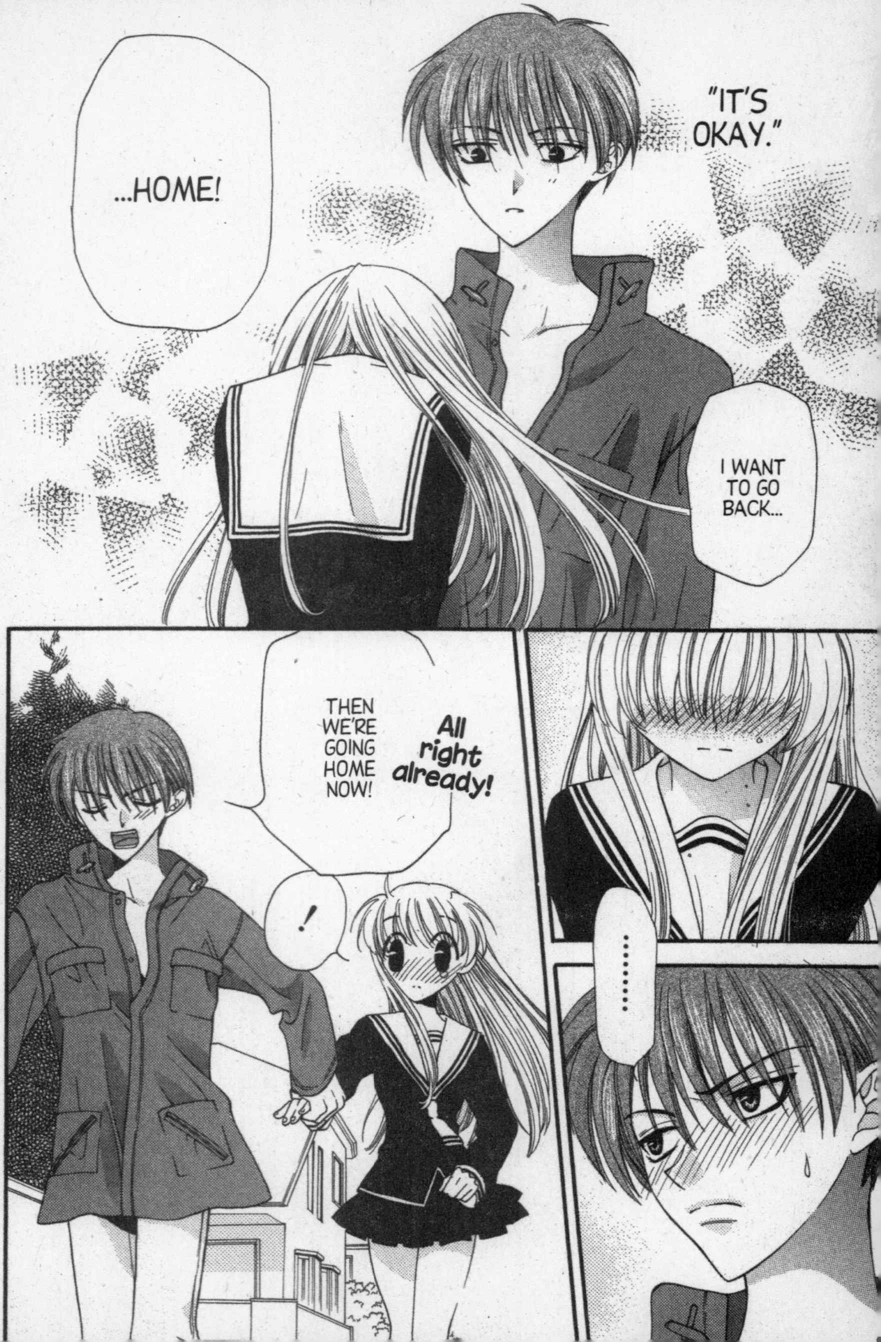
"IT'S OKAY."
I WANT TO GO BACK...
...HOME!
......
All right already!
THEN WE'RE GOING HOME NOW!
!

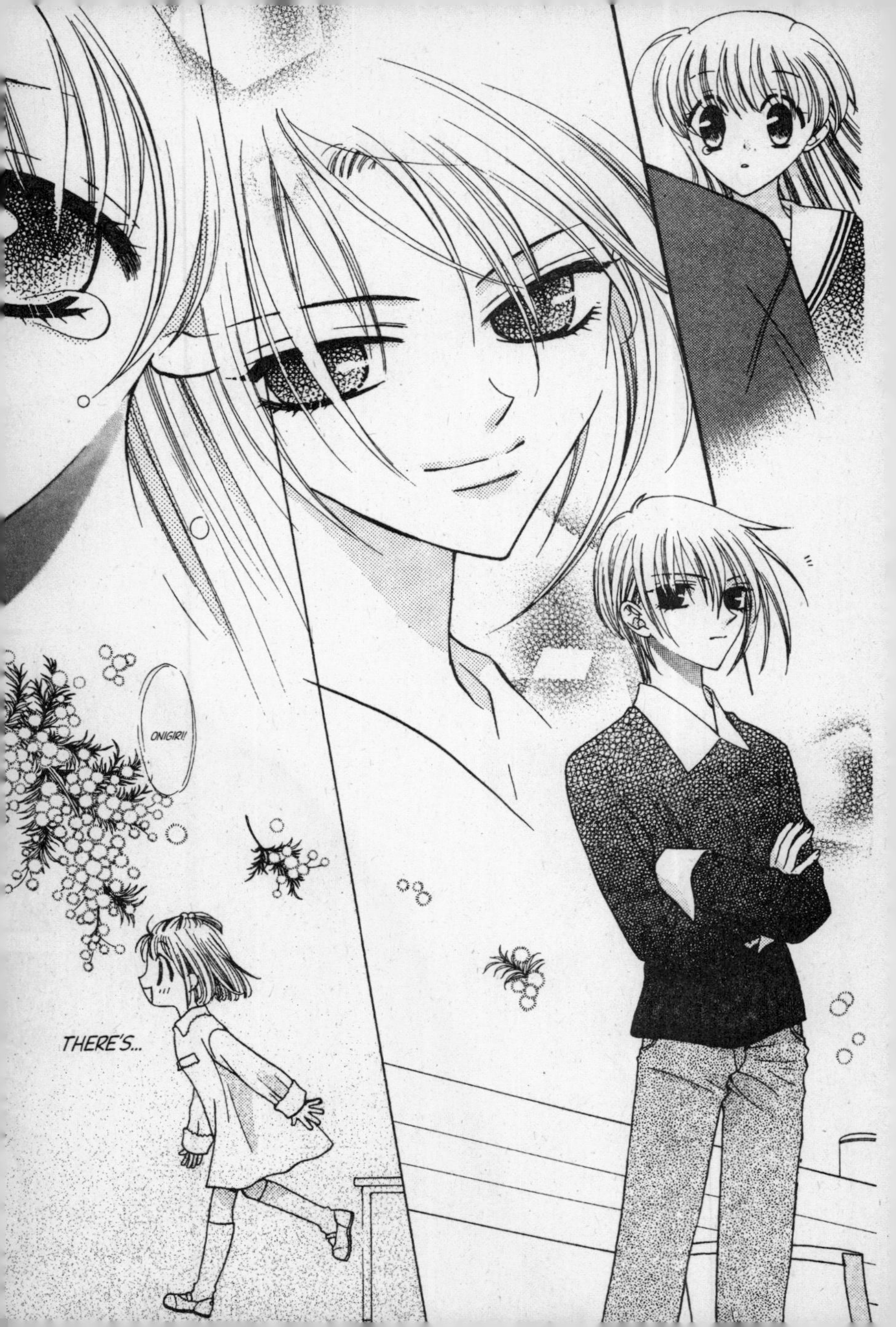
ONIGIRI!
THERE'S...

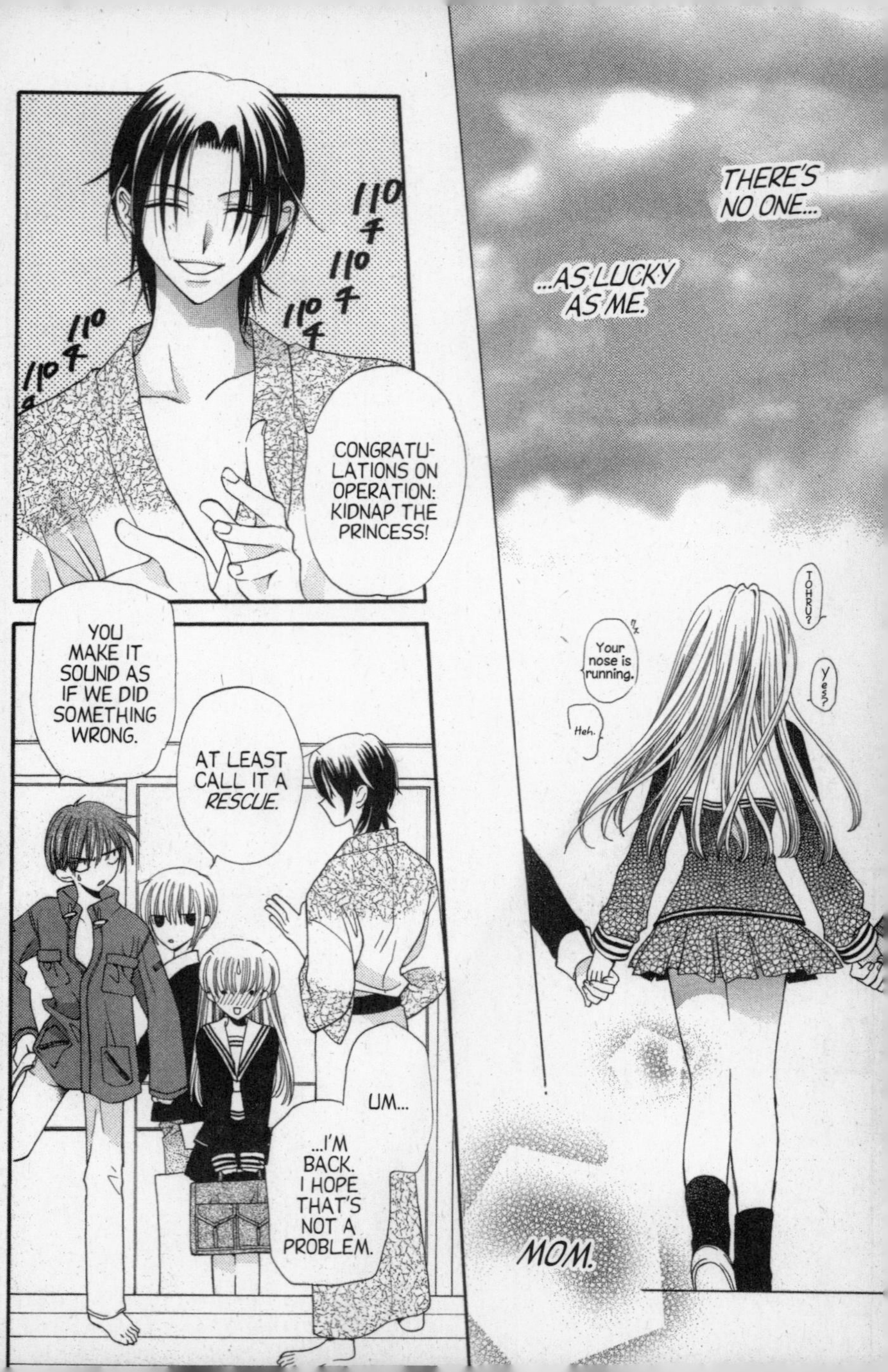
THERE'S NO ONE...
...AS LUCKY AS ME.
TOHRU?
Yes?
Your nose is running.
Heh.
MOM.
CONGRATU-LATIONS ON OPERATION: KIDNAP THE PRINCESS!
YOU MAKE IT SOUND AS IF WE DID SOMETHING WRONG.
AT LEAST CALL IT A *RESCUE.*
UM...
...I'M BACK. I HOPE THAT'S NOT A PROBLEM.

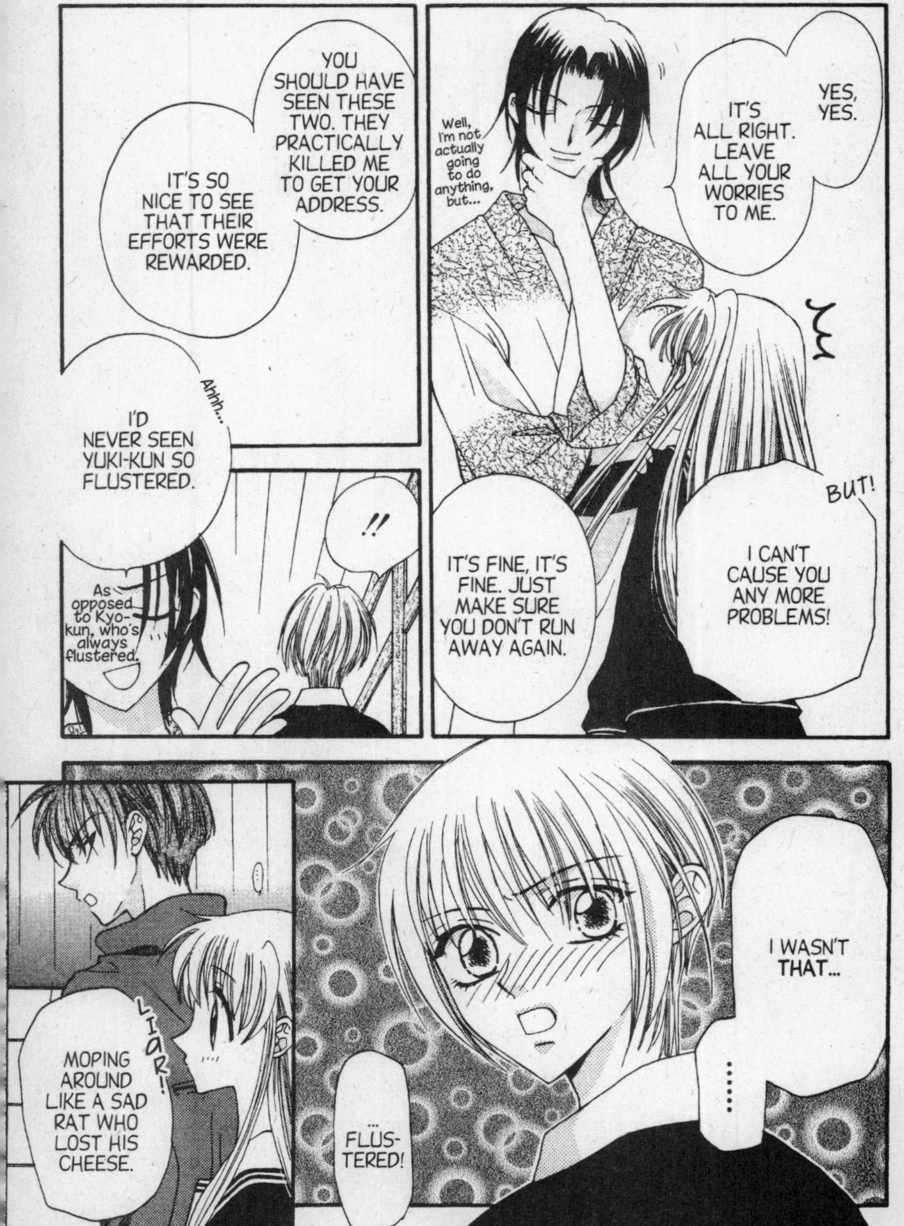
YES, YES.
IT'S ALL RIGHT. LEAVE ALL YOUR WORRIES TO ME.
Well, I'm not actually going to do anything, but...
BUT!
I CAN'T CAUSE YOU ANY MORE PROBLEMS!
IT'S FINE, IT'S FINE. JUST MAKE SURE YOU DON'T RUN AWAY AGAIN.
YOU SHOULD HAVE SEEN THESE TWO. THEY PRACTICALLY KILLED ME TO GET YOUR ADDRESS.
IT'S SO NICE TO SEE THAT THEIR EFFORTS WERE REWARDED.
!!
Ahhh...
I'D NEVER SEEN YUKI-KUN SO FLUSTERED.
As opposed to Kyo-kun, who's always flustered.
I WASN'T THAT...
......
FLÜS-TERED!
LIAR!
MOPING AROUND LIKE A SAD RAT WHO LOST HIS CHEESE.

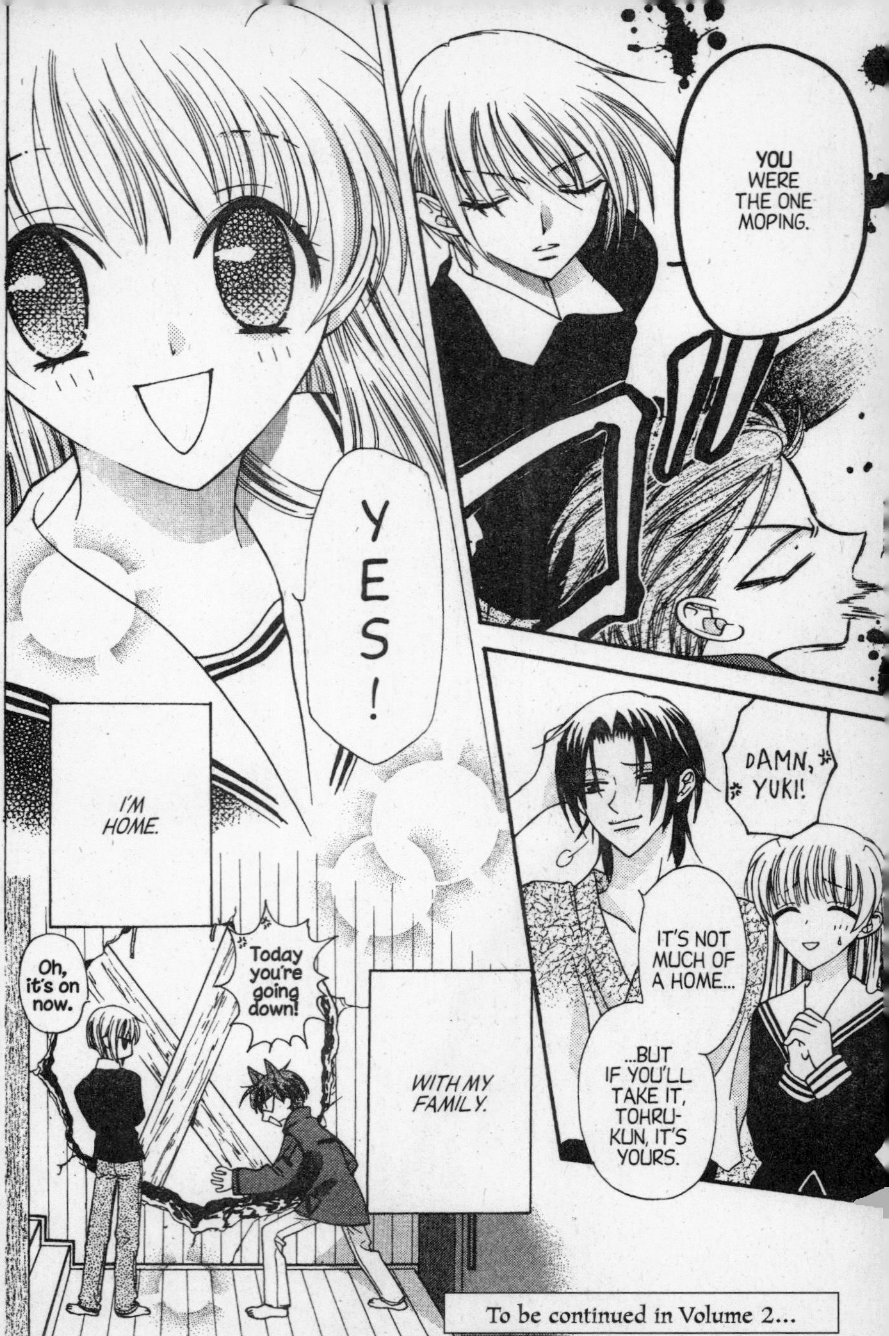
YOU WERE THE ONE MOPING.
DAMN, YUKI!
IT'S NOT MUCH OF A HOME...
...BUT IF YOU'LL TAKE IT, TOHRU-KUN, IT'S YOURS.
YES!
I'M HOME.
WITH MY FAMILY.
Today you're going down!
Oh, it's on now.

To be continued in Volume 2...

Omake Theater 4: This question isn't on the S.A.T....

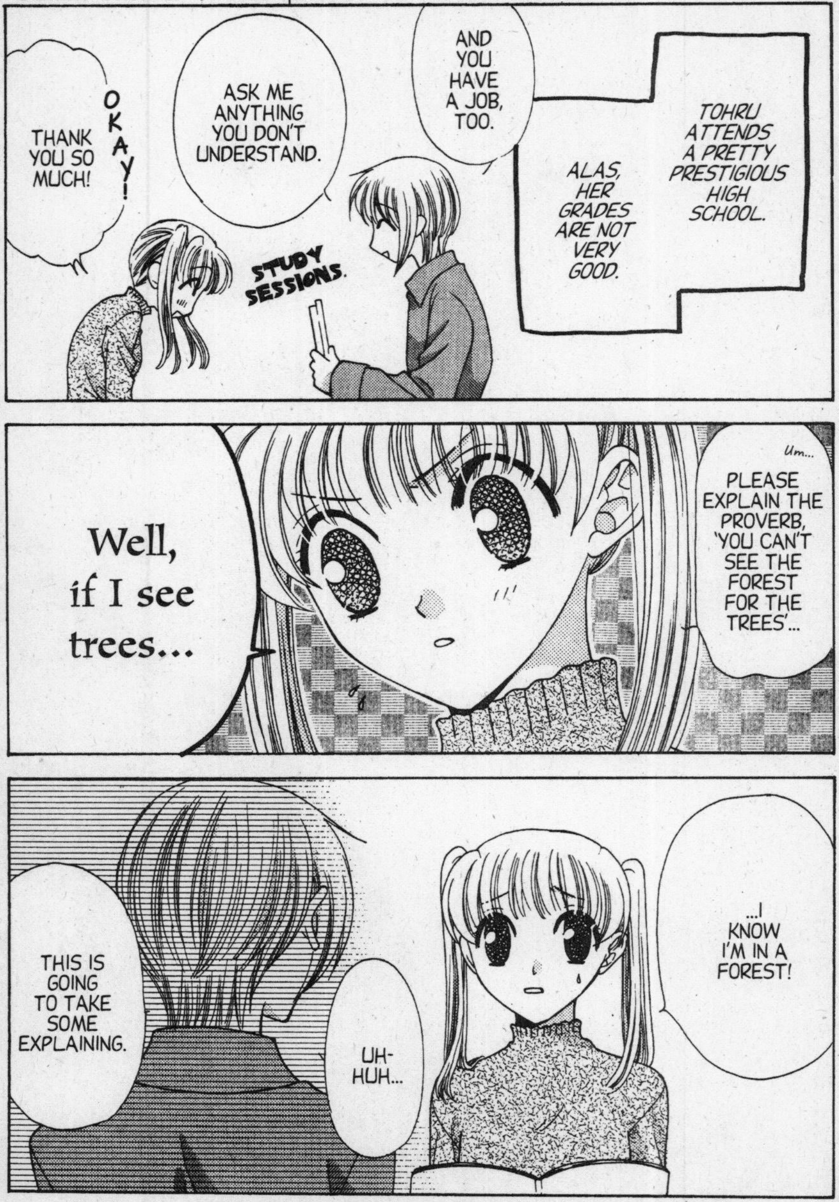
TOHRU ATTENDS A PRETTY PRESTIGIOUS HIGH SCHOOL.
ALAS, HER GRADES ARE NOT VERY GOOD.
AND YOU HAVE A JOB, TOO.
ASK ME ANYTHING YOU DON'T UNDERSTAND.
STUDY SESSIONS.
OKAY!
THANK YOU SO MUCH!
Um...
PLEASE EXPLAIN THE PROVERB, 'YOU CAN'T SEE THE FOREST FOR THE TREES'...
Well, if I see trees...
...I KNOW I'M IN A FOREST!
UH-HUH...
THIS IS GOING TO TAKE SOME EXPLAINING.

Correct answer: Sometimes it's easier to understand a situation if you look at it from a distance.

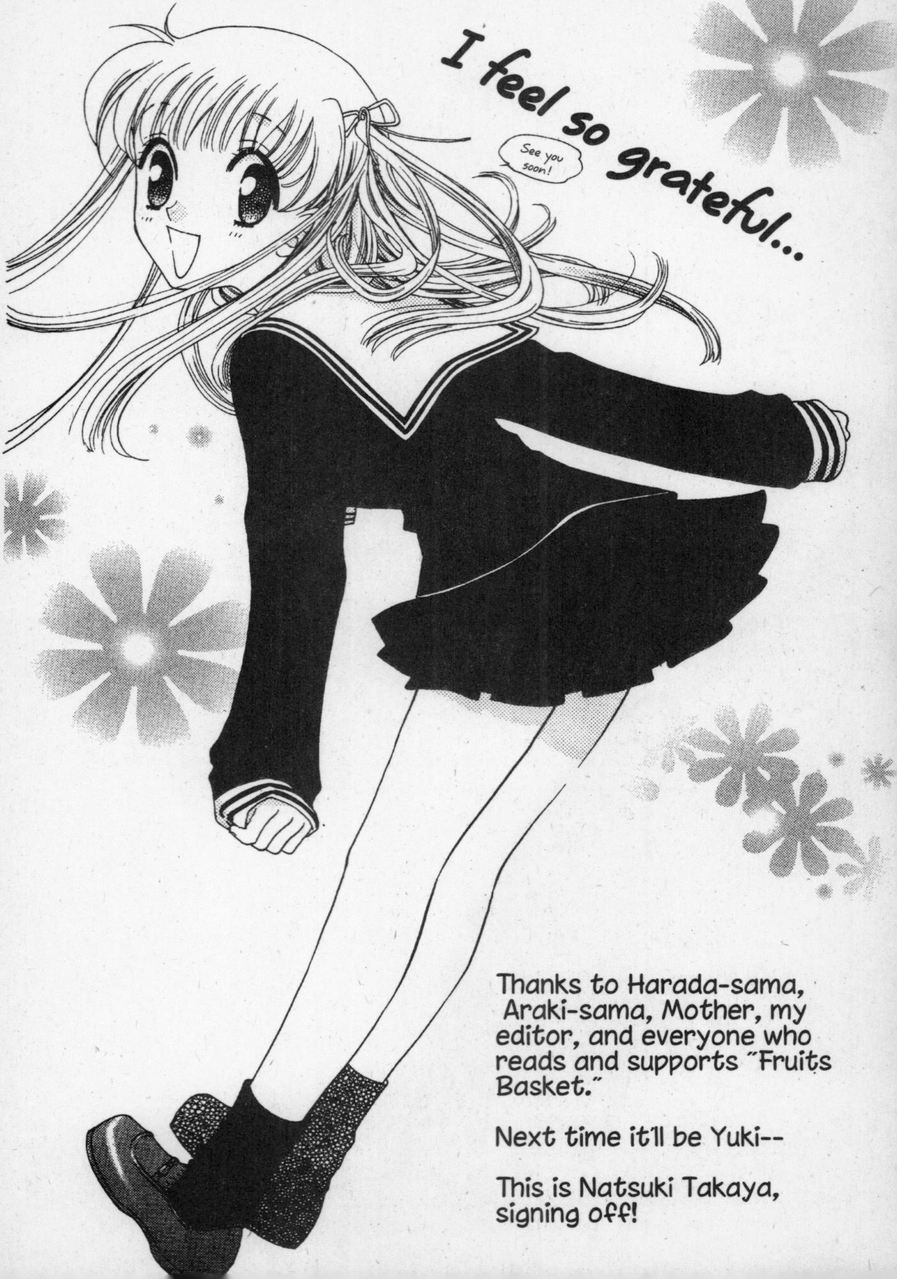
I feel so grateful...
See you soon!

Thanks to Harada-sama, Araki-sama, Mother, my editor, and everyone who reads and supports "Fruits Basket."

Next time it'll be Yuki--

This is Natsuki Takaya, signing off!

Next time in...

Fruits Basket
TOKYOPOP
2
Natsuki Takaya

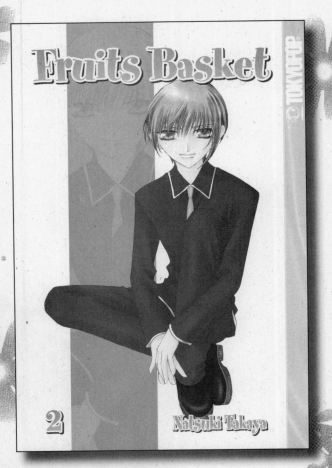

Old Friends and New Family

The Sohma family is just starting to get used to life with Tohru, but can they survive a sleepover visit by her two best friends without their secret being exposed? Things aren't any easier at school where crowd-shy Kyo must deal with sudden popularity—and a surprise visit by two other members of the Sohma clan!

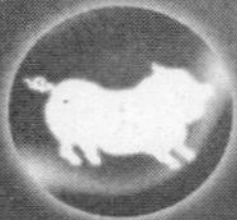

Boar

Years: 1971, 1983, 1995, 2007
Positive: reliable, sincere, tolerant
Negative: shy, short tempered

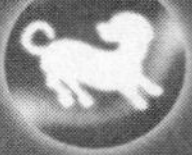

Dog

Years: 1970, 1982, 1994, 2006
Positive: honest, generous, faithful
Negative: quiet, cynical

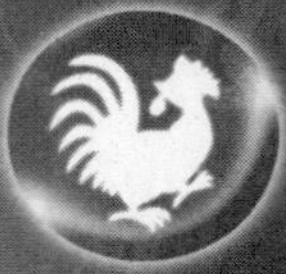

Rooster

Years: 1969, 1981, 1993, 2005
Positive: courageous, hardworking, skilled
Negative: arrogant, selfish

Monkey

Years: 1968, 1980, 1992, 2004
Positive: inventive, entertaining, magnetic personality
Negative: distrusting, untrusting

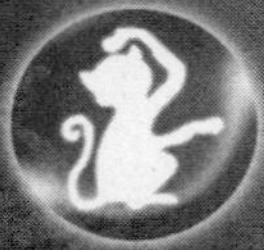

Dragon

Years: 1964, 1976, 1988, 2000
Positive: intelligent, enthusiastic, softhearted
Negative: bossy, loud

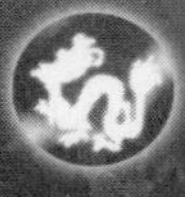

Sheep

Years: 1967, 1979, 1991, 2003
Positive: creative, honest, passionate
Negative: disorganized, timid

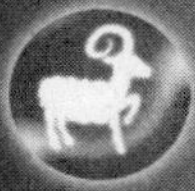

Snake

Years: 1965, 1977, 1989, 2001
Positive: romantic, clever, beautiful
Negative: vain, procrastinators

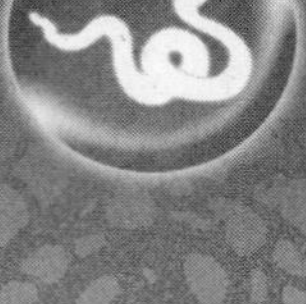

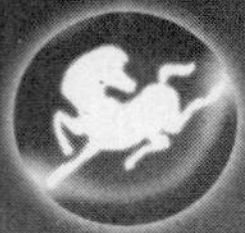

Horse

Years: 1966, 1978, 1990, 2002
Positive: cunning, adventurous, cheerful
Negative: impatient, selfish

Fruits Basket's

The Chinese Zodiac – Part 1: History Lesson

Fables, myths, and legends abound in every culture of the world. Some of the most ancient of them stem from a basic need to place some type of meaning on those events that are out of our control. The exact origins of the Chinese Zodiac remain a mystery, but their influence is still being felt even today.

The Chinese once viewed time as a cyclical journey consisting of highs and lows that would eventually come full circle. This concept of time would become the basis for the Chinese Lunar Calendar, a 12-year calendar built around 60-year cycles that were delegated by the longitude of the sun and the phases of the moon.

The calendar itself dates back to around 2637 B.C. and consists of 10 Heavenly Steams (elements with yin and yang characteristics) and 12 Earthly Branches (animals of the zodiac) that are clumped together to become the name of the year. When the steams and branches, also known as "Jikkan Junishi," are combined in sequential order, they do not repeat until 60 years have passed. So in essence no one person will ever see any given year more than twice in their own lifetime.

Unfortunately, much of the population was illiterate and unable to fully grasp the complexity of the calendar so the 12 Earthly Branches came to be represented by animals so that everyone could remember them better. The version of the calendar that has been passed down also incorporates the five Chinese elements (Metal, Water, Wood, Fire, and Earth) into its design. The elements themselves each have a yin and yang variation, but the zodiac animals are always either yin or yang. For example, an odd year is yin and an even year is yang.

Japan was introduced to the Chinese calendar in approximately 604 A.D. during the reign of the Empress Suiko-Tenno, when she made an active attempt to spread the many wonders of Buddhism throughout the island nation. By this time though, the calendar was all ready being used for a number of things including telling the time of day through two-hour intervals and even pointing out cardinal directions.

As time went on, the animals became the core basis of Asian astrology, which dictates that one's personality can be divined from the year in which they were born. When combined with the elemental aspects of the calendar, Chinese astrology can even point out which partner will be more dominant in a relationship. Needless to say, the vast majority of the population does not take this seriously anymore.

Still, the Chinese Zodiac does have its uses in modern society. Instead of being rude and asking someone how old they are, one would instead ask what their animal where they born under. With a little math—just add or subtract 12—you'll have your answer. And let us not forget the Chinese New Year, which is celebrated every year in either late January or early February.

Cow

Years: 1961, 1973, 1985, 1997
Positive: inspiring, conservative, natural born leaders
Negative: stubborn, unyielding personality

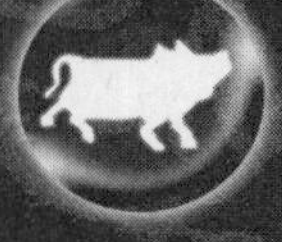

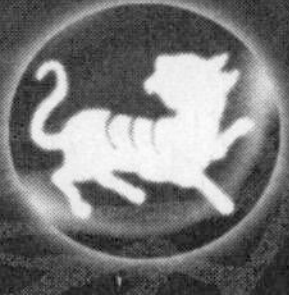

Tiger

Years: 1962, 1974, 1986, 1998
Positive: courageous, unpredictable, loving
Negative: overly aggressive, highly emotional

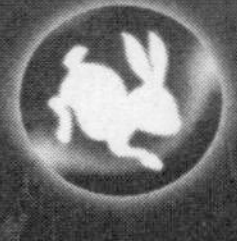

Rabbit

Years: 1963, 1975, 1987, 1999
Positive: affectionate, pleasant, talented
Negative: too sentimental, avoids conflict

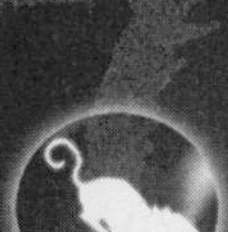

Rat

Years: 1960, 1972, 1984, 1996
Positive: imaginative, ambitious, generous to loved ones
Negative: hot-tempered,

A conversation with Laura Bailey.
the English voice of Tohru Honda

TOKYOPOP: Could you briefly explain the process of voice acting for Fruits Basket?

Laura Bailey: I, as an actress, become involved after the translated script has been completed and the director has an idea of what he wants from the episode. Justin Cook, my voice director on Fruits Basket, usually has pretty specific ideas and is great about filling me in on what's happening throughout the show. He'll give me the background of other characters and help me decide where Tohru is coming from during her interaction with others. That's especially helpful when I'm the first actor to record on an episode. All actors record separately due to the difficulty of ADR; but I always prefer to be the last to record so that I can have Justin play the other actors in my headphones when I go in. It's easier to be believable when you know what you're reacting to. One of the great things about Tohru was, though she had a lot of dialogue, most of it was spoken off screen. That helped to speed up recording because I didn't have to match mouth flaps and could use the timing that I wanted to. Often, on the narration, I could get through it in one take.

TP: When you first became involved with Fruits Basket, were you aware of the huge international following that the series has? What is it about Fruits Basket, do you think, that makes it such a fan favorite series with many viewers and readers outside of the usual shojo market?

LB: I had no idea Fruits Basket had the following it did, but I could tell from the first episode I watched that it wasn't an average series. I think what makes Fruits Basket so special is the depth of all the characters.

Laura Bailey

You genuinely care about every storyline.

TP: How did you prepare for the role of Tohru Honda? How was this character different from other anime characters that you've played?

LB: In preparing for the part, I researched the series on the Internet and watched the Japanese version. Tohru was the first innocent character I'd played. The more I researched, the more I fell in love with that innocence.

TP: How does the original Japanese performance influence your own interpretation of a character?

LB: Well, it helped me form a basis for Tohru's mannerisms and inflections. I think when the original is so wonderful, you don't want to stray from that. Why mess with a good thing, y'know?

TP: Many of Tohru's humble behaviors and speech patterns must have been very difficult to translate to English. What did you find most challenging about capturing her character in your performance?

LB: Actually, I was asked a similar question by Mr. Daichi (Japanese director) himself, during a panel discussion. He wanted to make sure that her sweetness and formal nature didn't get lost in the translation. I think that, while we in America don't have that same speech formality, the humble nature can still be communicated through inflections and tone. I guess the challenging part was just making sure to always use those softer inflections.

TP: What about Tohru's character do you most relate to? What do you find difficult to relate to?

LB: Her desire to turn any situation into a positive one—that's what I most connected with. Not to say that I always succeed ... but I certainly try to remain optimistic. I think it was her formal nature that I found most difficult. Luckily, John Burgmeier did a wonderful job with the dialogue, which made things easier.

TP: How is acting for anime different from other acting jobs you do?

LB: Well I can look like sin for one thing. I love that. And anime is the only thing I do in which I act after the fact. Dubbing is a craft unto itself; it takes a completely different approach. You don't always get to decide how you want to say a line, because your way doesn't work with the timing. Anime means taking something very specific, and making it work for you.

TP: Do you have a favorite anime or manga series?

LB: I feel like a cheese for saying so, but Fruits Basket is my favorite. When I found out you guys were releasing the manga in English, I was ecstatic.

TP: What's your zodiac animal? Are you happy being that animal or would you rather be something else?

LB: I'm a cock. I wouldn't change that either; just 'cause it's fun to say, "I'm a cock."

TP: Okay, I have to ask... If you were in Tohru's shoes and you had to pick one guy, who would you choose Kyo or Yuki?

LB: I don't know ... I've tried to make that choice about a thousand times. At first I thought Kyo because, c'mon, he's awesome. He's got the whole bad boy thing working for him; but then I think about Yuki, and how much he truly cares about Tohru and how wonderful a person he is ... and I'm back at square one. It's an endless circle.

TP: Tohru is a very emotional character who is often moved to tears of joy or sadness. Was it difficult to bring out her emotions out in your performance?

LB: It wasn't so much difficult as it was draining. In the last few episodes especially, Tohru goes though a lot of extreme emotions. Those days of recording were the hardest. The emotion you feel as the character attaches itself to you, so I left the booth very depressed and frustrated.

TP: What was it like working with the other members of the Fruits Basket cast? What was your involvement with the other actors?

LB: Justin did a great job of casting the show. When listening to the final product, I kept wishing that I had been able to be involved with their recording sessions as well. Luckily, I'm friends with a lot of the cast, so I could still tell them how much I enjoyed what they did.

TP: How did you feel when the series was over?

LB: I was so upset. I loved working on Fruits Basket; there's no doubt that I would jump at the chance to continue it.

TP: What was your first voice acting role for anime?

LB: The first thing I did was kid Dende on Dragonball Z. I was filling in for the woman who originally did that voice, as she wasn't available. It turns out, though, she came back to the studio after me, and rerecorded everything I'd done. Which really sucked, let me tell you. Soon after, though, I was cast as kid Trunks. So I guess it was all for the best in the end.

TP: Is there a favorite anime role that you've performed?

LB: Tohru. I just loved everything about her.

TP: What was the most challenging role you've ever played?

LB: That's a tough question. Either Tohru or Marlene in Blue Gender. Both had some intense moments throughout their series.

How much are you like Kyo?

And how can you be lucky in love?

Furuba-themed Personality Test

We'll chart your answers to a series of questions to see how much you're like Yuki, Kyo, or Shigure! The results can reveal things like your ideal job.

Q1:
How do you spend your days off?

A: I PREFER GOING OUT; IF I'M GOING TO WATCH A MOVIE, I GO TO A THEATER.

B: I PREFER STAYING IN; IF I'M GOING TO WATCH A MOVIE, I RENT A VIDEO.

Q2:
How do you feel about competition?

A: I CAN'T STAND TO LOSE!

B: AS LONG AS I HAVE FUN, IT'S OKAY!

Q3:
People say it's easy to tell what you're thinking.

A: YES.

B: NO.

Q4:
When you were in elementary school, what did you do for fun?

A: I PLAYED WITH EVERYONE OUTSIDE.

B: I WAS REALLY INTO PLAYING GAMES AT HOME.

Q5:
At cultural festivals and athletic meets, you wind up getting into the spirit of things even if you started off thinking they were a pain.

A: YES, FESTIVALS ARE EXCITING!

B: NO, THEY REALLY ARE A PAIN.

Q6:
You get absorbed in things you like, but you can't be bothered doing boring things.

A: YES.

B: NO.

Q7:
You've had an unrequited love for over a year.

A: YES.

B: NO.

Q8:
When something ticks you off, you take it out on other people.

A: YES.

B: NO.

Q9:
You don't mince words.

A: YES.

B: NO.

100% like Kyo
If you're 100% like Kyo, you're the reliable older-sister type. But your weakness is that you suddenly get tongue-tied around the person you like...

HOW TO BE LUCKY IN LOVE: Have confidence in yourself and be assertive!

70% like Kyo
If you're 70% like Kyo, you're cheerful and well-liked. But although you make friends easily, it might be hard for you to take a friendship to the next level.

HOW TO BE LUCKY IN LOVE: Casually express your love every day!

30% like Kyo
If you're 30% like Kyo, you may be too reserved to stand out much. The first step is to make sure the person you like knows who you are!

HOW TO BE LUCKY IN LOVE: Find out what you have in common to increase your opportunities to talk to your crush!

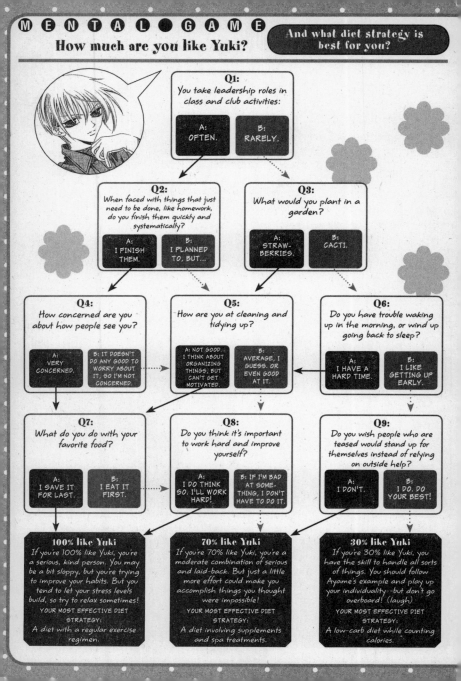

MENTAL GAME

How much are you like Yuki?

And what diet strategy is best for you?

Q1:
You take leadership roles in class and club activities:

A: OFTEN. → Q2

B: RARELY. → Q3

Q2:
When faced with things that just need to be done, like homework, do you finish them quickly and systematically?

A: I FINISH THEM. → Q4

B: I PLANNED TO, BUT... → Q5

Q3:
What would you plant in a garden?

A: STRAWBERRIES. → Q5

B: CACTI. → Q6

Q4:
How concerned are you about how people see you?

A: VERY CONCERNED. → Q7

B: IT DOESN'T DO ANY GOOD TO WORRY ABOUT IT, SO I'M NOT CONCERNED. → Q5

Q5:
How are you at cleaning and tidying up?

A: NOT GOOD. I THINK ABOUT ORGANIZING THINGS, BUT CAN'T GET MOTIVATED. → Q7

B: AVERAGE, I GUESS. OR EVEN GOOD AT IT. → Q8

Q6:
Do you have trouble waking up in the morning, or wind up going back to sleep?

A: I HAVE A HARD TIME. → Q5

B: I LIKE GETTING UP EARLY. → Q9

Q7:
What do you do with your favorite food?

A: I SAVE IT FOR LAST. → 100% like Yuki

B: I EAT IT FIRST. → Q8

Q8:
Do you think it's important to work hard and improve yourself?

A: I DO THINK SO. I'LL WORK HARD! → 100% like Yuki

B: IF I'M BAD AT SOMETHING, I DON'T HAVE TO DO IT. → 70% like Yuki

Q9:
Do you wish people who are teased would stand up for themselves instead of relying on outside help?

A: I DON'T. → 70% like Yuki

B: I DO. DO YOUR BEST! → 30% like Yuki

100% like Yuki

If you're 100% like Yuki, you're a serious, kind person. You may be a bit sloppy, but you're trying to improve your habits. But you tend to let your stress levels build, so try to relax sometimes!

YOUR MOST EFFECTIVE DIET STRATEGY:
A diet with a regular exercise regimen.

70% like Yuki

If you're 70% like Yuki, you're a moderate combination of serious and laid-back. But just a little more effort could make you accomplish things you thought were impossible!

YOUR MOST EFFECTIVE DIET STRATEGY:
A diet involving supplements and spa treatments.

30% like Yuki

If you're 30% like Yuki, you have the skill to handle all sorts of things. You should follow Ayame's example and play up your individuality--but don't go overboard! (laugh)

YOUR MOST EFFECTIVE DIET STRATEGY:
A low-carb diet while counting calories.

Furuba-themed Juusanshi Fortune-Telling

Step 1

Find Your Chinese Astrology Color

First, use the chart below to find your Furuba Chinese Zodiac color (you need to know your Chinese zodiac sign).

Chinese Zodiac Sign	Color
Rat	Pink
Ox	Green
Tiger	Red
Rabbit	Pink
Dragon	Red
Snake	Black
Horse	Green
Ram	Blue
Monkey	Yellow
Bird	Yellow
Dog	Blue
Boar	Black

How the fortune-telling works:

Step 1 will tell you what your Furuba Chinese Zodiac color is, according to your Chinese Zodiac sign. Next, the chart in Step 2 will indicate your blood type number (you need to know your blood type, too!). Once you have both pieces of information, go to Step 3 to determine your Juusanshi Sign.

This fortune-telling game adds the Year of the Cat to the zodiac, since we're dealing with Furuba. It indicates your romance "type", and which character you're compatible with!

ONCE YOU'VE LOOKED UP YOUR COLOR AND NUMBER, GO TO STEP 3!

This has no relation to wave fortune-telling.

HEY, HANAJIMA— NORMALLY I HATE GIRLY STUFF LIKE FORTUNE TELLING...
...BUT I WOULDN'T MIND IF YOU PREDICTED WHETHER OR NOT I'LL BEAT YUKI.
...OKAY.

Step 2

Find Your Blood Type Number

Start with Q1 and follow the arrows as you answer the questions.
The number you end up with is your blood type number.

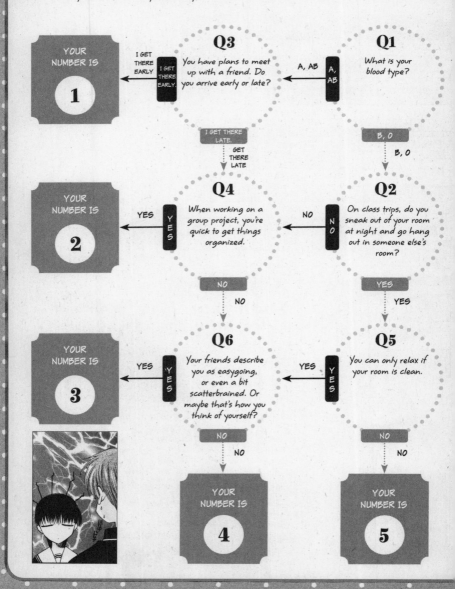

Q1

What is your blood type?

A, AB → **Q3**

B, O → **Q2**

Q3

You have plans to meet up with a friend. Do you arrive early or late?

I GET THERE EARLY → YOUR NUMBER IS **1**

I GET THERE LATE → **Q4**

Q4

When working on a group project, you're quick to get things organized.

YES → YOUR NUMBER IS **2**

NO → **Q6**

Q2

On class trips, do you sneak out of your room at night and go hang out in someone else's room?

NO → **Q4**

YES → **Q5**

Q5

You can only relax if your room is clean.

YES → **Q6**

NO → YOUR NUMBER IS **5**

Q6

Your friends describe you as easygoing, or even a bit scatterbrained. Or maybe that's how you think of yourself?

YES → YOUR NUMBER IS **3**

NO → YOUR NUMBER IS **4**

Step 3

Use your color and number to find your Juusanshi Sign!

Your Juusanshi Sign is based on the number and color you identified in Steps 1 and 2. The character you're most compatible with also indicates the sign of people with whom you're generally most compatible.

COLOR	NUMBER	JUUSANSHI SIGN	COLOR	NUMBER	JUUSANSHI SIGN
Red	1	**Cat**	Pink	1	**Dragon**
Red	2	**Snake**	Pink	2	**Ox**
Red	3	**Monkey**	Pink	3	**Rat**
Red	4	**Ram**	Pink	4	**Rat**
Red	5	**Rabbit**	Pink	5	**Rabbit**
Black	1	**Cat**	Green	1	**Cat**
Black	2	**Snake**	Green	2	**Ox**
Black	3	**Monkey**	Green	3	**Tiger**
Black	4	**Ram**	Green	4	**Dragon**
Black	5	**Boar**	Green	5	**Boar**
Yellow	1	**Cat**	Blue	1	**Rat**
Yellow	2	**Horse**	Blue	2	**Horse**
Yellow	3	**Rat**	Blue	3	**Tiger**
Yellow	4	**Bird**	Blue	4	**Bird**
Yellow	5	**Dog**	Blue	5	**Dog**

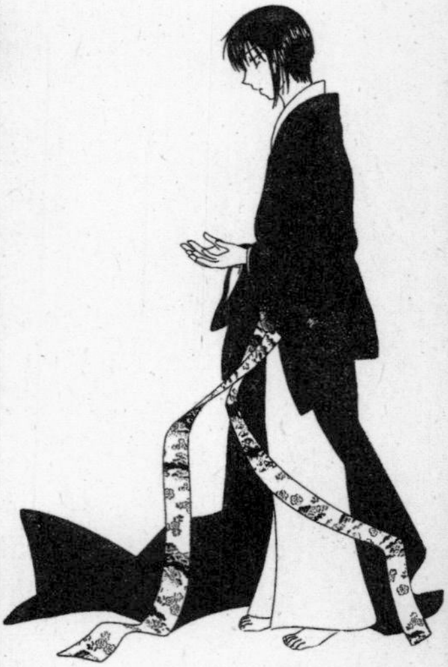

Juusanshi Descriptions

Your romance "type," and which character you're most compatible with.

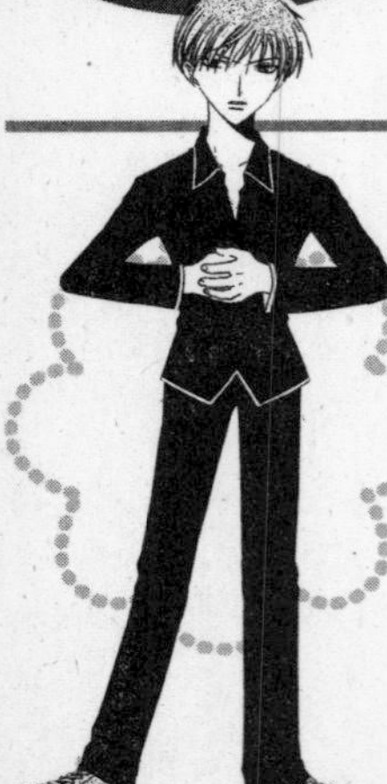

An explanation of your approach to romance, and which of the male Furuba characters is your best match.

Cat Type

You're a bit dense when it comes to romance--you may be completely oblivious to it when someone has feelings for you. However, once you fall in love, your heart will belong completely to that special person.

•YOUR MOST COMPATIBLE *FURUBA* CHARACTER•

Your most compatible character is Momiji. You rush headlong into situations, and sometimes it gets you hurt; Momiji's inner strength and cheerfulness will cushion life's blows.

Rat Type

When you're in love, you're very serious and a bit awkward. You put the other person's happiness first, so you watch out for them. You also have a hidden sloppy side, so you tend to look for a romantic partner who isn't a perfectionist.

•YOUR MOST COMPATIBLE *FURUBA* CHARACTER•

You tend to be reserved when it comes to love, so outgoing, forceful people like Ayame are a perfect balance for you. Taking things too seriously can wear you out, but matching Ayame's pace can open up whole new worlds!

Ox Type

You have a big heart, but you may not experience sudden flares of romance. On the other hand, your capacity to love just one person for a very long time is its own flavor of passion. You also have a tendency to change your interests and style to be more like the person you love.

•YOUR MOST COMPATIBLE *FURUBA* CHARACTER•

Your ability to see through other people's selfishness makes us think Kyo is a good match! His intense personality won't frighten you off, and you have the power to bring out the kindness hidden under his rough behavior.

Tiger Type

You probably express your love passively. Even if you like someone, you often won't tell them; instead, you'll wait for them to approach you. Be careful not to let opportunity pass you by!

•YOUR MOST COMPATIBLE *FURUBA* CHARACTER•

You are compatible with Hiro! He can seem bold or even self-important, but he's kind and prone to worrying. He's a perfect balance for someone like you, who wants to be protected.

Rabbit Type

You do everything you can for the person you love. You go out of your way to find gifts or to plan events to make them happy, and charm them with your smile.

•YOUR MOST COMPATIBLE *FURUBA* CHARACTER•

You are perfectly compatible with Kureno! His composure and maturity compensate for your exuberance and playfulness, and he can rein you in if you get a bit out of control.

Dragon Type

You have your own feelings under control, and don't force your opinions on others. You're so quiet that the people around you may be surprised when you have romantic feelings for someone, but that very restraint probably makes you popular.

•YOUR MOST COMPATIBLE *FURUBA* CHARACTER•

Yuki is an ideal match for you--your intellectual, peaceful aura appeals to Yuki's need for calm surroundings. The two of you would be a couple with a sympathetic, stable love.

Snake Type

You're the energetic sort, and other people trust you. Your love is naturally intense, and you express it frankly; you use every method you can think of to catch the attention of the person you love.

•YOUR MOST COMPATIBLE *FURUBA* CHARACTER•

Because you're so vibrant and overwhelming, we think Hatori is a natural match for you. His calm personality will help keep you from rushing into things, and being with him will probably help you settle down a little.

Horse Type

You come across as calm and composed, but you're capable of loving so intensely that you'll sacrifice anything for the person you love--and sometimes you may be badly hurt as a result.

•YOUR MOST COMPATIBLE *FURUBA* CHARACTER•

You love too strongly for your own good, so Hatsuharu is perfect for you: his heart is big enough to not be overwhelmed by your feelings. Simply being with him may be enough to give you some peace of mind.

Ram Type

No matter how much you love someone, you can't just be honest and admit it. But your attitude reveals your feelings, and the person you love--and everyone else around you--will notice your emotions right away.

•YOUR MOST COMPATIBLE *FURUBA* CHARACTER•

Yuki is your perfect partner. He's very sensitive about other people, and will notice your feelings right away. It's safe for you to entrust him with your heart.

Monkey Type

Your personality is so hesitant that people might never suspect you can confess your feelings to someone you *like*--but when the crucial moment comes, you can surprise them with your boldness. You may well win them over!

•YOUR MOST COMPATIBLE *FURUBA* CHARACTER•

You're easygoing in some ways, and so is Shigure--which could make a solid match! They say that no one ever knows what Shigure is thinking, but being around him will help you grow as a person.

Bird Type

You don't rely on anyone else, and you love patiently. If you fall in love with someone whose heart belongs to someone else, you'll quietly back down. But if you try being selfish once in a while, you never know what could come of it!

•YOUR MOST COMPATIBLE *FURUBA* CHARACTER•

Because you tend to suppress your own feelings, we think Hatsuharu would be ideal for you. He tries so hard to understand other people's emotions that you can't help but be honest with him, which would help you relax.

Dog Type

Many people are attracted to your mature aura, but the truth is that you have a selfish streak. If you do date anyone, it doesn't last long. But if you really fall in love, that love could last your entire life.

•YOUR MOST COMPATIBLE *FURUBA* CHARACTER•

When it comes right down to it, you only really care about the person you love. Ritsu, who has trouble seeing past himself, is perfect for you. It's the kind of relationship that other people might not understand, but what matters is that it works for the two of you.

Boar Type

You're the type to rush headlong into things, and you love wholeheartedly. Your cheerful love doesn't weigh heavily on people or hold them back, which means you can have a good relationship with almost anyone.

•YOUR MOST COMPATIBLE *FURUBA* CHARACTER•

You're most compatible with Kyo! His personality is a bit rough, but you know yourself well enough that you won't be intimidated by it. You can deal with his intensity, and may even be able to help him think more like you do.

GAME OF LIFE

This "Game of Life" is based on events in Furuba.
You can play it by yourself or with friends!

Furuba-themed Game of Life

Start

Start here to play the Furuba Game of Life! (You start with 50,000 yen.)

I'M SO EXCITED!
LET'S GO!!

1 Tonight you're having hamburger for dinner. (minus 500 yen)

2 Hana-chan uses waves to tell your fortune. (minus 7,000 yen)

WHY ARE YOU LOOKING AWAY?!!
YOU'RE... VERY SUPER-STITIOUS, AREN'T YOU?
......

3 Tonight you're having curry for dinner. (minus 500 yen)

4 You hit your head really hard at the haunted house! They charge you 10,000 yen to cover your medical bill. (minus 10,000 yen) + (lose one turn)

IT'S NO GOOD. AT THIS RATE...
...SHE'LL DIE!
EEK! WHAT'S THAT?!
IT'S...
...ALL
THERE'S NO POINT IF THE SOUNDS ARE GOING TO SCARE YOU!!

5 Uo-chan and Hana-chan buy you a swimsuit. (plus 5,000 yen)

TH—
THANK YOU SO MUCH.
I'LL... I'LL TAKE GOOD CARE OF IT!

6 Tonight you're having nira-tama for dinner. (minus 500 yen)

7 Tonight you're having shark fin for dinner. (minus 500 yen)

8 Mitchan writes a suicide note in front of your house. (minus 5,000 yen)

...BUT YOUR DAUGHTER MITSURU CAN NO LONGER BEAR THE HARASSMENT OF A CERTAIN AUTHOR...
tremble
MITCHAN—
...SAN?

HOW TO PLAY

(YOU'LL NEED)

- Pencil
- Die
- Something to use for pawns
- Calculator (optional, if you're not confident about math)

(RULES)

- You start with 50,000 yen.
- Roll the die and move your pawn forward the number of spaces shown on the die.
- Follow the instructions written on the space you land on.
- When you reach the "Finish", the player with the most money wins.
- The player who gets there last has to play a penalty game!

9

You are invited to stay at a Sohma hot springs inn. (plus 10,000 yen)

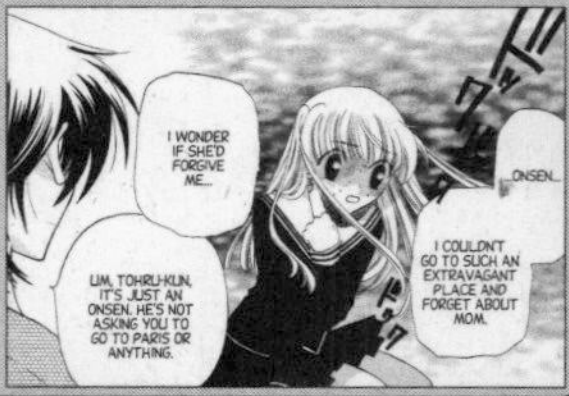
...ONSEN...
I COULDN'T GO TO SUCH AN EXTRAVAGANT PLACE AND FORGET ABOUT MOM.
I WONDER IF SHE'D FORGIVE ME...
UM, TOHRU-KUN, IT'S JUST AN ONSEN. HE'S NOT ASKING YOU TO GO TO PARIS OR ANYTHING.

10

Tonight you're having a gyoza combo for dinner. (minus 500 yen)

11

Ayame embroiders something idiotic on your clothes. (minus 7,000 yen)

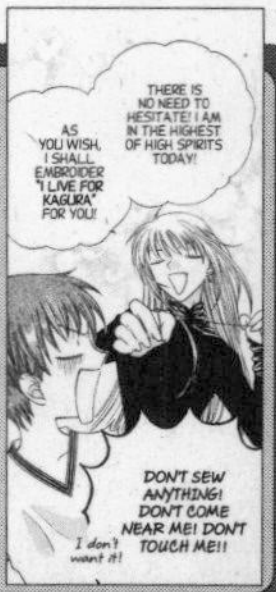
THERE IS NO NEED TO HESITATE! I AM IN THE HIGHEST OF HIGH SPIRITS TODAY!
AS YOU WISH, I SHALL EMBROIDER "I LIVE FOR KAGURA" FOR YOU!
DON'T SEW ANYTHING! DON'T COME NEAR ME! DON'T TOUCH ME!!!
I don't want it!

12

Tonight you're having hand-rolled sushi for dinner. (minus 500 yen)

13

You are given ribbons as a White Day gift. (plus 5,000 yen)

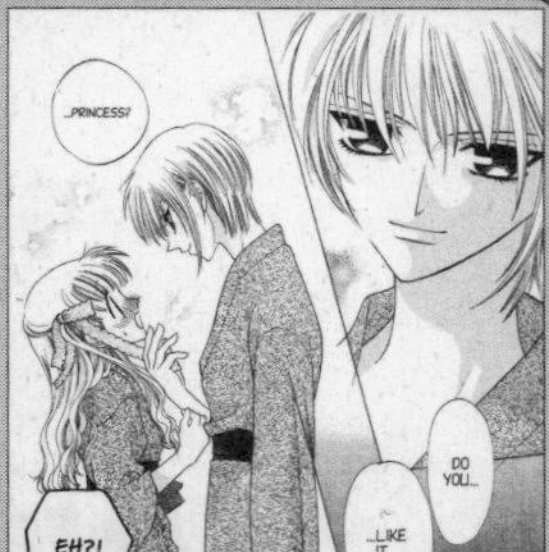
...PRINCESS?
DO YOU...
...LIKE IT...
EH?!

14

Tonight you're having soumen for dinner. (minus 500 yen)

22

You smash a watermelon with your bare hands! ...and hurt yourself. (minus 10,000 yen)

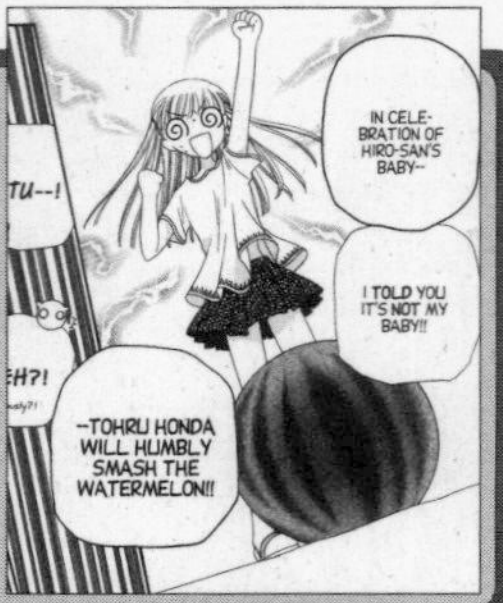
IN CELEBRATION OF HIRO-SAN'S BABY--
I TOLD YOU IT'S NOT MY BABY!!
EH?!
--TOHRU HONDA WILL HUMBLY SMASH THE WATERMELON!!

23

You get hit by a skyrocket firework. (minus 15,000 yen)

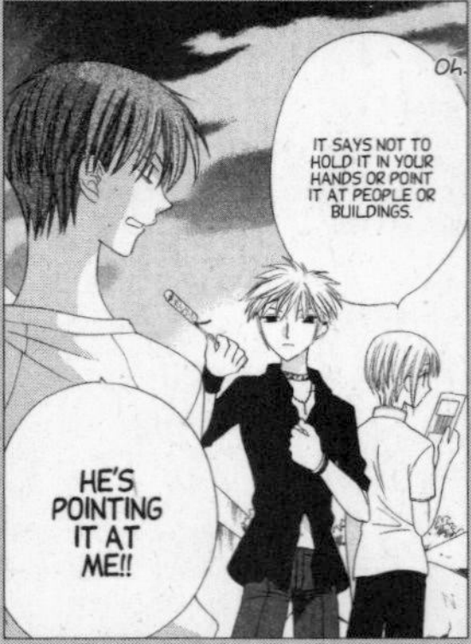
Oh.
IT SAYS NOT TO HOLD IT IN YOUR HANDS OR POINT IT AT PEOPLE OR BUILDINGS.
HE'S POINTING IT AT ME!!

24

You get infected by Ritchan's panic, and lose some years off your life. (minus 20,000 yen)

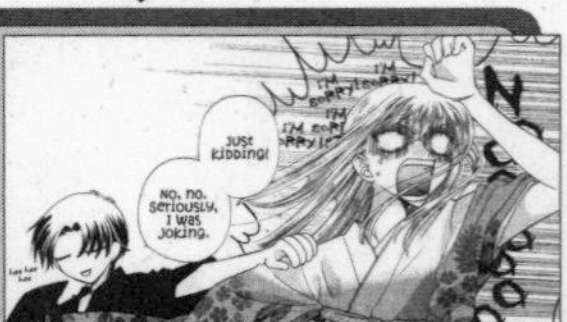
Just kidding!
No, no, seriously, I was joking.

20 You are invited to the Sohma beach house. (plus 10,000 yen)

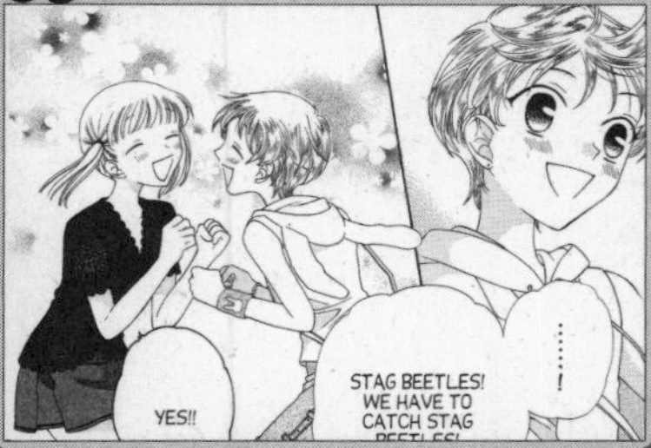
......!
STAG BEETLES! WE HAVE TO CATCH STAG
YES!!

19 Snack time: pancakes! (minus 500 yen)

18 You come down with a cold! (minus 3,000 yen) + (lose one turn)

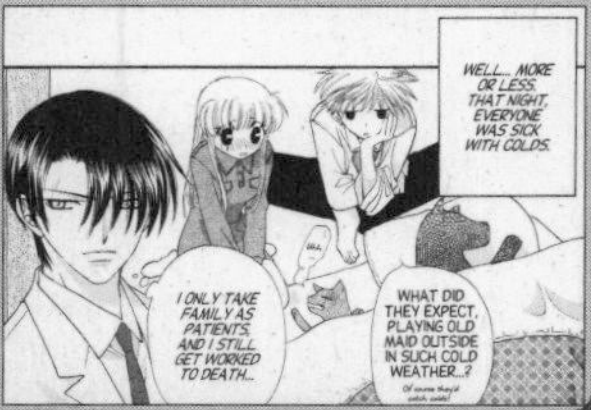
WELL... MORE OR LESS. THAT NIGHT, EVERYONE WAS SICK WITH COLDS.
WHAT DID THEY EXPECT, PLAYING OLD MAID OUTSIDE IN SUCH COLD WEATHER...?
I ONLY TAKE FAMILY AS PATIENTS, AND I STILL GET WORKED TO DEATH...

17 Tonight you're having tororo soba for dinner. (minus 500 yen)

16 Uh oh! Megumi Hanajima learns your real name!! (minus 10,000 yen) + (go back two spaces)

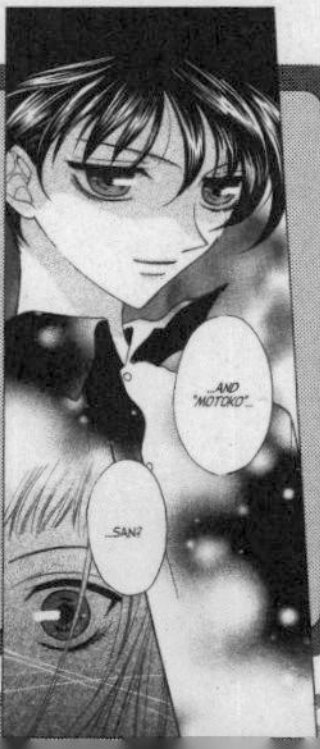
...AND "MOTOKO"...
...SAN?

21 Tonight you're having monja-yaki for dinner. (minus 500 yen)

The loser has to play this penalty game!

Roll the die to discover your penalty. See if you can manage it without bothering anyone.

- ◆If you roll 1 or 2 ······························ Imitate Kimi
- ◆If you roll 3 or 4 ······························ Imitate Aaya
- ◆If you roll 5 or 6 ······························ Imitate Ritchan

Finish

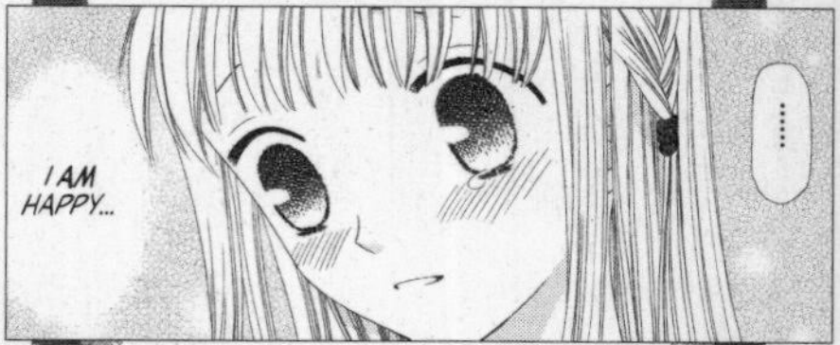
......
I AM HAPPY...

- ✱ First player to arrive ······························ Plus 10,000 yen
- ✱ Second player ······························ Plus 8,000 yen
- ✱ Third player ······························ Plus 6,000 yen

※Players who don't mind being called ingrates can sell the "ribbons" and "swimsuit" they were given as gifts during the game for 5,000 yen.

15 Snack time: aburi-mochi! (minus 500 yen)

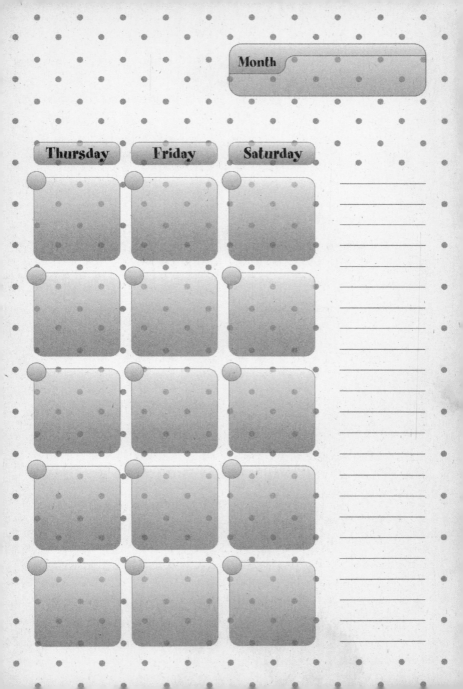

Month

Thursday	Friday	Saturday

Fruits Basket™ Planner

Sunday	Monday	Tuesday	Wednesday

Fruits Basket™

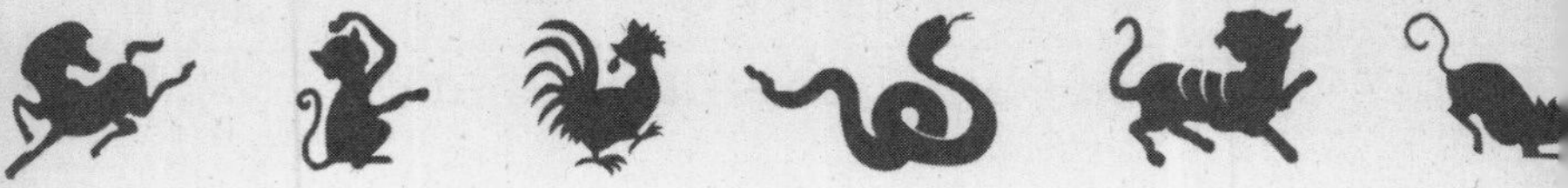

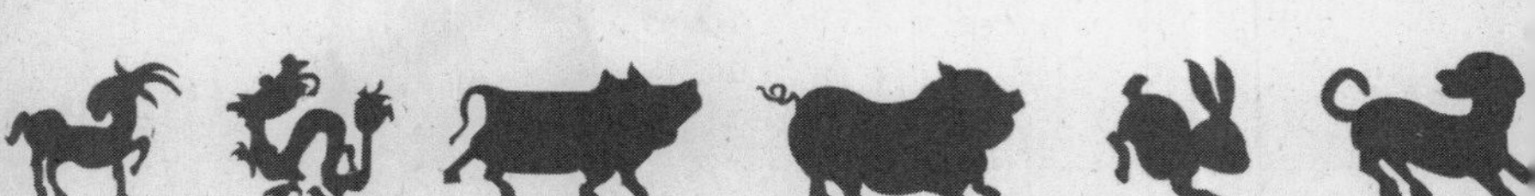

Coming in December 2008

Phantom Dream

From the Creator of Fruits Basket

Phantom Dream

Natsuki Takaya

GENEIMUSOU by Natsuki Takaya
© Natsuki Takaya 1994

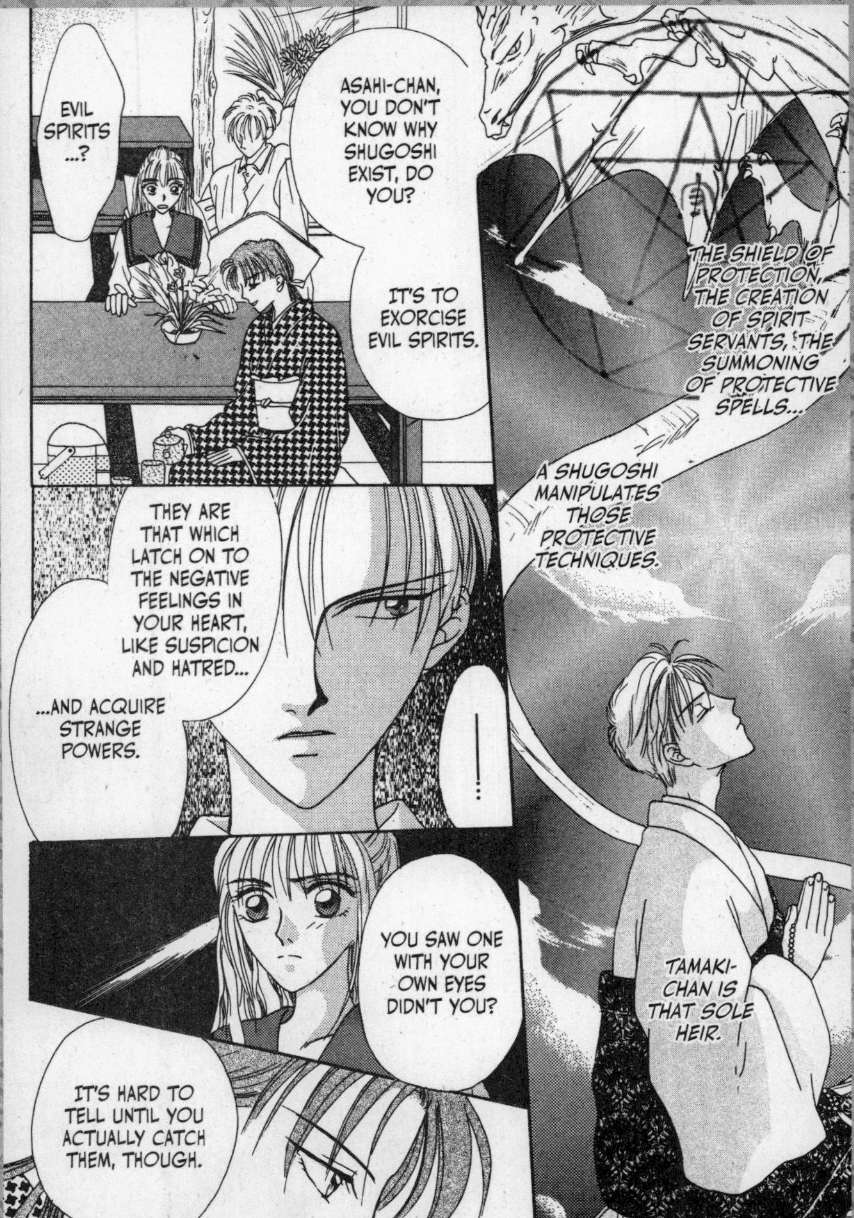
THE SHIELD OF PROTECTION, THE CREATION OF SPIRIT SERVANTS, THE SUMMONING OF PROTECTIVE SPELLS...
A SHUGOSHI MANIPULATES THOSE PROTECTIVE TECHNIQUES.
TAMAKI-CHAN IS THAT SOLE HEIR.
ASAHI-CHAN, YOU DON'T KNOW WHY SHUGOSHI EXIST, DO YOU?
IT'S TO EXORCISE EVIL SPIRITS.
EVIL SPIRITS ...?
THEY ARE THAT WHICH LATCH ON TO THE NEGATIVE FEELINGS IN YOUR HEART, LIKE SUSPICION AND HATRED...
...AND ACQUIRE STRANGE POWERS.
YOU SAW ONE WITH YOUR OWN EYES DIDN'T YOU?
IT'S HARD TO TELL UNTIL YOU ACTUALLY CATCH THEM, THOUGH.

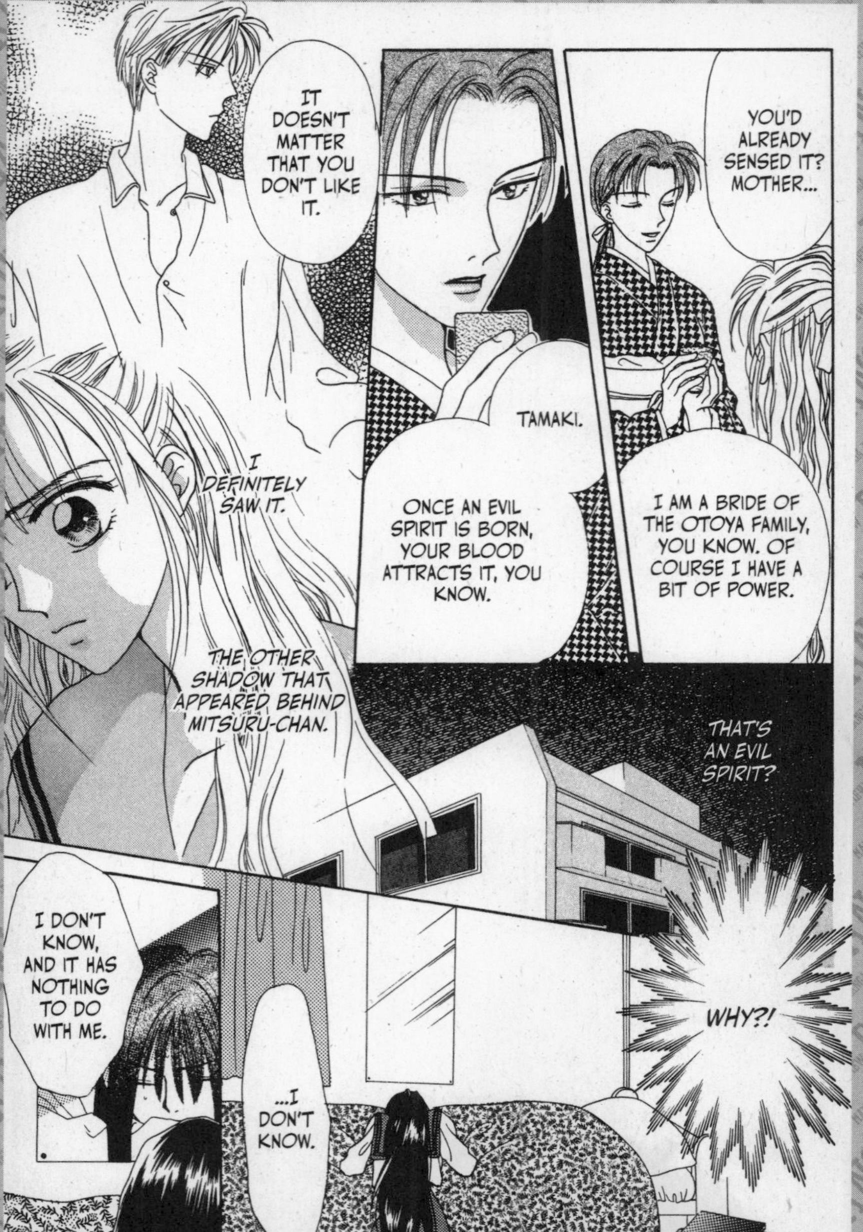
YOU'D ALREADY SENSED IT? MOTHER...
I AM A BRIDE OF THE OTOYA FAMILY, YOU KNOW. OF COURSE I HAVE A BIT OF POWER.
TAMAKI.
ONCE AN EVIL SPIRIT IS BORN, YOUR BLOOD ATTRACTS IT, YOU KNOW.
IT DOESN'T MATTER THAT YOU DON'T LIKE IT.
I DEFINITELY SAW IT.
THE OTHER SHADOW THAT APPEARED BEHIND MITSURU-CHAN.
THAT'S AN EVIL SPIRIT?
WHY?!
...I DON'T KNOW.
I DON'T KNOW, AND IT HAS NOTHING TO DO WITH ME.

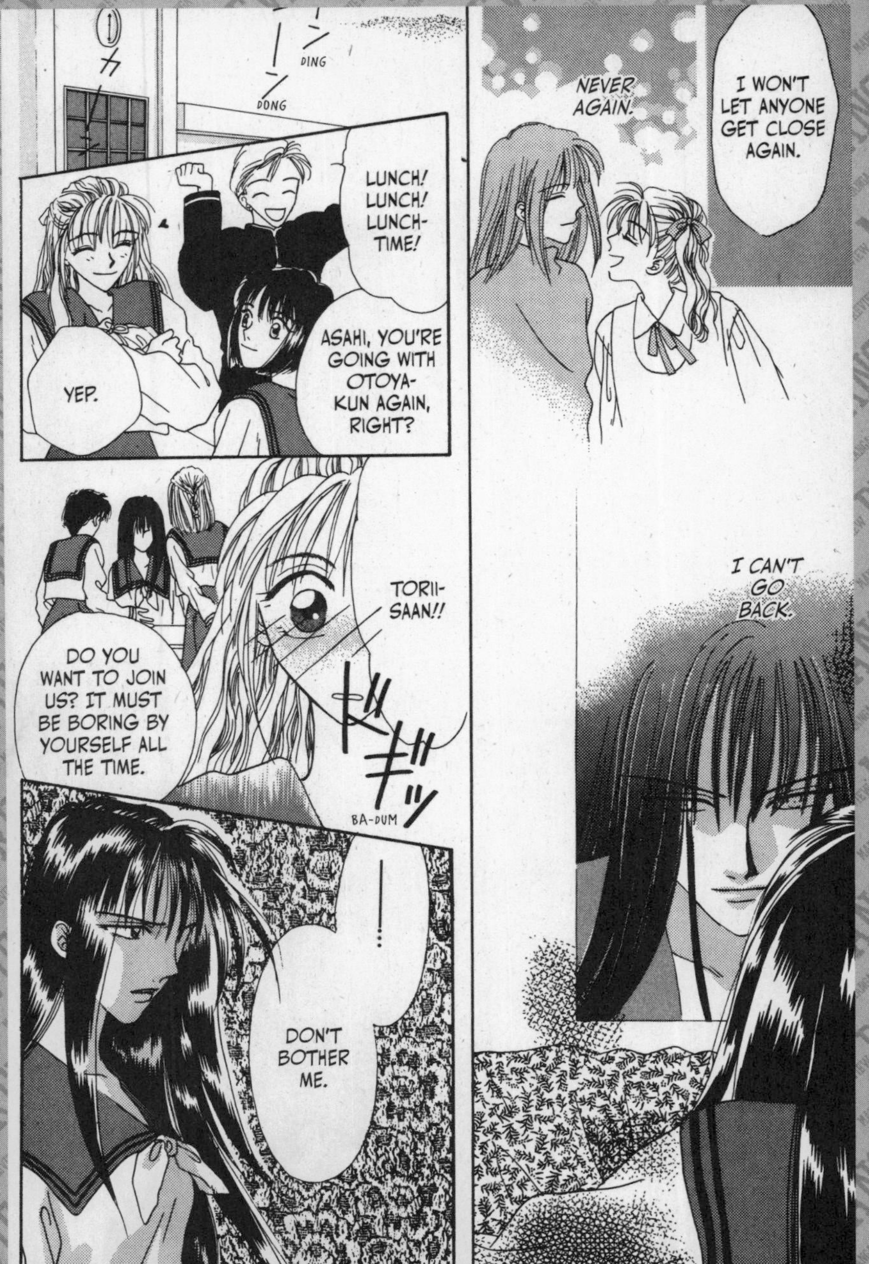
I WON'T LET ANYONE GET CLOSE AGAIN.
NEVER AGAIN.
I CAN'T GO BACK.
DING
DONG
LUNCH! LUNCH! LUNCH-TIME!
ASAHI, YOU'RE GOING WITH OTOYA-KUN AGAIN, RIGHT?
YEP.
TORII-SAAN!!
DO YOU WANT TO JOIN US? IT MUST BE BORING BY YOURSELF ALL THE TIME.
BA-DUM
......
DON'T BOTHER ME.

SHE'S COLD...

IT'S HARD TO GET CLOSE TO TORII-SAN, ISN'T IT...?

HEY...

YEP.

THE PERSON I THOUGHT OF LIKE A MOTHER...

I DID WISH I COULD SEE HER, BUT...

I DIDN'T WANT TO SEE HER LIKE THIS.

· · · · · ·

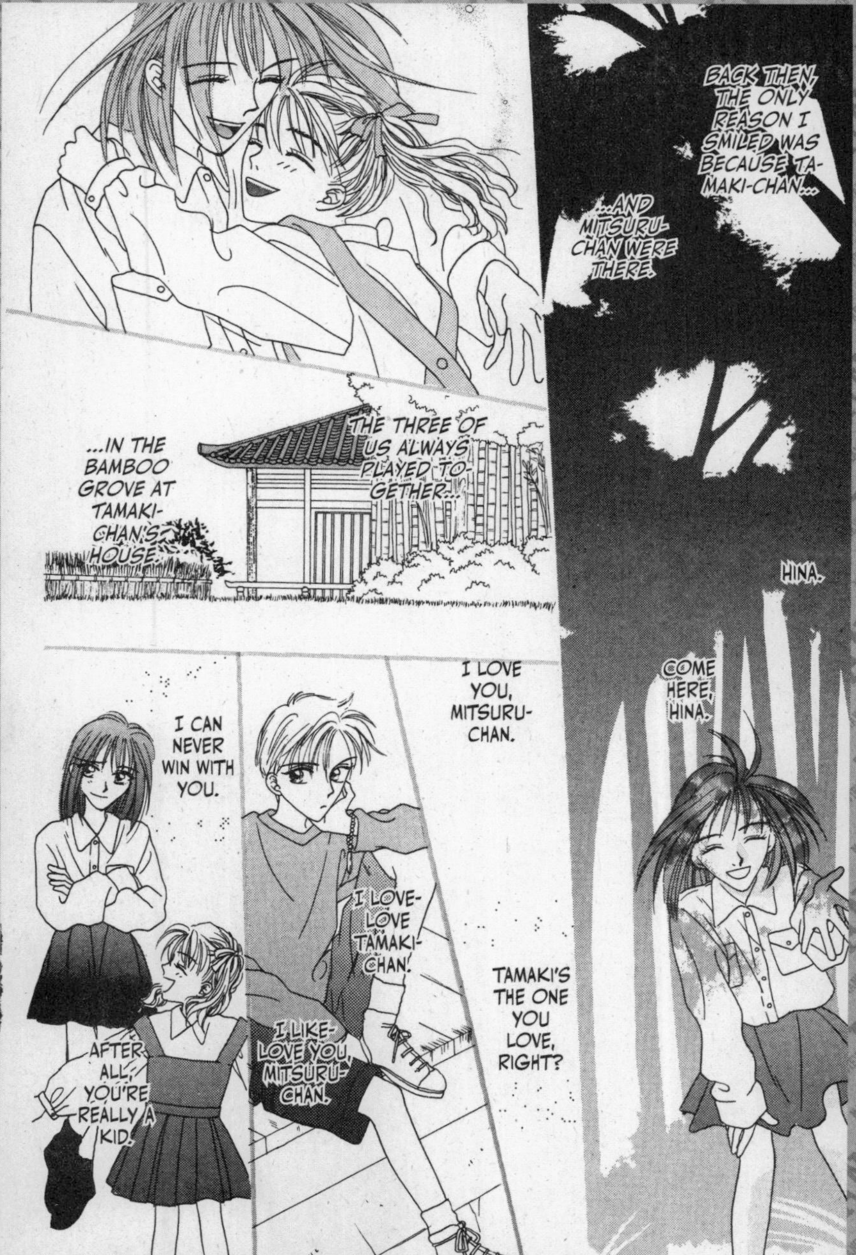

BACK THEN, THE ONLY REASON I SMILED WAS BECAUSE TA-MAKI-CHAN...
...AND MITSURU-CHAN WERE THERE.
HINA.
COME HERE, HINA.
THE THREE OF US ALWAYS PLAYED TO-GETHER...
...IN THE BAMBOO GROVE AT TAMAKI-CHAN'S HOUSE.
I LOVE YOU, MITSURU-CHAN.
TAMAKI'S THE ONE YOU LOVE, RIGHT?
I LOVE-LOVE TAMAKI-CHAN!
I LIKE-LOVE YOU, MITSURU-CHAN.
I CAN NEVER WIN WITH YOU.
AFTER ALL, YOU'RE REALLY A KID.

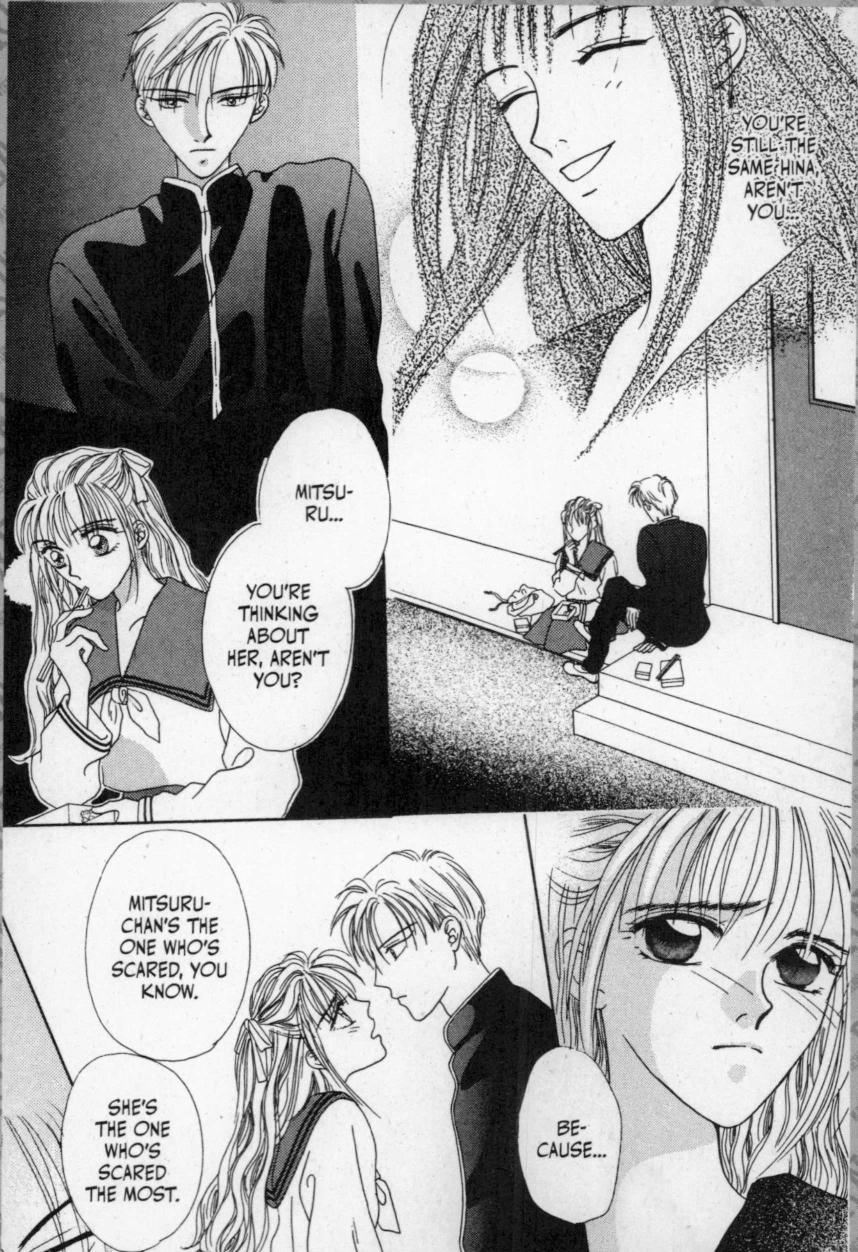
YOU'RE STILL THE SAME, HINA, AREN'T YOU...
MITSU-RU...
YOU'RE THINKING ABOUT HER, AREN'T YOU?
BE-CAUSE...
MITSURU-CHAN'S THE ONE WHO'S SCARED, YOU KNOW.
SHE'S THE ONE WHO'S SCARED THE MOST.

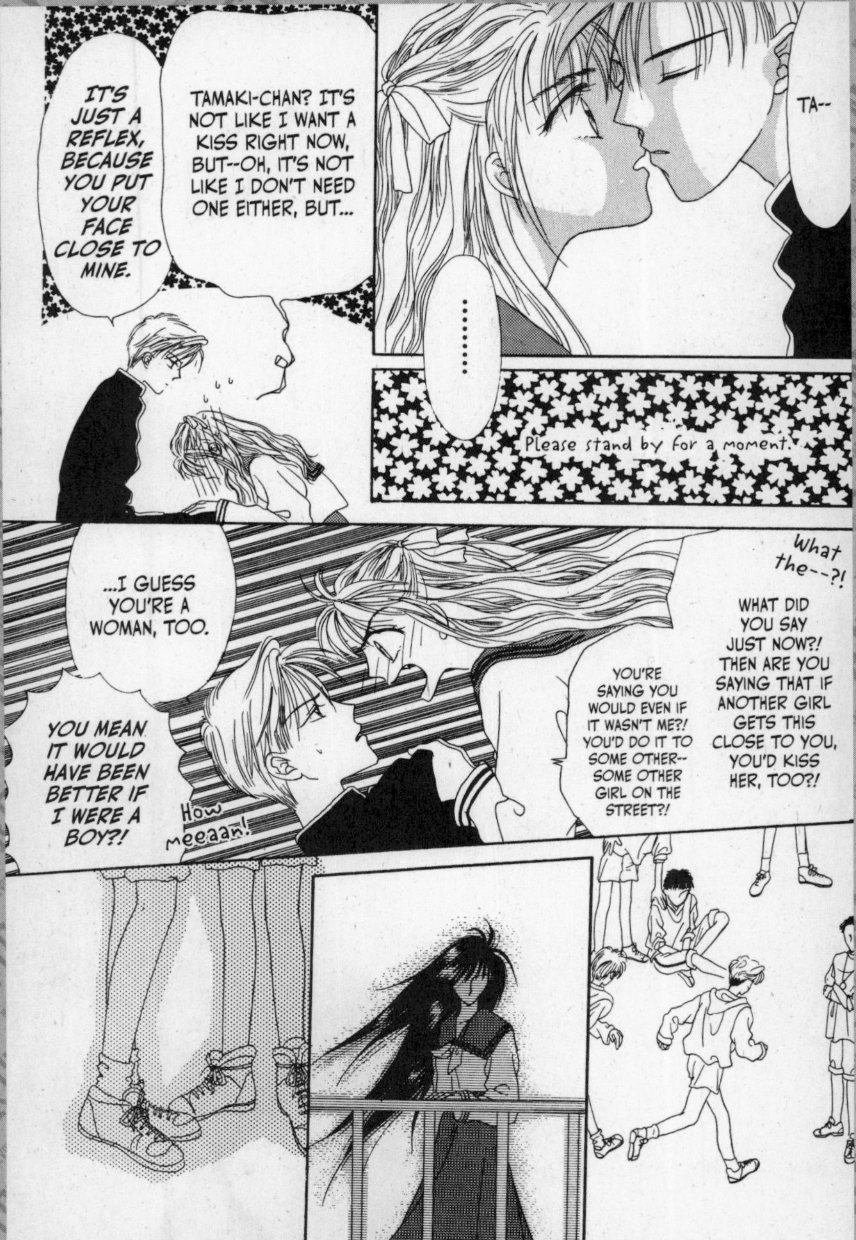
TA--
......
Please stand by for a moment.
TAMAKI-CHAN? IT'S NOT LIKE I WANT A KISS RIGHT NOW, BUT--OH, IT'S NOT LIKE I DON'T NEED ONE EITHER, BUT...
IT'S JUST A REFLEX, BECAUSE YOU PUT YOUR FACE CLOSE TO MINE.
...I GUESS YOU'RE A WOMAN, TOO.
What the--?!
WHAT DID YOU SAY JUST NOW?! THEN ARE YOU SAYING THAT IF ANOTHER GIRL GETS THIS CLOSE TO YOU, YOU'D KISS HER, TOO?!
YOU'RE SAYING YOU WOULD EVEN IF IT WASN'T ME?! YOU'D DO IT TO SOME OTHER-- SOME OTHER GIRL ON THE STREET?!
YOU MEAN IT WOULD HAVE BEEN BETTER IF I WERE A BOY?!
How meeaan!

STOP!

This is the back of the book. You wouldn't want to spoil a great ending!

This book is printed "manga-style," in the authentic Japanese right-to-left format. Since none of the artwork has been flipped or altered, readers get to experience the story just as the creator intended. You've been asking for it, so TOKYOPOP® delivered: authentic, hot-off-the-press, and far more fun!

DIRECTIONS

If this is your first time reading manga-style, here's a quick guide to help you understand how it works.

It's easy... just start in the top right panel and follow the numbers. Have fun, and look for more 100% authentic manga from TOKYOPOP®!

1
2
3
4
5
6
7
8
9
10

漫画革命

LEADING THE MANGA REVOLUTION